Lecture Notes in Computer Science 15537

Founding Editors

Gerhard Goos
Juris Hartmanis

Editorial Board Members

Elisa Bertino, *Purdue University, West Lafayette, IN, USA*
Wen Gao, *Peking University, Beijing, China*
Bernhard Steffen, *TU Dortmund University, Dortmund, Germany*
Moti Yung, *Columbia University, New York, NY, USA*

The series Lecture Notes in Computer Science (LNCS), including its subseries Lecture Notes in Artificial Intelligence (LNAI) and Lecture Notes in Bioinformatics (LNBI), has established itself as a medium for the publication of new developments in computer science and information technology research, teaching, and education.

LNCS enjoys close cooperation with the computer science R & D community, the series counts many renowned academics among its volume editors and paper authors, and collaborates with prestigious societies. Its mission is to serve this international community by providing an invaluable service, mainly focused on the publication of conference and workshop proceedings and postproceedings. LNCS commenced publication in 1973.

Esra Erdem · Germán Vidal
Editors

Practical Aspects of Declarative Languages

27th International Symposium, PADL 2025
Denver, CO, USA, January 20–21, 2025
Proceedings

 Springer

Editors
Esra Erdem
Sabanci University
Istanbul, Türkiye

Germán Vidal
Universitat Politècnica de València
Valencia, Valencia, Spain

ISSN 0302-9743   ISSN 1611-3349 (electronic)
Lecture Notes in Computer Science
ISBN 978-3-031-84923-7   ISBN 978-3-031-84924-4 (eBook)
https://doi.org/10.1007/978-3-031-84924-4

© The Editor(s) (if applicable) and The Author(s), under exclusive license to Springer Nature Switzerland AG 2025

This work is subject to copyright. All rights are solely and exclusively licensed by the Publisher, whether the whole or part of the material is concerned, specifically the rights of translation, reprinting, reuse of illustrations, recitation, broadcasting, reproduction on microfilms or in any other physical way, and transmission or information storage and retrieval, electronic adaptation, computer software, or by similar or dissimilar methodology now known or hereafter developed.
The use of general descriptive names, registered names, trademarks, service marks, etc. in this publication does not imply, even in the absence of a specific statement, that such names are exempt from the relevant protective laws and regulations and therefore free for general use.
The publisher, the authors and the editors are safe to assume that the advice and information in this book are believed to be true and accurate at the date of publication. Neither the publisher nor the authors or the editors give a warranty, expressed or implied, with respect to the material contained herein or for any errors or omissions that may have been made. The publisher remains neutral with regard to jurisdictional claims in published maps and institutional affiliations.

This Springer imprint is published by the registered company Springer Nature Switzerland AG
The registered company address is: Gewerbestrasse 11, 6330 Cham, Switzerland

If disposing of this product, please recycle the paper.

Preface

This volume contains the papers presented at the 27th International Symposium on Practical Aspects of Declarative Languages (PADL 2025). The symposium was held on 20–21 January 2025 in Denver, Colorado, USA, co-located with the 52nd ACM SIGPLAN Symposium on Principles of Programming Languages (POPL 2025).

PADL is a well-established forum for researchers and practitioners to present original work emphasizing novel applications and implementation techniques for all forms of declarative programming, including functional and logic programming, databases and constraint programming, and theorem proving. PADL 2025 especially welcomed new ideas and approaches related to applications, design, and implementation of declarative languages going beyond the scope of the past PADL symposia, for example, advanced database languages and contract languages, as well as verification and theorem proving methods that rely on declarative languages.

Originally established as a workshop (PADL 1999 in San Antonio, Texas), the PADL series developed into a regular annual symposium; other previous editions took place in Boston, Massachusetts (2000), Las Vegas, Nevada (2001), Portland, Oregon (2002), New Orleans, Louisiana (2003), Dallas, Texas (2004), Long Beach, California (2005), Charleston, South Carolina (2006), Nice, France (2007), San Francisco, California (2008), Savannah, Georgia (2009), Madrid, Spain (2010), Austin, Texas (2012), Rome, Italy (2013), San Diego, California (2014), Portland, Oregon (2015), St. Petersburg, Florida (2016), Paris, France (2017), Los Angeles, California (2018), Lisbon, Portugal (2019), New Orleans, Louisiana (2020), online (2021), Philadelphia, Pennsylvania (2022), Boston, Massachusetts (2023), and London, UK (2024).

The 15 papers in this volume, including 14 regular papers and one short paper, were selected by the Programme Committee from 26 submissions. Each of the PADL 2025 submissions received three reviews and was discussed electronically, using the EquinOCS conference system, by the Programme Committee before a final decision was made. The reviewing process for PADL 2025 was double-anonymous, and only authors of the eventually accepted papers have been revealed.

The accepted papers span a range of topics related to functional and logic programming, including some novel applications of Answer Set Programming, language extensions, runtime monitoring, program transformations, type-checking, and applications of declarative programming techniques to artificial intelligence and machine learning, among others.

We were also honored to include the two invited talks by Yanhong A. Liu (Stony Brook University, NY), "Solvers, unite! A simple unified semantics for reasoning with assurance and agreement", and Umut A. Acar (Carnegie Mellon University, PA), "Bridging Safety and Performance", in the PADL 2025 program.

The symposium was supported and sponsored by the Association of Logic Programming (ALP), the Association for Computing Machinery (ACM), and the Artificial

Intelligence Journal (AIJ). We thank all who contributed to the success and the exciting program of PADL 2025. This includes the authors of submissions; the ten external reviewers, who provided timely expert reviews; and, of course, the 30 members of the Program Committee. We are particularly grateful to Marina De Vos, Marco Gavanelli, and Enrico Pontelli for their invaluable advice and support.

December 2024

Esra Erdem
Germán Vidal

Organization

Program Committee Chairs

Erdem, Esra	Sabancı University, Turkey
Vidal, Germán	Universitat Politècnica de València, Spain

Program Committee Members

Akgün, Özgür	University of St Andrews, UK
Amin, Nada	Harvard University, USA
Balduccini, Marcello	Saint Joseph's University, USA
Banbara, Mutsunori	Nagoya University, Japan
Benac Earle, Clara	Universidad Politécnica de Madrid, Spain
Biernacka, Małgorzata	University of Wrocław, Poland
Carro, Manuel	IMDEA Software Institute and Universidad Politécnica de Madrid, Spain
Castro, Laura M.	University of A Coruña, Spain
Gebser, Martin	University of Klagenfurt, Austria
Gupta, Gopal	University of Texas at Dallas, USA
Hanus, Michael	Kiel University, Germany
Inclezan, Daniela	Miami University, USA
Izmirlioglu, Yusuf	University of Roehampton, UK
Janhunen, Tomi	Tampere University, Finland
Komendantskaya, Ekaterina	Heriot-Watt University and Southampton University, UK
Lanese, Ivan	University of Bologna, Italy
Leuschel, Michael	Heinrich-Heine-Universität Düsseldorf, Germany
Nishida, Naoki	Nagoya University, Japan
Pardo, Alberto	Universidad de la República, Uruguay
Pontelli, Enrico	New Mexico State University, USA
Sabuncu, Orkunt	TED University and Potassco Solutions, Turkey
Saribatur, Zeynep G.	TU Wien, Austria
Schrijvers, Tom	KU Leuven, Belgium
Tarau, Paul	University of North Texas, USA
Titolo, Laura	Code Metal, USA
Tóth, Melinda	Eötvös Loránd University, Hungary
Vennekens, Joost	KU Leuven, Belgium

Westrick, Sam New York University, USA
Zangari, Jessica Università della Calabria, Italy
Zhou, Neng-Fa CUNY Brooklyn College and Graduate Center, USA

Additional Reviewers

Ballesteros González, Ignacio IMDEA Software Institute and Universidad Politécnica de Madrid, Spain
Byrd, William University of Alabama at Birmingham, USA
Feliú, Marco A. AMA/NASA LaRC, USA
Lukács, Dániel Eötvös Loránd University, Hungary
Olarte, Carlos Université Sorbonne Paris Nord, France
Orosz, Tamás Eötvös Loránd University, Hungary
Retchin, Matthew Harvard University, USA
Sanna, Rafaello Harvard University, USA
Ugarte Guzmán, Tania Fernanda KU Leuven, Belgium
Yli-Jyrä, Anssi Tampere University, Finland

Invited Talks

Solvers, Unite!
A Simple Unified Semantics for Reasoning with Assurance and Agreement

Yanhong A. Liu

Stony Brook University, Stony Brook, NY, USA
liu@cs.stonybrook.edu

Abstract. Complex reasoning problems are most clearly and easily specified using logic rules, but require recursive rules with aggregation such as count and sum and more for practical applications. Unfortunately, the meaning of such rules has been a significant challenge, with many disagreeing semantics, implemented in different classes of solvers and rule engines.

This talk examines a simple unified semantics for reasoning with assurance and agreement—with which the power of different classes of solvers and rule engines can be united—and consists of three main parts:

1. An introduction to complex reasoning problems expressed using logic rules, with recursion, negation, quantification, and aggregation; the key idea of a simple unified semantics, supporting simple expression of different assumptions; and how it unifies different prior semantics.
2. An overview of the precise rule language; the formal semantics, called Founded Semantics and Constraint Semantics [2, 3], or Founded + Constraint Semantics (FCS) for short here, supporting efficient and precise inference over aggregation even with approximation; and the properties of the semantics.
3. An exploration of a wide range of challenging examples, including the well-known problem of company control and extended win-not-win games. FCS is simple and matches the desired results in all cases.

Additionally, we compare 10 different classes of solvers and rule engines and discuss the different semantics they compute and how their power can be united. Such combined power for problem solving and question answering with assurance and agreement is an essential complement to LLMs [1].

References

1. Liu, Y.A.: Rigorous language models for trustworthy AI. In: Integrating Reasoning Systems for Trustworthy AI: Proceedings of the 4rd Workshop on Logic and Practice of Programming (LPOP), pp. 33–36. https://arxiv.org/abs/2410.19738 (2024)

2. Liu, Y.A., Stoller, S.D.: Founded semantics and constraint semantics of logic rules. J. Logic Comput. **30**(8), 1609–1638 (2020). https://arxiv.org/abs/1606.06269
3. Liu, Y.A., Stoller, S.D.: Recursive rules with aggregation: a simple unified semantics. J. Logic Comput. **32**(8), 1659–1693 (2022). https://arxiv.org/abs/2007.13053

Bridging Safety and Performance

Umut A. Acar

Carnegie Mellon University, USA
umut@cmu.edu

Abstract. As computer scientists, we have long wrestled with a perceived trade-off between safety and performance. Choosing performance meant using low-level languages, which help optimize for performance but at the expense of safety. Choosing safety meant using high-level languages, which guarantee safety at the expense of performance. Historically, we have chosen performance over safety. This choice has not aged well, because societal significance and economic costs of safety has been steadily increasing. Therefore, it is (past) time to challenge this rigid dichotomy. Obvious question is: why can't we have both?

In this talk, I show that we can have both safety and performance, by developing programming languages and systems that integrate both. I present two advances in this direction by considering classic problems. First, I show that parallel functional programming languages, which are traditionally regarded as safe but slow, can deliver impressive performance. Second, I show that parallel programming languages, including both functional and procedural, can automatically and safely optimize their own performance, reducing reliance on labor-intensive manual optimizations. The method underpinning these advances blends several "ingredients":

1. "Theory A" (algorithms and complexity, a.k.a., "Turing" theory) for asymptotic efficiency,
2. "Theory B" (theory of programming, a.k.a., "Church" theory) for safety, and
3. system building and empirical computer science for practical efficiency.

Contents

On Bridging Prolog and Python to Enhance an Inductive Logic Programming System 1
    Vítor Santos Costa and Miguel Areias

Type-Checking Heterogeneous Sequences in a Simple Embeddable Type System 18
    Jim Newton

The Scenic Route to Deforestation: An Exercise in Applying Parametricity in Curry 35
    Vincent Robinson and Steven Libby

MOLA: A Runtime Verification Engine Factory by (Meta-)interpreting Embedded DSLs 53
    Felipe Gorostiaga, Martin Ceresa, and César Sánchez

SM-Based Semantics for Answer Set Programs Containing Conditional Literals and Arithmetic 71
    Zachary Hansen and Yuliya Lierler

A Practical Approach to Handling Tabular Data in Logic 88
    Robin De Vogelaere, Kylian Van Dessel, and Joost Vennekens

Automated Playing of Survival Video Games with Commonsense Reasoning 104
    Bryant Hargreaves, Dan N. Nguyen, Keegan Krimbell, and Gopal Gupta

Checking Concurrency Coding Rules 113
    Lars-Åke Fredlund, Ángel Herranz, and Julio Mariño

A Weighted Bipolar Argumentation Framework and Its ASP-Based Implementation 130
    Yan Yan, Junru Li, Fangzhou Liu, Zerong Wang, and Zhizheng Zhang

Haskell Based Spreadsheets 146
    Ignacio Ballesteros, Luis Eduardo Bueso de Barrio, and Julio Mariño

Leveraging LLM Reasoning with Dual Horn Programs 163
    Paul Tarau

ASP for Language Documentation and Reclamation: A Derivational
Stemming Tool for Myaamia 179
   Daniela Inclezan, Hunter Lockwood, Anita Baral, Jitendra Sharma,
   and Pratiksha Shrestha

Enhancing a Hierarchical Graph Rewriting Language Based on MELL
Cut Elimination 196
   Kento Takyu and Kazunori Ueda

C3G: Causally Constrained Counterfactual Generation 215
   Sopam Dasgupta, Farhad Shakerin, Joaquín Arias, Elmer Salazar,
   and Gopal Gupta

Exploring Answer Set Programming for Provenance Graph-Based Cyber
Threat Detection: A Novel Approach 233
   Fang Li, Fei Zuo, and Gopal Gupta

Author Index 249

On Bridging Prolog and Python to Enhance an Inductive Logic Programming System

Vítor Santos Costa[✉][iD] and Miguel Areias[iD]

CRACS/INESC TEC, Department of Computer Science, Faculty of Sciences,
University of Porto, Rua do Campo Alegre, 1021/1055, 4169-007 Porto, Portugal
{vscosta,miguel.areias}@fc.up.pt

Abstract. Prolog is a programming language that provides a high-level approach to software development. Python is a versatile programming language that has a vast range of libraries including support for data analysis and machine learning tasks. We present a Prolog-Python interface that aims at exploiting Prolog deduction capabilities and Python's extensive libraries. Our novel interface was built using a divide and conquer methodology. In a first step, we implemented a set of `C++` classes that can be matched to Python classes; next, we used an interface generator to export the relevant classes. Finally, we use `C` code to actually convert between the two realms. In order to demonstrate the usefulness of the interface, we enhance an Inductive Logic Programming System with a visualization capabilities and show how to interface with a standard classifier.

Keywords: Prolog · Python · Inductive Logic Programming · Interoperability

1 Introduction

Prolog is a programming language that provides a high-level approach to programming through the use of a subset of First Order Logic [17]. Prolog relies on a very efficient querying mechanism, based on goal refutation for Horn clauses. Prolog systems complement this foundation with support for state capture and manipulation, and with mechanism for interaction. As Horn clause programs consist of a set of predicate definitions, this extra functionality is made available through "built-in" predicates; that is, through predicates that are defined as part of the Prolog implementation. Collections of these built-ins correspond to system libraries in traditional languages.

The design and implementation of these primitives is a large part of developing a Prolog system [11]. In fact, it is quite hard to support the different needs of the very diverse Prolog applications. One answer is to allow the user to build by herself some of these built-ins. To do so, the user will need to access the internal structure of the Prolog engine. The bidirectional protocol that defines how to access Prolog data-structures, on the one hand, and how logic programs may be allowed to manipulate external data, on the other hand, is called the *Foreign Language Interface* (FLI).

Most often, the FLI is designed to interface with programs that were written in the Prolog engine's language. Arguably, most widely used systems are based on *C* or *Java*, and so are the FLIs. Note that a single Prolog system may have several FLIs, either to support different languages or for compatibility [31].

We introduce an interface that connects Python with a Prolog system. Python is a very popular language, and at the moment dominates in areas such as machine learning. It includes a large collection of tools that can be well used in Logic Programming Systems. Python programs are organized as modules, that group related classes, which may contain variables and functions. Arguably, the natural unit of sharing are instances of classes, and goals, the instances of predicates. Our goal is to provide a mapping such that Prolog goals can be Python objects, and Python goals can be Prolog calls.

Next, we describe our approach. Python is object oriented making it cumbersome to use a *C* based interface. Thus, the first step was to build a *C++* interface for the Prolog system. We then used the SWIG interface generator to export the classes to Python. The classes in the *C++* interface are thus translated to classes in a Python module. SWIG is very good at re-targeting the interface, but is not very good at writing all the nitty-grid of the translation. We found out it was sensible to use a separate library to do the actual translation.

The paper is organized as follows. First, we briefly review prior work on Prolog FLIs: there has been extensive work on these interfaces, but often this is not documented. Next, we describe the three components in our design: the *C++* interface, the SWIG translator, and the support libraries. We then give an example of how the interface can be applied to improve an existing application. Last, we conclude and discuss further work.

2 Prolog and the World

Most Prolog systems provide a foreign language interface (FLI), both to extend the language with user-defined built-ins, and to allow Prolog to be embedded as a component in a larger system. As most Prolog systems were traditionally written in C, FLIs supported C/Prolog. Quintus Prolog was one of the first systems to include a full fledged FLI allowing passing integers, floats, terms and pointers to the external code [21]. SICStus Prolog follows similar principles, but has a richer set of base types and more support for handling terms. Interface predicates are declared from types and modes [7]. A similar approach is implemented by GNU-Prolog [12].

Most other Prolog systems FLIs are based on reading and writing terms, built with *C* code. B-Prolog provides access to the engine internals [34]; YAP provides a wrapper but essentially exports the functional approach used in inner routines [10]; SWI-Prolog provides a handle-based abstraction of unification [33];

Ciao also implements term construction and access routines [15]; ECL^{i}PS^e provides a more object-oriented flavor [19]; XSB provides two interfaces: one for direct access and the other for high-level access [24].

The advent of Java has generated interest in interfacing to other programming languages. There are two approaches: the client-server approach allows for distributed execution and is often more robust and cleaner. Examples include SICStus PrologBeans [1], InterProlog [6], and Prolog to R real [3]. Monolithic, or DLL based examples include Quintus Visual Prolog interface and the SWI-Prolog JPL [22]. The latter is a merge of a Prolog to Java and Prolog to Java interface and provides a very nice and complete API.

Python has also generated interest in the logic programming community. Bedevere was a SWIG [5] interface for GNU-Prolog, geared at Python [20]; similarly, pwig was developed for SWI-Prolog. Both rely on the C-interface [14]. py-xsb [4] exports the XSB FLI to a Python environment using ctypes. A more high-level approach is provided by PySWIP, that also uses Python ctypes to provides a module Prolog with most common operations [29].

The approaches presented so far rely on the system's FLI. Most FLIs provide only access to a system's functionality; these limitations are noticeable when trying to generate code that will run across systems [31]. A tighter integration with the external environment was proposed in Jinni [27] and Fluents [26]. External code embedding is also possible [32]. Finally, some authors would argue that object oriented logic languages provide a more natural integration with Object Oriented languages [8].

Janus is a Prolog-Python interface originally developed by Swift for XSB Prolog [25]. Janus was since adopted by SWI-Prolog and is the target of a joint effort between the XSB, SWI, and ciao communities [2]. ON the Prolog side, Janus provides a collection of built-in predicates, the `py_` family of predicates. These built-ins can execute arbitrary Python code and translate the results back to Prolog. Important examples are `py_call` that can call a Python method, and `py_iter` can be used to iterate over an object. In the specific case of SWI-Prolog one can also the quasi-quotation mechanism to inject Python code in the Prolog environment.

The Python to Prolog interface consists of five key classes: `query`, `apply`, `Term`, `Undefined`, and `PrologError`. The `query` and the `apply` classes serve the same goal, calling Prolog, but `query` is text based whereas `apply` is object based.

3 The C++ FLI

The *C++* FLI task is to wrap *C* data structures as classes. Next, we detail the main components that are concerned with term construction and manipulation, database management, and execution. Figure 1 describes graphically the class hierarchy of the interface.

Terms. The `PTerm` or `T` class exports handles to Prolog terms (type `Term` or `PTerm`). The sub-classes are `PApplterm`, `PPairterm`, and sub-classes for the usual

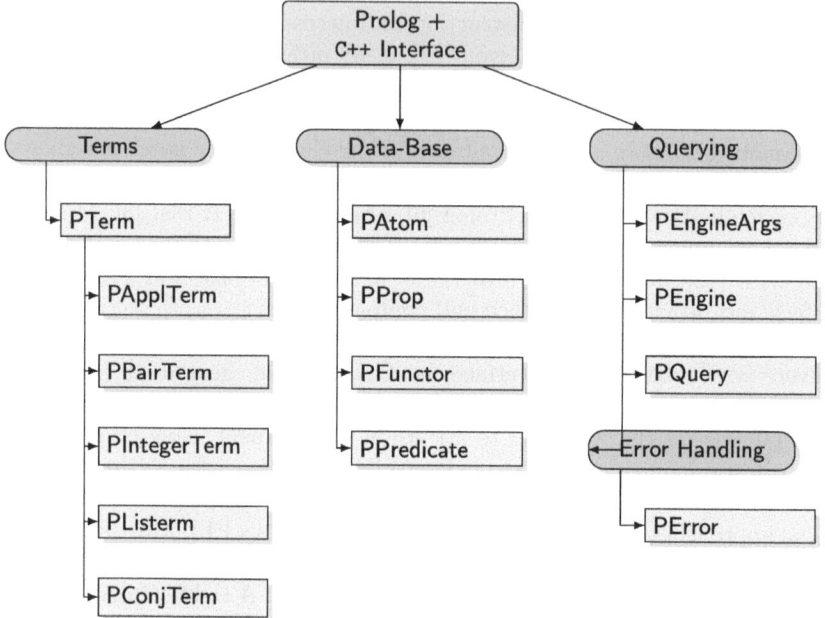

Fig. 1. Class structure of the C++ interface

types. PTerm is a collection of methods plus a handler pointing to the Prolog term.

```
protected:
  yhandle_t hdl; /// handle to term, equivalent to term_t
```

The private methods mk(Term t) generates the handle and copies it to this->hdl; the getter Term gt() fetches the term. As an example, term type checking is implemented through virtual methods such as isVar, that is defined by PTerm as

```
{ virtual bool isVar() { return IsVarTerm(gt()); } }
```

that is redefined by PIntegerTerm as:

```
bool isVar() { return false; }
```

The gt() method gets the Prolog term from the handler.

PTerm also provides interfaces for most term operations, e.g., to verify whether our object is a variant of a term t1, we simply write:

```
virtual P_Term variant(PTerm t1) { return P_Variant(gt(), t1.term()); }
```

Notice that as `gt()` is a private method, we use `term()` to construct the the external object.

The sub-classes do not have to be disjoint. The interface provides both `PPairTerm` that refers to a pair of terms, and `PListTerm` that is used to access a true list. The latter class allows for constructors such as:

```
PListTerm(std::vector<Term>).
```

The constructor uses an array with objects of `Term`. Whenever possible, one should avoid creating intermediate C++ objects. It is much more efficient to work with the engine C objects, and create a single C++ object as the final result.

The Prolog Database. Our approach assumes that the Prolog database is organised as a symbol table, where symbols are Prolog atoms. Atoms have a variable set of properties. One important property is `PFunctor`, that is special in the sense that functors themselves can have properties of type `PPredicate`. The classes `Patom`, `PProp`, `PFunctor`, and `PPredicate` wrap this functionality.

Run-Time. The run-time consists of three classes: `PEngine`, `PEngineArgs`, and `PQuery`. To boot the Prolog system, one must first fill the execution parameters at `PEngineArgs` and create an `PEngine` object, whose main task is to create `PQuery` object. The latter's main task is to create an iterator for query execution, and to provide access to the query state. There are several ways to start a query, the example below is used by the interpreter to run a query from user input:

```
PQuery(const char *s) :-
PPredicate(s, goal, names, (nts = a1_ptr()))
```

In this example, `PPredicate` is given the query string `s`, parses it, stores the goal's argument in the register array, uses call by reference to pass the map with the variable names, and finally returns itself. `PQuery` just needs to start the engine.

Error Handling. The `PError` class takes care of error objects. Errors are generated by all the Prolog components. In our approach, we assume that the Prolog system ensures a fair treatment by storing the error as a dictionary, and storing all the entries as constants or as text strings. Terms are presented as text.

4 The SWIG Translator

SWIG is a tool that promises that, if given a specification for a C or $C++$ library it will generate the corresponding stub in a target language, such as *Python*, or *Java*. In practice the specification details the data structures that are made visible in the library's header file. A simple example is:

```
%include "pt.hh"
```

This single line of code results in generating a set of Python classes, one per C++ class. The classes are really just stubs: they wrap the arguments and pass them to the source library.

Unfortunately, the wrappers just insulate the objects, and often we need too access fields or call methods. One solution is to extend SWIG with libraries for common data-structures:

```
%include stdint.i
%include std_string.i
%include std_vector.i
%include "pt.hh"
```

We now can use the methods for classes `int_t`, `std::string`, and `std::vector<T>` from within Python. Although SWIG supports *namespaces* and templates, but not full C++.

We can construct and manipulate PTerms, but objects of type `Term` are opaque. This is a problem because Prolog programs only manipulate terms; as such, all calls from Prolog to Python will have arguments of type Term. SWIG addresses this problem through *typemaps*, such as the one in the followup code:

```
% typemap(out) Term {
   return $result =
       prolog_to_python($1, false, 0, true);
}
%
```

Unfortunately, writing SWIG extensions eventually becomes very hard. The interface relies instead on auxiliary functions, *p2py* () (`prolog_to_python`) and *py2p* () (`python_to_prolog`) interactions. Table 1 describes the main rules: notice that these rules are applied recursively over terms or Python expressions.

4.1 From Prolog to Python

The function *p2py*() is the key to having transparent execution. It maps a Prolog term to a Python object as follows:

– Integers and other numbers map to integers (integer objects). Prolog atoms are used for two purposes: as symbols (e.g., `fail` is likely to refer to a built-in), and as text, e.g., `'Where twinkling in the dewy light'`, is probably text. Unfortunately, these roles are in no way guaranteed: we can use the atom `fail` to search for students who `failed` a course, and we could use the text as the name of a predicate. This confusion stems from the origins of Prolog and the Edinburgh syntax.

  There is no perfect solution to this problem. Our approach is:
  1. if the atom text can be a legal Python symbol, map it as symbol: return $pyLookup(str(t))$;

Table 1. Translation rules from Prolog to Python and from Python to Prolog; $vnames$ is the set of valid names for Python symbols

Prolog $\rightarrow$ p2py() $\rightarrow$	Python $\rightarrow$ py2p() $\rightarrow$	Prolog
int	int	int
float	float	float
true	True	true
false	False	false
none	None	none
atom $\in vnames$	symbol	atom
atom $\notin vnames$	string	–
string	string	string
$[A, B, \ldots, C]$	Python List	$[A, B, \ldots, C]$
$t(\ldots)$	Python Tuple	$t(\ldots)$
$\{k_1 : v_1, \ldots, k_n : v_n\}$	Python Dictionary	$\{k_1 : v_1, \ldots, k_n : v_n\}$
$F(a_1, ..., k_n = a_n)$ (compound term)	$\phi = F(a_1, ..., k_n = a_n)$ or Python Named Tuple	py2p(ϕ) $F(a_1, ..., k_n = a_n)$
A.B.F(...)	Function call obj	$ptr(\&obj)$

2. or alternatively, map it as a Python string (PyUnicode object): return $PyUnicode\_Str(str(t))$.

One alternative is to map atoms to symbols only if they are symbols in Python; the problem is that the atom may be translated in different ways as the program runs (in the worst case the translation will depend on the Python garbage collector).

- True lists are translated into Python lists (PyList objects). Prolog lists are linked lists, so the actual match for a Prolog list [1,2,3] should be an X such that:
t0 = [3,[]]
t1 = [2,t0]
X = [1,t1]
In practice, users expect list to match list, and that is what we support when atom [] matches the empty list: while list(t) .
- Terms of the form t(...) are translated to Python tuples (PyTuple). Python tuples are similar to Python lists, but whereas Python lists can expand, contract and be updated, tuples have fixed size and fixed arguments.
- Dictionaries: we assume that the Prolog system does not support dictionaries at the engine level, instead, it will translate a Python dictionary to a term of the form:
    { a1:t1, ... , am:tm, ... an:tn }.
This representation allow us to send dictionaries to Python and back.

- we still have to translate partial lists and compound terms. By default, Python does not construct compound terms; it evaluates functions (or methods). The interface thus tries T with functor named f, and arity a. It builds and execute the function call as follows:
  1. set $i \leftarrow a, args \leftarrow None, dict \leftarrow$
  2. search for an object of name f; proceed if the object is callable, otherwise certify it matches a named tuple: if it does, return the tuple otherwise an error;
  3. while $T[i] = (k = v)$, where k is an atom or a string $dict[k] = p2py(v)$ do $i \leftarrow i - 1$;
  4. create a tuple for the remaining arguments that must be represented: $args = (p2py(T[1]), \ldots, p2py(T[i]))$.
  5. execute the code and return $code(f)(args, dict)$
- Python uses $A.B.C$ to represent module/class/method hierarchy. We use the same syntax, taking advantage of the fact that early Prolog systems used the dot operator to represent a pair, so $A.B.C = [A|[B,C]]$. This makes the text close to Python. Drawbacks include overloading even more the dot character, and diverging from other packages.

Our approach goes a little bit further and defines ./2 as an existing predicate, so that we can write $A.B.C$ as a goal:

4.2 From Python to Prolog

The reverse function $py2p$ `python_to_prolog` follows the same guidelines as $p2py$:

- in Python there is no ambiguity about whether an object should be treated as a string or not. It is natural to map strings to strings, but it would be nice to translate to atoms, or list of codes or characters.
- If an object does not fit in the above mentioned rules, we assume that the Prolog system will pass the address of the object.

4.3 Assignment

The library supports two different forms of assignment:

- If the target is a variable, that is $V \leftarrow Exp$, we should bind the variable to the outcome of the $p2py$ call.
- If the target is an atom and the atom is an attribute or a key already existing in the symbol table, $A \leftarrow Exp$ should set the attribute to $p2py(T)$.
- If the target is a new atom create it in a system table, and then proceed as before.
- if the target is indexed, $A[I] \leftarrow Exp$, call $py2p$ to obtain either a variable or an address, and then proceed as before.

4.4 An Example

Next, we show a self-contained example of using the interface. The example was adapted from the seaborn package [30], based on matplotlib [16].

```
:- use_module(library(python)).
:- python_import(seaborn as sns).
:- python_import(matplotlib.pyplot as plt).

main :-
    penguins := sns.load_dataset( "penguins" ),
    sns.histplot(penguins, x="flipper_length_mm"),
    plt.show().
```

After loading the Prolog library, we import seaborn and bind the package to two symbols, seaborn and sns. The actual program starts by looking up sns in the system table, and then creates a function call with the function load_dataset() obtained from the module seaborn, a tuple with a string "penguins", and an empty dictionary. The result of the function is assigned to a new symbol, penguins. To call the procedure we lookup sns and build a function call by looking up histplot in seaborn, constructing a tuple with a single entry penguins, and a dictionary with a single entry with key "x" and value "flipper_length_mm". This call generates the plot. Finally, matplotlib is called to show the result plot in a physical device.

A more complex example is shown next, with corresponding output presented in Fig. 2.

4.5 Interface Libraries

The previous examples focused on the Prolog side. SWIG provides an extensive set of classes for the Python side, but as the classes are based on C++, it cannot take full advantage of the language. Thus, the Prolog system must include libraries to facilitate programming. We briefly discuss two of the most interesting techniques.

Iterators

```
class Query (PQuery):
    def __init__(self, engine, g):
        ...
    def __iter__(self):
        return self
    def done(self):
        gate = self.gate
        completed = gate == ...
        return completed
```

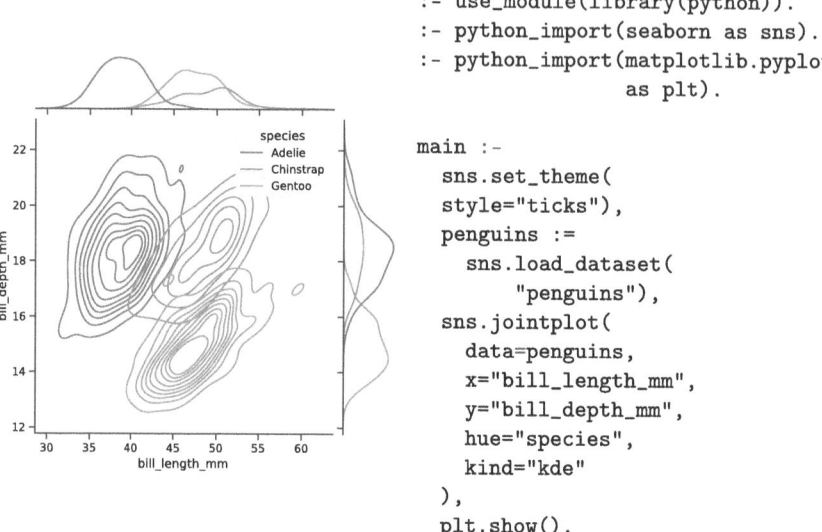

Fig. 2. Visualization of the Penguin dataset - showing the difference between three penguin species

```
def __next__(self):
    if self.done() or
       not self.next():
        raise StopIteration()
    return self
```

Iterators are classes that implement a sequence generation protocol. In this example, the class `Query` is a refinement of the C++ class that can be used it to enumerate solutions in a `for` or `while` loop.

The two key methods are `done` and `__next__`. They rely on PQuery to provide the last port or gate crossed. A call to `self.done()` checks whether a query us still active. `self.__next__()` either gets the next answer, or sends a signal to stop iterating.

Named Tuples. Named tuples are syntactically similar to Prolog terms, and we use them to give a Prolog flavor to Python code. By adding an iterator to a named tuple, we can have a Prolog goal:

```
class LoadLibrary(Predicate):
    def __init__(self, eng):
        self.engine = eng
        self.goal = namedtuple('load_library', 'name' )
```

```
def run(self, c):
    self.engine.run(self.goal(library(c)))

def __str__(self):
    return self.goal.__str__()
```

`load_library = LoadLibrary(PEngine).run`

This code allows to call `load_library("lists")`.

5 Pythonic Aleph

To conclude we show how the interface can be used to improve an existing application. Aleph [23] is an Inductive Logic Programming learning system, based on Progol [18]. Aleph implements relational machine-learning algorithms; the reference algorithm, `induce` generates a theory by following these steps:

- Choose an example, and collect literals that are connected to the example. Swap different constants by different variables and call the result *bottom clause*;
- select subsets from the example and pick the clause that best separate positives from negatives.

The `induce` algorithm implements greedy coverage removal, that is, examples covered by the chosen clause will be discarded from the step.

The bottom-clause dominates the search space. Its construction depends on the user-provided predicates plus mode declarations that structure the clause. Mode declarations are related, but quite different, from the usual mode declarations in logic programming [11]. As an example, consider the following two mode declarations for a chemical structure-activity dataset [9,13]:

```
:- modeb(*,atm(+drug,-atomid,#element,#integer, charge)).
:- modeb(*,symbond(+drug,+atomid,-atomid,#integer)).
```

The first argument can be largely ignored: it just says we should look for all the solutions. The main functors of the axioms argument, `atm` and `symbond` declare that we were going to use atoms and bounding in a molecule. The symbols `drug`, `atomid`, `element`, `integer` and `charge` name a set of disjoint concepts, the types, that will be associated with clause variables. Finally, the mode declarations are as follows, assuming we want to place a variable V at an argument A_i whose type is $\mathcal{T}$:

- +: V must have been used in a previous call C'. Moreover, if $A'_j = V$ then $type(A'_j) == \mathcal{T}$;
- -: V may be a new variable of type $\mathcal{T}$;
- #: A_i must be set to a constant of type $\mathcal{T}$.

The following example tries to clarify the application of modes:

```
active(Drug) :- atm(Drug, Atom, c, 4, Charge)).
active(Drug) :- symbond(Drug, Atom1, Atom2, 1)).
active(Drug) :- atm(Drug, Atom, c, 4, Charge)),
                symbond(Drug, Atom, Atom0, 1).
```

The first example receives the input variable *Drug* from the head, hence it obeys the modes. The second clause is illegal, because the second argument is input, and it is the first occurrence of *Atom*. The third clause calls *atm* and then *symbond*, making it legal.

The first step in the `induce` algorithm is to create a maximal conjunction of goals that **(i)** include the example and **(ii)** goals satisfy the input and constant declarations. The saturated clause can be seen as clause but also as a graph (or hypergraph) where the edges are nodes and the edges are mode-induced dependencies: generating rules is enumerating sub-graphs.

Aleph can display the bottom-clause as a text clause, but as the bottom clause can easily reach hundreds or thousands of nodes, it is difficult to extract any useful insights. An alternative is to use graph visualization. Next we show results from D3blocks [28], an interface between Python and the D3.js library.

```
firstgraph2d3(Edges,Nodes,_Groups,Colors,Weights,Names,Preds) :-
   maplist(split_edge, Edges, Sources, Targets),
   maplist(edge_weight, Edges, EWeights),
   d3 := d3blocks.'D3Blocks'(),
   df := pd.'DataFrame'.from_dict({"source":Sources,
     "target":Targets,
     "weight":EWeights}),
   d3.elasticgraph(df, filepath="./SatClause.html",
                   figsize=[3000,2000]),
   maplist(set_node(d3), Nodes, Preds, Colors, Names, Weights),
   d3.'Elasticgraph'.'D3graph'.show().

set_node(Whom, Node, Pred, Color, Name, Size) :-
   n := Whom.'Elasticgraph'.'D3graph'.node_properties[Node],
   n["tooltip"] := Pred,
   n["color"] := Color,
   n["label"] := Name,
   n["size"] := Size.
```

First, the edges are converted into a Pandas data-frame. This data-frame is the main structure for the search object `d3`. This object also stores nodes as the dictionary `node_properties`. Dictionaries are not guaranteed to always maintain key order. The Prolog code uses `map_list` to iterates over the nodes. The `set_node` predicate fetches this dictionary by using unification to combine the D3 object, the path to the properties dictionary, and the code key. Finally, we set the properties.

We use color to distinguish five type of predicates:

1. the seed is the concept we want to learn (dark green);
2. the attributes are properties of the compound (light blue).
3. entities are the atoms in the compound (red);
4. relations provide nearest of the structure of the graph, (light green)
5. constraints are relations between attributes, such as arithmetic comparisons between numeric attributes, like $A = 8$ or $B \leq 7.3$. (yellow).

The picture is centered in the example. There is a ring with the atom ls and an external ring with the boundings. Looking closely one can notice clusters of atoms, quite often hydrogens bonded to a larger atom. One can also observe that the boundings are always duplicates: for all $A_1 \to A_2$ there is a $A_2 \to A_1$. The bonds form a nice half-ring with a cluster of carbons on top. The attributes cluster to the left; they are totally independent from the rest of the network. There are many other opportunities for visualization in this application, namely within the search process. Figure 3 shows a snapshot of plot of a drug discovery application's bottom clause using the elastic graph algorithm.

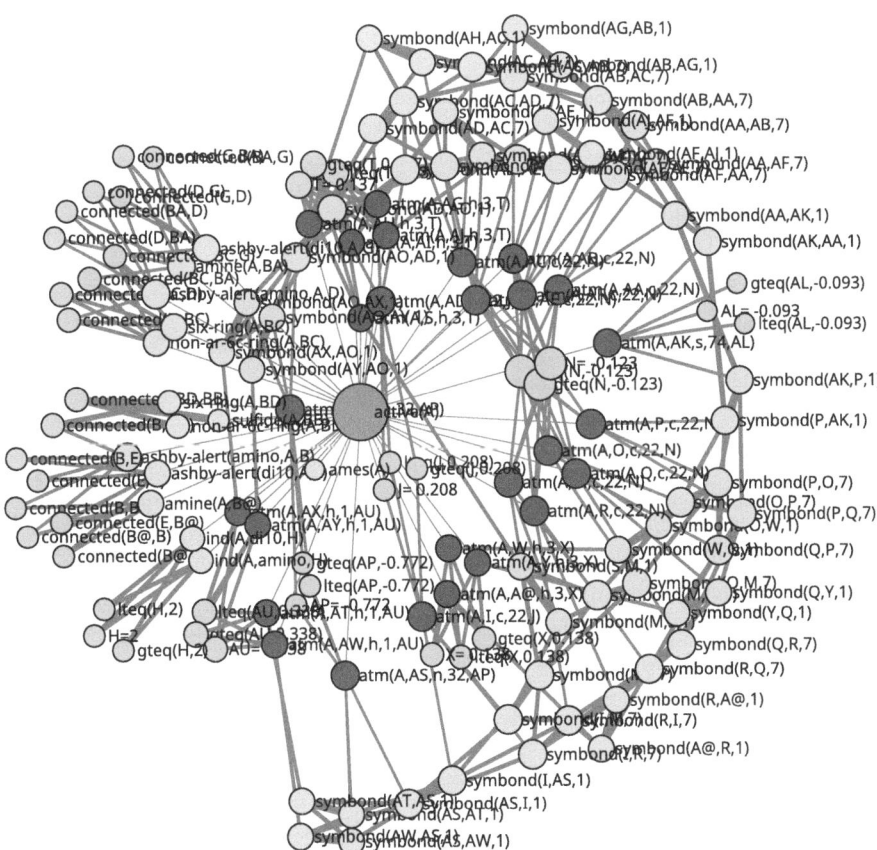

Fig. 3. A Bottom-Clause according to D3.js

Arguably, the relations described in the snapshot are too complex to be analyzed in a static visualization. However, the reader should keep in mind that D3.js is interactive, which for for molecular structure visualization offers significant advantages. D3.js enables precise control over the rendering of molecular diagrams, allowing for customizable layouts that accurately depict atom positions and bond types, including visual distinctions like bond thickness or color coding. Its interactivity supports also dynamic exploration, such as zooming, panning, and tool-tips for displaying the atomic properties, enhancing the user's engagement and understanding.

5.1 Other Applications

Often one tries to improve the leaner performance by seeing each clause in the theory as an attribute, so that the set of clauses become the attributes of a classifier. The next procedure learns an SVM classifier from a set of clauses plus a set of examples, and evaluates its performance on the training data:

```
learn :-
   findall(t(Train,Label),
       (example(_,Pol,Ex),
       ( Pol=pos -> Label = 1 ; Label = 0),
       findall(V,(clause(Ex,B),
                  (once(B)->V=1;V=0)),
              Train),
       ), TrainingData),
       maplist(zip,TrainingData,Data,Labels),
       clf := sklearn.svm.'SVC'(kernel= "linear".
                                class_weight="balanced").
       clf.fit(Data,  Labels),
        Scores := clf.predict_proba(Data).transpose()[1].tolist(),
       scipy.metrics.'RocCurveDisplay'.from_predictions(Labels,
                                                         Scores).
```

The algorithm constructs a list of labels, and a list of lists that represent the data (or examples) as bitmaps. The classifier is initialized, and trained according to the data and labels; the data is converted by the interface from Prolog list of lists to Python list with lists, and then by the NumPy library to an array. The reverse process is more complex because YAP does not convert NumPy matrices; we first transpose to extract the second column, next convert the NumPy vector to a list, and then pass the result to provide a first evaluation on the data set.

6   Conclusions

As the amount of reusable existing libraries keeps on growing, programming becomes more about connecting. This interface tries to take advantage of this trend, by making it as natural as possible to use both languages together.

The main challenge was the complexity of both environments. We used C++ to obtain object orientation, and SWIG to automatically cover the libraries. The "piano lifting" is still in C. Reference handling and documentation need work. Altogether, we hope that this work will be a step to exploit the overall advantages of Prolog systems, making Prolog more helpful, but also more fun.

As future work, we plan to compare the performance of our approach against Janus, the Prolog-Python interface originally developed by Swift for XSB Prolog, adopted by SWI-Prolog and the target of a joint effort between the XSB, SWI, and ciao communities.

Acknowledgments. This work is financed by National Funds through the Portuguese funding agency, FCT - Fundação para a Ciência e a Tecnologia, within projects UIDB/ 04434/2020, UIDP/04434/2020 and UIDB/50014/2020. DOI 10.54499/UIDB/50014/2020.

References

1. Carlsson, M., et al.: SICStus Prolog Users Manual (2022). https://sicstus.sics.se/sicstus/docs/latest4/html/prologbeans/
2. Andersen, C., Swift, T.: The Janus system: a bridge to new prolog applications. In: Warren, D.S., Dahl, V., Eiter, T., Hermenegildo, M.V., Kowalski, R.A., Rossi, F. (eds.) Prolog: The Next 50 Years. LNCS, vol. 13900, pp. 93–104. Springer, Cham (2023).https://doi.org/10.1007/978-3-031-35254-6_8
3. Angelopoulos, N., Santos Costa, V., Azevedo, J., Wielemaker, J., Camacho, R., Wessels, L.: Integrative functional statistics in logic programming. In: Sagonas, K. (ed.) PADL 2013. LNCS, vol. 7752, pp. 190–205. Springer, Heidelberg (2013). https://doi.org/10.1007/978-3-642-45284-0_13
4. Bartsch, G.: py-xsb (2004). https://github.com/gooofy/py-xsb
5. Beazley, D.M.: SWIG: an easy to use tool for integrating scripting languages with C and C++. In: Diekhans, M., Roseman, M. (eds.) Fourth Annual USENIX Tcl/Tk Workshop 1996, Monterey, California, USA, 10–13 July 1996. USENIX Association (1996)
6. Calejo, M.: InterProlog: towards a declarative embedding of logic programming in Java. In: Alferes, J.J., Leite, J. (eds.) JELIA 2004. LNCS (LNAI), vol. 3229, pp. 714–717. Springer, Heidelberg (2004). https://doi.org/10.1007/978-3-540-30227-8_64
7. Carlsson, M., Mildner, P.: Sicstus prolog - the first 25 years. Theory Pract. Log. Program. **12**(1–2), 35–66 (2012). https://doi.org/10.1017/S1471068411000482
8. Castro, S., Mens, K., Moura, P.: JPC: a library for categorising and applying interlanguage conversions between java and prolog. Sci. Comput. Program. **134**, 75–99 (2017). https://doi.org/10.1016/j.scico.2015.11.008
9. Chen, J., Muggleton, S.H., Santos, J.C.A.: Learning probabilistic logic models from probabilistic examples. Mach. Learn. **73**(1), 55–85 (2008). https://doi.org/10.1007/s10994-008-5076-4
10. Costa, V.S., Rocha, R., Damas, L.: The YAP prolog system. Theory Pract. Log. Program. **12**(1–2), 5–34 (2012). https://doi.org/10.1017/S1471068411000512
11. Deransart, P., Ed-Dbali, A., Cervoni, L.: Prolog - The Standard: Reference Manual. Springer, Heidelberg (1996). https://doi.org/10.1007/978-3-642-61411-8
12. Diaz, D., Abreu, S., Codognet, P.: On the implementation of GNU prolog. Theory Pract. Log. Program. **12**(1–2), 253–282 (2012). https://doi.org/10.1017/S1471068411000470

13. Finn, P., Muggleton, S., Page, D., Srinivasan, A.: Pharmacophore discovery using the inductive logic programming system Progol. Mach. Learn. **30**, 241–270 (1998)
14. no García, S.F.: PWIG wrapper and interface generator (2004). https://pwig.sourceforge.net/
15. Hermenegildo, M.V., et al.: An overview of ciao and its design philosophy. Theory Pract. Log. Program. **12**(1–2), 219–252 (2012). https://doi.org/10.1017/S1471068411000457
16. Hunter, J.D.: Matplotlib: a 2D graphics environment. Comput. Sci. Eng. **9**(3), 90–95 (2007)
17. Körner, P., et al.: Fifty years of prolog and beyond. Theory Pract. Log. Program. **22**(6), 776–858 (2022). https://doi.org/10.1017/S1471068422000102
18. Muggleton, S.H.: Inverting entailment and Progol. In: Furukawa, K., Michie, D., Muggleton, S.H. (eds.) Machine Intelligence 14, Proceedings of the Fourteenth Machine Intelligence Workshop, held at Hitachi Advanced Research Laboratories, Tokyo, Japan, pp. 135–190. Oxford University Press (1993)
19. Schimpf, J., Shen, K.: Ecl^{i}ps^e - from LP to CLP. Theory Pract. Log. Program. **12**(1–2), 127–156 (2012). https://doi.org/10.1017/S1471068411000469
20. Seward, A.J.: bedevere (2002). https://bedevere.sourceforge.net/
21. SICS Swedish ICT AB: Quintus Prolog Manual (2015). https://quintus.sics.se/isl/quintuswww/site/index.html
22. Singleton, P., Dushin, F.: JPL: a bidirectional Prolog/Java interface (2018). https://jpl7.org/
23. Srinivasan, A.: The aleph manual (2001)
24. Swift, T., Warren, D.S.: XSB: extending prolog with tabled logic programming. Theory Pract. Log. Program. **12**(1–2), 157–187 (2012). https://doi.org/10.1017/S1471068411000500
25. Swift, T., Andersen, C.: The Janus system: multi-paradigm programming in prolog and python. In: Pontelli, E., et al. (eds.) Proceedings 39th International Conference on Logic Programming, ICLP 2023, Imperial College London, UK, 9th–15th July 2023. EPTCS, vol. 385, pp. 241–255 (2023). https://doi.org/10.4204/EPTCS.385.24
26. Tarau, P.: Fluents: a refactoring of prolog for uniform reflection and interoperation with external objects. In: Lloyd, J., et al. (eds.) CL 2000. LNCS (LNAI), vol. 1861, pp. 1225–1239. Springer, Heidelberg (2000). https://doi.org/10.1007/3-540-44957-4_82
27. Tarau, P.: Agent oriented logic programming in jinni 2004. In: Haddad, H., Liebrock, L.M., Omicini, A., Wainwright, R.L. (eds.) Proceedings of the 2005 ACM Symposium on Applied Computing (SAC), Santa Fe, New Mexico, USA, 13–17 March 2005, pp. 1427–1428. ACM (2005). https://doi.org/10.1145/1066677.1067000
28. Taskesen, E.: D3blocks: the python library to create interactive and standalone D3JS charts (2022). https://towardsdatascience.com/d3blocks-the-python-library-to-create-interactive-and-standalone-d3js-charts-3dda98ce97d4/
29. Tekol, Y.: Pyswip (2023). https://github.com/yuce/pyswip
30. Waskom, M.L.: Seaborn: statistical data visualization. J. Open Sour. Softw. **6**(60), 3021 (2021)
31. Wielemaker, J., Costa, V.S.: On the portability of prolog applications. In: Rocha, R., Launchbury, J. (eds.) PADL 2011. LNCS, vol. 6539, pp. 69–83. Springer, Heidelberg (2011). https://doi.org/10.1007/978-3-642-18378-2_8
32. Wielemaker, J., Hendricks, M.: Why it's nice to be quoted: quasiquoting for Prolog. CoRR abs/1308.3941 (2013). http://arxiv.org/abs/1308.3941

33. Wielemaker, J., Schrijvers, T., Triska, M., Lager, T.: Swi-prolog. Theory Pract. Log. Program. **12**(1–2), 67–96 (2012). https://doi.org/10.1017/S1471068411000494
34. Zhou, N.: The language features and architecture of B-prolog. Theory Pract. Log. Program. **12**(1–2), 189–218 (2012). https://doi.org/10.1017/S1471068411000445

Type-Checking Heterogeneous Sequences in a Simple Embeddable Type System

Jim Newton[✉][iD]

EPITA Research Lab, 94270 Le Kremlin Becêtre, France
jnewton@lrde.epita.fr

Abstract. Heterogeneously typed sequences are supported in a wide range of programming languages, both dynamically and statically typed. These sequences often exhibit type patterns such as repetition, alternation, and optionality. The programmer needs a mechanism to *declare* and query adherence to this regularity. The theory of finite automata over finite alphabets was conceived for characterizing patterns in so-called regular languages, but does not exactly meet this challenge, because the set of potential elements of the sequences is infinite. In this article, we present a generalization of regular expressions called rational type expressions as a means of declaring regular patterns in heterogeneous sequences. We present procedures for constructing and manipulating symbolic finite automata, a generalization of classical finite automata, using a portable, simple, embeddable, type system. For type systems with subtyping, the subtype relation and type vacuity cannot always be computed programmatically. We provide a working, sound solution for constructing finite automata for type-based regular expressions even in cases where the subtype decidability relations is not computable retrospectively, but can be ensured by construction. We demonstrate the generality and portability of the system by providing implementations in Common Lisp, Clojure, Scala, and Python.

1 Introduction

Our goal is to declaratively describe a set of sequences (rational language) in a programming language based on regularities in the types of the sequence elements, and to efficiently decide membership of these rational languages at run-time.

This paper studies *rational type expressions* (RTEs) and the construction from RTE to symbolic, deterministic, finite automata (σDFA). RTEs are used to specify patterns in the types of the sequence elements, such as $(int \cdot str \cdot evenp)^*$, and σDFAs are used to efficiently decide the language induced by the RTE. The main challenges in the system are: (1) how to define types in a generic enough way to be usable in multiple programming languages, and (2) how to construct σDFA from an RTE despite limitations in the type system. For the first challenge, the system defines types using *a Simple Embeddable Type System* from Newton and Pommellet [27]. For the second challenge, we use Brzozowski style derivative-based construction, and we solve the challenge of overlapping

© The Author(s), under exclusive license to Springer Nature Switzerland AG 2025
E. Erdem and G. Vidal (Eds.): PADL 2025, LNCS 15537, pp. 18–34, 2025.
https://doi.org/10.1007/978-3-031-84924-4_2

types (decidable and otherwise) using Maximal Disjoint Type Decomposition (MDTD).

Before looking into the theory and implementation, we introduce the rational type expression (RTE) and the deterministic, complete, symbolic, finite automaton (σDFA) simply with an extended example, Sect. 2.

1.1 Motivation

Statically typed languages, such as Java or C++, support sequences of fixed types such as `Array[String]`, e.g., `("ab","cd","xyz")`, or `List[Double]`, e.g., `(1.0,1.1,1.2)`. In a language whose type system forms a type lattice [14], it is possible to declare an `Array[String | Double]` designating a sequence such as `("ab",1.1,1.2,"cd","xyz")`, with each element either `String` or `Double`. More general still, languages such as Python [33] and Common Lisp [2], support sequences where any element may be an object of any inhabited type whatsoever.

Element types of *heterogeneous sequences* usually follow an implicit, tacit, pattern in the mind of the programmer and hopefully documented in the code comments. The programmer writes code assuming elements to be a certain type, or writes ad-hoc code to check the contents of the sequences at run-time.

Dynamically typed languages such as Common Lisp, Clojure [10,11], and Python commonly manipulate heterogeneous sequences. The Common Lisp type system, the Python `mypy` [17,32] library, and Clojure `spec` [19] allow the annotation of type hints, which can sometimes invoke run-time type checks or help IDEs provide useful development and debug feedback. However, these type systems are not rich enough to express regular patterns in sequences of mixed types.

Scala [28,29], a statically typed language with limited reflection [6], allows the program to manipulate sequences such as those coming from JSON [31], declared as `Seq[Any]`. Code pattern matches to implement `typecase` logic based on dynamic type meta-data from the JVM. [7].

What is lacking from many dynamic languages (or statically typed languages with sufficient reflection), and which we address in this article, is a mechanism for the programmer to declare the expected type patterns, allowing the sequences to be efficiently type-checked at run-time, and thereafter to allow application code the safety of making simplifying assumptions about the data in question.

1.2 Our Contribution

We present a technique for recognizing certain heterogeneous sequences based on the types of their constituent elements. The technique involves declaratively describing such sequences using so-called RTEs. The RTEs are used to construct symbolic finite automata [5], which are then used to validate and reason about finite sequences whose elements are taken from an infinite set of values supported in the programming language.

Our contributions in this article are as follows. We

1. Adapt theoretical description of D'Antoni and Veanes [5] and Keil and Thiemann [15] to heterogeneously typed sequences in programming languages.

2. Provide an algorithm for the maximal disjoint type decomposition, MDTD, which, by construction, avoids the problem of undecidability of subtyping.
3. Demonstrate constructions of σDFA recognizing Regular Type Expressions despite an incomplete subtype predicate.
4. Provide sample implementations in four programming languages: Scala, Clojure, Python, and Common Lisp.

1.3 Previous Work

In [20], Newton used deterministic finite automata (DFA) and RTEs to recognize heterogeneous Common Lisp sequences based on type patterns. The current work, generalizes the RTEs to a wider range of programming languages.

Clojure Spec [10,11,19] and `metosin` [9] support some forms of type pattern recognition. After conversations between experts on public forums it is not clear whether Spec is based on finite automata theory at all or rather on NFA (non-deterministic finite automata) work by Might et al. [18]. An NFA-based procedure (presumably using backtracking) would have at least polynomial complexity, whereas our approach offers linear complexity.

Christophe Grande authored `seqexp` [1] for Clojure, a regular pattern matching library. According to an interview with Grande, `seqexp` does not use a finite automata approach, suggesting that the size of resulting code would violate the JVM [7] limitation of function size susceptible to optimization.

The Brzozowski derivative and an algorithm to compute it for digital circuits was first presented in 1964 by Janusz Brzozowski [4]. Owens et al. [30] presented a *modern* version applied to regular pattern recognition for sequences of characters. Owens noted that a practical obstacle to using this approach is large computation time of generating large finite automata over excessively large alphabets. We ameliorate this problem by considering sets rather than individual values.

D'Antoni and Veanes [5] argue that the generalization retains many of the good properties of their finite-alphabet counterparts. D'Antoni and Veanes discuss a decomposition of types referred to as *Minterms(...), i.e., the set of maximal satisfiable Boolean combinations*. D'Antoni's set is a less optimized version of our MDTD algorithm, Sect. 5.4.

Grigore [8], Kennedy and Pierce [16], from Microsoft Research, discuss subtype decidability in Java [7], Scala [28,29], C#, and .NET Intermediate Language. The work curiously lacks citations for C# and .NET Intermediate Language, as if the reader is already intimately familiar with C# and .NET IL.

Hosoya, Vouillon, and Pierce [13] defined regular expression in the XDuce language, allowing static XML types to be defined recursively and hierarchically to describe the structure of XML documents. XDuce programs consume and manipulate XML [3] documents allowing the type checker to assure that the programmatic expressions are type correct according to the XML schema, DTD, XML-Schema *etc.*. RTEs as opposed to the XDuce, add such type checking ability to an existing dynamic type systems.

2 Symbolic Finite Automata

First we give an example of a σDFA. Section 2.1 provides formal definitions. Consider the three RTEs [26], r_1, r_3, and r_2, defined in (1), (2), and (3). The syntax should be intuitive to anyone already familiar with regular expressions.

$$r_1 = (int \cdot str \cdot evenp)^* \qquad (1)$$
$$r_2 = (int \cdot str \cdot str^* \cdot evenp)^* \qquad (2)$$
$$r_3 = (int \cdot str^* \cdot evenp)^* . \qquad (3)$$

RTE, r_1, represents the set of sequences of arbitrary (finite) length, each of which consists of zero or more occurrences: integer, string, even integer. RTE, r_2 allows the string to occur one or more times. Finally, in RTE, r_3, the string is allowed to occur 0 or more times. E.g., the sequence (11,"a",12,13,"a","b",14) matches r_3 and r_2, but not r_1; (11,"a",12,13,"a",14) matches all of them; and (11.5,12.6) matches none of three RTEs.

A finite automaton efficiently decides membership of a rational language. Analogous to classical finite automata theory [12], RTEs correspond to *symbolic finite automata* [5] (σDFA) over a possibly infinite alphabet, Σ. Transitions are labeled *symbolically* as subsets of the alphabet. In our case, Σ is the set of all values representable in a given programming language, including other sequences. RTEs, r_1 and r_2, are implemented in Fig. 1 [left] and [right] respectively, r_1 being represented by a deterministic automaton and r_2 non-deterministic. The σDFA for r_3 is shown in Fig. 2 [left].

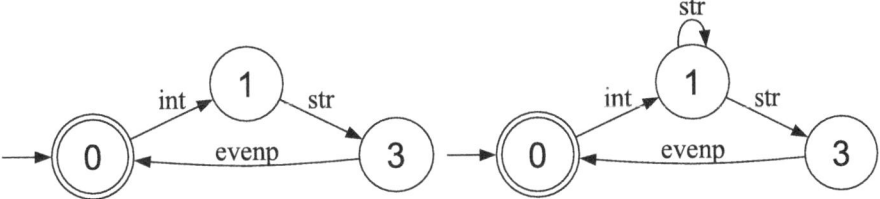

Fig. 1. σDFA for RTEs: [left] $r_1 = (int \cdot str \cdot evenp)^*$ and [right] non-deterministic automaton for $r_2 = (int \cdot str \cdot str^* \cdot evenp)^*$

We have chosen to work with deterministic automata, as opposed to non-deterministic, as they allow operations such as negation and intersection, and vacuity/habitation checks as well as disjoint and subset relations. Even though construction of DFAs can be slow and highly depends the syntactic representation of the regular expression, the time complexity of the membership decision is linear in length of sequence in question, constant in memory complexity, and no longer a function of the representation of the RTE itself. This independence is important because arbitrarily large expression trees may *reduce* to the same, *small* RTE. Much of the work in σDFA construction focuses on preventing overlap between transitions, thus enforcing determinism.

2.1 σDFA Formally

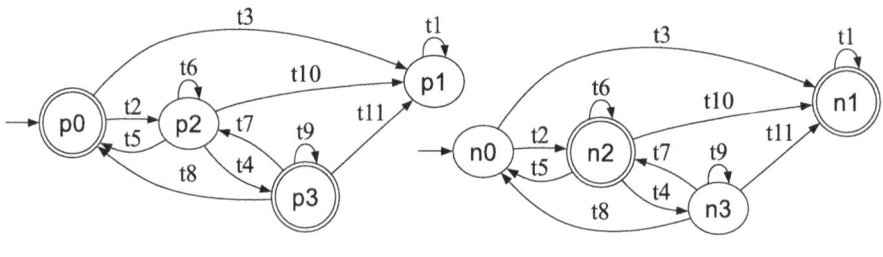

$$t_1 = \Sigma$$
$$t_2 = int$$
$$t_3 = \overline{int}$$
$$t_4 = str \cap evenp$$

$$t_5 = \overline{str \cap evenp}$$
$$t_6 = str \cap \overline{evenp}$$
$$t_7 = (int \cap \overline{evenp})$$
$$\cup (str \cap \overline{evenp})$$

$$t_8 = \overline{int} \cap \overline{str} \cap evenp$$
$$t_9 = (int \cap evenp)$$
$$\cup (str \cap evenp)$$
$$t_{10} = \overline{str} \cap \overline{evenp}$$
$$t_{11} = \overline{int} \cap \overline{str} \cap \overline{evenp}$$

Fig. 2. σDFAs A_p and A_n: [left] A_p is σDFA for RTE Eq. (3), $r_3 = (int \cdot str^* \cdot evenp)^*$; [right] A_n is σDFA for RTE $!r_3$.

The finite automata in Fig. 2 are called a *symbolic deterministic complete finite automata* (σDFA). A σDFA differs from a classical finite automaton in two significant ways. (1) The alphabet, Σ, may be infinite; and (2) each transition is labeled by a symbol representing a possibly infinite subset of Σ.

A *symbolic finite automaton* is a structure: $A = (\Sigma, \Upsilon, Q, q_0, F, T)$ where:

1. Σ is a possibly countably infinite set of *objects*.
2. Υ is a set of *symbols*, each designating a subset of Σ.
3. Q is a finite set of *states*.
4. $q_0 \in Q$ is the *initial* state.
5. $F \subseteq Q$ is the set of *accepting* states.
6. $T \subseteq Q \times \Upsilon \times Q$ is a set of transitions.

If $\nu \in \Upsilon$, let $[\![\nu]\!]$ denote the designated subset of Σ; $\nu \in \Upsilon \implies [\![\nu]\!] \subseteq \Sigma$.

A transition, $(q, \nu, r) \in T$, is also denoted $q \xrightarrow{\nu} r$. We refer to q as the *origin* of the transition, r as the *target*, and $\nu \in \Upsilon$ as the *label*.

A *partition* of Σ is a set of mutually disjoint, possibly empty subsets of Σ whose union is Σ.

If for each $q \in Q$, the set of labels of transitions having q as origin designates a partition of Σ, then A is called a *complete, deterministic, symbolic, finite automaton* on Σ, or simply a σDFA.

The definition of partition is non-conventional in order to avoid an annoying incoherence between theoretical partition and computed partition. In particular given two labels $\nu_1, \nu_2 \in \Upsilon$, the set $\{\nu_1 \cap \nu_2, \overline{\nu_1} \cap \nu_2, \nu_1 \cap \overline{\nu_2}, \overline{\nu_1} \cap \overline{\nu_2}\}$ is called the *standard partition* ($\overline{\nu_i}$ denotes set complement) and fulfills *our* definition of partition because the sets are mutually disjoint by construction, and their union is Σ, despite the possibility that any of the four intersections be empty.

A transition $\textcircled{q} \xrightarrow{\nu} \textcircled{r}$ is called *satisfiable* if $[\![\nu]\!]$ is inhabited ($[\![\nu]\!] \neq \emptyset$); otherwise it is called *non-satisfiable*. It is called *indeterminate* if it cannot be determined whether $[\![\nu]\!] = \emptyset$. The challenge of determining programmatically whether a transition is satisfiable is addressed in Sect. 5.1.

3 Rational Expressions

We accept the following definitions, borrowed from classical finite automata theory [12]. A length-n ($n \geq 0$) *sequence* is a function $\{0, 1, \ldots, n-1\} \to \Sigma$. A *language* is any set of finite-length sequences. The set of all finite-length sequences is called Σ^*. The symbol () represents the empty sequence. Two sequences, s, t can be concatenated to form a new sequence, $s \cdot t$. Similarly, two languages, L_1 and L_2 can be concatenated to form $L_1 \cdot L_2 = \{s \cdot t \mid s \in L_1, t \in L_2\}$. If $x \in \Sigma$, and s is a length-n sequence, then the *cons*, $x :: s = (x) \cdot s$, thus extending the sequence to length $n+1$. Finally, the Kleene star of a language, L^*, is the set of all finite concatenations of zero or more sequences from L.

A *rational type expression* or RTE is defined as any expression as defined below which represents (recognizes) a language on Σ. Let f and g be RTEs, recognizing languages $[\![f]\!]$ and $[\![g]\!]$. Let Υ be a set of symbols such that $\{\Sigma, \emptyset\} \subset \Upsilon$: $\nu \in \Upsilon \implies [\![\nu]\!] \subseteq \Sigma$. The following rules recursively define all RTEs.

RTE	Language	RTE	Language	RTE	Language
$\emptyset$	$\emptyset$	$f \cdot g$	$[\![f]\!] \cdot [\![g]\!]$	f^*	$[\![f]\!]^*$
ε	$\{()\}$	$f + g$	$[\![f]\!] \cup [\![g]\!]$	$\lfloor \nu \rfloor$	$\{(a) \mid a \in [\![\nu]\!]\}$
Σ	$\{(a) \mid a \in \Sigma\}$	$f \,\&\, g$	$[\![f]\!] \cap [\![g]\!]$	$!f$	$\Sigma^* \setminus [\![f]\!]$

The set of all sequences *recognized* by an RTE is called its *language*.

4 Programming Language Supporting RTEs

Even if finite automata theory is more general, we will restrict our discussion to objects and sequences representable in a given programming language. Σ will be the set of values expressible in some programming language, and Σ^* denotes the set of all finite, non-cyclic sequences whose values come from Σ. Suppose further that the programming language supports a set of built-in types and user-defined types, and a set, Υ_0, of symbols such as `int` and `str` which allow an application program to perform run-time type membership checks. We suppose that the programming language provides a mechanism for performing type membership and subtype checks in terms of the symbols in Υ_0. For example, in Scala `classOf[Number].isAssignableFrom(classOf[Integer])` and in Python `isinstance(42,int)` both return a Boolean *true*.

4.1 A Simple Embeddable Type System

Different programming languages make different assumptions about types. Newton and Pommellet [27] presented a *Simple Embeddable Type System* (SETS) which we use here. SETS keeps the type system simple enough to implement in a wide range of programming languages, and specifies that types already designatable in the programming language are accepted as atomic types in SETS. This type system suffices for our needs; although some limitations are described in Sect. 4.4. A formal definition of SETS can be found in [27], but we summarize it here.

A *type* is defined as any set of values, *i.e.* any subset of Σ.

We distinguish a *type* from a *type designator*. We typically denote a type designator by the symbol, ν, and the corresponding type by $[\![\nu]\!]$. The set of all types is 2^Σ, while the set of all type designators is denoted by, Υ, and is recursively defined as follows.

1. **Hosted types**: $\Upsilon_0 \subseteq \Upsilon$.
2. **Terminal types**: $\Sigma, \emptyset \in \Upsilon$ representing the universal and empty types.
3. **Singleton types**: $\forall a \in \Sigma$, $\{a\} \in \Upsilon$, with $[\![\{a\}]\!] = \{a\}$.
4. **Predicates**: for any decidable function $f : \Sigma \to \{true, false\}$, implemented in the host language, $Sat(f) \in \Upsilon$ with $[\![Sat(f)]\!] = \{x \in \Sigma \mid f(x) = true\}$.
5. **Union**: if $\nu_1, \nu_2 \in \Upsilon$, then $\nu_1 \cup \nu_2 \in \Upsilon$ with $[\![\nu_1 \cup \nu_2]\!] = [\![\nu_1]\!] \cup [\![\nu_2]\!]$.
6. **Intersection**: if $\nu_1, \nu_2 \in \Upsilon$, then $\nu_1 \cap \nu_2 \in \Upsilon$ with $[\![\nu_1 \cap \nu_2]\!] = [\![\nu_1]\!] \cap [\![\nu_2]\!]$.
7. **Complement**: if $\nu \in \Upsilon$, then $\overline{\nu} \in \Upsilon$ with $[\![\overline{\nu}]\!] = \overline{[\![\nu]\!]} = \{x \in \Sigma \mid x \notin [\![\nu]\!]\}$.

With a clever choice of f, $Sat(f)$ may designate the same set as other composed types in SETS, albeit with less reasoning power; *e.g.*, it is impossible to determine whether $[\![Sat(f)]\!] \subseteq [\![Sat(g)]\!]$ or if $\overline{[\![Sat(f)]\!]} \cap \overline{[\![Sat(g)]\!]}$ is inhabited.

A programming language specific API must implement type designators and $\in$ (Boolean, decidable), $\subseteq$ (semi-Boolean[1]) procedures. *E.g.*, in scala-rte [25] and in python-rte [24] type designators are implemented as class `SimpleTypeD` and subclasses thereof; while in clojure-rte [22] they are implemented as s-expressions. Type designators (type specifiers) are native to Common Lisp. An inhabited semi-Boolean predicate can be implemented as $\nu \subseteq \emptyset$, or in a more clever way depending on the programming language.

4.2 The Problematic Subtype Relation

Why is the subtype relation important? Knowing the subtype relation is critical for proving other relations between types. We can prove types ν and μ equivalent

---
[1] By *semi-Boolean*, we mean function which returns *true*, *false*, or *dont-know*.

by proving $(\nu \subseteq \mu) \wedge (\mu \subseteq \nu)$. ν is provably vacuous, if we can prove $\nu \subseteq \emptyset$. ν and μ are provably disjoint, if we can prove $\nu \cap \mu \subseteq \emptyset$.

The fact that the subtype relation is not always decidable exacerbates the challenge to guaranteed determinism. For example, the set of even integers, evenp, is a subset of the set of integers. However, evenp is disjoint from the set of strings. The fact that we cannot *decide* this programmatically, means we compute types such as $t_7 = (int \cap \overline{evenp}) \cup (str \cap \overline{evenp})$ in Fig. 2. The component $(int \cap \overline{evenp})$ is reasonable, however the component $(str \cap \overline{evenp})$ is superfluous as all even integers are necessarily not strings.

We would like to represent $t_7 = (int \cap \overline{evenp}) \cup str$, but we cannot. Worse still, in the figure, transitions $(p_2) \xrightarrow{t_{10}} (p_1)$ and $(p_2) \xrightarrow{t_5} (p_3)$ are constructed to guarantee determinism—the two types are disjoint by construction. The type, $t_4 = str \cap evenp$, is empty; consequently the transition is unsatisfiable, and thus state (p_3) is useless. We would like to eliminate (p_3) along with all transitions to and from it; unfortunately, we cannot—lacking an omniscient oracle.

In Fig. 2, the transitions leaving each state are labeled with mutually disjoint, but suboptimal types. *E.g.*, state (p_2) has four exiting transitions: t_4, t_5, t_6, and t_{10} which are mutually disjoint and a partition: $t_4 \cup t_5 \cup t_6 \cup t_{10} = \Sigma$.

4.3 Pragmatic Solution to the Subtype Problem

Our solution to the subtype problem is to employ a *semi-Boolean* subtype predicate. SETS (Sect. 4.1) proposes a type system equipped with a pragmatic subtype ($\subseteq$) semi-Boolean predicate which returns *true*, *false*, or *dont-know*, nevertheless equipped with a true-Boolean membership predicate ($\in$).

One might suppose that the inability to universally determine subtype or disjoint type relations will inevitably lead to non-deterministic transitions, but it does not. For σDFAs, undecidable does not imply non-deterministic. Why? Because given two types μ and ν, it is guaranteed *by construction* that the sets in the standard partition, $\mu \cap \nu$, $\mu \cap \overline{\nu}$, $\overline{\mu} \cap \nu$, and $\overline{\mu} \cap \overline{\nu}$ are mutually disjoint. These are disjoint independent of whether $\mu \subseteq \nu$, or whether μ and ν are disjoint. An example of transitions, disjoint by construction, can be seen with state (p_2) as was explained in Sect. 4.2.

Indeterminate transitions, leading to useless states, are common, as seen with the *evenp* type in Sect. 4.2. These indeterminate transitions do not cause misbehavior at run-time. Even if slightly inefficient, at run-time the evenp predicate returns true a, given an even integer, and false otherwise.

Undecidable subtype relations, and consequently unsatisfiable transitions, lead to challenges in minimization. Whereas classical finite automata are always uniquely minimizable, σDFAs are not. Case in point, as discussed in Sect. 4.2, the system cannot eliminate state (p_3), even though the only transition leading to it is unsatisfiable.

It may occur (albeit not in this example) that certain transitions reference equivalent types; *e.g.* $t_4 = str$ and $t_6 = str \cap \overline{evenp}$. These equivalent types, may prevent some σDFAs from being optimally minimized, in that certain equivalent states cannot be recognized as such. However, we are guaranteed by construction that two such transitions never appear leaving the same state, else the automaton would fail to be deterministic.

Minimization of σDFAs is an open question which requires more research. We will address this topic no further in the current article. We only mention it here because the impossibility of minimization can lead to sub-optimal σDFA, as well as compile-time and run-time inefficiencies.

4.4 Limitations of SETS

The type system we describe in Sect. 4.1 and used throughout our research lacks features some programmers might expect. Readers might wonder whether SETS is an appropriate interface to serve as a robust foundation of RTEs. We believe it is perfectly sufficient for the following reasons.

SETS does not explicitly mention tuple types, but exposes the tuple type built-into the language if available, e.g., in Scala, `SAtomic(Tuple2[Int, Double])`.

SETS does not attempt to robustly express function types such as $\nu \to \mu$ as such would violate the axioms of SETS. SETS demands that the type membership predicate return a Boolean, and that the subtype predicate return a semi-Boolean. Suppose function $f : \alpha_1 \to \beta_1$. Asking whether $f \in \alpha_2 \to \beta_2$, requires a subtype check $(\alpha_1 \to \beta_1) \subset (\alpha_2 \to \beta_2)$, obtaining a semi-Boolean. Thus the function type membership predicate would need to be a semi-Boolean. This limitation is not actually troublesome in practice, for none of the languages we have used in our research (Common Lisp, Clojure, Scala, Python) have a runtime operator to test whether a given function is an element of a type $\nu \to \mu$.

SETS cannot know when additional types are defined at run-time, thus invalidating a memoized result. In Java, such loading is possible via run-time loading of `jar` files. Because of this issue, the Scala implementation of SETS can be configured in `open-world-view` or `closed-world-view`. In `closed-world-view`, we assume that no additional types will be defined. Thus if ν and μ are the only subclasses of τ, then $\tau \setminus (\nu \cup \mu)$ can be reduced to $\emptyset$.

SETS supports types such as $Sat(f)$ which wrap predicates of arbitrary complexity. Thus we cannot reason about the computation complexity of a type membership query such as $x \in Sat(f)$.

5 Brzozowski Derivative Construction of σDFA

In this section we present a generalization of the Brzozowski derivative which is the principal tool needed for the Brzozowski σDFA construction.

While Brzozowski/Owens [4,30] defined $\partial_a r$ (the derivative of regular expression, r, with respect to letter $a \in \Sigma$), we present $\partial_\nu r$ for type $\nu \in \Upsilon$.

Let r be an RTE and $\nu \in \Upsilon$ be a type designator, then the RTE $\partial_\nu r$, the *derivative* of r *with respect to* ν is defined such that $[\![\partial_\nu r]\!] = \{s \in \Sigma^* \mid \exists h \in [\![\nu]\!], h :: s \in [\![r]\!]\}$.

Consider the RTE from Eq. (3): $r_3 = (int \cdot str^* \cdot evenp)^*$. Each sequence in $[\![r_3]\!]$ is either () or begins with an int. $\partial_{int}\, r_3$ is the set recognized by

$$\partial_{int}\,(int \cdot str^* \cdot evenp)^* = str^* \cdot evenp \cdot (int \cdot str^* \cdot evenp)^*$$

because if we take the subset of $[\![r_3]\!]$ containing sequences starting with an int, which is $[\![r_3]\!] \setminus \{()\}$, then strip off the head (an int) from each sequence; each of the remaining tails consists of zero or more str followed by $evenp$, then followed by zero or more occurrences of $(int \cdot str^* \cdot evenp)$.

We wish to compute a derivative of an RTE by recursively applying reduction rules in Fig. 3. We introduce subtype based rules (10), (11) and (12) which generalize equivalence based rules which Owens [30] stated.

$$\partial_\nu \emptyset = \partial_\nu \varepsilon = \emptyset \qquad (4)$$
$$\partial_\nu (r^*) = \partial_\nu r \cdot r^* \qquad (5)$$
$$\partial_\nu (r + s) = \partial_\nu r + \partial_\nu s \qquad (6)$$
$$\partial_\nu (r \,\&\, s) = \partial_\nu r \,\&\, \partial_\nu s \qquad (7)$$
$$\partial_\nu !r = !\partial_\nu r \qquad (8)$$

$$\partial_\nu (r \cdot s) = \begin{cases} (\partial_\nu r) \cdot s & \text{if } () \notin [\![r]\!] \\ (\partial_\nu r) \cdot s + \partial_\nu s & \text{if } () \in [\![r]\!] \end{cases} \qquad (9)$$

$$\partial_\nu \lfloor \mu \rfloor = \varepsilon \quad \text{if } [\![\nu]\!] \subseteq [\![\mu]\!] \qquad (10)$$
$$\partial_\nu \lfloor \mu \rfloor = \emptyset \quad \text{if } [\![\nu]\!] \cap [\![\mu]\!] = \emptyset \qquad (11)$$
$$\partial_\nu \lfloor \mu \rfloor \quad \text{otherwise, no rule defined} \qquad (12)$$

Fig. 3. Brzozowski Derivative Rules. For Equation (8) see Sect. 5.3. Variables, ν and μ represent type designators, $[\![\nu]\!], [\![\mu]\!] \subseteq \Sigma$; while r and s represent RTEs.

Owens [30] and Keil [15] also give similar recursive rules for computing *nullability*, detecting whether $() \in [\![r]\!]$, as well as $1^{st}(r)$ which is set of symbols which appear as first positions in a regular expression, *i.e.* the set of type designators to which (10) and (11) will be applied. We omit these rules here for lack of space.

5.1 Support for Overlapping Types

The Brzozowski construction for finite alphabets does not encounter the problem of overlapping types, because every letter in the alphabet is distinct. On the contrary, in our case, the *labels* under considerations designate types which correspond to subsets of Σ. Two types might be related by a subtype relation, or a disjoint relation. We have extended the Brzozowski method to accommodate intersecting types. Rather than calculating the derivative at each state with respect to each (possibly intersecting) type mentioned in the RTE, instead we calculate a disjoint set of types, then compute the derivatives with respect to this potentially larger set of disjoint types. The exact set of disjoint types, and the manner to compute it is discussed in Sect. 5.4.

The derivative rules, (4) through (12), are similar to those Owens [30] mentions. We have replaced a rule from the treatment from Owens, which was $\partial_a b = \varepsilon$ whenever $a \neq b$ with a generalization. This rule as Owens states, does not hold when regular expressions are generalized to RTEs. Our generalization is the introduction of Equations (10), (12), and 3: When computing $\partial_\nu \lfloor \mu \rfloor$ we must consider several cases: $\nu \subseteq \mu$, in which case rule (11) applies and $\partial_\nu \lfloor \mu \rfloor$ reduces to ε; or $\nu \cap \mu = \emptyset$, in which case rule (11) applies and $\partial_\nu \lfloor \mu \rfloor$ reduces to $\emptyset$. If $\nu \not\subseteq \mu$ and $\nu \cap \mu \neq \emptyset$, then we define no rule to compute the derivative. The algorithm must avoid any such an attempted computation.

A caveat of our enhanced algorithm is that we must determine whether $\nu \subseteq \mu$ or whether $\nu \cap \mu = \emptyset$. This poses a challenge: the subtype relation, and thus the equivalence and disjoint relation, are sometimes undecidable. One might naively think that if we deconstruct the type designators ν and μ (as discussed in Sect. 4.3) to the standard partition, $\{\nu \cap \mu, \nu \cap \overline{\mu}, \overline{\nu} \cap \mu, \overline{\nu} \cap \overline{\mu}\}$, then the undecidability problem would be averted. Unfortunately, there is no guarantee that the subtype procedure in the host language nor the subtype procedure in SETS (Sect. 4.1) is sufficiently clever to subsequently determine all subtype relations necessary. E.g., the subtype procedure does not inherently know *ex post facto* that the types in question were generated by a partitioning algorithm.

We do not attempt to solve the undecidability problem, rather we solve the problem of computing the derivative in our MDTD algorithm (Sect. 5.4), which assures knowledge of subtype and disjointness *by construction*. I.e., every time we need to compute $\partial_\nu \lfloor \mu \rfloor$, we know by construction that either $\nu \subseteq \mu$ or $\nu \cap \mu = \emptyset$; moreover, we know which of the two holds.

Our extension step has two positive effects on the algorithm. 1) it enforces determinism, *i.e.*, we ensure that all the transitions *leaving* a state specify disjoint types, and 2) it forces our treatment of the problem to comply with the assumptions required by the Brzozowski/Owens algorithm.

5.2 Constructing States and Transitions

Algorithm 1 specifies the construction of a σDFA from an RTE. The algorithm can be summarized as follows. The initial state, q_0 represents the given RTE, r. Each subsequent state represents some n^{th} derivative, $\partial_\nu^{[n]} r \; \forall \nu \in \varUpsilon$. Brzozowski [4,30] argues that the set of all such derivatives is finite.

We wish to compute the states and transitions of the σDFA A_p in Fig. 2 [left] corresponding to Eq. (3), $r_3 = (int \cdot str^* \cdot evenp)^*$. We name the states $p_0 \ldots p_3$ to distinguish the states from A_n [left] which we will call $n_0 \ldots n_3$. Step 1: construct the initial state (p_0) corresponding to r_3. Step 2: compute $MDTD(\{int\})$, because int is the only type which may appear as first element of a sequence contained in $[\![r_3]\!]$. MDTD returns the partition $\varPi = \{int, \overline{int}\}$. Step 3: compute $\{p_1, p_2\} = \{\partial_\nu r_3 \mid \nu \in \{\overline{int}, int\}\}$ as in (13) and (14), by applying rules (5), (9), (10), and (11):

During the computation of (13) and (14), we encounter the computation of $\partial_{\overline{int}} \lfloor int \rfloor$ and $\partial_{int} \lfloor int \rfloor$. As explained in Sect. 5.1, $\partial_{int} \lfloor int \rfloor = \varepsilon$, because $[\![int]\!] \subseteq [\![int]\!]$, rule (10); and $\partial_{\overline{int}} \lfloor int \rfloor = \emptyset$, because $[\![\overline{int}]\!] \cap [\![int]\!] = \emptyset$, rule (11).

Input: r : an RTE
Output: Components of a σDFA as in Section 2.1.
begin

$q_0 \leftarrow \text{new } State(r)$; $T \leftarrow ()$; $Q \leftarrow \{q_0\}$
$W \leftarrow \{q_0\}$ // working list states
while $W \neq \emptyset$ **do**

$q_1 \leftarrow$ any element from W
$W \leftarrow W \setminus \{q_1\}$
for $\nu \in MDTD(1^{st}(q_1.expression))$ // $1^{st}()$ see Owens [30]
do

$d \leftarrow \partial_\nu(q_1.expression)$ // reduced to canonical form
if $d \neq \emptyset$ // if not the empty language
then

if $\exists\, q_2 \in Q$ such that $q_2.expression = d$ **then**
   $T \leftarrow (q_1, \nu, q_2) :: T$ // transition
else
   $q_2 \leftarrow \text{new } State(d)$
   $T \leftarrow (q_1, \nu, q_2) :: T$
   $W \leftarrow q_2 :: W$
   $Q \leftarrow q_2 :: Q$

$F \leftarrow \{q \in Q \mid () \in [\![q.expression]\!]\}$ // see Owens [30]
return (Q, q_0, F, T)

Algorithm 1: Compute DFA by Brzozowski derivative

Having computed the RTEs, p_1 and p_2, we create two new states (in the σDFA), labeled (p_1) and (p_2), and add two transitions, one for each derivative: $(p_0) \xrightarrow{int} (p_2)$ and $(p_0) \xrightarrow{\overline{int}} (p_1)$, using the values of ν as the respective labels.

We process the constructed states in any order. Resulting derivative computations are shown in Fig. 4. As we encounter RTEs not yet seen, we simply add them to a to-do list. The only types which can be the first element of a sequence in $[\![p_2]\!]$ are str and $evenp$, so when we process (p_2), we compute $MDTD(\{str, evenp\})$, using Algorithm 2, to obtain the partition $\Pi = \{str \cap evenp,\ \overline{str} \cap evenp,\ str \cap \overline{evenp},\ \overline{str} \cap \overline{evenp}\}$, and the additional information in Fig. 5, which provides the subtype and disjoint relations needed to apply reduction rules (10) and (11), when computing $\{\partial_\nu p_2 \mid \nu \in \Pi\}$.

Finally, we decide which states are *accepting*. A state associated with RTE r is accepting if $() \in [\![r]\!]$. Thus the accepting states are q_0 and q_3; $() \in [\![r_3]\!]$, $() \notin [\![q_1]\!]$, $() \notin [\![q_2]\!]$, and $() \in [\![q_3]\!]$. Owens [30], provides a simple algorithm for deciding whether $\varepsilon \subseteq [\![r]\!]$; we omit the algorithm in this article.

$$\begin{aligned}
p_0 &= r_3 & &= (int \cdot str^* \cdot evenp)^* \\
p_1 &= \partial_{t_3} p_0 & &= \partial_{\overline{int}} p_0 = \emptyset & &(13) \\
p_2 &= \partial_{t_2} p_0 & &= str^* \cdot evenp \cdot (int \cdot str^* \cdot evenp)^* & &(14) \\
p_3 &= \partial_{t_4} p_2 & &= \partial_{str \cap evenp} p_2 \\
& & &= str^* \cdot evenp \cdot (int \cdot str^* \cdot evenp)^* \\
& & &\quad + (int \cdot str^* \cdot evenp)^* & &(15)
\end{aligned}$$

$$\begin{aligned}
\partial_\nu p_1 &= \emptyset \quad \forall \nu \\
\partial_{t_6} p_2 &= p_2 \\
\partial_{t_5} p_2 &= p_0 \\
\partial_{t_{10}} p_2 &= p_1 \\
\partial_{t_7} p_3 &= p_2 \\
\partial_{t_9} p_3 &= p_3 \\
\partial_{t_8} p_3 &= p_0 \\
\partial_{t_{11}} p_3 &= p_1
\end{aligned}$$

Fig. 4. Computation of Transitions of σDFA in Fig. 2.

Type designator	Supertypes	Disjoint types
$str \cap evenp$	$\Sigma, str, evenp$	$\emptyset, \overline{str}, \overline{evenp}$
$str \cap \overline{evenp}$	$\Sigma, str, \overline{evenp}$	$\emptyset, \overline{str}, evenp$
$\overline{str} \cap evenp$	$\Sigma, \overline{str}, evenp$	$\emptyset, str, \overline{evenp}$
$\overline{str} \cap \overline{evenp}$	$\Sigma, \overline{str}, \overline{evenp}$	$\emptyset, str, evenp$

Fig. 5. MDTD computation for types: $\{str, evenp\}$.

5.3 Constructing a σDFA from a Negated RTE

We consider (8) in more detail. Keil and Thiemann [15] address the question: under which conditions $\partial_\nu !r = !\partial_\nu r$? They argue that the equivalence holds whenever $\bigcup_{a \in \llbracket \nu \rrbracket} \llbracket \partial_{\{a\}} r \rrbracket = \bigcap_{a \in \llbracket \nu \rrbracket} \llbracket \partial_{\{a\}} r \rrbracket$, and that condition is valid whenever ν is selected from a partition of a union of types which appear as a $1^{st}(r)$, which is what our MDTD algorithm (Sect. 5.4) enforces.

The identity, $\partial_\nu !r = !\partial_\nu r$, can also be seen visually in A_p and A_n, Fig. 2 [left] and [right] respectively. In order for A_n to accept the language complementary to A_p, the underlying graph structures of the two σDFAs must be isomorphic except that state acceptance is toggled. Consequently, state (n_0) corresponds to the RTE $!p_0$; i.e., $n_0 = !p_0$. For the Brzozowski construction to be valid the RTE associated with (n_2) must be $\partial_{t_2} n_0$; i.e. $n_2 = \partial_{t_2} n_0$.

How do we know that $n_2 = !\partial_\nu p_0$? Because the language of state (n_2) is the complement of the language of state (p_2); i.e. $\llbracket n_2 \rrbracket = \overline{\llbracket p_2 \rrbracket}$.

$$\llbracket \partial_{t_2} !p_0 \rrbracket = \llbracket \partial_{t_2} n_0 \rrbracket = \llbracket n_2 \rrbracket = \overline{\llbracket p_2 \rrbracket} = \overline{\llbracket \partial_{t_2} p_0 \rrbracket}.$$

5.4 Maximal Disjoint Type Decomposition (MDTD)

Newton [21] presented a streamlined algorithm to compute MDTD (Maximal Disjoint Type Decomposition) which creates other artifacts useful in σDFA construction especially in light of undecidability of subtype or disjoint procedures.

Input: $\mathcal{M}$: a set of type designators
Output: $(\mathcal{U}, \mathcal{S})$: a pair as described in Section 5.4.
begin
  $\mathcal{S} \leftarrow \{(\top, \{\top\}, \{\bot\})\}$ // working list of triples
  for $\mu \in \mathcal{M}$ **do**
    for $(\nu, f, d) \in \mathcal{S}$ **do**
      $\mathcal{S} \leftarrow \mathcal{S} \setminus \{(\nu, f, d)\}$ // remove triple from $\mathcal{S}$
      if $\mu \cap \nu = \emptyset$ **then**
        $\mathcal{S} \leftarrow (\nu, f, \mu :: d) :: \mathcal{S}$ // ν and μ are disjoint
      else if $\overline{\mu} \cap \nu = \emptyset$ **then**
        $\mathcal{S} \leftarrow (\nu, \mu :: f, d) :: \mathcal{S}$ // $\nu \subseteq \mu$
      else
        $\mathcal{S} \leftarrow (\mu \cap \nu, \mu :: f, d) :: \mathcal{S}$ // $\mu \cap \nu \subseteq \mu$
        $\mathcal{S} \leftarrow (\overline{\mu} \cap \nu, f, \mu :: d) :: \mathcal{S}$ // $\overline{\mu} \cap \nu$ and μ are disjoint

  $\mathcal{U} \leftarrow$ set of first elements of each 3-tuple in $\mathcal{S}$
  return $(\mathcal{U}, \mathcal{S})$

Algorithm 2: Compute MDTD of given $\mathcal{M}$.

Given a set of potentially intersecting type designators, $\mathcal{M} = \{\mu_1, \mu_2, \ldots, \mu_n\}$, Algorithm 2 computes a pair, $(\Pi, \mathcal{S})$, where $\mathcal{S}$ is meta-data described below, and $\Pi = \{\nu_1, \nu_2, \ldots, \nu_m\}$ is a new set of type designators designating a partition of Σ, such that for $i \leq m$, and $j \leq n$, either $[\![\nu_i]\!] \subseteq [\![\mu_j]\!]$ or $[\![\nu_i]\!] \cap [\![\mu_j]\!] = \emptyset$.

Algorithm 2 has a limitation that there may be $\nu_i, \nu_j \in \Pi$ such that $[\![\nu_i]\!] = [\![\nu_j]\!] = \emptyset$, because the subset predicate may return *dont-know*; see Sect. 4.3.

MDTD has worst-case (time and space) complexity $\Omega(2^{|\mathcal{M}|})$, if the final else is taken every time through the inner loop. Any alternate algorithm must also have worst-case, exponential complexity, because in the worst case, a set of size $2^{|\mathcal{M}|}$ must be computed. We say Ω, because we are ignoring the complexity of the vacuity/disjoint checks, which only worsen the complexity. However, the complexity is quadratic if $\mathcal{M}$ is already a partition of its union.

As mentioned above, the return value of Algorithm 2 contains as meta-data a set, $\mathcal{S}$, of triples, (ν, f, d): ν is an element of the partition, Π; f is a set of factors, each of which is a guaranteed supertype of ν, even if the subtype predicate is not able to detect it; and d is a set of type designators, each of which is guaranteed disjoint with ν, even if (especially if) the disjoint predicate is not capable of detecting the fact.

6 Sample Implementations

```
def evenp(x: Any): Boolean =
  x match {
    case y: Int => y % 2 == 0
    case _ => false
  }
val even = SSatisfies(evenp,"even")
val int = Atomic(classOf[Int])
val str = Atomic(classOf[String])
val r0 = (int ++ str ++ even).*
val r1 = int ++ str.* ++ even).*
```

```
val dfa = r1.toDfa()
val s1= Seq(1,"hello",3)
val s2= Seq(1,"hello","world",2,
            3,4,
            5,"hello",6)
val s3 = Seq(1.1, 1.2, 1.3)

r0.contains(s1) // Some(false)
dfa.simulate(s2) // Some(true)
dfa.simulate(s3) // None
```

Fig. 6. Scala code for constructing r_1 and r_3 Eqs. (1) and (3). `r0.contains(s1)` asks whether `s1` is in the language of the RTE, while `dfa.simulate(s2)` asks whether `s2` is in the language of the σDFA.

One of the goals of our project is to design RTE abstractly enough to be implementable in multiple programming languages. As a proof of concept, we provide open source implements for RTE and its support libraries in Common Lisp [2], Scala [28,29], Clojure [10,11], and Python [33]. The original implementation is a Common Lisp library `cl-rte` [23], first presented in [20]. The Clojure (`clojure-rte` [22]) and Scala (`scala-rte` [25]) libraries extend the Clojure and Scala type systems, which are already extensions of the type system of the JVM. The Python library, `python-rte` [24], extends the built-in Python type system.

In this article we suppress most of the specifics of these implementations. We invite the reader to download the code from the links provided. Figure 6 shows a small example of how RTEs can be used in a Scala program.

In each of these `*-rte` libraries, users may specify RTEs based on fundamental types in the language, or user defined classes. The language-level types are interfaced to RTE via SETS serving as a wrapper recognizable by the RTE implementation code. The implementations provide Brzozowski σDFA constructions to convert the RTE (expression tree) into a σDFA, including APIs for manipulating RTEs, such as inversion, intersection, union, determinization, minimization, extraction (extracting an RTE from a σDFA [34, sec 2.4.2]), vacuity checks, etc.

7 Conclusion and Perspectives

We have presented a foundation sufficient for implementing RTEs in various programming languages using an adaptation of the Brzozowski construction algorithm. Two challenges for implementing RTE in a host language are representing and computing with types in the host language, and converting a set of overlapping types to a partition of the value space. We have proposed SETS (Sect. 4.1) and MDTD (Sect. 5.4) as solutions to these challenges, along with sample implementations in Common Lisp, Clojure, Scala, and Python.

An important strength of our type system is that many questions are answered with three-way logic. For types ν and μ, we distinguish $\nu \subseteq \mu$ (ν is proven to be a subtype of μ), $\nu \not\subseteq \mu$ (ν is proven NOT to be a subtype of μ), and dont-know (we were unable to prove or disprove $\nu \subseteq \mu$). This three-way logic extends into the question of habitation of rational languages. For example, given an σDFA it might be that every computation path from q_0 to a final state passes through at least one indeterminate transition–not provably satisfiable and not provably non-satisfiable. In this case we cannot determine whether the language of the σDFA is inhabited.

References

1. Seqexp: regular expressions for sequences (2014). https://github.com/cgrand/seqexp
2. Ansi: American National Standard: Programming Language – Common Lisp. ANSI X3.226:1994 (R1999) (1994)
3. Bray, T., Paoli, J., Sperberg-McQueen, C.M., Maler, E., Yergeau, F.: Extensible markup language (XML) 1.0 (fifth edition). W3C Recommendation (2008). http://www.w3.org/TR/REC-xml/
4. Brzozowski, J.A.: Derivatives of regular expressions. J. ACM **11**(4), 481–494 (1964). https://doi.org/10.1145/321239.321249
5. D'Antoni, L., Veanes, M.: The power of symbolic automata and transducers. In: Computer Aided Verification, 29th International Conference (CAV 2017). Springer (2017). https://www.microsoft.com/en-us/research/publication/power-symbolic-automata-transducers-invited-tutorial/
6. EPFL: Scala Reflection Library 2.12.0 (2016). https://www.scala-lang.org/api/2.12.0/scala-reflect/scala/reflect/runtime/index.html
7. Gosling, J., Joy, B., Steele, G.L., Bracha, G., Buckley, A.: The Java Language Specification, Java SE 8 Edition, 1st edn. Addison-Wesley Professional (2014)
8. Grigore, R.: Java generics are turing complete. CoRR abs/1605.05274 (2016). http://arxiv.org/abs/1605.05274
9. Heikkilä, M.: Malli, Metosin (2022). https://github.com/metosin/malli
10. Hickey, R.: The Clojure programming language. In: Proceedings of the 2008 Symposium on Dynamic Languages, p. 1. ACM (2008)
11. Hickey, R.: A history of clojure. Proc. ACM Program. Lang. **4**(HOPL) (2020). https://doi.org/10.1145/3386321
12. Hopcroft, J.E., Motwani, R., Ullman, J.D.: Introduction to Automata Theory, Languages, and Computation, 3rd edn. Addison-Wesley Longman Publishing Co., Inc., Boston (2006)
13. Hosoya, H., Vouillon, J., Pierce, B.C.: Regular expression types for XML. ACM Trans. Program. Lang. Syst. **27**(1), 46–90 (2005). https://doi.org/10.1145/1053468.1053470
14. Newton, J., Sébastien Doeraene, L.P.: Union types in scala 3 (2020). https://contributors.scala-lang.org/t/union-types-in-scala-3/4046
15. Keil, M., Thiemann, P.: Symbolic solving of extended regular expression inequalities. In: Raman, V., Suresh, S.P. (eds.) 34th International Conference on Foundation of Software Technology and Theoretical Computer Science (FSTTCS 2014).

Leibniz International Proceedings in Informatics (LIPIcs), vol. 29, pp. 175–186. Schloss Dagstuhl – Leibniz-Zentrum für Informatik, Dagstuhl (2014). https://doi.org/10.4230/LIPIcs.FSTTCS.2014.175
16. Kennedy, A., Pierce, B.C.: On decidability of nominal subtyping with variance. In: International Workshop on Foundations and Developments of Object-Oriented Languages (FOOL/WOOD) (2007). https://www.microsoft.com/en-us/research/publication/on-decidability-of-nominal-subtyping-with-variance/
17. Lehtosalo, J.: The MyPy project (2022). http://mypy-lang.org
18. Might, M., Darais, D., Spiewak, D.: Parsing with derivatives: a functional pearl. In: Proceedings of the 16th ACM SIGPLAN International Conference on Functional Programming, ICFP 2011, pp. 189–195. Association for Computing Machinery, New York (2011). https://doi.org/10.1145/2034773.2034801
19. Miller, A.: Spec Guide (2022). https://clojure.org/guides/spec
20. Newton, J.: Representing and computing with types in dynamically typed languages. Ph.D. thesis, Sorbonne University (2018)
21. Newton, J.: An elegant and fast algorithm for paritioning types. In: European Lisp Symposium, Amsterdam, Netherlands (2023)
22. Newton, J.: Regular type expressions for clojure (2024). github.com/jimka2001/clojure-rte
23. Newton, J.: Regular type expressions for common lisp (2024). github.com/jimka2001/cl-rte
24. Newton, J.: Regular type expressions for python (2024). github.com/jimka2001/python-rte
25. Newton, J.: Regular type expressions for scala (2024). github.com/jimka2001/scala-rte
26. Newton, J., Demaille, A., Verna, D.: Type-checking of heterogeneous sequences in common lisp. In: European Lisp Symposium, Kraków, Poland (2016)
27. Newton, J., Pommellet, A.: A portable, simple, embeddable type system. In: European Lisp Symposium. Online, Everywhere (2021)
28. Odersky, M., et al.: The Scala language specification (2004)
29. Odersky, M., Zenger, M.: Scalable component abstractions. In: Sigplan Notices - SIGPLAN, vol. 40, pp. 41–57 (2005). https://doi.org/10.1145/1103845.1094815
30. Owens, S., Reppy, J., Turon, A.: Regular-expression derivatives re-examined. J. Funct. Program. **19**(2), 173–190 (2009)
31. Pezoa, F., Reutter, J.L., Suarez, F., Ugarte, M., Vrgoč, D.: Foundations of JSON schema. In: Proceedings of the 25th International Conference on World Wide Web, WWW 2016, pp. 263–273. International World Wide Web Conferences Steering Committee, Republic and Canton of Geneva, CHE (2016).https://doi.org/10.1145/2872427.2883029
32. Rak-amnouykit, I., McCrevan, D., Milanova, A., Hirzel, M., Dolby, J.: Python 3 types in the wild: a tale of two type systems. In: Proceedings of the 16th ACM SIGPLAN International Symposium on Dynamic Languages, DLS 2020, pp. 57–70. Association for Computing Machinery, New York (2020).https://doi.org/10.1145/3426422.3426981
33. van Rossum, G., Drake, F.L.: The Python Language Reference Manual. Network Theory Ltd. (2011)
34. Sakarovitch, J.: Elements of Automata Theory. Cambridge University Press, USA (2009)

The Scenic Route to Deforestation
An Exercise in Applying Parametricity in Curry

Vincent Robinson and Steven Libby[✉]

University of Portland, Portland, OR 97203, USA
{robinsma25,libbys}@up.edu

Abstract. Parametricity and free theorems are a powerful tool for proving the correctness of optimizations. There has been some investigation of incorporating free theorems for functional logic languages, including a proof of the parametricity theorem for a sub-language of Curry. In this paper we explore the consequences of adding one optimization, shortcut deforestation, to a Curry compiler. We describe the optimization and give a proof of correctness. While proving the correctness of the optimization, we explore the application of parametricity and free theorems to Curry. This leads to some of the more surprising aspects of functional logic programming.

1 Introduction

Recently there has been a renewed interest in the efficient execution of functional logic programs [5–7,16]. This has proven to be a rich area of new ideas. We examine shortcut deforestation, which is a common functional programming optimization, and apply it to the Curry language.

Curry is a lazy functional logic programming language. It combines the efficient execution of functional programming with the general search strategies of logic programming, and has an optimal evaluation strategy [2]. Syntactically it is similar to Haskell, but with the addition of a choice operator (?) and free variables with the *free* clause.

There are many examples of the utility of functional logic programs from constraint solving to parsing to GUI development. [3,4,8,13] Functional logic programming allows us to attack problems in new ways, but it comes at the cost of efficiency. Most of the optimizations that work in a functional language like Haskell, do not directly apply to Curry.

In this paper, we correct this situation, at least for shortcut deforestation. Libby [15] showed that the optimization was effective at speeding up Curry programs, but was only able to show that the optimization was valid in limited cases in Curry. The aim of this paper it to show that shortcut deforestation is correct in a much more general setting.

The rest of the paper is organized as follows: in the next section we describe the optimization and how it was proved correct with parametricity; next, we re-introduce the CuMin and SaLT languages [18]; after this, we turn

$$
\begin{aligned}
&foldr\ k\ z\ []   &&= z \\
&foldr\ k\ z\ (x:xs)   &&= x\ \text{`}k\text{`}\ foldr\ k\ z\ xs \\
\\
&build\ g   &&= g\ (:)\ [] \\
\\
&anyOf\ xs   &&= foldr\ (?)\ failed\ xs \\
\\
&map\ f\ xs   &&= build\ (\lambda c\ n \to foldr\ (\lambda a\ b \to c\ (f\ a)\ b)\ n\ xs)
\end{aligned}
$$

Fig. 1. Definition of map and anyOf using foldr and build

our attention to proving the correctness of the optimization; we prove successively stronger results using dinaturality and free theorems; finally, we conclude by discussing the efficacy of the optimization in Curry.

2 Background

Deforestation is a technique to remove intermediate data structures from functional programs. Consider the expression $anyOf\ (map\ f\ xs)$ where $anyOf$ and map are defined as follows.

$$
\begin{aligned}
&anyOf   &&:: [a] \to a \\
&anyOf\ (x:xs)   &&= x\ ?\ anyOf\ xs \\
\\
&map   &&:: (a \to b) \to [a] \to [b] \\
&map\ f\ []   &&= [] \\
&map\ f\ (x:xs)   &&= f\ x\ :\ map\ f\ xs
\end{aligned}
$$

The result of our expression is to arbitrarily pick a value from the list, and apply the function f to it. While this is an elegant formulation, it is not efficient. We apply f to every value in the list, and construct an entirely new list. This second list is entirely superfluous, and could easily be removed.

$$anyMap\ f\ (x:xs) = f\ x\ ?\ anyMap\ f\ xs$$

This is an example of deforestation. The intermediate list is removed, and we return the value we want. Wadler's original implementation of deforestation [23] was complex and suffered from termination issues when dealing with recursive functions. A more economical example was given by Gill et al. [12]. The key insight is that we can rewrite many list processing functions as a combination of *foldr* and *build* as seen in Fig. 1. The *build* function produces a list using a function g, and the *foldr* function consumes the list. We avoid giving a type to *build* for the same reason as Gill et al. [12]. Since Curry uses Hindley-Milner typing, we cannot express the type of *build* so we must define the function as a primitive in the compiler. We can rewrite both *anyOf* and *map* using *build* and *foldr*. While this is a less intuitive way to write list processing functions, the advantage is that we can derive the following theorem:

Theorem 1. *Let τ be a closed type. For any function g of the type*

$$g :: (\tau \to \beta \to \beta) \to \beta \to \beta$$

the following holds for all expressions $z :: v$ and $k :: \tau \to v \to v$:

$$foldr\ k\ z\ (build\ g) \equiv g\ k\ z$$

After applying this to our previous example, we can immediately simplify the expression, which leads to a nearly identical definition to *anyMap*.

$$anyOf\ (map\ f\ xs)$$
$$\Rightarrow \boxed{foldr}\ (?)\ failed\ (\boxed{build}\ (\lambda c\ n \to foldr\ (\lambda a\ b \to c\ (f\ a)\ b)\ n\ xs))$$
$$\Rightarrow (\lambda c\ n \to foldr\ (\lambda a\ b \to c\ (f\ a)\ b)\ n\ xs)\ (?)\ failed$$
$$\Rightarrow foldr\ (\lambda a\ b \to (f\ a)\ ?\ b)\ failed\ xs$$

Shortcut deforestation has been an effective optimization in GHC for many years. It also comes with a simple proof of correctness. Theorem 1 is a direct consequence of the free theorem for g [12]. This is often cited as one reason why free theorems are so useful.

While this is a good result for Haskell, we do not have an analogous result for Curry. Our derivation above may not even be correct. In fact, there are several cases where sharing and non-determinism conspire to make Theorem 1 invalid in Curry, as we will see in the next section. We need a corresponding version of parametricity for Curry. Fortunately much of this work has already been done. We build on the work of Mehner et al. [18] for our result.

Free theorems are an application of Reynold's abstraction theorem [20], which Wadler renames the parametricity theorem [22]. By defining a relation on each type in our program, we can derive theorems about a function directly from its type. These theorems are colloquially called "free theorems". This is a powerful technique for reasoning about functional programs, so naturally we would like to apply this strategy to Curry. The theory of parametricity has come a long way for functional logic languages in recent years. Mehner et al. [18] present a version of the parametricity for the language CuMin, which is a sublanguage of Curry. Later, Voigtländer [21] showed a system to automatically derive free theorems strictly from a type that is compatible with Mehner's work.

Determining a function's free theorem from its type can be technical, so we provide an example with the free theorem for g. We need two concepts from "Theorems for Free". First, we interpret the type of an expression as a relation on that expression. The hope is that if $e_1 :: t$ and $e_2 :: t$, then $(e_1, e_2) \in t$ iff $e_1 \downarrow e_2$. That is, e_1 and e_2 are related if they reduce to the same value. The second concept is that we can build up relations for more complicated types. if $f :: a \to b$

and $f' :: a \to b$, then $(f, f') \in a \to b$, iff for all $(x, x') \in a$, $(f\ x, f'\ x') \in b$. We say that f and f' are related if they take related inputs to related outputs. We can reason about parametric expressions the same way. $(g, g') \in \forall X.F(X)$ for some type expression F involving X, iff for any relation R and types A and A', we have $(g_A, g'_{A'}) \in R$. In other words, polymorphic expression are related if they take related types to related values.

We give a brief derivation of Theorem 1 as an example of deriving free theorems. We look at the type of the function $g :: \forall \beta.(\tau \to \beta \to \beta) \to \beta \to \beta$. First we pick a function $h :: b \to b'$ to be the relation β. Next we pick an arbitrary $c :: \tau \to \beta \to \beta$. If $(y, y') \in h$ we have $(c\ x\ y, c\ x\ y') \in h$, or, since h is a function, $h\ (c\ x\ y) = c\ x\ (h\ y)$. We can apply the same reasoning to g. if $(n, n') \in h$ and $(c, c') \in \tau \to h \to h$, then $(g\ c\ n,\ g\ c'\ n') \in h$. Rewriting using the fact that h is a function we find that if $h\ (c\ x\ y) = c\ x\ (h\ y)$ then $h\ (g\ c\ n) = g\ c'\ (h\ n)$. Finally, we specialize h to $foldr\ k\ z$, c to $(:)$, n to $[]$ and c' to k. This leaves us with the theorem. if $foldr\ k\ z\ (x : y) = k\ x\ (foldr\ k\ z\ y)$ then $foldr\ k\ z\ (g\ (:)\ []) = g\ k\ (foldr\ k\ z\ [])$. We note that our condition is part of the definition of $foldr$, and we recall that the definition for $build$ is $build\ g = g\ (:)\ []$ and that $foldr\ k\ z\ [] = z$. This gives us the final result $foldr\ k\ z\ (build\ g) = g\ k\ z$. This line of reasoning is very powerful for functional languages. Unfortunately, it does not work for Curry as we will see in the next section.

3   Adapting *foldr/build* to Curry

When trying to adapt free theorems from functional languages to Curry, we run into a number of problem. Free theorems as formulated for functional languages simply do not work in functional logic languages [9]. Even with these problems, the naive assumption that *foldr/build* will apply to Curry is surprisingly good, since there are only a few situations in which the original *foldr/build* transformation does not work in Curry.

A simple way to cause the *foldr/build* transformation to fail is to use the choice function (?) in k and manipulate where that nondeterministic choice is made in g. Consider the following definitions:

$g\ c\ n = \text{let}\ c' = c\ 2\ \text{in}\ c'\ (c'\ n)$

$k\ a\ \ \ = (\lambda b \to a + b)\ ?\ (\lambda b \to a * b)$

$z\ \ \ \ \ = 4$

If we apply *foldr/build* to get $g\ k\ z$, the let binding $c' = c\ 2$ chooses c' to be either $\lambda b \to a + b$ or $\lambda b \to a * b$, which is then used twice to construct the expressions $2 + (2 + 4)$ and $2 * (2 * 4)$, resulting in the values 8 and 16. The let binding introduces sharing by making a nondeterministic choice and using it multiple times. On the other hand, $build\ g$ constructs the list $[2, 2, 4]$, which causes $foldr\ k\ z\ (build\ g)$ to expand to $k\ 2\ (k\ 2\ 4)$. This expression has no sharing between the two k's, so the expressions $2 + (2 * 4)$ and $2 * (2 + 4)$ are also constructed, resulting in the values 8, 10, 12, and 16. Clearly, *foldr/build* is not valid in this instance since the transformation introduces sharing, causing some results to be lost.

The previous example was able to induce sharing by partially applying k, but sharing can also occur with a fully applied k when recursive let bindings are used. For instance:

$$g\ c\ n = \mathsf{let}\ c' = c\ 1\ c'\ \mathsf{in}\ c'$$
$$k\ a\ b = (a:b)\ ?\ (a+1:b)$$
$$z\quad = [\,]$$

In this case, $take\ 2\ (g\ k\ z)$ returns $[1,1]$ and $[2,2]$, which is due to sharing in c' creating the infinite lists $[1,1,\ldots]$ and $[2,2,\ldots]$. However, sharing still cannot occur in $foldr$, so $take\ 2\ (foldr\ k\ z\ (build\ g))$ returns $[1,1]$, $[1,2]$, $[2,1]$, and $[2,2]$.

Any nondeterminism in k that makes sharing possible can clearly break $foldr/build$. However, some types of nondeterminism are permissible. We can leverage the concept of *multi-determinism* [9,18], which requires that k be a choice of deterministic functions $k_1\ ?\ k_2\ ?\ \ldots\ ?\ k_n$. For instance, the following function is multi-deterministic whereas the previous two k functions are not:

$$k = (\lambda a\ b \to a+b)\ ?\ (\lambda a\ b \to a*b)$$

Intuitively, this solves the problem because the nondeterministic choice between k functions takes place only once when g is called, making it impossible for g to induce any sharing.

Given that nondeterministic k can break $foldr/build$, it is natural to wonder whether nondeterminism in g can cause similar problems. However, we have no cause for concern because g is only used once on either side of the $foldr/build$ equivalence. Therefore, there can be no issues with nondeterministic choices in g being shared in ways that change the behavior of the program.

Another notable case in which the equivalence seems to break down is when g uses free variables. For instance, consider the following:

$$g\ c\ n = \mathsf{let}\ u\ \mathsf{free}\ \mathsf{in}\ u$$
$$k\quad = (||)$$
$$z\quad = \mathsf{True}$$

In the case of $g\ k\ z$, the free variable u generates the values True and False and halts. On the other hand, in $foldr\ k\ z\ (build\ g)$ u generates every possible value of type [Bool], which causes the program to diverge. Moreover, the result will never be False.

This issue is akin to another issue discussed in Gill et al. [12] for the functional version of $foldr/build$. They found that the translation fails when g contains (:) and [] rather than c and n, such as in the following:

$$g\ c\ n = [1,2]$$
$$k\quad = (+)$$
$$z\quad = 0$$

$$P ::= D; P \mid D$$
$$D ::= f :: \kappa\tau; f\ x_1 \ldots x_n = e$$
$$\kappa ::= \forall^\varepsilon \alpha.\,\kappa \mid \forall^* \alpha.\,\kappa \mid$$
$$\tau ::= \alpha \mid \mathsf{Bool} \mid \mathsf{Nat} \mid [\tau] \mid (\tau,\tau') \mid \tau \to \tau'$$
$$e ::= x \mid f_{\tau_1\ldots\tau_k} \mid e_1\ e_2 \mid \mathsf{let}\ x = e_1\ \mathsf{in}\ e_2 \mid n \mid e_1 + e_2 \mid e_1 \mathbin{\hat{=}} e_2$$
$$\mid (e_1,e_2) \mid \mathsf{case}\ e\ \mathsf{of}\ \langle (x,y) \to e_1 \rangle$$
$$\mid \mathsf{True} \mid \mathsf{False} \mid \mathsf{case}\ e\ \mathsf{of}\ \langle \mathsf{True} \to e_1; \mathsf{False} \to e_2 \rangle$$
$$\mid \mathsf{Nil}_\tau \mid \mathsf{Cons}(e_1,e_2) \mid \mathsf{case}\ e\ \mathsf{of}\ \langle \mathsf{Nil} \to e_1; \mathsf{Cons}(x,y) \to e_2 \rangle$$
$$\mid \mathsf{failure}_\tau \mid \mathsf{anything}_\tau$$

Fig. 2. Syntax of CuMin

Indeed, *foldr k z (build g)* returns 3 while *g k z* returns [1, 2]: these do not even have the same type, let alone the same value. However, this issue immediately disappears if *g* is given a polymorphic type. In the above example, [1, 2] is not of type β, so *g* will not typecheck.

Similarly in our example, the return value of *g* is generated by the free variable without using *c* or *n*, thus the theorem breaks down. However, free variables in current versions of Curry require the type class Data [14], so if *g* uses free variables of type β, it must have the type $g :: (\mathsf{Data}\ \beta) \Rightarrow (\tau \to \beta \to \beta) \to \beta \to \beta$ This is not the type of *g* used in the *foldr/build* theorem because β is now overloaded and not a purely polymorphic type. Therefore, our example with free variables does not typecheck either. Free theorems can be stated for types in the presence of polymorphic free variables, but the above example demonstrates that *foldr/build* is not generally valid with this modified type of *g*. Because *g* must have a polymorphic type, free variables will not be relevant for any of the remainder of the paper.

As a result of this exploration, it seems that the only restriction we need to place on the *foldr/build* transformation in order to make it valid in Curry is to require that *k* be multi-deterministic. Of course, we need more rigorous arguments to prove this, rather than mere intuition.

4 Spicing Things up with CuMin and SaLT

We build on the work of Mehner et al. [18] to provide the basis for parametricity and free theorems from which we prove *foldr/build*. They introduce two languages: CuMin, a simplified sub-language of Curry, and SaLT, which makes CuMin's nondeterminism explicit with set types and primitive operations for working with them. We prove the *foldr/build* equivalence for CuMin by translating it to equivalent code in SaLT, from which we derive the necessary free theorem to prove *foldr/build* in SaLT.

$$P ::= D; P \mid D$$
$$D ::= f :: \kappa\tau; f = e$$
$$\kappa ::= \forall^\varepsilon \alpha.\,\kappa \mid \forall^* \alpha.\,\kappa \mid$$
$$\tau ::= \alpha \mid \mathsf{Bool} \mid \mathsf{Nat} \mid [\tau] \mid (\tau, \tau') \mid \tau \to \tau' \mid \{\tau\}$$
$$e ::= x \mid \lambda x :: \tau.\,e \mid f_{\tau_1 \ldots \tau_k} \mid e_1\ e_2 \mid n \mid e_1 + e_2 \mid e_1 \mathrel{\hat{=}} e_2$$
$$\mid (e_1, e_2) \mid \mathsf{case}\ e\ \mathsf{of}\ \langle (x,y) \to e_1 \rangle$$
$$\mid \mathsf{True} \mid \mathsf{False} \mid \mathsf{case}\ e\ \mathsf{of}\ \langle \mathsf{True} \to e_1; \mathsf{False} \to e_2 \rangle$$
$$\mid \mathsf{Nil}_\tau \mid \mathsf{Cons}(e_1, e_2) \mid \mathsf{case}\ e\ \mathsf{of}\ \langle \mathsf{Nil} \to e_1; \mathsf{Cons}(x, y) \to e_2 \rangle$$
$$\mid \{e\} \mid e_1 \ni x \bigcup e_2 \mid \mathsf{failure}_\tau \mid \mathsf{anything}_\tau$$

Fig. 3. Syntax of CuMin and SaLT

The syntax of CuMin and SaLT can be found in Figs. 2 and 3, as defined in [18]. CuMin is more or less a subset of Curry with many niceties like pattern matching, lambda abstractions, and where clauses removed. There are a few substantial deviations from Curry that must be noted. First, polymorphic function types require for-all clauses and explicit type instantiation. For-all with no restrictions on what types they can bind to are ε-tagged, if the type variables cannot be bound to function or set types. We will often omit the latter when they are easy to infer. Pattern matching is explicitly represented with case expressions, and lambda abstractions must be rewritten as top-level functions instead. CuMin is similar, although not identical to, the intermediate representation FlatCurry [1].

Finally, nondeterministic failure is represented, naturally, as the $\mathsf{failure}_\tau$ primitive. Using these tools, we can construct a choice function ($\cup$) that works the same way as Curry's (?) function:

$(\cup) :: \forall \alpha.\, \alpha \to \alpha \to \alpha;$
$(\cup)\ x\ y = \mathsf{case}\ \mathsf{anything}_{\mathsf{Bool}}\ \mathsf{of}\ \langle \mathsf{True} \to x; \mathsf{False} \to y \rangle$

Lastly, CuMin does not support recursive let bindings where a variable appears in its own definition, such as using let $x = [\,] ? (0 : x)$ in x to create the lists $[\,] ? [0, 0, \ldots]$. This is a fundamental restriction compared to Curry, rather than a mere loss of syntactic sugar. Recursive let bindings cannot always be rewritten using other constructs such as recursive functions. In particular, choices are shared in recursive let bindings, but not across recursive calls.

SaLT shares much of the same syntax as CuMin, but rather than being nondeterministic, SaLT is fully deterministic and represents CuMin's nondeterministic values as sets of values using the set type $\{\tau\}$. In SaLT, $\mathsf{failure}_\tau$ corresponds to the single value $\bot$, whereas $\mathsf{anything}_\tau$ corresponds to the set of all values of type τ. Similarly, CuMin values are translated to singleton sets containing that value in SaLT. For example, True is translated to $\{\mathsf{True}\}$. Reifying nondeterminism in the type system and syntax allows SaLT to use traditional equational reasoning, something that is invalid in CuMin and Curry.

SaLT forms new sets out of existing ones via the indexed union operator $e_1 \ni x \bigcup e_2$. As its syntax implies, this operator corresponds intuitively to the mathematical notation $\bigcup_{x \in e_1} e_2$, that is, the union of each set e_2 formed using each x in e_1. We can create the operations *smap* and $\{\_\}$ via the following definitions:

$smap :: \forall \alpha. \forall \beta. (\alpha \to \beta) \to \{\alpha\} \to \{\beta\};$
$smap = \lambda f. \lambda s. s \ni c \bigcup \{f\ c\}$

$\{\_\} :: \forall \alpha. \alpha \to \{\alpha\};$
$\{\_\} = \lambda x. \{x\}$

The *smap* function operates on sets similarly to the *map* function for lists, and $\{\_\}$ is the nondeterministic identity function. Both of these functions are quite useful for proving free theorems when set types are involved.

As seen in the above example, SaLT includes lambda abstractions $\lambda x :: \tau. e$. These subsume certain features provided by CuMin, namely let expressions and parameters on top-level functions, so SaLT does not include those. As in the above, we usually drop the type annotation on the lambda parameter for simplicity.

We can translate from CuMin to SaLT via the translation functions $\lceil \cdot \rceil$ for expressions and $\lfloor \cdot \rfloor$ for types from Mehner et al. [18].

The SaLT code generated by this translation is semantically equivalent to the CuMin code [18]. Hence, any properties that can be proved about the translated SaLT code must also be true for the original CuMin code.

Note how these translations convert a CuMin function of the form $f :: \tau \to \tau'$ to a SaLT function $f :: \{\tau \to \{\tau'\}\}$. However, if f is multi-deterministic, then the SaLT function can be rewritten such that it has the type $f' :: \{\tau \to \tau'\}$, where τ' is not a set type, corresponding to a choice of deterministic functions. More generally, a function f is multi-deterministic if it has type $f :: \{\tau_1 \to \cdots \to \tau_n \to \tau'\}$.

We also define *inner-nondeterminism*, which corresponds to the notion of a function that must be deterministic when partially applied, but may be nondeterministic when fully applied. For example, the function $f :: \{\tau_1 \to \{\tau_2 \to \{\tau_3\}\}\}$ is fully nondeterministic whereas $f' :: \tau_1 \to \tau_2 \to \{\tau_3\}$ is inner-nondeterministic. Formally, a function f is inner-nondeterministic if it can be given the type $f :: \tau_1 \to \cdots \to \tau_n \to \{\tau'\}$. Inner-nondeterministic functions are easier to reason about than fully nondeterministic functions because of their simplified types. Hence, we will use inner-nondeterminism heavily when simplifying translated SaLT code. We can turn any nondeterministic function $f = \lambda x_1. \ldots . \lambda x_n. e$ into an inner-nondeterministic function $\hat{f}$ with the following definition.

$\hat{f} = \lambda x_1. \ldots . \lambda x_n. f \ni f' \bigcup x_1 \ni x_1' \bigcup \ldots x_n \ni x_n' \bigcup f'\ x_1'\ \ldots\ x_n'$

$$\lceil x \rceil = \{x\} \qquad \lceil n \rceil = \{n\}$$
$$\lceil \mathsf{True} \rceil = \{\mathsf{True}\} \qquad \lceil \mathsf{False} \rceil = \{\mathsf{False}\}$$
$$\lceil \mathsf{failure}_\tau \rceil = \{\mathsf{failure}_{\lfloor \tau \rfloor}\} \qquad \lceil \mathsf{anything}_\tau \rceil = \mathsf{anything}_{\lfloor \tau \rfloor}$$
$$\lceil \mathsf{Nil}_\tau \rceil = \{\mathsf{Nil}_{\lfloor \tau \rfloor}\} \qquad \lceil f_{\tau_1 \ldots \tau_n} \rceil = f_{\lfloor \tau_1 \rfloor \ldots \lfloor \tau_n \rfloor}$$
$$\lceil \mathsf{Cons}(e_1, e_2) \rceil = \lceil e_1 \rceil \ni x_1 \bigcup \lceil e_2 \rceil \ni x_2 \bigcup \{\mathsf{Cons}(x_1, x_2)\}$$
$$\lceil \mathsf{let}\ x = e_1\ \mathsf{in}\ e_2 \rceil = \lceil e_1 \rceil \ni x \bigcup \lceil e_2 \rceil$$
$$\lceil e_1 + e_2 \rceil = \lceil e_1 \rceil \ni x_1 \bigcup \lceil e_2 \rceil \ni x_2 \bigcup \{x_1 + x_2\}$$
$$\lceil e_1 \mathrel{\hat{=}} e_2 \rceil = \lceil e_1 \rceil \ni x_1 \bigcup \lceil e_2 \rceil \ni x_2 \bigcup \{x_1 \mathrel{\hat{=}} x_2\}$$
$$\lceil e_1\ e_2 \rceil = \lceil e_1 \rceil \ni x_1 \bigcup \lceil e_2 \rceil \ni x_2 \bigcup x_1\ x_2$$
$$\lceil (e_1, e_2) \rceil = \lceil e_1 \rceil \ni x_1 \bigcup \lceil e_2 \rceil \ni x_2 \bigcup \{(x_1, x_2)\}$$
$$\lceil \mathsf{case}\ e\ \mathsf{of}\ \langle (x,y) \to e_1 \rangle \rceil = \lceil e \rceil \ni c \bigcup \mathsf{case}\ c\ \mathsf{of}\ \langle (x,y) \to \lceil e_1 \rceil \rangle$$
$$\lceil \mathsf{case}\ e\ \mathsf{of}\ \langle \mathsf{True} \to e_1; \mathsf{False} \to e_2 \rangle \rceil =$$
$$\lceil e \rceil \ni c \bigcup \mathsf{case}\ c\ \mathsf{of}\ \langle \mathsf{True} \to \lceil e_1 \rceil; \mathsf{False} \to \lceil e_2 \rceil \rangle$$
$$\lceil \mathsf{case}\ e\ \mathsf{of}\ \langle \mathsf{Nil} \to e_1; \mathsf{Cons}(x,y) \to e_2 \rangle \rceil =$$
$$\lceil e \rceil \ni c \bigcup \mathsf{case}\ c\ \mathsf{of}\ \langle \mathsf{Nil} \to \lceil e_1 \rceil; \mathsf{Cons}(x,y) \to \lceil e_2 \rceil \rangle$$
$$\lfloor \mathsf{Bool} \rfloor = \mathsf{Bool} \quad \lfloor \alpha \rfloor = \alpha \quad \lfloor (\tau, \tau') \rfloor = (\lfloor \tau \rfloor, \lfloor \tau' \rfloor)$$
$$\lfloor \mathsf{Nat} \rfloor = \mathsf{Nat} \quad \lfloor [\tau] \rfloor = [\lfloor \tau \rfloor] \quad \lfloor \tau \to \tau' \rfloor = \lfloor \tau \rfloor \to \{\lfloor \tau' \rfloor\}$$
$$\begin{bmatrix} f :: \kappa\ \tau_1 \to \cdots \to \tau_n \to \upsilon; \\ f\ x_1 \ldots x_n = e \end{bmatrix} = \begin{array}{l} f :: \kappa \{\lfloor \tau_1 \rfloor \to \cdots \to \tau_n \to \upsilon \rfloor\}; \\ f = \{\lambda x_1 :: \lfloor \tau_1 \rfloor. \cdots \{\lambda x_n :: \lfloor \tau_n \rfloor. \lceil e \rceil\} \cdots\} \end{array}$$

Fig. 4. Translation functions from CuMin to SaLT

Additionally, it is sometimes useful to allow for a set of inner-nondeterministic functions, such as in the case of $f' :: \{\tau_1 \to \tau_2 \to \{\tau_3\}\}$. We call this *multi-inner-nondeterminism*.

Finally, a word or two must be said about the semantics of SaLT. Every type in SaLT forms a pointed partially ordered set, or *poset* for short. These sets are partially ordered by the relation $\sqsubseteq$ where $\mathbf{x} \sqsubseteq \mathbf{y}$ if $\mathbf{y}$ is at least as defined as $\mathbf{x}$, with $\bot$ as the least defined element. Lower sets and down sets are given their standard definitions [11]. The set of all lower sets of a poset P is denoted $\mathcal{P}_\ell(P)$, which is itself a poset (Fig. 4).

If we have a relation R between posets P_1 and P_2, we define the relation $\mathcal{P}_\mathcal{R}(R)$[1] as follows: two lower sets $A \in \mathcal{P}_\ell(P_1)$ and $B \in \mathcal{P}_\ell(P_2)$ are related by $\mathcal{P}_\mathcal{R}(R)$ if:

---

[1] In [18], the notation $\mathcal{P}_\ell(R)$ is used for this relation, which can result in potential confusion between it and the construction for the set of all lower sets. Hence, we prefer the notation $\mathcal{P}_\mathcal{R}(R)$.

$$\forall \mathbf{a} \in A.\ \exists \mathbf{a'} \in A.\ (\mathbf{a} \sqsubseteq \mathbf{a'} \wedge \exists \mathbf{b} \in B.\ (\mathbf{a'}, \mathbf{b}) \in P)$$
$$\forall \mathbf{b} \in B.\ \exists \mathbf{b'} \in B.\ (\mathbf{b} \sqsubseteq \mathbf{b'} \wedge \exists \mathbf{a} \in A.\ (\mathbf{a}, \mathbf{b'}) \in P)$$

This allows A and B to be related without requiring every $\mathbf{a} \in A$ and $\mathbf{b} \in B$ to be related, which is necessary for the definition of parametricity. Lastly, we define the relation R to be *strict* if $(\bot, \bot) \in R$ and *whole* if $(P_1, P_2) \in \mathcal{P}_\mathcal{R}(R)$.

This gives us the tools we need to summarize the denotational semantics of SaLT, given in more detail in Mehner et al. [18]. First, the denotation of a type τ is a poset containing all the values of that type. This is written as $[\![\tau]\!]_\theta$, where θ is a type environment mapping type variables to posets. A type τ is *closed* if it contains no polymorphic type variables, in which case the denotation of the type may be written as just $[\![\tau]\!]_\varnothing$.

The denotation of an expression $e :: \tau$ is the value that the expression evaluates to, which is an element of $[\![\tau]\!]_\theta$. These semantics proceed in two stages. The first stage is written as $[\![e]\!]^i_{\theta,\sigma}$, where θ is the same as in the type semantics and σ is a term environment mapping variables $x :: \upsilon$ to values $\sigma(x) \in [\![\upsilon]\!]_\theta$. This stage puts a finite limit on the number of nested function calls that can be performed. For each nested call, the step index i is decremented. Once i reaches zero, $[\![f]\!]^0_{\theta,\sigma}$ simply returns $\bot$ for any function f, allowing no further function calls to be performed.

An important property of these semantics is that they are monotone with respect to σ and i. Binding variables to more defined values or increasing i cannot result in a value that is less defined. This fact is essential to our proof of *foldr/build*.

Next, if $e :: \{\tau\}$, we can lift this restriction on recursive calls by defining a second stage of semantics as $[\![e]\!]_{\theta,\sigma} = \bigcup_{i \in \mathbb{N}} [\![e]\!]^i_{\theta,\sigma}$. These semantics are also monotone with respect to σ. We have to be careful because it only makes sense to use the semantics if e is a set. Luckily, this is not a problem because we can use $[\![\{e\}]\!]^i_{\theta,\sigma}$ if necessary.

We say that two expressions e_1 and e_2 are *semantically equivalent*, written as $e_1 \equiv e_2$, if $[\![e_1]\!]_{\theta,\sigma} = [\![e_2]\!]_{\theta,\sigma}$ for set typed e_1 and e_2 or $[\![\{e_1\}]\!]_{\theta,\sigma} = [\![\{e_2\}]\!]_{\theta,\sigma}$ otherwise. Note that $e_1 \equiv e_2$ is implied by $[\![e_1]\!]^i_{\theta,\sigma} = [\![e_2]\!]^i_{\theta,\sigma}$, but the converse is not necessarily true.

If we have a SaLT function $f :: \tau \to \tau'$, then $[\![f]\!]^i_{\theta,\sigma}$ corresponds to a relation between posets $[\![f]\!]^i_{\theta,\sigma} \subseteq [\![\tau]\!]_\theta \times [\![\tau']\!]_\theta$. If we apply $\mathcal{P}_\mathcal{R}$ to this relation, we get the convenient fact $[\![smap\ f]\!]^{i+1}_{\theta,\sigma} = \mathcal{P}_\mathcal{R}([\![f]\!]^i_{\theta,\sigma})$. This means we can also apply the notions of strict and whole relations to SaLT functions: the function f is strict if f failure$_\tau \equiv$ failure$_{\tau'}$ and whole if $smap\ f$ anything$_\tau \equiv$ anything$_{\tau'}$.

After translating our main theorem to SaLT, we end up with the code in Fig. 5. If we have a multi-deterministic function g, we can create a new function $\hat{g}$ to represent one of the non-deterministic branches. With the translation work out of the way, we turn our attention to figuring out how to prove *foldr/build* in SaLT.

$$g :: \forall \beta. \{(\tau \to \beta \to \beta) \to \{\beta \to \{\beta\}\}\} \quad foldr :: \forall \alpha. \forall \beta. (\alpha \to \beta \to \beta) \to \beta \to [\alpha] \to \beta;$$
$$foldr = \lambda k. \lambda z. \lambda \ell.$$
$$\hat{g} :: \forall \beta. (\tau \to \beta \to \beta) \to \beta \to \{\beta\};$$
$$\hat{g} = \lambda c. \lambda n. g \ni g' \bigcup g' \; c \ni s \bigcup s \; n \qquad \text{case } \ell \text{ of } \langle \text{ Nil} \qquad \to z;$$
$$\text{Cons}(x, xs) \to$$
$$k \; x \; (foldr \; k \; z \; xs)\rangle$$

$$build \; \hat{g} \ni c \bigcup \{foldr \; k \; z \; c\} \equiv \hat{g} \; k \; z$$

Fig. 5. SaLT adjusted for multi-determinism and new $\hat{g}$ function

5 A First Attempt with Dinaturality

Proving free theorems by unravelling the parametricity definition can often be tedious or difficult. Instead, we turn to the work of Mehner et al. [18] to automatically generate a free theorem for g by taking turns swapping out the polymorphic subexpressions *in* and *out* with an arbitrary function h:

Theorem 2 (Conjuring Theorem). *Let $e :: \tau$ be an expression of closed type that may nevertheless contain subexpressions of type α. Also let $h :: \varepsilon \to \varepsilon'$ be a strict function that is also whole if α is $*$-tagged, and define variables in $:: \varepsilon \to \alpha$ and out $:: \alpha \to \varepsilon'$. Then the following holds:*

$$e[\alpha \mapsto \varepsilon, in \mapsto id_\varepsilon, out \mapsto h] \equiv e[\alpha \mapsto \varepsilon', in \mapsto e, out \mapsto id_{\varepsilon'}]$$

If an appropriate e could be constructed using *in* and *out*, then proving *foldr*/*build* might be significantly easier. Finding such an e is difficult by hand, but fortunately a way of deriving such an expression automatically via the concept of dinaturality is provided by Voigtländer [21]. Given a function $f :: \forall \alpha. \tau$ that we want to prove a free theorem for, the function *mono* defined in [21] can be used to generate an appropriate e via $mono_{in,out}(\tau) \; f$. Theorem 2 can then be applied to e to provide the final free theorem. Although the resulting equivalence is not guaranteed to be as general as the statement proved by standard parametricity, we could hope that it is still general enough to prove our result.

By Theorem 2 the type of $\hat{g}$ gives us the following expression e.

$$e = (\lambda p. (smap \; out) \circ p \circ in) \circ \hat{g} \circ (\lambda q. (\lambda r. in \circ r \circ out) \circ q)$$

where $p :: \beta \to \{\beta\}$, $q :: \tau \to \varepsilon' \to \varepsilon$, and $r :: \varepsilon' \to \varepsilon$. Therefore, $e :: (\tau \to \varepsilon' \to \varepsilon) \to \varepsilon \to \{\varepsilon'\}$. Now we set to instantiating this result. Set $\varepsilon = [\tau]$ and $\varepsilon' = \upsilon$, and consider the expression $e' = e \; f \; n$ for some $f :: \tau \to \upsilon \to [\tau]$ and $n :: [\tau]$:

$$e' \equiv (\hat{g} \; (\lambda a. \lambda b. in \; (f \; a \; (out \; b))) \; (in \; n)) \ni c \bigcup \{out \; c\}$$

By applying Theorem 2, this becomes

$$(\hat{g} \; (\lambda a. \lambda b. f \; a \; (h \; b)) \; n) \ni c \bigcup \{h \; c\} \equiv \hat{g} \; (\lambda a. \lambda b. h \; (f \; a \; b)) \; (h \; n)$$

$$\Delta_{\rho,\alpha} = \rho(\alpha)$$
$$\Delta_{\rho,\mathsf{Nat}} = \{(\mathbf{n},\mathbf{n}) \mid \mathbf{n} \in [\![\mathsf{Nat}]\!]_\varnothing\}$$
$$\Delta_{\rho,\mathsf{Bool}} = \{(\mathbf{b},\mathbf{b}) \mid \mathbf{b} \in [\![\mathsf{Bool}]\!]_\varnothing\}$$
$$\Delta_{\rho,\{\tau\}} = \mathcal{P}_\mathcal{R}(\Delta_{\rho,\tau})$$
$$\Delta_{\rho,\tau \to \tau'} = \{(\mathbf{f},\mathbf{g}) \in [\![\tau \to \tau']\!]_{\theta_1} \times [\![\tau \to \tau']\!]_{\theta_2} \mid \forall (\mathbf{x},\mathbf{y}) \in \Delta_{\rho,\tau}.\,(\mathbf{f}\,\mathbf{x},\mathbf{g}\,\mathbf{y}) \in \Delta_{\rho,\tau'}\}$$
$$\Delta_{\rho,[\tau]} = \{(\mathbf{x}_1 : \cdots : \mathbf{x}_n : \mathbf{e}, \mathbf{y}_1 : \cdots : \mathbf{y}_n : \mathbf{e}) \mid n \geq 0,\, (\mathbf{x}_i,\mathbf{y}_i) \in \Delta_{\rho,\tau},\, \mathbf{e} \in \{\bot,[\,]\}\}$$
$$\Delta_{\rho,(\tau,\tau')} = \{(\bot,\bot)\} \cup \{((\mathbf{l}_1,\mathbf{r}_1),(\mathbf{l}_2,\mathbf{r}_2)) \mid (\mathbf{l}_1,\mathbf{l}_2) \in \Delta_{\rho,\tau},\, (\mathbf{r}_1,\mathbf{r}_2) \in \Delta_{\rho,\tau'}\}$$

Fig. 6. Definitions of the parametricity relation

This looks enticingly similar to the free theorem derived for g in Gill et al. [12]. However, we can see the first signs of a problem: instead of having an $f :: \tau \to [\tau] \to [\tau]$ on one side and an $f' :: \tau \to \upsilon \to \upsilon$ on the other, we instead have the same function f on both sides with the strange hybrid type $f :: \tau \to \upsilon \to [\tau]$ required by the type of e. If we set $h = \textit{foldr}\ k\ z$ and $n = \mathsf{Nil}_\tau$, then this equivalence becomes

$$(\hat{g}\ (\lambda a.\,\lambda b.\,f\ a\ (\textit{foldr}\ k\ z\ b))\ \mathsf{Nil}_\tau) \ni c \bigcup \{\textit{foldr}\ k\ z\ c\} \equiv \hat{g}\ (\lambda a.\,\lambda b.\,\textit{foldr}\ k\ z\ (f\ a\ b))\ z$$

And now we are stuck. Somehow, we must turn the first argument of $\hat{g}$ into $(:)$ on the left side and k on the right. If we added the highly restrictive constraint $\upsilon = [\tau]$ and set $f = (:)$, we could simplify the expression into the form

$$(\hat{g}\ (\lambda a.\,\lambda b.\,a : (\textit{foldr}\ k\ z\ b))\ \mathsf{Nil}_\tau) \ni c \bigcup \{\textit{foldr}\ k\ z\ c\}$$
$$\equiv \hat{g}\ (\lambda a.\,\lambda b.\,k\ a\ (\textit{foldr}\ k\ z\ b))\ z$$

However, this leads to a dead end. To get the *foldr/build* equivalence from this expression, we would also have to impose the restriction $\textit{foldr}\ k\ z\ b \equiv b$, which requires $k \equiv (:)$ and $z \equiv \mathsf{Nil}_\tau$. The resulting theorem is not useful at all, since it boils down to $\hat{g} \equiv \hat{g}$, which is a tautology. Dinaturality does not result in an equivalence that is powerful enough to prove the *foldr/build* theorem.

6 Proving *foldr/build* with Parametricity

With dinaturality untimately failing to produce a proof for us, we must turn to the parametricity definition to get our free theorem for *foldr/build*. Unravelling parametricity worked for the functional version of *foldr/build*, so it seems hopeful that we can adapt it to parametricity as defined in SaLT.

Parametricity in SaLT for a type τ is defined by the relation $\Delta_{\rho,\tau}$ as given in [18]. Here, ρ is a mapping between type variables α and relations $R \subseteq [\![\alpha]\!]_{\theta_1} \times [\![\alpha]\!]_{\theta_2}$. Relations in ρ are always required to be strict, and if α is *-tagged, then the relation must also be whole. The definitions of the parametricity relation for each type are shown in Fig. 6. Using these definitions, we can restate a simplified version of the parametricity theorem from [18]:

Theorem 3 (Parametricity for SaLT). *Let there be a SaLT term* $e :: \tau$, *and let* θ_1, σ_1 *and* θ_2, σ_2 *be appropriate pairs of type and term environments. Also let* ρ *be a mapping from type variables to strict relations that are also whole for* $*$-*tagged type variables. If for all variables* $x :: \upsilon$ *in* e *we have* $(\llbracket x \rrbracket^i_{\theta_1,\sigma_1}, \llbracket x \rrbracket^i_{\theta_2,\sigma_2}) \in \Delta_{\rho,\upsilon}$, *then* $(\llbracket e \rrbracket^i_{\theta_1,\sigma_1}, \llbracket e \rrbracket^i_{\theta_2,\sigma_2}) \in \Delta_{\rho,\tau}$ *for all* $i \in \mathbb{N}$.

To prove *foldr/build* using parametricity, we prepare a lemma for unravelling the parametricity definition in ways that are directly useful to our proof. Most of these are standard, and similar facts could be stated about tuple and list types.

Lemma 1. *Let* $h :: \varepsilon \to \varepsilon$ *be a strict function, and* $\rho' = \rho[\alpha \mapsto \llbracket h \rrbracket^i_{\varnothing,\varnothing}]$ *with appropriate values for* $\theta_1, \theta_2, \sigma_2, \sigma_2, \rho$, *and closed type* υ.

1. If $\left(\llbracket e_1 \rrbracket^i_{\theta_1,\sigma_1}, \llbracket e_2 \rrbracket^i_{\theta_2,\sigma_2}\right) \in \Delta_{\rho,\upsilon}$, then $\llbracket e_1 \rrbracket^i_{\theta_1,\sigma_1} = \llbracket e_2 \rrbracket^i_{\theta_2,\sigma_2}$; that is, $\Delta_{\rho,\upsilon}$ is the identity relation.
2. If $\left(\llbracket e_1 \rrbracket^i_{\theta_1,\sigma_1}, \llbracket e_2 \rrbracket^i_{\theta_2,\sigma_2}\right) \in \Delta_{\rho',\alpha}$, then $\llbracket h\ e_1 \rrbracket^i_{\theta_1,\sigma_1} = \llbracket e_2 \rrbracket^i_{\theta_2,\sigma_2}$.
3. If $\left(\llbracket f_1 \rrbracket^i_{\theta_1,\sigma_1}, \llbracket f_2 \rrbracket^i_{\theta_2,\sigma_2}\right) \in \Delta_{\rho',\tau \to \tau'}$,
   $\forall (\mathbf{a}_1, \mathbf{a}_2) \in \Delta_{\rho',\tau}.\ \left(\llbracket f_1\ a_1 \rrbracket^i_{\theta_1,\sigma_1[a_1 \mapsto \mathbf{a}_1]}, \llbracket f_2\ a_2 \rrbracket^i_{\theta_2,\sigma_2[a_2 \mapsto \mathbf{a}_2]}\right) \in \Delta_{\rho',\tau'}$.
4. If $\left(\llbracket f_1 \rrbracket^i_{\theta_1,\sigma_1}, \llbracket f_2 \rrbracket^i_{\theta_2,\sigma_2}\right) \in \Delta_{\rho',\upsilon \to \tau'}$,
   $\forall \mathbf{a} \in \llbracket \upsilon \rrbracket_\theta.\ \left(\llbracket f_1\ a \rrbracket^i_{\theta_1,\sigma_1[a \mapsto \mathbf{a}]}, \llbracket f_2\ a \rrbracket^i_{\theta_2,\sigma_2[a \mapsto \mathbf{a}]}\right) \in \Delta_{\rho',\tau'}$.
5. If $\left(\llbracket f_1 \rrbracket^i_{\theta_1,\sigma_1}, \llbracket f_2 \rrbracket^i_{\theta_2,\sigma_2}\right) \in \Delta_{\rho',\alpha \to \tau'}$,
   $\forall \mathbf{a} \in \llbracket \varepsilon \rrbracket_\theta.\ \left(\llbracket f_1\ a \rrbracket^i_{\theta_1,\sigma_1[a \mapsto \mathbf{a}]}, \llbracket f_2\ (h\ a) \rrbracket^i_{\theta_2,\sigma_2[a \mapsto \mathbf{a}]}\right) \in \Delta_{\rho',\tau'}$.
6. If $\left(\llbracket e_1 \rrbracket^i_{\theta_1,\sigma_1}, \llbracket e_2 \rrbracket^i_{\theta_2,\sigma_2}\right) \in \Delta_{\rho',\{\alpha\}}$, then $\llbracket e_1 \ni c \bigcup \{h\ c\} \rrbracket^i_{\theta_1,\sigma_1} = \llbracket e_2 \rrbracket^i_{\theta_2,\sigma_2}$.

Proof. Properties 2 and 3 follow directly from the definition of $\Delta_{\rho',\tau}$. Properties 4 and 5 are special cases of 3 that apply 1 and 2 to their input type. Property 6 is true by merit of the fact that $\Delta_{\rho',\{\alpha\}} = \mathcal{P}_\mathcal{K}(\llbracket h \rrbracket^i_{\varnothing,\varnothing}) = \llbracket smap\ h \rrbracket^{i+1}_{\varnothing,\varnothing}$. Hence $\llbracket smap\ h\ e_1 \rrbracket^{i+1}_{\theta_1,\sigma_1} = \llbracket e_1 \ni c \bigcup \{h\ c\} \rrbracket^i_{\theta_1,\sigma_1} = \llbracket e_2 \rrbracket^i_{\theta_2,\sigma_2}$.

Property 1 is an expected fact about parametricity which can be demonstrated by induction. In the case of $\Delta_{\rho,\{\tau\}}$, the induction hypothesis tells us that $\Delta_{\rho,\tau}$ is the identity relation over $\llbracket \tau \rrbracket_\theta$. Therefore $\Delta_{\rho,\{\tau\}} = \llbracket smap\ f \rrbracket^{i+1}_{\varnothing,[f \mapsto \Delta_{\rho,\tau}]}$ which is the identity relation over $\llbracket \{\tau\} \rrbracket_\theta$. $\square$

It is notable that the only set types that this lemma can work with are simple ones like $\{\alpha\}$ or closed $\{\upsilon\}$. Absent are any ways of dealing with sets of polymorphic functions like $\{\alpha \to \{\alpha\}\}$ because $\Delta_{\rho',\alpha \to \{\alpha\}}$ is not necessarily a function, and hence it cannot be used in $\llbracket smap\ f \rrbracket^{i+1}_{\varnothing,[f \mapsto \Delta_{\rho',\tau}]}$. This shows that converting our SaLT functions to inner-nondeterministic form is not merely a cosmetic change, but actually makes it possible for Lemma 1 to work with it. With this lemma, we are finally equipped to prove *foldr/build*.

Proposition 1 (Multi-deterministic SaLT *foldr/build*). *Let τ be a closed type. If we have the function*

$$\hat{g} :: \forall \beta.\, (\tau \to \beta \to \beta) \to \beta \to \{\beta\}$$

then the following holds for all expressions $z :: \upsilon$ and $k :: \tau \to \upsilon \to \upsilon$:

$$\textit{build } \hat{g} \ni c \bigcup \{\textit{foldr } k\ z\ c\} \equiv \hat{g}\ k\ z$$

Proof. Let $h :: \varepsilon \to \varepsilon'$ be a strict function, and let $\rho' = \rho[\beta \to [\![h]\!]^i_{\varnothing,\varnothing}]$ with appropriate values for $\theta_1, \theta_2, \sigma_2, \sigma_2, \rho$. By parametricity as given in Theorem 3,

$$([\![\hat{g}_\varepsilon]\!]^i_{\theta_1,\sigma_1}, [\![\hat{g}_{\varepsilon'}]\!]^i_{\theta_2,\sigma_2}) \in \Delta_{\rho',(\tau \to \beta \to \beta) \to \beta \to \{\beta\}}$$

Then, by unravelling parametricity via Lemma 1, the following holds for all $f :: \tau \to \varepsilon \to \varepsilon$ and $f' :: \tau \to \varepsilon' \to \varepsilon'$:

$$\forall a :: \tau.\, \forall b :: \varepsilon.\, h\ (f\ a\ b) \equiv f'\ a\ (h\ b)$$
$$\implies \forall b :: \varepsilon.\, \hat{g}\ f\ b \ni c \bigcup \{h\ c\} \equiv \hat{g}\ f'\ (h\ b)$$

Now, choose $h = \textit{foldr } k\ z$ (which is strict), $f = (:)$, and $f' = k$. This gives us

$$\forall a :: \tau.\, \forall b :: [\tau].\, \textit{foldr } k\ z\ (a : b) \equiv k\ a\ (\textit{foldr } k\ z\ b)$$
$$\implies \forall b :: [\tau].\, \hat{g}\ (:)\ b \ni c \bigcup \{\textit{foldr } k\ z\ c\} \equiv \hat{g}\ k\ (\textit{foldr } k\ z\ b)$$

The left side follows from the definition of *foldr*. Therefore, we can set $b = \textit{Nil}_\tau$, and since $\hat{g}\ (:)\ \textit{Nil}_\tau \equiv \textit{build } \hat{g}$ and $\textit{foldr } k\ z\ \textit{Nil}_\tau \equiv z$, we get

$$\textit{build } \hat{g} \ni c \bigcup \{\textit{foldr } k\ z\ c\} \equiv \hat{g}\ k\ z$$

which is the SaLT *foldr/build* equivalence itself. □

Aside from the extra handling needed for the set type in $\hat{g}$, this proof is almost identical to the one for the functional version of *foldr/build* in [12]. This is enough to prove out theorem where k is -multi-deterministic.

7 Allowing Nondeterminism in *foldr/build*

Earlier in our investigation about whether *foldr/build* could be adapted to Curry, we found that a properly constructed g could cause the transformation to break if k were nondeterministic. Notably, in the case of inner-nondeterministic k, a recursive let binding could be used to break the transformation.

However, this counterexample is not applicable to CuMin, which does not support recursive let. Intuitively, there is no other way to break *foldr/build* with inner-nondeterministic k because there is no way to cause sharing of the nondeterministic choice $c' = c\ x\ y$ in g without reusing c' in its own definition. This leads to a stronger version of out theorem that allows some nondeterminism in k.

To prove this more general version of *foldr/build*, we need to make appropriate modifications to our SaLT code to account for the new type of k. The only change we need to make to Fig. 5 is to give k the more general inner-nondeterministic type $k :: \tau \to \upsilon \to \{\upsilon\}$. From here we need to update the type of g and *foldr* to accept the more generalized type.

We would like to prove this equivalence using a free theorem, but this requires some consideration. Earlier *foldr* was deterministic because k was deterministic as well. Since we set $h = foldr\ k\ z$ in the proof for Proposition 1, parametricity instantiated $\hat{g}$ as $(\hat{g}_\tau, \hat{g}_\upsilon)$ because $h :: \tau \to \upsilon$. Now, however, *foldr* is nondeterministic. If we tried an identical proof, we would end up with $\hat{g}$ instantiated as $(\hat{g}_\tau, \hat{g}_{\{\upsilon\}})$. This seems to be a problem because plain equational reasoning cannot turn $\hat{g}_{\{\upsilon\}}$ into the $\hat{g}_\upsilon$ required by the *foldr/build* theorem.

However, just as we related $\hat{g}_\tau$ and $\hat{g}_{\{\upsilon\}}$ by using the free theorem for $\hat{g}$, we can relate $\hat{g}_\upsilon$ and $\hat{g}_{\{\upsilon\}}$ by reusing the same theorem. We simply require an appropriate function for $h :: \upsilon \to \{\upsilon\}$. Since we need to relate deterministic values to their nondeterministic counterparts, $\{\_\}$ seems to be the perfect candidate. With this idea, we can prove our new generalized version of *foldr/build*.

Proposition 2 (Multi-inner-nondeterministic SaLT *foldr/build*). *Let τ be a closed type. If we have the function*

$$\hat{g} :: \forall \beta. (\tau \to \beta \to \{\beta\}) \to \beta \to \{\beta\}$$

then the following holds for all expressions $z :: \upsilon$ and $k :: \tau \to \upsilon \to \{\upsilon\}$:

$$build\ \hat{g} \ni c \bigcup foldr\ k\ z\ c \equiv \hat{g}\ k\ z$$

Proof. Let $h :: \varepsilon \to \varepsilon'$ be a strict function, and let $\rho' = \rho[\beta \to [\![h]\!]^i_{\varnothing,\varnothing}]$ with appropriate values for $\theta_1, \theta_2, \sigma_2, \sigma_2, \rho$. By unravelling parametricity on $\hat{g}$ via Theorem 3 and Lemma 1, we get the following equivalence for all $f :: \tau \to \varepsilon \to \{\varepsilon\}$ and $f' :: \tau \to \varepsilon' \to \{\varepsilon'\}$:

$$\forall a :: \tau. \forall b :: \varepsilon.\ f\ a\ b \ni c \bigcup \{h\ c\} \equiv f'\ a\ (h\ b)$$
$$\implies \forall b :: \varepsilon.\ \hat{g}\ f\ b \ni c \bigcup \{h\ c\} \equiv \hat{g}\ f'\ (h\ b)$$

Now we set $h = foldr\ k\ z$ and $f = (:)$. We cannot set $f' = k$ directly because $f' :: \tau \to \{\upsilon\} \to \{\{\upsilon\}\}$, so we instead set $f' = k'$ where k' is defined as $k' = \lambda a.\ \lambda b.\ b \ni c \bigcup \{k\ a\ c\}$. This gives us the following equivalence:

$$\forall a :: \tau. \forall b :: [\tau].\ a : b \ni c \bigcup \{foldr\ k\ z\ c\} \equiv k'\ a\ (foldr\ k\ z\ b)$$
$$\implies \forall b :: [\tau].\ \hat{g}\ (:)\ b \ni c \bigcup \{foldr\ k\ z\ c\} \equiv \hat{g}\ k'\ (foldr\ k\ z\ b)$$

This is implied by the definition of *foldr* after expanding the definitions of (:) and k' on the left side of the equivalence and simplifying. By setting $b = \text{Nil}_\tau$ and recognizing $\hat{g}\ (:)\ \text{Nil}_\tau \equiv build\ \hat{g}$ and $foldr\ k\ z\ \text{Nil}_\tau \equiv \{z\}$, we end up with the simplified equivalence

$$build\ \hat{g} \ni c \bigcup foldr\ k\ z\ c \equiv \hat{g}\ k'\ \{z\} \ni s \bigcup s$$

The left side matches up with the left side of the *foldr/build* equivalence, so we can turn our attention to the second instantiation of $\hat{g}$'s free theorem. Set $h = \{\_\}$, $f = k$, and $f' = k'$:

$$\forall a :: \tau. \forall b :: \varepsilon. k\ a\ b \ni c \bigcup \{\{c\}\} \equiv k'\ a\ \{b\}$$
$$\implies \forall b :: \varepsilon. \hat{g}\ k\ b \ni c \bigcup \{\{c\}\} \equiv \hat{g}\ k'\ \{b\}$$

The left hand side follows directly after expanding k' and simplifying [18]. Now, on the right side of the equivalence, we set $b = z$. After simplification, this gives us $\hat{g}\ k\ z \equiv \hat{g}\ k'\ \{z\} \ni s \bigcup s$ The left side matches up with the right side of the *foldr/build* equivalence. Since the right sides are the same for both instantiations of $\hat{g}$'s free theorem, $build\ \hat{g} \ni c \bigcup foldr\ k\ z\ c \equiv \hat{g}\ k\ z$ □

To complete our new theorem, we need to state the CuMin version of Proposition 2. We could just add the restriction that k be multi-inner-nondeterministic, but we can do better by making a wrapper function $\hat{k}$ that does this for us with $\hat{k}\ a\ b = k\ a\ b$

We can force k to fit the form of 2 since any k can be converted to a inner-nondeterministic function $\hat{k}$ by fully applying its arguments. Now, this means that $\hat{k}$ must appear on both sides of the *foldr/build* equivalence, but it is easily demonstrated that $foldr\ \hat{k}\ z\ \ell \equiv foldr\ k\ z\ \ell$ by converting $\hat{k}$ to SaLT and checking that both are equivalent using the definition of *foldr* found in Fig. 5.

This allows us to state a fully generalized functional logic CuMin *foldr/build* theorem with the same power as the functional *foldr/build*:

Theorem 4 (Nondeterministic CuMin *foldr/build*). *Let τ be closed and*

$$g :: \forall \beta. (\tau \to \beta \to \beta) \to \beta \to \beta$$

then for all expressions $z :: \upsilon$ and $k :: \tau \to \upsilon \to \upsilon$ with $\hat{k}$ as defined above:

$$foldr\ k\ z\ (build\ g) \equiv g\ \hat{k}\ z$$

If additionally k is multi-inner-nondeterministic, then:

$$foldr\ k\ z\ (build\ g) \equiv g\ k\ z$$

8 Related Work and Conclusion

In this paper, we presented a proof of correctness for shortcut deforestation in a functional logic setting. This work is built heavily on the work of Gill et al., Mehner et al., and Voigtländer [12,18,21]. Deforestation has proved to be a useful technique for both Haskell and Curry. In the RICE compiler, [15] deforestation was shown to have an average of 15% improvement by itself, with further improvements when combined with other optimizations [17]. This proof gives us an opportunity to apply shortcut deforestation in even more cases.

While shortcut deforestation is certainly effective, it is not the current state of the art. Stream fusion [10] is a more general optimization that is currently implemented in GHC. There is still a lot of work to do to implement stream fusion in a Curry compiler. First, the correctness of stream fusion needs to be established for functional logic languages. Even with this, there are no implementations of Curry that contain the required optimizations to make stream fusion worthwhile. Specifically, we would need a compiler to support constructor specialization [19] and static argument transformation [10]. Currently no Curry compiler supports either of these optimizations. This makes shortcut deforestation an ideal middle ground for optimizing Curry programs.

The proof of correctness of shortcut deforestation suggests that the SaLT language is a good framework for exploring the properties of functional logic programs. In fact, we believe that SaLT might be a good intermediate representation language in a Curry compiler. However, there is currently a flaw in this plan. The semantics of both CuMin and SaLT do not allow for a recursive let binding. It was shown [18] that non-determinism can subsume general recursion, however it remains unclear if recursive let bindings can be incorporated into this scheme. We suspect that the semantics would require a substantial alteration.

This proof is a step forward in optimizing functional logic program. While we have focused on Curry for this paper, we believe that these techniques should apply to other functional logic languages as well.

References

1. Albert, E., Hanus, M., Huch, F., et al.: Operational semantics for declarative multi-paradigm languages. J. Symb. Comput. **40**(1), 795–829 (2005). https://doi.org/10.1016/j.jsc.2004.01.001. ISSN 0747-7171
2. Antoy, S., Echahed, R., Hanus, M.: A needed narrowing strategy. J. ACM **47**(4), 776–822 (2000). https://doi.org/10.1145/347476.347484. ISSN 0004-5411
3. Antoy, S., Hanus, M.: Functional logic design patterns. In: Hu, Z., Rodríguez-Artalejo, M. (eds.) FLOPS 2002. LNCS, vol. 2441, pp. 67–87. Springer, Heidelberg (2002). https://doi.org/10.1007/3-540-45788-7_4
4. Antoy, S., Hanus, M.: New functional logic design patterns. In: Kuchen, H. (ed.) WFLP 2011. LNCS, vol. 6816, pp. 19–34. Springer, Heidelberg (2011). https://doi.org/10.1007/978-3-642-22531-4_2
5. Antoy, S., Jost, A.: A new functional-logic compiler for curry: sprite. CoRR abs/1608.04016 (2016)
6. Augustsson, L., et al.: The verse calculus: a core calculus for functional logic programming. Proc. ACM Program. Lang. **7**(ICFP) (2023). https://doi.org/10.1145/3607845
7. Böhm, J., Hanus, M., Teegen, F.: From non-determinism to goroutines: a fair implementation of curry in Go. In: Proceedings of the 23rd International Symposium on Principles and Practice of Declarative Programming, PPDP 2021. Association for Computing Machinery, Tallinn (2021). https://doi.org/10.1145/3479394.3479411. ISBN 9781450386890
8. Caballero, R., López-Fraguas, F.J.: A functional-logic perspective of parsing. In: Middeldorp, A., Sato, T. (eds.) FLOPS 1999. LNCS, vol. 1722, pp. 85–99. Springer, Heidelberg (1999). https://doi.org/10.1007/10705424_6. ISBN 978-3-540-47950-5

9. Christiansen, J., Seidel, D., Voigtländer, J.: Free theorems for functional logic programs. In: Proceedings of the 4th ACM SIGPLAN Workshop on Programming Languages Meets Program Verification, PLPV 2010, pp. 39–48. Association for Computing Machinery, Madrid (2010). https://doi.org/10.1145/1707790.170779. ISBN 9781605588902
10. Coutts, D., Leshchinskiy, R., Stewart, D.: Stream fusion: from lists to streams to nothing at all. In: Proceedings of the 12th ACM SIGPLAN International Conference on Functional Programming, ICFP 2007, pp. 315–326. Association for Computing Machinery, Freiburg (2007). https://doi.org/10.1145/1291151.1291199. ISBN 9781595938152
11. Davey, B.A., Priestley, H.A.: Introduction to Lattices and Order, 2nd edn. Cambridge University Press (2002)
12. Gill, A., Launchbury, J., Peyton Jones, S.L.: A short cut to deforestation. In: Proceedings of the Conference on Functional Programming Languages and Computer Architecture, FPCA 1993, pp. 223–232. Association for Computing Machinery, Copenhagen (1993). https://doi.org/10.1145/165180.165214. ISBN 089791595X
13. Hanus, M.: A functional logic programming approach to graphical user interfaces. In: Pontelli, E., Santos Costa, V. (eds.) PADL 2000. LNCS, vol. 1753, pp. 47–62. Springer, Heidelberg (1999). https://doi.org/10.1007/3-540-46584-7_4
14. Hanus, M., Teegen, F.: Adding Data to curry. In: Hofstedt, P., Abreu, S., John, U., Kuchen, H., Seipel, D. (eds.) INAP/WLP/WFLP -2019. LNCS (LNAI), vol. 12057, pp. 230–246. Springer, Cham (2020). https://doi.org/10.1007/978-3-030-46714-2_15. ISBN 978-3-030-46713-5
15. Libby, S.: Making curry with rice: an optimizing compiler for curry. Ph.D. thesis. Portland State University (2022)
16. Libby, S.: Rice curry compiler (2022). https://github.com/slibby05/rice
17. Libby, S.: RICE: an optimizing curry compiler. In: Hanus, M., Inclezan, D. (eds.) PADL 2023. LNCS, vol. 13880, pp. 3–19. Springer, Cham (2023). https://doi.org/10.1007/978-3-031-24841-2_1. ISBN 978-3-031-24841-2
18. Mehner, S., et al.: Parametricity and proving free theorems for functional- logic languages. In: Proceedings of the 16th International Symposium on Principles and Practice of Declarative Programming, PPDP 2014, pp. 19–30. Association for Computing Machinery, Canterbury (2014). https://doi.org/10.1145/2643135.2643147. ISBN 9781450329477
19. Peyton Jones, S.: Call-pattern specialisation for Haskell programs. SIGPLAN Not. **42**(9), 327–337 (2007). https://doi.org/10.1145/1291220.1291200. ISSN 0362-1340
20. Reynols, J.C.: Types, abstraction and parametric polymorphism. In: Mason, R.E.A. (ed.) Information Processing 1983. IFIP Congress Series, vol. 9, pp. 513–523. Elsevier Science Publishers B.V., Amsterdam (1983)
21. Voigtländer, J.: Free theorems simply, via dinaturality. In: Hofstedt, P., Abreu, S., John, U., Kuchen, H., Seipel, D. (eds.) INAP/WLP/WFLP -2019. LNCS (LNAI), vol. 12057, pp. 247–267. Springer, Cham (2020). https://doi.org/10.1007/978-3-030-46714-2_16. ISBN 978-3-030-46713-5
22. Wadler, P.: Deforestation: transforming programs to eliminate trees. Theor. Comput. Sci. **73**(2), 231–248 (1990). http://www.sciencedirect.com/science/article/pii/030439759090147A. ISSN 0304-3975
23. Wadler, P.: Theorems for free!. In: Proceedings of the Fourth International Conference on Functional Programming Languages and Computer Architecture, FPCA 1989, pp. 347–359. Association for Computing Machinery, Imperial College (1989). https://doi.org/10.1145/99370.99404. ISBN 0897913280

MOLA: A Runtime Verification Engine Factory by (Meta-)interpreting Embedded DSLs

Felipe Gorostiaga[1,2], Martin Ceresa[1(✉)], and César Sánchez[1]

[1] IMDEA Software Institute, Pozuelo de Alarcón s/n, 28223 Madrid, Madrid, Spain
martin.ceresa@imdea.org
[2] CIFASIS, Rosario, Argentina

Abstract. Runtime verification (RV) is a formal monitoring technique that uses formal specifications to create monitors. Stream runtime verification (SRV) extends RV from Boolean observations and verdicts to diverse data, allowing much richer monitors. This expressivity is challenging for developers of monitoring engines, so SRV tools end up fixing a collection of data theories for an application domain, and require significant overhead to incorporate new datatypes. Recent results allow incorporating Haskell datatypes transparently into generic SRV engines through the use of an embedded DSL, but the resulting syntax is conditioned by Haskell, every new monitor requires recompilation and error reporting is cryptic.

In this paper, we introduce MOLA, a generic implementation of an SRV engine that uses reflection in Haskell to implement a *universal interpreter* that offers data-theory extensibility and type guarantees as well as a simple syntax with useful error reports. MOLA introduces the role of *data-theory engineer*, who easily defines datatypes for each application domain and compiles MOLA into a specialized engine. The resulting tool is then used by *specification engineers* who define monitors that the engine can evaluate without recompilation. Hence, MOLA finally realizes the promise of SRV to provide a clean separation between datatypes and temporal engines.

1 Introduction

Runtime Verification (RV) [3,19,22] is an area of formal methods that studies the dynamic analysis of formal specifications against a single trace of execution. Compared to static techniques like model checking [8,9,29], RV sacrifices

---

This work was funded in part by PRODIGY Project (TED2021-132464B-I00)—funded by MCIN/AEI/10.13039/501100011033/and the European Union NextGenerationEU/PRTR—by the DECO Project (PID2022-138072OB-I00)—funded by MCIN/AEI/10.13039/501100011033 and by the ESF, as well as by a research grant from Nomadic Labs and the Tezos Foundation.

© The Author(s), under exclusive license to Springer Nature Switzerland AG 2025
E. Erdem and G. Vidal (Eds.): PADL 2025, LNCS 15537, pp. 53–70, 2025.
https://doi.org/10.1007/978-3-031-84924-4_4

completeness to get an applicable extension of testing and debugging of reactive systems. The main problems studied in RV are: (1) how to generate monitors from formal specifications and (2) evaluating single execution traces against monitors [34].

Early RV languages were based on well-established specification languages from static verification, for example logics like LTL [23] or past LTL adapted for finite paths [4,12,20], regular expressions [1,33], rule-based languages [2] or rewriting [31]. All these specification languages were introduced in static verification where it is crucial to have decidable decision problems, and thus, observations and verdicts are typically Boolean values.

Stream Runtime Verification (SRV) generalizes monitoring algorithms from Boolean observations and verdicts to arbitrary data-theories and operations. Languages for SRV, pioneered by LOLA [11], are rich RV languages where monitors are declaratively defined using equations that relate input and output streams, offering a theoretical *clean separation between time dependencies and data operations*. Data-theories, in the SRV terminology, are similar to universal algebras in the sense that they consist of constructor symbols to build typed expressions along with the interpretation of these symbols. SRV monitoring algorithms collect and store data at runtime and apply a sequence of operations defined by the data theories to compute a final verdict. LOLA specifications can have future references and can be defined from infinite streams.

Example 1. Given a Boolean observation s, the past LTL formula $\diamondsuit s$ is *false* until the first time s is *true* and *true* thereafter. This can be defined in LOLA as

$$once\_s = once\_s[-1|\mathit{false}] \vee s[\mathbf{now}],$$

which defines an output Boolean stream $once\_s$ as the disjunction between its own previous value (or *false* at the initial instant), written as ($once\_s[-1|\mathit{false}]$), and the current value of s, written as $s[\mathbf{now}]$. This specification can be adapted to count how many times s has been true in the past:

$$c\_once\_s = c\_once\_s[-1|0] + (\textbf{if } s[\mathbf{now}] \textbf{ then } 1 \textbf{ else } 0)$$

These example illustrate how LOLA uses time shifts (written between brackets) and operators from the data-theories of Booleans and integers.

Most SRV research [10,14,21] has focused on implementing efficient temporal engines (in terms of the data stored or the operations performed), promising that the clean separation of data and monitoring engines will allow extending the tools to new data-theories. However, in practice, these extensions require modifying parsers, internal representations, and evaluation functions in the runtime system. In particular, every value in the data-theory has a corresponding syntax in the language, and thus, the parser needs to be aware of syntax tokens at the same time that the engine needs to be able to interpret symbols at runtime. As result, a large part of the programming effort when building SRV tools is devoted to implementing and maintaining data, and most tools end up supporting only a few hard-wired data-theories, with little or no reuse between application domains.

Incorporating Data-Theories from Haskell Datatypes. To alleviate the problem of extending SRV engines with new data-theories, [7] introduced *lift deep embeddings*, implemented in the tool HLOLA [17] as a Haskell eDSL. Lift deep embeddings incorporate Haskell datatypes as data-theories for SRV languages. The temporal engine is implemented focusing only on the temporal structure of specifications while abstracting away all concrete data operations through a clever use of generics. Moreover, using Haskell as a host language for HLOLA enables many Haskell features, like recursion, clear syntax, a module system, and strong typing.

Example 2. The specifications from Ex. 1 are implemented in HLOLA as follows:

```
1  s :: Stream Bool
2  s = Input "s"
3
4  once_s :: Stream Bool
5  once_s = "once_s" =: once_s :@ (-1, Leaf False) || Now s
6
7  c_once_s :: Stream Bool
8  c_once_s = "c_once_s"
9             =: once_s :@ (-1, Leaf False) + if Now s then 0 else 1
```

HLOLA overrides many usual functions such as the Boolean disjunction (||), addition (+) and **if** · **then** · **else** · to improve legibility. The extensibility of HLOLA has enabled multiple application domains. For example, HLOLA is used as a fundamental building block in [36] to implement the guidance of UAVs, and [24] uses HLOLA to implement intrusion detection policies based on network activity. Moreover, HLOLA can be used itself as a data-theory to enable dynamic parameterization, nested monitors and to create monitors on-the-fly [18,24].

Unfortunately, the implementation of HLOLA using deep lift embedding has some short-comings due to specifications being in fact Haskell programs. First, compiling Haskell programs is necessary *for each new monitor specification*. Second, errors are Haskell errors which tend to be cryptic for end users. Finally, the syntax of HLOLA inevitably diverges from LOLA syntax revealing some implementation details required by the use of Haskell generics. This is a major practical drawback because the users of RV tools are interested in describing monitors easily, and need not be expert Haskell programmers.

In this paper, we solve these issues by building a meta interpreter that can be specialized into a monitor interpreter once data-theories are fixed. Data-theories are first defined concisely by *data-theory engineers* for a given application domain. These data-theories are then *compiled once* together with the engine to generate an interpreter for specifications (monitors) that can use the data-theories described. Specification engineers then write conventional LOLA specifications without further recompilation. The main contribution of this paper is a new language and tool called MOLA, solving the syntax obscurity problem, the need for recompilation and the cryptic error reporting present in HLOLA. MOLA is a factory of SRV engines, where each engine is the result of specializing the temporal engine for a concrete collection of data-theories. We exploit modern functional language capabilities, available in Haskell, to build meta-interpreters in the application domain of RV.

Example 3. The MOLA specifications for Ex. 1 is:

```
1 input Bool s
2 output Bool once_s = once_s[-1|False] || s[now]
3 output Int c_once_s = c_once_s[-1|False] + if s[now] then 0 else 1
```

Related Work. Other stream runtime verification engines using features from the functional programming community are:

- *The Lucid Synchrone experiment* [6], which presents a way to transparently lift OCaml functions to stream functions, in the usual point-wise way, as well as OCaml datatypes and pattern-matching features. The language defines a mechanism for functions, called sequential functions, that depend on the history of their inputs. Compared to Lola, HLOLA and MOLA, Lucid does not allow future references. In particular, stream accesses and offsets do not exist, and only functions lifted for stream manipulation.
- *Copilot* [28], which is a Haskell implementation that offers a collection of stream transformers, does not allow explicit time accesses and offsets, similar to Lucid. Copilot focuses on real-time correct C code generation.
- *Haski: IoT Programming in Haskell* [35], which focuses on IoT devices and information flow capabilities. As for Copilot and Lucid, Haski does not present explicit time constraints but uses streams as semantics model under-the-hood. Aside from the time model, Haski follows a monadic approach, deviating from a more declarative approach followed by LOLA.
- HLOLA [17], which implements lift-deep embeddings [7] to bring Haskell datatypes as data-theories but at the price of polluting the input syntax, requiring recompilation and suffering from obscure error reporting.

Other SRV tools are TeSSLa [10], Striver [16]—both real-time stream languages—and Lola2.0 [13]—which extends LOLA with special constructs for runtime parameterization. All these languages still support only limited data-types, hard-wired in their parser, AST and runtime systems. Similarly, R2U2 [30]—based on a variation of metric interval temporal logic (MITL) for finite (real-time) traces—is restricted to Boolean values.

The rest of the paper is structured as follows: we revisit LOLA and the tool HLOLA in Sect. 2. The main contribution of this paper, MOLA is introduced in Sect. 3, and compared with LOLA and HLOLA in Sect. 4. Finally, Sect. 5 concludes.

2 Preliminaries. LOLA and HLOLA

The LOLA Specification Language. We introduce SRV using LOLA [11,32], a language for specifications. LOLA specifications declare equations that describe the relation between streams of input values and streams of output values. The LOLA online monitoring algorithm incrementally computes values for the output streams as it is fed values for the input streams. The basic elements of LOLA are data-theories and offset expressions.

Data-Theories. LOLA represents data using multi-sorted first-order interpreted theories, called data-theories in the LOLA terminology. These are finite collections of interpreted *sorts* and finite collections of interpreted function symbols. For example, the data-theory of natural numbers uses two sorts: *Nat* and *Bool* plus constant symbols 0, 1, 2, $\cdots$ of sort *Nat* and *true* and *false* of sort *Bool*, as well as functions +, *, and other algebraic operations with their usual interpretations. Other function symbols in the theory of natural numbers are predicates $<$, $\leq$, and other binary relations, defining symbols of type $Nat \times Nat \to Bool$. We assume that all theories include equality, the sort *Bool*, and a ternary predicate **if** $\cdot$ **then** $\cdot$ **else** $\cdot$ of type $Bool \times T \times T \to T$ for every sort T. We use $e : T$ to represent that e has sort T, and we typically use $\mathcal{T}$ to refer to the data-theory of a given specification, usually set by context.

Offset Expressions. The offset expression $v[k|d]$ refers to the value of the stream associated with variable v shifted k time steps from the current time. The value d is the default value used in case the time shift results in a moment before the beginning or after the end of time (for finite streams[1]). We use $v[\mathbf{now}]$ to refer to the 0 offset expression. In this case, a default value is not necessary because no illegal time instant results by shifting 0 steps.

Stream expressions are expressions built using variables and constructors from a set of data-theories. For example, the expression $(x[-1|\mathit{false}] \vee x)$ is a stream expression of sort *Bool* and $(y[\mathbf{now}] + y[3|5] * 7)$ is a stream expression of sort *Nat* where x is a stream expression of sort *Bool* and y is a stream of sort *Nat* in the environment. We omit the sort and data-theories of an expression when they are clear from context.

Specifications in LOLA are written as equation systems between input and output variables. We write $t_i = e_i(s_1, \ldots, s_m, t_1, \ldots t_n)$ to emphasize that equation e_i depends on *all* input and output streams including t_i itself.

Example 4. Consider Ex.1, with input streams $\{s : Bool\}$. The specification of $once\_s$ has output streams $\{once\_s : Bool\}$ and equation

$$once\_s = once\_s[-1|\mathit{false}] \vee s[\mathbf{now}].$$

The specification of c_once_s has output streams $\{c\_once\_s : Nat\}$ and equation

$$c\_once\_s = c\_once\_s[-1|0] + (\mathbf{if}\ s[\mathbf{now}]\ \mathbf{then}\ 1\ \mathbf{else}\ 0).$$

---
[1] LOLA accepts infinite streams.

The semantics of LOLA specifications is defined in terms of evaluation models [11] which are assignments of streams of values to each stream variable such that they respect the equations. Not all syntactically valid LOLA specifications are correct, because one could write circular specifications where there is not a unique solution, or there are many solutions[2]. However, a simple algorithm that checks cicularities within the temporal dependencies between expressions in LOLA specifications determines when specifications are correct [11,32] and have a unique output for every input.

HLOLA, a LOLA Extensible Engine. HLOLA [17] is an implementation of the language LOLA which allows importing datatypes from Haskell as data-theories. HLOLA lifts Haskell datatypes into LOLA data-theories employing a technique called *lift deep embedding* [7]. HLOLA also obtains from Haskell high-level features such as static parameterization to obtain concrete streams as the output of functions. In HLOLA, users define the temporal logic operators and pack them as libraries, while in other SRV tools libraries would require ad-hoc constructs that are already provided by Haskell. Using eDSLs brings the usual benefits beyond data-theories, including leveraging Haskell's parsing, compiling, type-checking, and modularity.

In HLOLA, input streams are just typed names. During the evaluation, the engine looks up the names of input streams in its environment and fetches their corresponding values at a given instant when needed. Output steams in HLOLA are typed names and their type-matching defining expressions. The values of these streams are computed incrementally following their corresponding expressions. HLOLA specifications are Haskell programs, and thus, type correct. When the engine reads values from the environment, it also parses and type checks them, raising an error if the type of an input value is not the expected.

Lift Deep Embedding in Action. To incorporate data-theories transparently, concrete types are abstracted away in the eDSL. For example, we should be able to use the *Boolean* data-theory without adding the constructors that a conventional deep embedding would require. The main idea of the lift deep embedding is to embed Haskell datatypes along with two stream runtime primitives. The resulting expressions are *values* and *function applications*, plus two additional stream access primitives representing offset expressions, as in LOLA. The resulting datatype resembles *Free Applicative Functors* [5] and *high-order abstract syntax* [27].

HLOLA defines stream expressions in Haskell as a parametric datatype `Expr` with a polymorphic argument domain. The term `e :: Expr d` represents an expression `e` over domain `d`. For example, to use the `Int` domain, we use `Expr Int` automatically instantiated inside Haskell borrowing its type `Int`. The `Expr` datatype in Haskell has the following constructors: `Leaf`, `App`, `Now` and `(:@)`. The constructor `Leaf` contains an element of the theory; `App` is the application of a *function* expression to a *value* expression; `Now` represents the value of a stream at the current instant; and `(:@)` (read as *at*) represents the value of a stream at a

---
[2] Examples are `a = a[now]` and `a = not a[now]`.

different instant in time. These constructions enable us to lift operations from domain values to expressions of type **Expr** directly. For example, we can create an expression that represents the sum of two **Expr Int** without defining a dedicated type of expression. The ability to map values into expressions avoids the definition of each constructor in the data-theory making extensions transparent.

The specification from Ex. 1 in plain HLOLA is:

```
s, once_s :: Stream Bool
s = Input "s"
once_s = Output ("once_s",
    App (App (Leaf (||)) (once_s :@ (-1, Leaf False))) (Now s))
```

The expression of once_s uses the function (||) from the data-theory and applies it to the previous value of once_s, using **False** as default value and applying the result to the current value of s. This style of writing declarations is cumbersome and error-prone, so HLOLA leverages the expressive power of Haskell to alleviate these issues and make the specifications more amenable. Using function overloading and infix operator one can define the following equivalent specification:

```
s, once_s :: Stream Bool
s = Input "s"
once_s = "once_s" =: once_s :@ (-1, Leaf False) || Now s
```

HLola Limitations. Implementation of HLOLA as an eDSL in Haskell comes with some important drawbacks.

Notation. First, the syntax of HLOLA diverges notably from that of LOLA. Since the syntax of eDSLs is inherited from the host language and only a few simple constructs are defined, the HLOLA eDSL is familiar for Haskell programmers but idiosyncratic for specification engineers.

Compilation. Second, every HLOLA specification has to be compiled with a Haskell compiler. If one writes the specification for once_s, and later modifies the specification, then the entire engine (that is, HLOLA) must be recompiled together with the new specification. We solve this problem in this paper, only requiring recompilation when new data-theories are used. Changing data-theories only occurs when new application domains are introduced but not when new monitors are defined in existing application domains.

Errors. Errors in HLOLA specification are reported at compilation time as Haskell errors. For example, if one forgets to tag the name of a stream, Haskell will consider it an expression definition and report a corresponding error. Given:

```
s, once_s :: Stream Bool
s = Input "s"
once_s = once_s :@ (-1, Leaf False) || Now s
```

generates the error mesage *"Couldn't match type: Expr Bool with: Stream Bool"*, which does not hint at the real problem in the specification.

Similarly, incorrectly using the postfix notation $s[\mathbf{now}]$ natural of LOLA:

```
1 s, once_s :: Stream Bool
2 s = Input "s"
3 once_s :: Stream Bool
4 once_s = "once_s" =: once_s :@ (-1, Leaf False) || s Now
```

results in the following Haskell error *"Couldn't match expected type: (Stream a0 -> Expr a0) -> Expr Bool with actual type: Stream Bool. The function 's' is applied to one value argument, but its type 'Stream Bool' has none"*.

3 Mola: A Factory of Lola Monitoring Engines

MOLA is a meta interpreter of LOLA specifications that uses HLOLA under-the-hood[3]. LOLA assumes that there is a fixed data-theory [32]. However, in practice different application domains require different concrete data-theories.

HLOLA offers the flexibility to incorporate data-theories at the price of diverging from LOLA, requiring recompilation for every new specification. In contrast, MOLA reconciles the syntax of LOLA and the flexibility to add new data-theories of HLOLA. In MOLA, data-theories are not fixed at the core of the language but are defined programmatically by *data-theory designers*. Once the data-theory engineer defines a set of data-theories $\mathcal{T}$ useful in the application domain, MOLA is compiled into an interpreter of $\mathcal{T}$-LOLA specifications which uses HLOLA as the underlying SRV engine.

In this section, we explain the design and implementation of MOLA. We show how MOLA reuses the HLOLA evaluation engine and static analyzer. We show MOLA internal untyped stream representation and how we can translate MOLA expressions into well typed HLOLA stream expressions. When designing this translation we made several pragmatic decisions keeping in mind that the end users are LOLA specification engineers.

3.1 Mola Generic Internal Data Representation

Following HLOLA expressions (see Sect. 2), MOLA parses equation definitions into names bound to untyped expressions, ignoring types while keeping the applicative and temporal structure of expressions. These expressions are similar to trees used in graph-reduction schemes and G-machines [26], but with special temporal nodes:

```
1 data SExpr = SLeaf String  | SApp SExpr SExpr
2                            | SNow SExpr    | SAt SExpr SExpr SExpr
```

LOLA specifications are parsed as lists of stream definitions captured by the following type `StreamDef`:

---

[3] MOLA is available at (github website removed to preserve author anonymity).

```
1 data StreamDef = SD {name :: String, ty :: String, body :: Maybe SExpr}
```

Using datatypes **SExpr** and **StreamDef**, MOLA abstracts the structure of the input LOLA specifications as uninterpreted symbols and plain strings, but with enough temporal information to decide whether the input specifications is valid (by checking cycles [32]).

Recall the MOLA specification for the LTL property $\Diamond s$ from Ex.1:

```
1 input Bool s
2 output Bool once_s = once_s[-1|False] || s[now]
```

The MOLA parser creates the following two **StreamDef** values:

```
1 SD { name = "s"     , ty = "Bool", body = Nothing}
2 SD { name = "once_s", ty = "Bool"
3     , body = Just (SApp (SApp (SLeaf "||") (SAt "once_s" "-1" "false"))
4                         (SNow "s"))
5     }
```

The code above captures the structure of an HLOLA specification but lacks the interpretation of the symbols for types, functions and values from the theory.

3.2 From Data-Theories to Haskell Datatypes

Inside the engine of MOLA, uninterpreted function and value symbols in data-theories accessible at runtime are interpreted as Haskell values. So, we can have runtime errors, ask Feli. A theory is captured as a table that maps symbols to their interpretations, an algebra for each sort linking data-theories in LOLA with datatypes in Haskell.

MOLA uses internally the following datatype to hide types:

```
1 data KnownValue where KV :: a -> KnownValue
```

and a type **Theory** mapping symbols to well-typed known values:

```
1 type Theory = Map String KnownValue
```

We bind sort symbols to their interpreted Haskell types using proxies:

```
1 data Proxy a
2 data KnownType where KT :: Proxy a -> KnownType
```

After mapping symbols to their Haskell interpretation, we can interpret and monitor MOLA specifications with HLOLA as the backend.

Example 5. With all the above definitions, we can define a version of the Boolean data-theory in MOLA as follows:

```
1 values = [ ("true", KV True), ("false", KV False)
2          , ("not", KV not)  , ("||", KV (||))    , ("&&", KV (&&))]
3 sorts  = [("Bool" , KT (Proxy :: Proxy Bool))]
```

Now MOLA can traverse the body of the output stream once_s from Ex.1 building the HLOLA expression by looking up the data-theory symbols in the theory table, translating the original parsed body:

```
1 SApp (SApp (SLeaf "||") (SAt "once_s" "-1" "false")) (SNow "s")
```

into the HLOLA expression:

```
1 App (App (Leaf (||)) (once_s :@ (-1, False))) (Now s)
```

of type **Expr Bool**. Integers are part of the meta theory of LOLA.

When interpreting MOLA streams, their names are bound to their definitions in a table of streams, so they can be accessed by themselves or by other streams. MOLA streams can be recursive, for example, the stream once_s refers to the stream s and also to once_s itself.

Given a list of stream definitions of type **StreamDef** and a theory, MOLA creates HLOLA streams of type **Stream** and expressions of type **Expr** using the Haskell `reflection` package[4] to ensure that each function and value are of their expected type.

We have implemented a simple type checking algorithm that detects type mismatches and reports them nicely to the user.

3.3 Adding Polymorphic Constructions

The previous definitions are not enough to support polymorphism, as there is no way to decide the type of functions associated with symbols based on their context. Polymorphism is extensively used in LOLA specifications, for example in conditional statements or in the equivalence operator. To regain polymorphism in MOLA, we modify the type of theories **Theory** to associate each symbol to both a potentially polymorphic type and a function that given concrete types for each type variable returning their corresponding **KnownValue**. To avoid annotating each term in a specification with its concrete type, we implement type inference and type checking using the Haskell `unification-fd` package[5].

We introduce the following datatype to represent polymorphic types within MOLA:

```
1 data PT = Const String | Var String | PTApp PT PT
```

Then, the new definition of **Theory** is the following:

```
1 data ThEntry = TE { ty :: PT, val :: KnownValue }
2 type Theory = Map String ThEntry
```

Some polymorphic functions impose restrictions on the concrete types that they accept using Constraints. MOLA defines a handful of constraints that polymorphic functions can refer to and uses the package `constraints`[6] to access the

---
[4] Reflection in Hackage. https://hackage.haskell.org/package/reflection.
[5] Wren Romano, Unification-FD in Hackage https://hackage.haskell.org/package/unification-fd.
[6] Constraint in Hackage. https://hackage.haskell.org/package/constraints.

dictionaries of concrete datatypes of a given theory. In particular, polymorphic functions in MOLA can use the following constraints **Eq**, **Ord Show**, **FromJSON**, **Read**, **ToJSON**, and **Default**[7].

Given a specification, MOLA traverses lists of stream definitions inferring the concrete type of each expression, since MOLA has context information to select a concrete implementation for polymorphic functions, and applying the interpreted functions to their interpreted arguments, effectively reducing the application graph. The tool also performs type-checking to make sure that stream definitions match their expected type. At the end of this process, MOLA computes a list of HLOLA stream definitions (potentially parametric) i.e. functions with an arbitrary number of arguments returning HLOLA streams of type **Stream** in the end.

Exploiting the Read Type-Class Trick. To improve LOLA syntax even further using Haskell, MOLA tries to read symbols guessing their types using the **Read** type-class. This is particularly useful when writing data-theories because it enables theory designers to avoid assigning interpretations to valid common strings like numbers, simply define or derive the **Read** class for custom datatypes.

4 MOLA vs. HLOLA Specifications

We compare in this section MOLA and HLOLA specifications to illustrate how MOLA offers a much cleaner syntax to define LOLA specifications, while HLOLA specifications are closer to Haskell programs.

For this purpose, we define MOLA and HLOLA specifications for the same monitor based on a blockchain application. This monitor inspects the execution of the Juster smart contract, a decentralized betting platform deployed in the Tezos blockchain [15]. Juster is a decentralized application that allows users to bet on events that represent the changes of certain cryptocurrency prices within a given time interval. Users get a reward if their predictions are correct and loose their bet otherwise. The Juster administrator opens events that users can bet on and closes these after the betting interval ended, distributing the earnings accordingly. Since the information of the blockchain is public and immediately available, we can define monitors assessing properties about the behavior of the decentralized applications using SRV.

We consider the following LOLA specification, designed to monitor the Juster platform assessing that: (1) only open events are closed and only closed events are open, and (2) there are less than 100 open events at any given time. The monitor receives events tagged with an identifier **eventId** and with the kind of event which can be either **Open**, **Close** or **Other**.

We use the following five data-theories: Booleans, EventId, Operation, Integers and Sets of EventId, with the values and functions to manipulate them. Our specification has two input stream variables, $\{eventId : \mathsf{EventId}, operation :$

---

[7] Constraints were selected following basic LOLA assumptions and the input/output nature of monitors.

Operation}, and three output stream variables, {*open_events* : {EventId}, *few_events* : Bool, *right_order* : Bool}. Our monitor is defined by the following LOLA specification:

$$open\_events = \textbf{if } operation[\textbf{now}] \equiv \mathsf{Open}$$
$$\text{else if } operation[\textbf{now}] \equiv \mathsf{Close}$$
$$\text{then } eventId[\textbf{now}] \setminus \{open\_events[-1|\emptyset]\}$$
$$\text{else } \{open\_events[-1|\emptyset]\}$$
$$few\_events = |open\_events[\textbf{now}]| < 100$$
$$right\_order = (operation[\textbf{now}] \equiv \mathsf{Close}) \leftrightarrow$$
$$(eventId[\textbf{now}] \in open\_events[-1|\emptyset])$$

We now elaborate the data-theories used. In LOLA, we can describe each sort and symbol interface as follows (leaving aside Booleans and Integers sorts to simplify the presentation, which are standard):

$$\mathsf{GroundSorts} = \{ \mathsf{Boolean, EventId, Operation, Integer} \}$$
$$\mathsf{Sorts} \quad\quad = \mathsf{GroundSorts} \cup \{Set_i \mid i \in \mathsf{GroundSorts}\}$$
$$\mathsf{Operation} \quad = \{(Open \mapsto \epsilon), (Close \mapsto \epsilon), (Other \mapsto \epsilon)\}$$
$$\mathsf{EventId} \quad\quad = \mathsf{Integer}$$

The LOLA definitions above are mathematical pseudocode and it is not clear how to provide a way to define new sorts in a concrete implementation. Hence, most SRV engines data-theories are either hard-coded internally or built from predefined data-theories using simple constructors.

In HLOLA, we can define the theories above leveraging datatypes from Haskell. We bring Booleans and Integers from the Haskell prelude and Sets from a standard library. Then, we define the following custom datatypes:

```
1 type EventId = Int
2 data Operation = Open | Close | Other
3   deriving (Show,Generic,Read,ToJSON,Eq,FromJSON)
```

With these definitions we are ready to define the specification in HLOLA:

```
1 spec :: Specification
2 spec = [out few_events]
3
4 eventId :: Stream EventId
5 eventId = Input "eventId"
6 operation :: Stream Operation
7 operation = Input "operation"
8
9 open_events :: Stream (Set EventId)
10 open_events = "open_events" =:
11   let prevopen = open_events :@ (-1, Leaf empty) in
12   if Now operation === Leaf Open
13     then insert <$> Now eventId <*> prevopen
14     else if Now operation === Leaf Close
```

```
15      then delete <$> Now eventId <*> prevopen
16    else prevopen
17
18 few_events :: Stream Bool
19 few_events = "few_events" =: (size <$> Now open_events) < 100
20
21 right_order :: Stream Bool
22 right_order = "right_order" =:
23    let prevopen = open_events :@ (-1, Leaf empty) in
24    (Now operation === Leaf Close)===(member <$> Now eventId <*> prevopen)
```

The syntax of the HLOLA specification above is polluted by Haskell idiosyncrasies, but in exchange, defining its data-theories is straightforward.

Compared to HLOLA, the syntax of the equivalent MOLA specification is clean and more amenable, matching the LOLA intended syntax.

```
1 input EventId eventId
2 input Operation operation
3 define {EventId} open_events =
4   if operation[now] == Open
5     then insert(eventId[now], openevents[-1|{}])
6   else if operation[now] == Close
7     then delete(eventId[now], openevents[-1|{}])
8   else openevents[-1|{}]
9 output Bool few_events = size(openevents[now]) < 100
10 output Bool right_order =
11   (operation[now] == Close) == member(eventId[now], openevents[-1|{}])
```

The role of the data-theory engineer consists on deciding the Haskell datatypes to be used as data-theories for the application domain and specialize MOLA accordingly, generating a tool that can read MOLA specifications without recompilation and perform the monitoring activity. The custom datatypes in MOLA can borrow native and third-parties datatypes, so it preserves the extensibility of the data-theory from HLOLA. For the previous example, in MOLA we define and manually add the datatypes to the data-theory as follows:

```
1 type EventId = Int
2 data Operation = Open | Close | Other
3   deriving (Show,Generic,Read,ToJSON,Eq,FromJSON)
4
5 -- No need for values.
6 sorts = [("EventId" , KT (Proxy :: Proxy EventId)) ,
7          ("Operation" , KT (Proxy :: Proxy Operation))]
```

We just add two entries to the theory table binding the symbols "EventId" and "Operation" of the newly defined datatypes to the types **EventId** and **Operation** respectively. We do not have to add the specific values **Open**, **Other**, and **Close** because the types **EventId** and **Operation** are instances of the class **Read**. Moreover, MOLA already provides several predefined data-theories, such as Integers, Booleans, Lists and Sets, which is why it is not necessary to incorporate the datatypes and functions to manipulate these data-theories by hand.

However, if we want to part from the notation defined by those classes, we need to define our own. For example adding the following line:

```
1  values = [("openE", KV Open),("closeE", KV Close),("otherE", KV Other)]
```

We can see the difference between how MOLA and HLOLA operate comparing how they are invoked. In HLOLA, we need to compile specifications along with the SRV engine, then we execute the compiled program (monitor) and consume inputs, which means that the execution order is as follows:

```
HLola$ $EDITOR Spec1.hs; stack install; HLola input1.txt
HLola$ $EDITOR Spec2.hs; stack install; HLola input2.txt
```

Even if `Spec1.hs` and `Spec2.hs` share the same data-theories, the Haskell compiler must be invoked for every specification. In MOLA, first the interpreter is specialized with the data-theory:

```
Mola$ $EDITOR MyTheory.hs; stack install;
```

and then the specs can be simply run:

```
Mola$ $EDITOR Spec1.mola; Mola Spec1.mola input1.txt
Mola$ $EDITOR Spec2.mola; Mola Spec2.mola input2.txt
```

There is no need to recompile MOLA when we change the specification unless we update the data-theories.

5 Conclusions and Future Work

We presented MOLA, a meta interpreter for LOLA specifications and a factory of monitoring engines, where each engine is specialized with a data-theory for a given application domain. MOLA finally fulfills entirely the SRV promise [11] of a clean separation between data-theories and the temporal engine. We based our meta interpreter on the tool HLOLA which uses the lift deep embedding principle to implement data-theories as Haskell datatypes and harnesses the great abstraction level of Haskell to produce efficient and concise monitors. MOLA has two users: (1) data theory engineers, who design the data-theories to be used in a given application domain with the power to use and build Haskell data-types, and then compile MOLA into a stand-alone tool. (2) specification engineers, who write monitors at their own level of abstraction. In this sense, MOLA is the first meta interpreter of LOLA specifications enjoying at the same time the usability of LOLA and the flexibility of lift deep embedding based tools like HLOLA.

HLOLA is a concise and efficient stream runtime verification engine. HLOLA supports specifications for both online and offline monitoring, real-time event streams, and advanced features like reatroactive-parametrization and spawing new monitors on-the-fly based on new evidence found dynamically. MOLA benefits from all HLOLA features and, following the same principle as in HLOLA, borrows from Haskell a mature ecosystem along with its inference and typing algorithms instead of re-implementing them. With MOLA preserving the syntax of LOLA, we expect the community to finally enjoy writing specifications in their lovely declarative SRV language with little to no effort.

Future Work. In addition to having experimental data showing MOLA performance and practical usage, we propose the following research directions to simplify the use of MOLA and improve its acceptance in the runtime verification community.

Data-Theory Specification Language. We shifted the need of using Haskell from specifications to the design of data-theories. Our next steps are identifying key concepts when defining new data-theories, common patterns, to simplify the job of data-theory engineers with a specialized language.

Functions in Specs. We are already working on a new MOLA (and LOLA) keyword **function** that allows defining pure functions within specifications. Such functions are interpreted and do not require recompilation, being readily available in stream definitions. For example, in the following specification:

```
1 input Int s
2 output Int r = succ(s)
3 function Int succ <n Int> = n+1
```

The function succ would be added to the data-theory table when the specification is processed and bound to the Haskell function \ n -> n + 1 so that it can be used in the definition of r as any other function in the theory.

Strengthen the Interaction Between MOLA *and* HLOLA. We can use a stream defined using native HLOLA in a MOLA specification by simply adding it to the theory table. We are working on the dual direction: a new stream constructor of HLOLA**External :: String -> Stream** a as a placeholder that allows us to refer to streams in HLOLA that will be defined in MOLA at a later stage.

Beyond LOLA. Since we have separated the AST of HLOLA from the parser (we only parse the application graph) we can easily define multiple parsers for MOLA. For example, we can let the application of function f to parameters x and y be written as f x y as in Haskell or as f(x,y) like in other programming languages. We can define the application of a parametric stream s to parameters a and b as s<a><b> instead of a normal function application as in HLOLA.

We are working on the implementation of parsers for third-party languages that are known to be subsumed by LOLA, such as rule-based languages and logic-based languages. For example, one such parser would interpret Past-LTL properties and use the HLOLA eDSL as a backend, and without modifying anything else, we would be able to parse properties like H(p || (q U r)), which represents the Past-LTL property $\boxdot(p \vee (q\,\mathcal{U}\,r))$, and generate a monitor based on HLOLA.

Certified C Monitors with MOLA. There exists a variation of HLOLA called MC-LOLA, in the spirit of the monitoring tool Copilot [25,28] that transpiles HLOLA code into certified C code that can later be compiled into an efficient monitor of LOLA using a C compiler. In MC-LOLA, functions and values available in the specification data-theories, $\mathcal{T}$, are determined by those available in C and are not arbitrary functions and values from Haskell. Since the parser of MOLA is agnostic of the underlying engine (be it HLOLA or MC-LOLA), we plan to investigate the use of MOLA to generate MC-LOLA specifications providing the functions and values of C used in useful MC-LOLA specifications as data-theory.

References

1. Asarin, E., Caspi, P., Maler, O.: Timed regular expressions. J. ACM **49**(2), 172–206 (2002)
2. Barringer, H., Goldberg, A., Havelund, K., Sen, K.: Rule-based runtime verification. In: Proceedings of VMCAI'04. LNCS, vol. 2937, pp. 44–57. Springer, Venice (2004)
3. Bartocci, E., Falcone, Y. (eds.): Lectures on Runtime Verification - Introductory and Advanced Topics, LNCS, vol. 10457. Springer, Heidelberg (2018). iSBN 978-3-319-75631-8
4. Bauer, A., Leucker, M., Schallhart, C.: Runtime verification for LTL and TLTL. ACM T. Softw. Eng. Meth. **20**(4), 14 (2011)
5. Capriotti, P., Kaposi, A.: Free applicative functors. EPTCS **153**, 2–30 (2014). https://doi.org/10.4204/EPTCS.153.2
6. Caspi, P., Hamon, G., Pouzet, M.: Real-Time Systems: Models and verification – Theory and tools, chap. Synchronous Functional Programming with Lucid Synchrone. ISTE (2007)
7. Ceresa, M., Gorostiaga, F., Sánchez, C.: Declarative stream runtime verification (hLola). In: Oliveira, B.C.S. (ed.) APLAS 2020. LNCS, vol. 12470, pp. 25–43. Springer, Cham (2020). https://doi.org/10.1007/978-3-030-64437-6_2
8. Clarke, E.M., Emerson, E.A.: Design and synthesis of synchronization skeletons using branching time temporal logic. In: Proceedings of Workshop on Logic of Programs, pp. 52–71 (1981)
9. Clarke, E.M., Grunberg, O., Peled, D.A.: Model Checking. MIT Press, Cambridge (1999)
10. Convent, L., Hungerecker, S., Leucker, M., Scheffel, T., Schmitz, M., Thoma, D.: TeSSLa: temporal stream-based specification language. In: Massoni, T., Mousavi, M.R. (eds.) SBMF 2018. LNCS, vol. 11254, pp. 144–162. Springer, Cham (2018). https://doi.org/10.1007/978-3-030-03044-5_10
11. D'Angelo, B., et al.: LOLA: runtime monitoring of synchronous systems. In: Proceedings of TIME'05, pp. 166–174. IEEE (2005)
12. Eisner, C., Fisman, D., Havlicek, J., Lustig, Y., McIsaac, A., Van Campenhout, D.: Reasoning with temporal logic on truncated paths. In: Hunt, W.A., Somenzi, F. (eds.) CAV 2003. LNCS, vol. 2725, pp. 27–39. Springer, Heidelberg (2003). https://doi.org/10.1007/978-3-540-45069-6_3

13. Faymonville, P., Finkbeiner, B., Schirmer, S., Torfah, H.: A stream-based specification language for network monitoring. In: Falcone, Y., Sánchez, C. (eds.) RV 2016. LNCS, vol. 10012, pp. 152–168. Springer, Cham (2016). https://doi.org/10.1007/978-3-319-46982-9_10
14. Faymonville, P., Finkbeiner, B., Schwenger, M., Torfah, H.: Real-time stream-based monitoring. CoRR arxiv:1711.03829 (2017)
15. Goodman, L.M.: Tezos – a self-amending crypto-ledger (2014). https://www.tezos.com/whitepaper.pdf
16. Gorostiaga, F., Sánchez, C.: Striver: stream runtime verification for real-time event-streams. In: Colombo, C., Leucker, M. (eds.) RV 2018. LNCS, vol. 11237, pp. 282–298. Springer, Cham (2018). https://doi.org/10.1007/978-3-030-03769-7_16
17. Gorostiaga, F., Sánchez, C.: HLola: a very functional tool for extensible stream runtime verification. In: TACAS 2021. LNCS, vol. 12652, pp. 349–356. Springer, Cham (2021). https://doi.org/10.1007/978-3-030-72013-1_18
18. Gorostiaga, F., Sánchez, C.: Nested monitors: monitors as expressions to build monitors. In: Feng, L., Fisman, D. (eds.) RV 2021. LNCS, vol. 12974, pp. 164–183. Springer, Cham (2021). https://doi.org/10.1007/978-3-030-88494-9_9
19. Havelund, K., Goldberg, A.: Verify your runs. In: Meyer, B., Woodcock, J. (eds.) VSTTE 2005. LNCS, vol. 4171, pp. 374–383. Springer, Heidelberg (2008). https://doi.org/10.1007/978-3-540-69149-5_40
20. Havelund, K., Roşu, G.: Synthesizing monitors for safety properties. In: Katoen, J.-P., Stevens, P. (eds.) TACAS 2002. LNCS, vol. 2280, pp. 342–356. Springer, Heidelberg (2002). https://doi.org/10.1007/3-540-46002-0_24
21. Leucker, M., Sánchez, C., Scheffel, T., Schmitz, M., Schramm, A.: TeSSLa: runtime verification of non-synchronized real-time streams. In: Proceedings of the 33rd Symposium on Applied Computing (SAC'18), pp. 1925–1933. ACM (2018)
22. Leucker, M., Schallhart, C.: A brief account of runtime verification. J. Logic Algebr. Progr. **78**(5), 293–303 (2009)
23. Manna, Z., Pnueli, A.: Temporal Verification of Reactive Systems: Safety. Springer, New York (1995)
24. Pedregal, P., Gorostiaga, F., Sánchez, C.: A stream runtime verification tool with nested and retroactive parametrization. In: Katsaros, P., Nenzi, L. (eds.) Runtime Verification, pp. 351–362. Springer, Cham (2023). https://doi.org/10.1007/978-3-031-44267-4_19
25. Perez, I., Dedden, F., Goodloe, A.: Copilot 3. Technical Report. NASA/TM-2020-220587, NASA Langley Research Center (2020)
26. Peyton Jones, S.: The Implementation of Functional Programming Languages. Prentice Hall Internaltional (UK) Ltd. (1987). https://www.microsoft.com/en-us/research/publication/the-implementation-of-functional-programming-languages-2/, chapters also by: Philip Wadler, Programming Research Group, Oxford; Peter Hancock, Metier Management Systems, Ltd.; David Turner, University of Kent, Canterbury
27. Pfenning, F., Elliott, C.: Higher-order abstract syntax. SIGPLAN Not. **23**(7), 199–208 (1988). https://doi.org/10.1145/960116.54010
28. Pike, L., Goodloe, A., Morisset, R., Niller, S.: Copilot: a hard real-time runtime monitor. In: Barringer, H., Falcone, Y., Finkbeiner, B., Havelund, K., Lee, I., Pace, G., Roşu, G., Sokolsky, O., Tillmann, N. (eds.) RV 2010. LNCS, vol. 6418, pp. 345–359. Springer, Heidelberg (2010). https://doi.org/10.1007/978-3-642-16612-9_26
29. Queille, J.P., Sifakis, J.: Specification and verification of concurrent systems in CESAR. In: Dezani-Ciancaglini, M., Montanari, U. (eds.) Programming 1982.

LNCS, vol. 137, pp. 337–351. Springer, Heidelberg (1982). https://doi.org/10.1007/3-540-11494-7_22
30. Reinbacher, T., Rozier, K.Y., Schumann, J.: Temporal-logic based runtime observer pairs for system health management of real-time systems. In: Ábrahám, E., Havelund, K. (eds.) TACAS 2014. LNCS, vol. 8413, pp. 357–372. Springer, Heidelberg (2014). https://doi.org/10.1007/978-3-642-54862-8_24
31. Roşu, G., Havelund, K.: Rewriting-based techniques for runtime verification. Autom. Softw. Eng. **12**(2), 151–197 (2005)
32. Sánchez, C.: Online and offline stream runtime verification of synchronous systems. In: Colombo, C., Leucker, M. (eds.) RV 2018. LNCS, vol. 11237, pp. 138–163. Springer, Cham (2018). https://doi.org/10.1007/978-3-030-03769-7_9
33. Sen, K., Roşu, G.: Generating optimal monitors for extended regular expressions. ENTCS **89**(2), 226–245 (2003)
34. Sánchez, C., et al.: A survey of challenges for runtime verification from advanced application domains (beyond software). Formal Methods Syst. Des. **54**(3), 279–335 (2019). https://doi.org/10.1007/s10703-019-00337-w
35. Valliappan, N., Krook, R., Russo, A., Claessen, K.: Towards secure iot programming in haskell. In: Proceedings of the 13th ACM SIGPLAN International Symposium on Haskell, Haskell 2020, pp. 136–150. Association for Computing Machinery, New York (2020). https://doi.org/10.1145/3406088.3409027
36. Zudaire, S., Gorostiaga, F., Sánchez, C., Schneider, G., Uchitel, S.: Assumption monitoring using runtime verification for UAV temporal task plan executions. In: Proceedings of IEEE International Conference on Robotics and Automation (ICRA'21). IEEE (2021)

SM-Based Semantics for Answer Set Programs Containing Conditional Literals and Arithmetic

Zachary Hansen[✉][iD] and Yuliya Lierler[iD]

University of Nebraska Omaha, Omaha, NE 68106, USA
zachhansen@unomaha.edu

Abstract. Modern answer set programming solvers such as CLINGO support advanced language constructs that improve the expressivity and conciseness of logic programs. Conditional literals are one such construct. They form "subformulas" that behave as nested implications within the bodies of logic rules. Their inclusion brings the form of rules closer to the less restrictive syntax of first-order logic. These qualities make conditional literals useful tools for knowledge representation. In this paper, we propose a semantics for logic programs with conditional literals and arithmetic based on the SM operator. These semantics do not require grounding, unlike the established semantics for such programs that relies on a translation to infinitary propositional logic. The main result of this paper establishes the precise correspondence between the proposed and existing semantics.

Keywords: Answer Set Programming · Conditional Literals · Semantics

1 Introduction

Answer Set Programming (ASP) [24,25] is a declarative programming paradigm that has been applied within a variety of challenging and high-consequence systems such as explainable donor-patient matching [6], space shuttle decision support systems [2,3], train scheduling [1], robotics [16], and automated fault diagnosis [29]. ASP programs are concise, human-readable, and benefit from well-defined semantics rooted in mathematical logic – these qualities make ASP programs attractive candidates for formal verification [5]. Providing high levels of assurance regarding program behavior is particularly crucial for safety-critical applications. This paper is part of a research stream with the long-term goal of supporting rigorous verification of ASP systems.

Conditional literals are powerful language features for knowledge representation. Originating in the LPARSE grounder [27], these languages features are now also supported by the answer set solver CLINGO [14,15]. Intuitively, they represent a nested implication within the body of an ASP rule [17]. Rules with conditional literals concisely express knowledge that may be difficult to otherwise encode. For instance, conditional literals are widely employed in meta-programming – Listings 4–7 in "How to build your own ASP-based system?!" by Kaminski et al. [20] define meta encodings which compute the classical and supported models of reified logic programs; these encodings rely heavily on conditional literals.

Conditional literals may also make programs easier to formally verify by reducing the number of auxiliary or inessential predicates in a program. Consider Listing 1.1, which contains a typical encoding of the graph coloring problem.

Listing 1.1. Graph coloring problem encoding.
```
1  {asg(V, C)} :- vtx(V), col(C).
2  :- asg(V, C1), asg(V, C2), C1 != C2.
3  colored(V) :- asg(V,C).
4  :- vtx(V), not colored(V).
5  :- asg(V1, C), asg(V2, C), edge(V1, V2).
```

The program in this listing can be simplified by replacing lines 3–4 with the following *constraint* (a rule with an empty head) containing a conditional literal:

$$:\text{-} \; not \; asg(V, C) : col(C); vtx(V). \tag{1}$$

This simplification is attractive since it eliminates the auxiliary predicate *colored*/1 (introduced in line 3 for the sole purpose of stating the subsequent constraint in line 4). We will use rule (1) as a running example in the remainder of the paper.

Typically, the semantics of programs with variables are defined indirectly, via a procedure called *grounding*. Grounding turns a given program with variables into a propositional one. Then, semantics are defined for the resulting propositional program. This hampers our ability to reason about the behavior of programs independently of a specific grounding context. In 2011, Ferraris, Lee, and Lifschitz proposed semantics for answer set programs that bypasses grounding [13]. They introduced the SM operator, which turns a program (or, rather, the first-order logic formula associated with the considered program) into a classical second-order formula. The Herbrand models of this formula coincide with the answer sets of the original program.

Since then, that approach has been generalized to cover such features of ASP input languages as aggregates [7,10], arithmetic [8,21], and conditional literals [17]. Yet, all of these features were addressed independently of the others. This paper helps to close that gap. Here, we introduce grounding-free SM operator-based semantics for logic programs containing *both* conditional literals and arithmetic, combining ideas from earlier work on these features [8,17,21]. We also show that the proposed characterization coincides with the existing semantics for such programs based on grounding to infinitary propositional logic [15]; these are the semantics adhered to by CLINGO.

One of the advantages of the SM-based characterization is that it enables us to construct proofs of correctness in a modular way that does not rely on grounding the program with respect to a specific instance of input data. For instance, this style of verification – which exploits the SM operator's ability to divide programs into modules – has been employed to demonstrate the adherence of Graph Coloring, Hamiltonian Cycle, and Traveling Salesman problems to natural language specifications [5,9]. This paper extends the class of programs for which such arguments can be constructed.

Section 2 defines the language of logic programs considered, and Sect. 3 provides the essence of the SM characterization for logic programs with conditional literals and arithmetic. Section 4 reviews the established semantics for programs with conditional literals and arithmetic, which relies on a translation from logic programs to infinitary propositional formulas. The main results of this paper –Theorems 1 and 2 – are given in Sect. 5, connecting our SM-based semantics to the established semantics.

2 Syntax of Logic Programs

We now present the language of logic programs considered in this paper. It can be viewed as a fragment of the Abstract Gringo (AG) language [15]; equivalently, it can be viewed as an extension of the mini-GRINGO language [21] to rules whose bodies may contain conditional literals.

We assume a *(program) signature* with three countably infinite sets of symbols: *numerals*, *symbolic constants* and *variables*. We also assume a 1-to-1 correspondence between numerals and integers; the numeral corresponding to an integer n is denoted by $\overline{n}$. A syntactic expression is *ground* if it contains no variables. A ground expression is *precomputed* if it contains no operation names. *Terms* are defined recursively:

- Numerals, symbolic constants, variables, or either of the special symbols *inf* and *sup* are terms;
- if t_1, t_2 are program terms and $\circ$ is one of the *operation names*

$$+ \quad - \quad \times \quad / \quad \backslash \quad .. \tag{2}$$

then $t_1 \circ t_2$ is a term (we write $-t$ to abbreviate the term $\overline{0} - t$);
- if t_1 is a program term, then $|t_1|$ is a term.

We assume that a total order on ground terms is chosen such that

- *inf* is its least element and *sup* is its greatest element,
- for any integers m and n, $\overline{m} < \overline{n}$ iff $m < n$, and
- for any integer n and any symbolic constant c, $\overline{n} < c$.

A comparison is an expression of the form $t_1 \prec t_2$, where t_1 and t_2 are terms and $\prec$ is one of the comparison symbols:

$$= \quad \neq \quad < \quad > \quad \leq \quad \geq \tag{3}$$

An *atom* is an expression of the form $p(\mathbf{t})$, where p is a symbolic constant and $\mathbf{t}$ is a list of program terms. A *basic literal* is an atom possibly preceded by one or two occurrences of *not*. A *conditional literal* is an expression of the form

$$H : l_1, \ldots, l_m,$$

where H is either a comparison, a basic literal, or the symbol $\bot$ (denoting falsity) and $l_1, \ldots, l_m$ is a list of basic literals and comparisons. We often abbreviate such an expression as $H : \mathbf{L}$. If $m = 0$, then the preceding ":" is dropped (so that the program stays CLINGO-compliant [15]). We view basic literals and comparisons as conditional literals with an empty list of conditions, i.e., $m = 0$. A *rule* is an expression of the form

$$Hd :\!\!- B_1, \ldots, B_n, \tag{4}$$

where

- Hd is either an atom (a normal rule), or an atom in braces (a choice rule), or the symbol $\bot$ (a constraint);
- each B_i ($1 \leq i \leq n$) is a conditional literal.

We call the symbol :- a *rule operator*. We call the left hand side of the rule operator the *head*, the right hand side of the rule operator the *body*. The symbol $\bot$ may be omitted from the head, resulting in an empty head. Such rules are called *constraints*. If the body of the rule is empty, the rule operator will be omitted, resulting in a *fact*. A *program* is a finite set of rules.

3 Semantics of Logic Programs via the SM Operator

Here, we introduce the SM operator-based semantics for logic programs written in the syntax of Sect. 2. Subsections reviewing necessary concepts are prefixed by the word *preliminaries*. The introduction of these semantics is split into two parts. The first part is given in Sect. 3.1, where a translation from a logic program to a many-sorted first order theory is provided. This section builds on earlier translations by Fandinno et al. [8, 12] and Hansen and Lierler [17]. Section 3.2 provides us with the details of the second part, where we start by reviewing the SM operator and conclude with the definition of answer sets for the considered logic programs. These programs are translated into first-order theories and then the SM operator is applied. Certain models of the resulting formula that we call "standard" correspond to answer sets.

3.1 Translation τ^* Extended

In this section, we introduce an extension of the τ^* translation from logic programs to many-sorted first-order theories (we refer to the introduced extension with the same symbol τ^*). This extension combines elements of the most recent incarnation of the τ^* transformation [12] with the translation ϕ for conditional literals [17]. Following the example of past work [7], we extend the τ^B component of the τ^* translation with special treatment for global variables.

Preliminaries: The Target Language of τ^*. A *signature* σ consists of *function* and *predicate* constants in addition to a set of *sorts*. For every sort s, a many-sorted interpretation $\mathscr{I}$ has a non-empty universe $|\mathscr{I}|^s$ (we further assume that there are infinitely many variables for each sort). A reflexive and transitive *subsort* relation $\prec$ is defined on the set of sorts such that when sort $s_1 \prec s_2$, an interpretation $\mathscr{I}$ satisfies the condition $|\mathscr{I}|^{s_1} \subseteq |\mathscr{I}|^{s_2}$. The *function signature* of every function constant f consists of a tuple of *argument sorts* $s_1, \ldots, s_n$, and *value sort* s, denoted by $s_1 \times \cdots \times s_n \to s_{n+1}$.

Object constants are function constants with $n = 0$, their function signature contains only a value sort. Similarly, the *predicate signature* of every predicate constant p is a tuple of argument sorts $s_1 \times \cdots \times s_n$. A predicate constant whose predicate signature is the empty tuple is called a *proposition*. The *arity* of a function or predicate signature with n argument sorts is n.

Terms of a signature σ are constructed recursively from function constants. Atomic formulas are built similar to the standard unsorted logic with the restriction that in a term $f(t_1,\ldots,t_n)$ (an atom $p(t_1,\ldots,t_n)$, respectively), the sort of term t_i must be a subsort of the i-th argument of f (of p, respectively). In addition, $t_1 = t_2$ is an atomic formula if the sorts of t_1 and t_2 have a common supersort. The notion of satisfaction is analogous to the unsorted case with the restriction that an interpretation maps a term to an element in the universe of its associated sort.

Our translation τ^* transforms a logic program Π written in the syntax of Sect. 2 into a first-order sentence with equality over a signature σ_Π of *two sorts*. The first sort is called the *program sort* (denoted s_p); all program terms are of this sort. The second sort is called the *integer sort* (denoted s_i); it is a subsort of the program sort. Specifically, the variables of s_i range over numerals. Variants of X,Y,Z will denote variables of sort s_p and variants of I,J,M,N will denote integer variables. Bold face variants will denote lists of variables. To define the remainder of this signature, we must introduce the concepts of *occurrences* and *global variables*.

A *predicate symbol* is a pair p/n, where p is a symbolic constant and n is a non-negative integer. About a program or other syntactic expression, we say that a predicate symbol p/n *occurs* in it if it contains an atom of the form $p(t_1,\ldots,t_n)$.

A variable is *global* in a conditional literal $H : \mathbf{L}$ if it occurs in H but not in $\mathbf{L}$. Thus, any variables in basic literals or comparisons are also global. A variable is global in a rule if it is global in any of the rule's expressions. All non-global variables in an expression are called *local*.

For a program Π, signature σ_Π contains:

1. all precomputed terms as object constants of the program sort; a precomputed constant is assigned the sort s_i iff it is a numeral;
2. all predicate symbols occurring in Π as predicate constants with all arguments of the sort s_p;
3. the comparison symbols other than equality and inequality as predicate constants with predicate signature $s_p \times s_p$ (we will use infix notation for constructing these atoms);
4. function constants $+$, $-$, and $\times$ with function signature $s_i \times s_i \to s_i$, and function constant $|\cdot|$ with function signature $s_i \to s_i$;

Preliminaries: Values of Terms. In the language of Sect. 2, a term may have one value (as in $3+5$), many values (as in $3+1..5$), or no values (as in $a+3$). Thus, for every program term t, we define a formula $val_t(Z)$, where Z is a program variable with no occurrences in t. It indicates that Z is a value of t.

- if t is a numeral, symbolic constant, program variable, inf, or sup, then $val_t(Z)$ is $Z = t$;
- if t is $|t_1|$, then $val_t(Z)$ is $\exists I (val_{t_1}(I) \land Z = |I|)$;
- if t is $(t_1 \circ t_2)$, where $\circ$ is one of $+$, $-$, or $\times$, then $val_t(Z)$ is

$$\exists IJ(Z = I \circ J \land val_{t_1}(I) \land val_{t_2}(J))$$

where I, J are fresh integer variables;

- if t is t_1/t_2 then $val_t(Z)$ is

$$\exists IJK(val_{t_1}(I) \wedge val_{t_2}(J) \wedge F_1(IJK) \wedge F_2(IJKZ))$$

where $F_1(IJK)$ is

$$K \times |J| \leq |I| < (K+\overline{1}) \times |J|$$

and $F_2(IJKZ)$ is

$$(I \times J \geq \overline{0} \wedge Z = K) \vee (I \times J < \overline{0} \wedge Z = -K)$$

- if t is $t_1 \setminus t_2$ then $val_t(Z)$ is

$$\exists IJK(val_{t_1}(I) \wedge val_{t_2}(J) \wedge F_1(IJK) \wedge F_3(IJKZ))$$

where $F_3(IJKZ)$ is

$$(I \times J \geq \overline{0} \wedge Z = I - K \times J) \vee (I \times J < \overline{0} \wedge Z = I + K \times J)$$

- if t is $t_1..t_2$ then $val_t(Z)$ is

$$\exists IJK(Z = K \wedge I \leq K \leq J \wedge val_{t_1}(I) \wedge val_{t_2}(J))$$

where $I \leq K \leq J$ is an abbreviation for $I \leq K \wedge K \leq J$.

Translation τ^*. We now describe a translation τ^* that converts a program into a finite set of first-order sentences. It will be helpful to consider additional notation. For a tuple of terms $t_1, \ldots, t_k$, abbreviated as $\mathbf{t}$, and a tuple of variables $V_1, \ldots, V_k$, abbreviated as $\mathbf{V}$, we use $val_{\mathbf{t}}(\mathbf{V})$ to denote the formula

$$val_{t_1}(V_1) \wedge \cdots \wedge val_{t_k}(V_{t_k}).$$

Now we introduce $\tau_{\mathbf{Z}}^B$. It extends the τ^B translation [12] with a translation for conditional literals. We use the $\mathbf{Z}$ subscript to denote the set of global variables present in a rule. Given a list $\mathbf{Z}$ of global variables in some rule R, we define $\tau_{\mathbf{Z}}^B$ for all elements of R as follows:

1. $\tau_{\mathbf{Z}}^B(\bot)$ is $\bot$;
2. $\tau_{\mathbf{Z}}^B(p(\mathbf{t}))$ is $\exists \mathbf{V}(val_{\mathbf{t}}(\mathbf{V}) \wedge p(\mathbf{V}))$ for every basic literal $p(\mathbf{t})$;
3. $\tau_{\mathbf{Z}}^B(not\ p(\mathbf{t}))$ is $\exists \mathbf{V}(val_{\mathbf{t}}(\mathbf{V}) \wedge \neg p(\mathbf{V}))$ for every basic literal $not\ p(\mathbf{t})$;
4. $\tau_{\mathbf{Z}}^B(not\ not\ p(\mathbf{t}))$ is $\exists \mathbf{V}(val_{\mathbf{t}}(\mathbf{V}) \wedge \neg\neg p(\mathbf{V}))$ for every basic literal $not\ not\ p(\mathbf{t})$
5. $\tau_{\mathbf{Z}}^B(t_1 \prec t_2)$ is $\exists Z_1 Z_2(val_{t_1}(Z_1) \wedge val_{t_2}(Z_2) \wedge Z_1 \prec Z_2)$ for every comparison $t_1 \prec t_2$;
6. $\tau_{\mathbf{Z}}^B(\mathbf{L})$ is $\tau_{\mathbf{Z}}^B(l_1) \wedge \cdots \wedge \tau_{\mathbf{Z}}^B(l_m)$ for a list $\mathbf{L}$ of basic literals and comparisons;
7. $\tau_{\mathbf{Z}}^B(H : \mathbf{L})$ is

$$\forall \mathbf{x} \left(\tau_{\mathbf{Z}}^B(\mathbf{L}) \rightarrow \tau_{\mathbf{Z}}^B(H) \right)$$

for every conditional literal $H : \mathbf{L}$ with local variables $\mathbf{x}$ occurring in the body of R.

In what follows, for each rule R, $\mathbf{Z}$ denotes the list of the global variables of R, and $\mathbf{V}$ denotes a list of fresh, alphabetically first program variables. We now define the translation τ^*.

1. For a basic rule R of the form $p(\mathbf{t})$:- $B_1,\ldots,B_n$, its translation $\tau^* R$ is

$$\widetilde{\forall}\left(val_\mathbf{t}(\mathbf{V}) \wedge \tau_\mathbf{Z}^B(B_1) \wedge \cdots \wedge \tau_\mathbf{Z}^B(B_n) \to p(\mathbf{V})\right).$$

2. For a choice rule R of the form $\{p(\mathbf{t})\}$:- $B_1,\ldots,B_n$, its translation $\tau^* R$ is

$$\widetilde{\forall}\left(val_\mathbf{t}(\mathbf{V}) \wedge \tau_\mathbf{Z}^B(B_1) \wedge \cdots \wedge \tau_\mathbf{Z}^B(B_n) \wedge \neg\neg p(\mathbf{V}) \to p(\mathbf{V})\right).$$

3. For a constraint R of the form $\bot$:- $B_1,\ldots,B_n$, its translation $\tau^* R$ is

$$\forall \mathbf{Z}\left(\tau_\mathbf{Z}^B(B_1) \wedge \cdots \wedge \tau_\mathbf{Z}^B(B_n) \to \bot\right).$$

4. For every program Π, its translation $\tau^* \Pi$ is the first-order theory containing $\tau^* R$ for each rule R in Π.

Example 1. For a list of global variables $\{V\}$, $\tau_{\{V\}}^B$ (not $asg(V, C)$: $col(C)$) is

$$\forall C(\exists Z(Z = C \wedge col(Z)) \to \exists Z Z_1 (Z = V \wedge Z_1 = C \wedge \neg asg(Z, Z_1)))$$

Thus, the translation of rule (1) is

$$\forall V(\tau_{\{V\}}^B (not\ asg(V,\ C)\ :\ col(C)) \wedge \exists Z(Z = V \wedge vtx(Z)) \to \bot).$$

3.2 Semantics via Many-Sorted SM

Preliminaries: The SM Operator for Many-Sorted Signatures. This subsection reviews an extension of the SM operator [13] to the many-sorted setting [7]. This operator is applied to a set of (many-sorted) first-order sentences corresponding to the *formula representation* of a logic program to obtain a set of (many-sorted) second-order sentences. Models of this set respecting certain assumptions (such as a Herbrand interpretation of symbolic constants) capture the stable models of the original logic program. We use τ^* to obtain the formula representation of a program in a specific many-sorted signature σ_Π, and apply SM to the result to characterize stable models of the program.

If p and u are predicate constants or variables with the same predicate signature, then $u \leq p$ stands for the formula

$$\forall \mathbf{W}(u(\mathbf{W}) \to p(\mathbf{W})),$$

where $\mathbf{W}$ is an n-tuple of distinct object variables. If $\mathbf{p}$ and $\mathbf{u}$ are tuples $p_1,\ldots,p_n$ and $u_1,\ldots,u_n$ of predicate constants or variables such that each p_i and u_i have the same predicate signature, then $\mathbf{u} \leq \mathbf{p}$ stands for the conjunction $(u_1 \leq p_1) \wedge \cdots \wedge (u_n \leq p_n)$, and $\mathbf{u} < \mathbf{p}$ stands for $(\mathbf{u} \leq \mathbf{p}) \wedge \neg(\mathbf{p} \leq \mathbf{u})$. For any many-sorted first-order formula F and a list $\mathbf{p}$ of predicate constants, by $\text{SM}_\mathbf{p}[F]$ we denote the second-order formula

$$F \wedge \neg \exists \mathbf{u}\left((\mathbf{u} < \mathbf{p}) \wedge F^*(\mathbf{u})\right)$$

where $\mathbf{u}$ is a list of distinct predicate variables $u_1,\ldots,u_n$ of the same length as $\mathbf{p}$, such that the predicate signature of each u_i is the same as the predicate signature of p_i, and $F^*(\mathbf{u})$ is defined recursively:

- $F^* = F$ for any atomic formula F that does not contain members of $\mathbf{p}$,
- $p_i(\mathbf{t})^* = u_i(\mathbf{t})$ for any predicate symbol p_i belonging to $\mathbf{p}$ and any list $\mathbf{t}$ of terms,
- $(F \wedge G)^* = F^* \wedge G^*$,
- $(F \vee G)^* = F^* \vee G^*$,
- $(F \to G)^* = (F^* \to G^*) \wedge (F \to G)$,
- $(\forall x F)^* = \forall x F^*$,
- $(\exists x F)^* = \exists x F^*$.

Definition 1. *For a many-sorted first-order sentence F from signature σ, the models of $SM_{\mathbf{p}}[F]$ are called the $\mathbf{p}$-stable models of F. For a set Γ of first-order sentences, the $\mathbf{p}$-stable models of Γ are the $\mathbf{p}$-stable models of the conjunction of all formulas in Γ.*

The list $\mathbf{p}$ of predicates of a $\mathbf{p}$-stable model are called *intensional* – "belief" in these predicates is minimized. Predicates that are not intensional are called *extensional*.

Answer Sets via Standard Interpretations. Recall from Sect. 3.1 that τ^* maps a program Π with intensional predicates $\mathbf{p}$ into a formula within signature σ_Π of two sorts. We now consider a special type of interpretation of σ_Π (a *standard* interpretation) to restrict the models of $SM_{\mathbf{p}}[\tau^*\Pi]$ to exactly the stable models of Π.

A standard interpretation $\mathscr{I}$ satisfies that

1. the universe $|\mathscr{I}|^{s_p}$ is the set of all precomputed terms;
2. the universe $|\mathscr{I}|^{s_i}$ is the set of all numerals;
3. $\mathscr{I}$ interprets every precomputed term t as t;
4. $\mathscr{I}$ interprets $\overline{m} + \overline{n}$ as $\overline{m+n}$, and similarly for subtraction and multiplication;
5. $\mathscr{I}$ interprets $|\overline{n}|$ as $\overline{|n|}$;
6. $\mathscr{I}$ interprets every comparison $t_1 \prec t_2$, where t_1 and t_2 are precomputed terms, as true iff the relation $\prec$ holds for the pair (t_1, t_2).

For a standard interpretation $\mathscr{I}$, we use $A(\mathscr{I})$ to denote the unique set of precomputed atoms to which $\mathscr{I}$ assigns the value *true*.

Definition 2. *Let Π be a program and let $\mathbf{p}$ be a list of some predicate symbols occurring in Π other than the comparison symbols. Then, for a standard interpretation $\mathscr{I}$, we call $A(\mathscr{I})$ a $\mathbf{p}$-answer set of Π when $\mathscr{I}$ is a $\mathbf{p}$-stable model of $\tau^*\Pi$. When $\mathbf{p}$ is the list of all predicate symbols occurring in Π other than the comparison symbols, then we simply call a $\mathbf{p}$-answer set of Π an answer set of Π.*

In the sequel, we illustrate how answer sets as defined here coincide with the notion of what we later call gringo answer sets. Yet, it is interesting to note that SM-operator based semantics enable a more flexible understanding of a $\mathbf{p}$-answer set that distinguishes intensional (namely, $\mathbf{p}$) and extensional predicate symbols.

4 Review: Semantics of Logic Programs via Infinitary Propositional Logic

Truszczyński (2012) provides a characterization of logic program semantics in terms of infinitary propositional logic (IPL) and illustrates the precise relation to the SM-based characterization [28]. IPL is a useful technical device due to its close relation to the grounding procedure implemented by answer set solver CLINGO. In this section, we review IPL and the infinitary logic of here-and-there, which are important tools for establishing the results of this paper. Unless otherwise specified, P and its variants are used to denote IPL formulas, whereas $\mathscr{P}$ and its variants denote sets of IPL formulas. Finally, we introduce *gringo answer sets*, which constitute the established semantic characterization of logic programs with conditional literals and arithmetic.

4.1 Infinitary Formulas

A *propositional signature* Σ is a set of propositional atoms. For every nonnegative integer r, *(infinitary) formulas* over Σ of rank r are defined recursively:

- every atom from Σ is a formula of rank 0,
- if $\mathscr{P}$ is a set of formulas, and r is the smallest nonnegative integer that is greater than the ranks of all elements of $\mathscr{P}$, then $\mathscr{P}^\wedge$ and $\mathscr{P}^\vee$ are formulas of rank r,
- if P and P' are formulas, and r is the smallest nonnegative integer that is greater than the ranks of P and P', then $P \to P'$ is a formula of rank r.

$P \wedge P'$ is shorthand for $\{P,P'\}^\wedge$, and $P \vee P'$ is shorthand for $\{P,P'\}^\vee$. We use $\top$ and $\bot$ as abbreviations for $\emptyset^\wedge$ and $\emptyset^\vee$, respectively. Further, $\neg P$ stands for $P \to \bot$, and $P \leftrightarrow P'$ stands for $(P \to P') \wedge (P' \to P)$.

A *propositional interpretation* of Σ is a subset S of Σ. The *satisfaction relation* between a propositional interpretation and an infinitary formula is defined recursively:

- For every atom p from Σ, $S \models p$ if $p \in S$.
- $S \models \mathscr{P}^\wedge$ if, for every formula P in $\mathscr{P}$, $S \models P$.
- $S \models \mathscr{P}^\vee$ if there is a formula P in $\mathscr{P}$ such that $S \models P$.
- $S \models P \to P'$ if $S \not\models P$ or $S \models P'$.

4.2 Infinitary Logic of Here-and-There and Truszczyński Stable Models

An *HT-interpretation* of propositional signature Σ is an ordered pair $\langle S, S' \rangle$ of interpretations of Σ such that $S \subseteq S'$. The *satisfaction relation (ht-satisfaction)* between an HT-interpretation and an infinitary formula is defined recursively:

- For every atom p from Σ, $\langle S, S' \rangle \models p$ if $p \in S$.
- $\langle S, S' \rangle \models \mathscr{P}^\wedge$ if, for every formula P in $\mathscr{P}$, $\langle S, S' \rangle \models P$.
- $\langle S, S' \rangle \models \mathscr{P}^\vee$ if there is a formula P in $\mathscr{P}$ such that $\langle S, S' \rangle \models P$.
- $\langle S, S' \rangle \models P \to P'$ if
  1. $S' \models P \to P'$, and
  2. $\langle S, S' \rangle \not\models P$ or $\langle S, S' \rangle \models P'$.

An *HT-model* of an infinitary formula is an HT-interpretation that satisfies this formula. An *HT-model* of a set $\mathscr{P}$ of infinitary formulas is an HT-interpretation that satisfies all formulas in $\mathscr{P}$. Two infinitary formulas (sets of infinitary formulas) are *equivalent* when they have the same HT-models. An HT-interpretation of the form $\langle S, S \rangle$ is called *total*. An *equilibrium model* of a set $\mathscr{P}$ of infinitary formulas is a total HT-model $\langle S', S' \rangle$ of $\mathscr{P}$ such that for every proper subset S of S', $\langle S, S' \rangle$ is not an HT-model of $\mathscr{P}$.

An interpretation satisfies a set $\mathscr{P}$ of formulas (is a model of $\mathscr{P}$) if it satisfies all formulas in $\mathscr{P}$.

Definition 3. *For a set $\mathscr{P}$ of infinitary propositional formulas, we say that a propositional interpretation S is a Truszczyński stable model if $\langle S, S \rangle$ is an equilibrium model of $\mathscr{P}$.*

In the sequel, we may refer to a Truszczyński stable model of an infinitary propositional formula, where we identify this formula with a singleton set containing it.

4.3 Translation τ and Gringo Answer Sets

In this section we review the relevant components of τ [12,15]. It is due to note that the 2015 publication is the "official" source of the Abstract Gringo semantics and contains a τ translation for conditional literals, whereas the 2024 publication is more up-to-date with respect to the definitions of division, modulo, and absolute value adhered to by the latest versions of CLINGO.

An expression is *ground* if it does not contain variables. For every ground term t, the set of precomputed terms $[t]$ of its *values* is defined as follows:

- if t is a numeral, symbolic constant, or inf or sup then $[t]$ is $\{t\}$;
- if t is $|t_1|$, then $[t]$ is the set of numerals $\overline{|n|}$ for all integers n such that $\overline{n} \in [t_1]$;
- if t is $(t_1 \circ t_2)$, where $\circ$ is one of $+, -, \times$, then $[t]$ is the set of numerals $\overline{n_1 \circ n_2}$ such that $\overline{n_1} \in [t_1], \overline{n_2} \in [t_2]$;
- if t is (t_1/t_2), then $[t]$ is the set of numerals $\overline{round(n_1/n_2)}$ for all integers n_1, n_2 such that $\overline{n_1} \in [t_1], \overline{n_2} \in [t_2]$ and $n_2 \neq 0$;
- if t is $(t_1 \setminus t_2)$, then $[t]$ is the set of numerals $\overline{n_1 - n_2 \cdot round(n_1/n_2)}$ for all integers n_1, n_2 such that $\overline{n_1} \in [t_1], \overline{n_2} \in [t_2]$ and $n_2 \neq 0$;
- if t is $(t_1..t_2)$, then $[t]$ is the set of numerals $\overline{m}$ for all integers m such that, for some integers n_1, n_2

$$\overline{n_1} \in [t_1], \quad \overline{n_2} \in [t_2], \quad n_1 \leq m \leq n_2.$$

- if $\mathbf{t}$ is a tuple of terms $t_1, \ldots, t_n$ $(n > 0)$ then $[\mathbf{t}]$ is the set of tuples $\langle r_1, \ldots, r_n \rangle$ for all $r_1 \in [t_1], \ldots, r_n \in [t_n]$.

The function *round* is defined as:

$$round(n) = \begin{cases} \lfloor n \rfloor & \text{if } n \geq 0 \\ \lceil n \rceil & \text{if } n < 0 \end{cases} \tag{5}$$

A rule (or any other expression in a rule) is called *closed* if it contains no global variables. An *instance* of a rule R is any rule that can be obtained from R by substituting precomputed terms for all global variables.

To transform a closed rule R into a set of infinitary propositional formulas, translation τ is defined as follows:

1. $\tau(\bot)$ is $\bot$;
2. $\tau(p(\mathbf{t}))$ is the disjunction of atoms $p(\mathbf{r})$ over all tuples $\mathbf{r}$ in $[\mathbf{t}]$ for any ground atom $p(\mathbf{t})$, thus, $\tau(p(\mathbf{t}))$ is $p(\mathbf{t})$ if $\mathbf{t}$ is a tuple of precomputed terms;
3. $\tau(not\ A)$ is $\neg \tau A$ for any ground atom A;
4. $\tau(not\ not\ A)$ is $\neg\neg \tau A$ for any ground atom A;
5. $\tau(t_1 \prec t_2)$ is $\top$ if the relation $\prec$ holds between the terms r_1, r_2 for some r_1, r_2 such that $r_1 \in [t_1]$ and $r_2 \in [t_2]$, and $\bot$ otherwise;
6. $\tau(\mathbf{L})$ is $\tau(l_1) \wedge \cdots \wedge \tau(l_m)$ for a list $\mathbf{L}$ of basic or conditional literals;
7. for a closed conditional literal $H : \mathbf{L}$ occurring in the body of rule R, $\tau(H : \mathbf{L})$ is the conjunction of the formulas $\tau(\mathbf{L}_\mathbf{r}^\mathbf{x}) \to \tau(H_\mathbf{r}^\mathbf{x})$ where $\mathbf{x}$ is the list of variables occurring in the conditional literal, over all tuples $\mathbf{r}$ of precomputed terms of the same length as $\mathbf{x}$;
8. for an instance ρ of
   - a basic rule $p(\mathbf{t})$:- $B_1, \ldots, B_n$, its translation $\tau\rho$ is
   $$\tau(B_1 \wedge \cdots \wedge B_n) \to \bigwedge_{\mathbf{r} \in [\mathbf{t}]} p(\mathbf{r}); \tag{6}$$
   - a choice rule $\{p(\mathbf{t})\}$:- $B_1, \ldots, B_n$, its translation $\tau\rho$ is
   $$\tau(B_1 \wedge \cdots \wedge B_n) \to \bigwedge_{\mathbf{r} \in [\mathbf{t}]} (p(\mathbf{r}) \vee \neg p(\mathbf{r})); \tag{7}$$
   - a constraint $\bot$:- $B_1, \ldots, B_n$, its translation $\tau\rho$ is
   $$\neg\tau(B_1 \wedge \cdots \wedge B_n).$$

For any rule R of form (4), τR stands for the conjunction of the elements in the set of formulas that consists of $\tau\rho$ for all instances ρ of R. By definition, each of these instances (and thus the expressions occurring within them) are closed. For any program Π, $\tau\Pi$ is the set of the formulas τR for each R in Π.

Example 2. For instance, $\tau(not\ asg(v,C) : col(C))$ is

$$\{(col(c) \to \neg asg(v,c)) \mid c \in |I|^{s_p}\}^\wedge.$$

Thus, τ applied to rule (1) is

$$\{\neg(\tau(not\ asg(v,C) : col(C)) \wedge vtx(v)) \mid v \in |I|^{s_p}\}^\wedge.$$

Consider the syntax of the language presented in Sect. 2, which is a subset of the Abstract Gringo language, whose semantics are defined by the translation τ. The following definition is from Gebser et al. [15].

Definition 4. *We say that a set S of ground atoms is a gringo answer set of a program Π if S is a Truszczyński stable model of $\tau\Pi$.*

5 Connecting Semantics

Ultimately, this section shows that the answer sets as introduced in Definition 2 by means of the SM operator coincide with the gringo answer sets as provided by Definition 4. Before that, we review the process of converting first order sentences (typically denoted by variants of F and G) into infinitary formulas originally proposed by Truszczyński [28]. In addition, we review the concept of strong equivalence in the settings of IPL. Equipped with these notions, we show how, given a program Π, the application of the transformation by Truszczyński on $\tau^*\Pi$ results in an IPL formula that is strongly equivalent to the IPL formula obtained by $\tau\Pi$. This is the key step that helps us to establish our main result: answer sets (Definition 2) and gringo answer sets (Definition 4) coincide.

5.1 Preliminaries: From First Order Sentences to Infinitary Formulas

Truszczyński (2012) provides a definition of stable models for first-order sentences via a grounding procedure, which converts them into infinitary formulas [28, Section 3]. Later, this grounding process was generalized to many-sorted first-order formulas and extensional predicate symbols [7,8]. We review this generalization below. Prior to the review we introduce some necessary notation.

If $\mathscr{I}$ is an interpretation of a signature σ then by $\sigma^{\mathscr{I}}$ we denote the signature obtained from σ by adding, for every element d of a domain $|I|^s$, its *name* d^* as an object constant of sort s. The interpretation $\mathscr{I}$ is extended to $\sigma^{\mathscr{I}}$ by defining $(d^*)^{\mathscr{I}} = d$. The value $t^{\mathscr{I}}$ assigned by an interpretation $\mathscr{I}$ of $\sigma^{\mathscr{I}}$ to a ground term t over $\sigma^{\mathscr{I}}$ and the satisfaction relation between an interpretation of $\sigma^{\mathscr{I}}$ and a sentence over $\sigma^{\mathscr{I}}$ are defined recursively, in the usual way. If $\mathbf{d}$ is a tuple $d_1,\ldots,d_n$ of elements of domains of $\mathscr{I}$ then $\mathbf{d}^*$ stands for the tuple $d_1^*,\ldots,d_n^*$ of their names. If $\mathbf{t}$ is a tuple $t_1,\ldots,t_n$ of ground terms then $\mathbf{t}^{\mathscr{I}}$ stands for the tuple $t_1^{\mathscr{I}},\ldots,t_n^{\mathscr{I}}$ of values assigned to them by $\mathscr{I}$.

For an interpretation $\mathscr{I}$ and a list $\mathbf{p}$ of predicate symbols, by $\mathscr{I}^{\mathbf{p}}$ we denote the set of precomputed atoms $p(t_1,\ldots,t_k)$ satisfied by $\mathscr{I}$ where $p \in \mathbf{p}$. Let $\mathbf{p},\mathbf{q}$ be a partition of the predicate symbols in the signature. Then, the *grounding of a first-order sentence F with respect to an interpretation $\mathscr{I}$ and a set of intensional predicate symbols $\mathbf{p}$* (and extensional predicate symbols $\mathbf{q}$) is defined as follows:

1. $gr^{\mathbf{p}}_{\mathscr{I}}(\bot) = \bot$;
2. for $p \in \mathbf{p}$, $gr^{\mathbf{p}}_{\mathscr{I}}(p(t_1,\ldots,t_k)) = p((t_1^{\mathscr{I}})^*,\ldots,(t_k^{\mathscr{I}})^*)$;
3. for $p \in \mathbf{q}$, $gr^{\mathbf{p}}_{\mathscr{I}}(p(t_1,\ldots,t_k)) = \top$ if $p((t_1^{\mathscr{I}})^*,\ldots,(t_k^{\mathscr{I}})^*) \in I^{\mathbf{q}}$
   and $gr^{\mathbf{p}}_{\mathscr{I}}(p(t_1,\ldots,t_k)) = \bot$ otherwise;
4. $gr^{\mathbf{p}}_{\mathscr{I}}(t_1 = t_2) = \top$ if $t_1^{\mathscr{I}} = t_2^{\mathscr{I}}$ and $\bot$ otherwise;
5. $gr^{\mathbf{p}}_{\mathscr{I}}(F \otimes G) = gr^{\mathbf{p}}_{\mathscr{I}}(F) \otimes gr^{\mathbf{p}}_{\mathscr{I}}(G)$ if $\otimes$ is $\wedge, \vee$, or $\rightarrow$;
6. $gr^{\mathbf{p}}_{\mathscr{I}}(\exists X F(X)) = \{gr^{\mathbf{p}}_{\mathscr{I}}(F(u^*)) \mid u \in |\mathscr{I}|^s\}^{\vee}$ if X is a variable of sort s;
7. $gr^{\mathbf{p}}_{\mathscr{I}}(\forall X F(X)) = \{gr^{\mathbf{p}}_{\mathscr{I}}(F(u^*)) \mid u \in |\mathscr{I}|^s\}^{\wedge}$ if X is a variable of sort s.

Recall that $\neg F$ is an abbreviation for $F \rightarrow \bot$ so that $gr^{\mathbf{p}}_{\mathscr{I}}(\neg F) = \neg gr^{\mathbf{p}}_{\mathscr{I}}(F)$. For a first order theory Γ, we define $gr^{\mathbf{p}}_{\mathscr{I}}(\Gamma) = \{gr^{\mathbf{p}}_{\mathscr{I}}(F) \mid F \in \Gamma\}^{\wedge}$.

In the sequel, most of the references to the stated definition of grounding are in the context of standard interpretations. Given the conditions 3–5 of the definition of standard interpretations, we can simplify the definition of grounding by restating conditions 2, 3, 6, and 7, as follows

2. for $p \in \mathbf{p}$, $gr^\mathbf{p}_\mathscr{I}(p(t_1,\ldots,t_k)) = p(t_1^\mathscr{I},\ldots,t_k^\mathscr{I})$;
3. for $p \in \mathbf{q}$, $gr^\mathbf{p}_\mathscr{I}(p(t_1,\ldots,t_k)) = \top$ if $p(t_1^\mathscr{I},\ldots,t_k^\mathscr{I}) \in I^\mathbf{q}$
   and $gr^\mathbf{p}_\mathscr{I}(p(t_1,\ldots,t_k)) = \bot$ otherwise;
6. $gr^\mathbf{p}_\mathscr{I}(\exists X\, F(X)) = \{gr^\mathbf{p}_\mathscr{I}(F(u)) \mid u \in |\mathscr{I}|^s\}^\vee$ if X is a variable of sort s;
7. $gr^\mathbf{p}_\mathscr{I}(\forall X\, F(X)) = \{gr^\mathbf{p}_\mathscr{I}(F(u)) \mid u \in |\mathscr{I}|^s\}^\wedge$ if X is a variable of sort s.

5.2 Preliminaries: Strong Equivalence in the Infinitary Setting

The Truszczyński stable models of a set of infinitary logic formulas (Definition 3 in Sect. 4) can be characterized by an extension of equilibrium logic to the infinitary setting [18, Theorem 2]. This allows strong equivalence of infinitary (propositional) formulas to be defined as follows: About sets $\mathscr{P}_1$, $\mathscr{P}_2$ of infinitary formulas we say that they are *strongly equivalent* (denoted as $\mathscr{P}_1 \equiv_s \mathscr{P}_2$) to each other if, for every set $\mathscr{P}$ of infinitary formulas, the sets $\mathscr{P}_1 \cup \mathscr{P}$ and $\mathscr{P}_2 \cup \mathscr{P}$ have the same Truszczyński stable models [18]. About infinitary formulas P and P' we say that they are strongly equivalent if the singleton sets $\{P\}$ and $\{P'\}$ are strongly equivalent. Theorem 3 from that work shows that two sets of infinitary formulas are strongly equivalent if and only if they are equivalent in the infinitary logic of here-and-there. Sometimes, we will abuse the term *strong equivalence* or notation $\equiv_s$ by stating that a set of infinitary formulas is strongly equivalent to an infinitary formula, understanding that in such a case these two entities share the same HT-models.

5.3 Connecting Semantics

In this section, we present the main results of this paper, which relate our proposed semantics – the answer sets of Definition 2 – to the established semantics – the gringo answer sets of Definition 4. Propositions 1–3 are counterparts of Propositions 1–3 from earlier work by Lifschitz et al. [21] within the context of a different language of logic programs. In particular, conditional literals are part of the language considered here. We also allow the absolute value function symbol, and our definition of the values of terms of the form t_1/t_2 and $t_1 \setminus t_2$ differ. It is due to note that the most recent dialect of mini-GRINGO [12] uses a different definition of integer division than the one presented in earlier publications.

Let us start by reviewing some notation. For a program Π, we call a partition $\mathbf{p},\mathbf{q}$ of predicate symbols from the signature σ_Π (defined in Sect. 3.1) the *standard partition* if $\mathbf{p}$ contains all predicate symbols from Π and $\mathbf{q}$ contains every comparison symbol. It is easy to see that the standard partition is unique to program Π, and thus can be identified with its first element $\mathbf{p}$ (all predicate symbols but comparisons occurring in Π). For a formula F, variable Z, and term t, by F_t^Z we denote the result of substituting term t for variable Z. For instance, $val_a(Z)_b^Z$ results in formula $b = a$, where b and a are symbolic constants. In the case when substitution is applied to the formula of the form $val_t(Z)$, we often write $val_t(r)$ to denote $val_t(Z)_r^Z$. Intuitively, the formula $val_t(r)$ expresses that r is one of the values of t. This claim is formalized in Proposition 1 below. Note that in the statements of the propositions below, some program Π is assumed implicitly with its corresponding signature σ_Π.

Proposition 1. *Let $\mathscr{I}$ be a standard interpretation, and let $\mathbf{p}$ be the standard partition. Then, for any program variable Z, ground term t, and precomputed term r, the formula $gr^{\mathbf{p}}_{\mathscr{I}}(val_t(Z)^Z_r)$ is strongly equivalent to $\top$ if $r \in [t]$ and to $\bot$ otherwise.*

Recall from Sect. 2 that in our proposed language, a basic literal or comparison is a special type of conditional literal with an empty list of conditions. Thus, within our extension of the mini-GRINGO language, conditional literals form the main syntactic element. Proposition 1 helps us establish the following result:

Proposition 2. *Let $H : \mathbf{L}$ be a closed conditional literal with local variables $\mathbf{X}$. Then, for a standard interpretation $\mathscr{I}$, the standard partition $\mathbf{p}$, and a tuple of program variables $\mathbf{Z}$,*

$$gr^{\mathbf{p}}_{\mathscr{I}}\left(\tau^B_{\mathbf{Z}}(H : \mathbf{L})\right) \equiv_s \tau(H : \mathbf{L}).$$

Using the preceding proposition, we can conclude the following result:

Proposition 3. *For a rule R, standard interpretation $\mathscr{I}$, and the standard partition $\mathbf{p}$,*

$$gr^{\mathbf{p}}_{\mathscr{I}}(\tau^*(R)) \equiv_s \tau R.$$

We can extend Proposition 3 to programs:

Proposition 4. *For a program Π, standard interpretation $\mathscr{I}$, and the standard partition $\mathbf{p}$,*

$$gr^{\mathbf{p}}_{\mathscr{I}}(\tau^*(\Pi)) \equiv_s \tau\Pi.$$

The last proposition is an important result supporting one of the key theorems of this work, namely, Theorem 1. For a (many-sorted) first-order interpretation $\mathscr{I}$ and a set of predicates $\mathbf{p}$, we use $\mathscr{I}^{\mathbf{p}}$ to denote $A(\mathscr{I})$ restricted to atoms whose predicate symbols occur in $\mathbf{p}$.

Theorem 1. *Let Π be a program, and let $\mathbf{p}$ be the standard partition. Then, a set $\mathscr{I}^{\mathbf{p}}$ of precomputed atoms is a Truszczyński stable model of $gr^{\mathbf{p}}_{\mathscr{I}}(\tau^*\Pi)$ iff $\mathscr{I}^{\mathbf{p}}$ is a Truszczyński stable model of $\tau\Pi$.*

Proof. An immediate consequence of Proposition 4 is that, for a program Π and interpretation $\mathscr{I}$, $gr^{\mathbf{p}}_{\mathscr{I}}(\tau^*(\Pi)) \equiv_s \tau\Pi$. Thus, $gr^{\mathbf{p}}_{\mathscr{I}}(\tau^*(\Pi))$ and $\tau\Pi$ have the same HT-models. This implies that they have the same infinitary equilibrium models. Consequently, they have the same Truszczyński stable models due to Theorem 3 by Truszczyński [28].

Now that we have uncovered the connection between the infinitary formulas produced by $gr^{\mathbf{p}}_{\mathscr{I}}(\tau^*\Pi)$ and those produced by $\tau\Pi$, we use the result by Fandinno et al. (2020) reformulated below to connect the Truszczyński stable models of these formulas to the $\mathbf{p}$-stable models of $\tau^*\Pi$.

Proposition 5 *[8, Proposition 2]. For any finite two-sorted (target language) theory Γ, an interpretation $\mathscr{I}$, and list of predicate symbols $\mathbf{p}$, $\mathscr{I}$ is $\mathbf{p}$-stable model of Γ if and only if $\mathscr{I}^{\mathbf{p}}$ is a Truszczyński stable model of $gr^{\mathbf{p}}_{\mathscr{I}}(\Gamma)$.*

We are ready to state the main result of this section, connecting our SM-based semantics for programs with the established semantics reviewed in Sect. 4:

Theorem 2. *Let Π be a program and let* **p** *be the standard partition. Then, $A(\mathscr{I})$ is an answer set of Π iff $A(\mathscr{I})$ is a gringo answer set of Π.*

Proof. $A(\mathscr{I})$ is an answer set of Π
iff $\mathscr{I}$ is a **p**-stable model of $\tau^*\Pi$ (Definition 2; **p** is the standard partition)
iff $\mathscr{I}^\mathbf{p}$ is a Truszczyński stable model of $gr^\mathbf{p}_{\mathscr{I}}(\tau^*\Pi)$ (Proposition 5)
iff $\mathscr{I}^\mathbf{p}$ is a Truszczyński stable model of $\tau\Pi$ (Theorem 1)
iff $\mathscr{I}^\mathbf{p}$ is a gringo answer set of Π (Definition 4)
iff $A(\mathscr{I})$ is a gringo answer set of Π (**p** is the standard partition).

6 Conclusions and Future Work

In this paper we introduced semantics based on the SM operator for logic programs containing both conditional literals and arithmetic. The key result of this work – Theorem 2 – demonstrates that the definition of answer sets using our extension of the τ^* translation correctly characterizes the behavior of the answer set solver CLINGO.

The main intuition of the ϕ translation [17], which provided SM-based semantics for programs with conditional literals but *without* arithmetic, was that conditional literals in rule bodies behave like nested implications. Our proposed translation preserves this intuition. However, allowing for arithmetic in the language considered here made the argument of the correspondence between our definition of answer sets and gringo answer sets substantially more complex in comparison to the similar argument made for the case of translation ϕ. Specifically, the correspondence now relies on strong equivalence as opposed to syntactic identity.

The newly introduced SM-based semantics enables ASP practitioners to verify programs with conditional literals and arithmetic in the style of past work on modular verification [5,9]. The definition of **p**-answer sets offers greater flexibility (due to the possibility to distinguish intensional and extensional predicate symbols) than the traditional notion of gringo answer sets and supports this verification style. Furthermore, conditional literals can make programs more concise and easier to verify. For example, as illustrated in the Introduction, we can refactor Listing 1.1 to use a smaller set of predicate symbols by employing a conditional literal in constraint (1).

In future work we intend to investigate how the process of using conditional literals to eliminate auxiliary predicates can be generalized. Automated verification is another important direction for future work. Recent progress in this direction is manifested in the ANTHEM[1] system, which employs an automated theorem prover to establish strong [23] or external [11] equivalence of mini-GRINGO programs. We plan to extend the theory and implementation supporting both types of verification to the language presented in this paper. Similar verification tools include CCT [26] and LPEQ [4,19]. Future work will include detailed comparisons of such systems against ANTHEM.

---

[1] https://github.com/potassco/anthem.

Finally, it is worth investigating ways to simplify the formulas produced by our extension of τ^*. For instance, it is easy to see that the formulas in Example 1 contain several unnecessary existential quantifiers. By applying ht-equivalent simplifications, we obtain a considerably more readable translation:

$$\forall V \, (\forall C (col(C) \rightarrow \neg asg(V,C)) \wedge vtx(V) \rightarrow \bot).$$

Past work in this vein has been devoted to developing a "natural" translation v for a broad fragment of the mini-GRINGO language [22]. We plan to extend the v translation with conditional literals to make (automated) verification of programs easier.

Acknowledgments. We are grateful to Jorge Fandinno and Vladimir Lifschitz for their valuable comments, and to our anonymous reviewers for their feedback.

Disclosure of Interests. The authors have no competing interests.

References

1. Abels, D., Jordi, J., Ostrowski, M., Schaub, T., Toletti, A., Wanko, P.: Train scheduling with hybrid answer set programming. Theory Pract. Logic Program. **21**(3), 317–347 (2021). https://doi.org/10.1017/S1471068420000046
2. Balduccini, M., Gelfond, M.: Model-based reasoning for complex flight systems. In: Proceedings of Infotech@Aerospace (American Institute of Aeronautics and Astronautics) (2005)
3. Balduccini, M., Gelfond, M., Nogueira, M., Watson, R., Barry, M.: An a-prolog decision support system for the Space Shuttle. In: Working Notes of the AAAI Spring Symposium on Answer Set Programming (2001)
4. Bomanson, J., Janhunen, T., Niemelä, I.: Applying visible strong equivalence in answer-set program transformations. ACM Trans. Comput. Logic **21**(4) (2020). https://doi.org/10.1145/3412854
5. Cabalar, P., Fandinno, J., Lierler, Y.: Modular answer set programming as a formal specification language. Theory Pract. Logic Program. **20**(5), 767–782 (2020)
6. Cabalar, P., Muñiz, B., Pérez, G., Suárez, F.: Explainable machine learning for liver transplantation (2021). https://arxiv.org/abs/2109.13893
7. Fandinno, J., Hansen, Z., Lierler, Y.: Axiomatization of aggregates in answer set programming. In: Proceedings of the Thirty-Six National Conference on Artificial Intelligence (AAAI 2022). AAAI Press (2022)
8. Fandinno, J., Lifschitz, V., Lühne, P., Schaub, T.: Verifying tight logic programs with anthem and vampire. Theory Pract. Logic Program. **20**(5), 735–750 (2020)
9. Fandinno, J., Hansen, Z., Lierler, Y.: Arguing correctness of asp programs with aggregates. In: Gottlob, G., Inclezan, D., Maratea, M. (eds.) LPNMR 2022. LNCS, vol. 13416, pp. 190–202. Springer, Cham (2022). https://doi.org/10.1007/978-3-031-15707-3_15
10. Fandinno, J., Hansen, Z., Lierler, Y.: Axiomatization of non-recursive aggregates in first-order answer set programming. J. Artif. Intell. Res. **80**, 977–1031 (2024). https://doi.org/10.1613/jair.1.15786
11. Fandinno, J., Hansen, Z., Lierler, Y., Lifschitz, V., Temple, N.: External behavior of a logic program and verification of refactoring. Theory Pract. Logic Program. **23**(4), 933–947 (2023). https://doi.org/10.1017/S1471068423000200

12. Fandinno, J., Lifschitz, V., Temple, N.: Locally tight programs. Theory Pract. Log. Program. 1–31 (2024). https://doi.org/10.1017/S147106842300039X
13. Ferraris, P., Lee, J., Lifschitz, V.: Stable models and circumscription. Artif. Intell. **175**(1), 236–263 (2011)
14. Gebser, M., Kaminski, R., Kaufmann, B., Ostrowski, M., Schaub, T., Thiele, S.: A user's guide to gringo, clasp, clingo, and iclingo. http://potassco.org
15. Gebser, M., Harrison, A., Kaminski, R., Lifschitz, V., Schaub, T.: Abstract gringo. Theory Pract. Logic Program. **15**(4–5), 449–463 (2015). https://doi.org/10.1017/S1471068415000150
16. Gebser, M., et al.: Experimenting with robotic intra-logistics domains. Theory Pract. Logic Program. **18**(3–4), 502–519 (2018). https://doi.org/10.1017/S1471068418000200
17. Hansen, Z., Lierler, Y.: Semantics for conditional literals via the SM operator. In: Gottlob, G., Inclezan, D., Maratea, M. (eds.) LPNMR 2022. LNCS, vol. 13416, pp. 259–272. Springer, Cham (2022). https://doi.org/10.1007/978-3-031-15707-3_20
18. Harrison, A., Lifschitz, V., Pearce, D., Valverde, A.: Infinitary equilibrium logic and strongly equivalent logic programs. Artif. Intell. **246**, 22–33 (2017). https://doi.org/10.1016/j.artint.2017.02.002
19. Janhunen, T., Oikarinen, E.: LPEQ and DLPEQ—translators for automated equivalence testing of logic programs. In: Lifschitz, V., Niemelä, I. (eds.) LPNMR 2004. LNCS (LNAI), vol. 2923, pp. 336–340. Springer, Heidelberg (2003). https://doi.org/10.1007/978-3-540-24609-1_30
20. Kaminski, R., Romero, J., Schaub, T., Wanko, P.: How to build your own ASP-based system?! Theory Pract. Log. Program. 1–63 (2021). https://doi.org/10.1017/S1471068421000508
21. Lifschitz, V., Lühne, P., Schaub, T.: Verifying strong equivalence of programs in the input language of gringo. In: Proceedings of the 15th International Conference on Logic Programming and Non-monotonic Reasoning (2019). http://www.cs.utexas.edu/users/ai-lab?verification
22. Lifschitz, V.: Transforming gringo rules into formulas in a natural way. In: Faber, W., Friedrich, G., Gebser, M., Morak, M. (eds.) JELIA 2021. LNCS (LNAI), vol. 12678, pp. 421–434. Springer, Cham (2021). https://doi.org/10.1007/978-3-030-75775-5_28
23. Lifschitz, V., Pearce, D., Valverde, A.: Strongly equivalent logic programs. ACM Trans. Comput. Log. **2**(4), 526–541 (2001). https://doi.org/10.1145/383779.383783
24. Marek, V.W., Truszczyński, M.: Stable models and an alternative logic programming paradigm. In: Apt, K.R., Marek, V.W., Truszczynski, M., Warren, D.S. (eds.) The Logic Programming Paradigm. Artificial Intelligence, pp. 375–398. Springer, Heidelberg (1999)
25. Niemelä, I.: Logic programs with stable model semantics as a constraint programming paradigm. Ann. Math. Artif. Intell. **25**(3), 241–273 (1999). https://doi.org/10.1023/A:1018930122475
26. Oetsch, J., Seidl, M., Tompits, H., Woltran, S.: Testing relativised uniform equivalence under answer-set projection in the system ccT. In: Seipel, D., Hanus, M., Wolf, A. (eds.) INAP/WLP -2007. LNCS (LNAI), vol. 5437, pp. 241–246. Springer, Heidelberg (2009). https://doi.org/10.1007/978-3-642-00675-3_16
27. Syrjänen, T.: Cardinality constraint programs. In: Alferes, J.J., Leite, J. (eds.) JELIA 2004. LNCS (LNAI), vol. 3229, pp. 187–199. Springer, Heidelberg (2004). https://doi.org/10.1007/978-3-540-30227-8_18
28. Truszczynski, M.: Connecting first-order ASP and the logic FO(ID) through reducts. In: Erdem, E., Lee, J., Lierler, Y., Pearce, D. (eds.) Correct Reasoning. LNCS, vol. 7265, pp. 543–559. Springer, Heidelberg (2012). https://doi.org/10.1007/978-3-642-30743-0_37
29. Wotawa, F., Kaufmann, D.: Model-based reasoning using answer set programming. Appl. Intell. **52**(15), 16993–17011 (2022). https://doi.org/10.1007/s10489-022-03272-2

A Practical Approach to Handling Tabular Data in Logic

Robin De Vogelaere[1,2,3](✉), Kylian Van Dessel[1,2,3], and Joost Vennekens[1,2,3]

[1] KU Leuven, De Nayer Campus, Department of Computer Science, 2860 Sint-Katelijne-Waver, Belgium
{robin.devogelaere,kylian.vandessel,joost.vennekens}@kuleuven.be
[2] Leuven.AI, 3000 Leuven, Belgium
[3] Flanders Make @ KU Leuven, 3000 Leuven, Belgium

Abstract. In the declarative approach to problem solving, a widely recognised challenge is how best to capture the relevant domain knowledge in a formal knowledge base. A lot of research focuses on formalising the knowledge of domain experts, but in addition, a suitable knowledge base typically also needs to incorporate data coming from existing sources (e.g. a database or CSV file). This data is often extracted by means of *ad hoc* scripts, e.g. in a general-purpose imperative programming language. In this paper, we study this task from a logical perspective. We analyse how to derive a logical vocabulary from tabular data, in order to transform the data into a logical structure. As data from multiple sources often needs to be combined, this paper will further discuss the combination of multiple logical specifications. We conduct our study in the context of the IDP-Z3 reasoning engine for the FO(.) language, a rich extension of classical first-order logic. For this engine, we implement a new API called KeBAP (Knowledge-Base API for Python), which automates tasks such as deriving logical vocabulary from data tables and merging different data sources.

Keywords: knowledge representation · first-order logic · configuration problems

1 Introduction

Declarative systems have a proven track record in providing decision support for configuration problems. However, in order to create an application, data needs to be entered into a knowledge base. Often, such data is already available in a different format, leading to the creation of *ad hoc* scripts to extract the data from its original source and insert it into the knowledge base.

The first goal of the present publication is to study this task from a logical perspective. We analyse how to derive a logical vocabulary from tabular data, in order to transform the data into a logical structure. A further complication is that information might be contained in different sources. Here, issues may arise due to contradictions between sources or differences in scope. We will provide a framework to combine such knowledge bases while reducing the risk of introducing errors.

To show the viability of our approach, we create a demo[1] in which tabular data about laptops and processors is transformed into an online store. It allows customers to search for a suitable product in a very flexible way, using any combination of properties to constrain the search or as an optimisation criterion. Moreover, it also allows to easily create custom categories by means of a declarative definition. For example, if a shop keeper wants to introduce a "gaming laptop" category, they can simply write a rule specifying the criteria for such a laptop. If, over time, these criteria change, the rule can be modified, and only the laptops that meet the new criteria are selected without the need to modify any data for the individual laptops.

The implementation relies on our newly developed tool called KeBAP (Knowledge-Base API for Python). Leveraging existing systems, in particular the IDP-Z3 reasoning engine [6] and its Interactive Consultant interface [3], our KeBAP interface allows to implement the entire webshop demo in just ten lines of Python code.

This paper is structured as follows. Section 2 provides a brief overview of the IDP System and its corresponding declarative language FO(.). Section 3 will discuss the details of transforming data from a single tabular data source to FO(.). Next, Section 4 covers the various issues that might evolve from combining multiple data sources. Section 5 provides details on some additional steps to create a working configuration application/online shop from the imported knowledge base. Section 6 follows up by showing the implementation. Section 7 discusses related work. Finally, Section 8 provides some conclusions and directions for future work.

2 The IDP System and FO(.)

2.1 The IDP System

The IDP system [6] is a state-of-the-art knowledge-based system, which has been used to provide decision support in the context of configuration problems. Its latest iteration is IDP-Z3 [4]. The main characteristic that sets it apart from other knowledge-based systems is its strict adherence to the knowledge-base paradigm [7]. This paradigm states that a strict separation must be sought between the knowledge and any execution logic (i.e., inference tasks carried out on it). In other words, the knowledge base is a "bag of knowledge" and is in no way tied to a certain goal or specific application.

On top of IDP-Z3, the Interactive Consultant graphical user interface has been developed [3]. When provided with a knowledge base that specifies a configuration problem, the Interactive Consultant automatically generates a flexible user interface that can be used to interactively find a suitable configuration.

---

[1] https://interactive-consultant.idp-z3.be/?file=laptop.idp&ic=true.

This interface works by linking the actions that a user can take to appropriate logical inference tasks that can be performed on the knowledge base. It has been successfully used in, e.g., an application to determine the right adhesive to join different types of materials [13], and in machine component design [1].

2.2 FO(.) Specification

The knowledge representation formalism used by IDP is the FO(.) language [7], an extension of first-order logic with, amongst others: types, arithmetic, aggregates and inductive definitions.

A specification in FO(.) consists of three blocks. A *vocabulary* block declares the types, predicate and function symbols. A *structure* for a vocabulary contains an interpretation for all or some of its symbols. Finally, a *theory* block contains the actual formulas.

In addition to these three declarative blocks, a *procedure* block may also be added. This block contains Python code and is used to have the engine execute a specific inference task, such as a *model expansion* or *optimisation*.

The IDP system offers support for both *incomplete* functions and *partial* functions. The former refers to the case where the function is total, but not all values are known. In such a case, the system may be able to infer the missing values. The latter refers to the mathematical concept of partial functions, i.e., a function that is undefined for certain values in its domain (e.g., integer division is undefined for any pair $(x, 0)$ in its domain).

3 Creating an FO(.) Specification from Data

In this section, we consider the automatic translation from data into an FO(.) specification. We consider the case of tabular data, since this is an often occurring format, and many other data sources can be rendered in tabular form.

Our running example will be a simple table with three students who receive grades for three courses. Table 1 shows the data. Say we want to introduce a rule that states "a student has failed if they have received any grade lower than 10". In FO(.) we can formalise this as:

$$\forall s \in Student : fails(s) \Leftrightarrow \exists c \in \ Course : grade(s, c) < 10.$$

To actually identify failing students, we of course need input data. In a logical setting, this would take the form of a structure for part of the vocabulary of this formula, as shown in Listing 1.1 in FO(.) syntax. However, in practice, such data is often only available as a table, such as Table 1, and will need to be transformed to an appropriate structure. Often, this is done by *ad hoc* scripts. Our goal in this section is to study this task from a logical perspective in order to find more general relations between tabular data and its logical representation, that can be exploited to automate the translation between both formats.

Our analysis results in a number of reasonable assumptions that can be used to automatically transform a table into a suitable vocabulary and a structure for this vocabulary. Our practical implementation of course allows the user to override these default assumptions when needed.

Table 1. Student grades

Student	Course	Grade
r1	programming	10
r1	maths	7
r1	philosophy	16
r2	programming	11
r2	maths	13
r2	philosophy	14
r3	programming	12
r3	maths	15
r3	philosophy	15

Listing 1.1. Vocabulary and structure for student grades in FO(.)

```
vocabulary V {
    type Student
    type Course
    type Grade ⊆ Int

    grade: Student × Course → Grade
}
structure S:V {
    Student := {r1, r2, r3}.
    Course := {programming, maths, philosophy}.
    Grade := {0..20}.

    grade := {(r1, programming) → 10, (r1, maths) → 7,
    (r1, philosophy) → 16, (r2, programming) → 11,
    (r2, maths) → 13, (r2, philosophy) → 14,
    (r3, programming) → 12, (r3, maths) → 15,
    (r3, philosophy) → 15}.
}
```

3.1 Types

In a simple typed logic, each element of the domain belongs to precisely one type. The type system of FO(.) is slightly more complex, and also allows to declare one type as a subtype of another.

In our context, we do not know up-front which domain elements there are, but will need to extract this information from the table. Here, it is reasonable to assume that all "identifiers" (i.e., values that are not numbers) that appear in the table correspond to domain elements, and that identifiers that appear in the same column correspond to unique elements of the same type (in other words, we make the Unique Names Assumption). Moreover, we can also assume that a type contains no other elements apart from those that are identified in this way (i.e., we also make the Closed World Assumption).

Once we have a mapping from each column to a type, these assumptions allow us to automatically enumerate the set of objects in each type. However, in general, such a mapping need not be given, and deriving it from the table requires to make additional assumptions.

If a column contains only identifiers that appear nowhere else in the table, we will assume that this column corresponds to a separate type which has the same name as the column header. In our running example, this assumption suffices to correctly derive the types *Student* and *Course* from the table.

Columns with Overlapping Values. The case left to consider is that of the same identifier appearing in more than one column. Such an occurrence may simply be a name clash, in which two different elements of two different types happen to have the same identifier (e.g., the movie "Rocky" also has a character called "Rocky"). However, it is also possible that both occurrences are in fact intended to refer to the same domain element. For instance, in a table that represents a parent-child relation, the same person may occur in both the "parent" and "child" columns.

In this case, both columns can be of the same type (e.g., "Person" in the parent-child example) and the objects of this type are simply those that correspond to an identifier that appears in at least one of the two columns. However, the subtyping in FO(.)'s type system also allows to consider more complex possibilities, such one column being a subtype of the other (e.g., parents being a subtype of children). In the absence of explicit information, the safest assumption to make is that each of the two columns is a different subtype of some common supertype. This preserves the information about which elements were found in which column and provides the most flexibility for the user to write correct theories.

Numeric Data. The FO(.) language has both integers and real numbers as built-in data types. In addition, a user can also declare a custom subtype of either and define it as either a range or set of possible values. In the example, *Grade* $\subseteq \mathbb{Z}$ is such a type. It is defined as the range $[0, 20]$, which is how courses are graded at our university.

The type of a column cannot be automatically derived with certainty, but again some reasonable assumptions are possible. When making these assumptions, there is a trade-off between wanting to be as precise as possible, but at the same time not being too strict. In a sense, the "safest" option is to assume that each numeric column is of type $\mathbb{R}$, since that is technically never wrong. However, from a practical point of view, this reduces the possibility of catching errors (e.g., a user entering a grade as a percentage rather than as an integer $\in [0, 20]$) and may lead to quantifiers ranging over a much larger scope than intended, making problems computationally harder.

When only integers appear in a column, it therefore seems reasonable to assume that the column is of type $\mathbb{Z}$ or some subtype thereof. Mimicking our assumptions for the non-numeric case, we might assume that only values that actually appear are possible, but this seems less desirable in this case. For instance, suppose we want to define when a student obtains a perfect score: $\forall s \in Student : perfect\_score(s) \Leftrightarrow \exists c \in Course : grade(s,c) = 20$. If no student actually obtained a perfect score (yet), then our assumption would entail that 20 does not belong to the type $Score \subseteq \mathbb{Z}$ and this formula would actually contain a type error. Therefore, in the absence of additional information, we will just assume that the type of a column which contains only integer values is always the entire type $\mathbb{Z}$.

Boolean Columns. A final special case is a column containing boolean values. From a logical perspective, this corresponds to a predicate, so no special type should be created for such columns.

3.2 Functions and Predicates

A next question is how to actually represent the rows of the table. A straightforward option is to view the entire table as specifying a single relation, such as $hasGradeFor(Student, Course, Grade)$. In practice, a more fine-grained representation, in which the table is split up into multiple predicates/functions is often more useful. Indeed, this is also what happens in the vocabulary we originally chose for our example.

To construct such a vocabulary, it suffices to have a primary key for the table. We can then define a function $f : PrimaryKey \to T$ for every non-boolean column of type T and a predicate $p : PrimaryKey \to Bool$ for every boolean column. In our example, the pair of columns $(Student, Course)$ is a primary key and we indeed used the function $grade : Student \times Course \to Grade$.

If a primary key is not explicitly provided by the user, we could try to automatically construct one by looking for an appropriate set of columns, i.e., one whose values suffice to uniquely identify a row of the table. In practice, however, there would no guarantee that such a combination is really a correct primary key, and the values might not stay unique if more data were added to the table. We therefore believe that this is not a good option. A safer option is to introduce a new index column, specifically to serve as primary key. As Listing 1.2 shows, in the case of our example, the resulting vocabulary is less intuitive, but this nevertheless seems to be the best fully automated solution.

Listing 1.2. Grading example with indices

```
vocabulary V {
    type Student
    type Course
    type Grade ⊆ Int
    type Index ⊆ Int

    student: Index → Student
    course: Index → Course
    grade: Index → Grade
}

structure S:V {
    Student := {r1, r2, r3}.
    Course := {programming, maths, philosophy}.
    Grade := {0..20}.
    Index := {1..9}.
    student:= {1 → r1, 2 → r1, 3 → r1,
               4 → r2, 5 → r2, 6 → r2,
               7 → r3, 8 → r3, 9 → r3}.

    course := {1 → programming, 2 → maths, 3 → philosophy,
               4 → programming, 5 → maths, 6 → philosophy,
               7 → programming, 8 → maths, 9 → philosophy}.

    grade := {1 → 10, 2 → 7, 3 → 16,
              4 → 11, 5 → 13, 6 → 14,
              7 → 12, 8 → 15, 9 → 15}.
}
```

3.3 Dealing with Missing Values

A table may be missing values, either because it does not contain every possible value for the primary key, or because certain cells are empty. There are two possible causes for missing values: column(s) may be representing functions that are not total, or they may be representing total functions for which some values are unknown. In our example, the first case occurs if not every student takes every course, whereas the second case occurs if every student does take every course, but not all grades have already been entered into the table.

The FO(.) language allows to distinguish both cases: functions can be declared as partial instead of total, and it is possible to provide a partial enumeration of a total function. In the latter case, the function is defined for its entire domain, but its value is specified only for a subset thereof. The function's value for the remaining elements can then simply be left open (so that, e.g., a reasoning engine can fill these in), or a default value can assigned.

Without additional information, the safest option is to assume that a function with missing values is partial, because this will prevent reasoning engines from attempting to "guess" the missing values. In FO(.), a partial function has an explicit predicate which defines its domain. For instance, the situation in which not each student takes each course can be represented as:

$$grades : Student \times Course \rightarrow Grade \ (domain: \ takes\_course).$$

The modeller can then use this domain predicate $takes\_course$ to guard applications of the function.

For predicates, FO(.) only allows complete enumerations. The enumeration contains all values for which the predicate is true. Consequently, for a column with boolean values, cells with missing values will be treated as if they contain the value "false". For boolean columns with missing values, we, therefore, add the information as a conjunction instead of an enumeration, and add a second predicate that a user can use to check where a value was found in the data.

4 Combining Data Contained in Different Specifications

Data will often not be contained in a single table. For instance, in our laptop demo, the data comes from two different tables: one containing details on different CPUs, and another with laptop data, containing an identifier for the CPU, but no details on it. Using the previously described approach, both tables can separately be transformed into a logical specification, consisting of a vocabulary, structure and possibly also a theory. We now look at the question of how to combine two such specifications and consider two options: the first is to merge the specifications, while the second is to leave the separate specifications in place, but create links between them.

4.1 Merging Specifications

To merge two specifications, we need to combine their vocabularies. The challenge here is that the same symbol may appear in both vocabularies, which may either indicate that the same concept occurs in both specifications, but which may also be a name clash. For types, we can look at their enumeration to try to decide which of these is the case. If both enumerations are completely identical, it is safe to assume that both types are in fact intended to be the same. If none of the values overlap, a name clash is the most likely reason and one of the types must be renamed. If there is a partial overlap, we are essentially in the same situation as before when dealing with columns with partially overlapping sets of values. This suggests that the same solution is appropriate: assume that both types are in fact different, but that they are both subtypes of a common supertype. This solution is especially appropriate in this case, because it avoids the potential issue that functions which are total in (one of) the original specifications would no longer be total in the merged specification.

For functions and predicates, if their signature is the same in both vocabularies, it is safe to assume that they are the same symbol. If the signatures do not match, we are either dealing with a naming conflict and one of the functions or predicates must be renamed, or the signature must be updated. The latter can occur due to the subtyping approach we adopt to handle overlapping types. In such a case, we may end up with two "versions" of the same function signature, where each version refers to a different subtype of a more general supertype. This problem can be fixed by just using the supertype in the signature. After fixing the function's signature in this way, the enumeration of the function can be constructed by combining the two original enumerations.

If functions or predicates are not defined through enumeration, the modeller needs to check that merging both is in fact appropriate. This cannot be automated, since having a subtype relationship could in fact hide a naming conflict, i.e. the application of both definitions of the function or predicate could lead to inconsistencies.

4.2 Linking Separate Specifications

The previous section showed some of the complexities of merging different specifications together. If the type enumerations are not identical, care must be taken to ensure that the functions using these types still work after the merge operation. On top of that, the merge operation cannot handle contradictions. For this reason, merging specifications might not always be feasible or desirable. For instance, if two departments of a company are responsible for their own data, neither may be willing to 'correct' their data to fit the data of the other.

In such cases, we may prefer to work with two loosely-coupled specifications instead of combining them into a single specification. This approach has some advantages: information is nicely divided in different knowledge bases, which makes them easier to maintain. A user is still able to interact with the knowledge contained in the different knowledge bases (without even being aware of the distributed nature of the data) and information can be passed between the different knowledge bases as required. The downsides are that some overhead is required for this communication and that it is less easy to spot inconsistencies between specifications (if these were merged, any inconsistencies would prevent merging and would have been dealt with). Further, some case-specific modelling might be required. For instance, in the example below, an additional predicate is added to store the information we would like to pass. Our goal here is to provide the necessary tools to allow a programmer to easily manipulate data from specifications as required to pass information between them.

Returning to our laptop shop example, if a user selects information about the CPU, the system adds this to the CPU knowledge base and propagates the information to reduce the number of eligible CPUs. The results of this propagation are passed on to the specification about the laptops and the system uses this knowledge base to, again, reduce the number of eligible laptops. Vice versa, if the number of eligible laptops is reduced by selecting a value for a non-CPU parameter, this may provide information on which CPUs remain possible according to the laptop knowledge base. This list can be passed back to the CPU knowledge base and any CPUs that do not occur in the list can be removed from the eligible CPUs. A further propagation step could reveal further information on the remaining possibilities for the reduced list of eligible CPUs.

To check what information can be passed, we take the intersection of the vocabularies of both specifications. This is the common terminology. For our CPU example this would only be the identifiers for the CPUs (e.g. type Processor). A predicate for this type could be introduced in each knowledge base to store the information from the other. E.g. $impossible\_CPU : Processor \rightarrow Bool$. In the CPU specification, this constraint is defined by reference to the constants that store the user choices, i.e. a CPU is impossible if its characteristics contradict any user choice. In the laptop specification, this predicate is initially empty. If over the course of a user's interaction with the system CPUs become impossible, this information is added to the enumeration and the consequences are obtained through propagation.

Our application is ideally suited to allow such an approach to work, because it provides functionality to manipulate data contained in specifications in Python. This means that we could write the application logic in Python, but rely on the IDP system for any inference on the specification(s).

This solution works well for the intended application, a configuration problem with a user interface that propagates user choices at runtime. Further research is needed to study how we can approach linking specifications from a logical perspective, which will improve its generalisation over inference tasks and different types of problems.

5 Further Requirements for a Working Online Shop

In order to create a useful specification, it is not sufficient to simply transform the data to a specific format. We briefly introduce two innovations to the IDP system introduced by our implementation KeBAP (Knowledge-Based API for Python).

5.1 User Choices and Standardised Constraints

The goal of a configuration system, such as our laptop shop, is to find a product that best matches the user's requirements. Let us introduce a constant $laptop$ of type $Laptop$ to designate the product that we are looking for. Following our import of the table data, we can assume that we have a function for each of the features that a laptop might have. For instance, a laptop has a screen diameter, so we have a function $diameter : Laptop \rightarrow \mathbb{R}$. However, in order to find suitable laptops, we also need to know which diameter the user actually wants. We can represent this by a constant such as $diameter\_ : () \rightarrow \mathbb{R}$ (here, we append an underscore to avoid a name clash). This allows us to then express the constraint:

$$diameter\_ = diameter(laptop)$$

In other words, the required diameter and the diameter of the selected laptop should be equal.

Of course, we do not only need to do this for the screen diameter of a laptop, but also for every other feature of interest. KeBAP introduces functionality to automatically create the constants and associated constraints for all functions with the same domain.

5.2 Precalculating Definitions

In the laptop shop demo, one of the benefits of our knowledge-based approach is that it is easy to define new concepts based on the existing features of laptops. Suppose, for instance, that we would like to add the information that a laptop with processor speed ≥ 4.8 and ≥ 16GB of memory can be considered a "gaming laptop". In our data table, we could add an additional boolean column "Gaming laptop" to explicitly enumerate this concept. However, by importing the data table into the logical world, we can simply add a new definition such as:

$$\forall l \in Laptop : GamingLaptop(l) \Leftrightarrow processor\_speed(l) \geq 4.8 \wedge memory(l) \geq 16$$

This is obviously much clearer, more compact and easier to maintain.

One possible downside, however, is that for large data tables, such a logical definition may introduce additional computational overhead, that may slow down an interactive system. Therefore, we also provide the ability to calculate the results of the definitions up front and store them for later reuse. In this way, the predicates must only be recalculated if the definitions are updated. Our API allows modellers to easily insert or remove the precalculated information as needed.

6 Implementation and Demo

We have implemented the KeBAP system, which offers the functionalities described above. It is available as open source[2]. Our approach has been to make the functionality customisable, while at the same time providing reasonable defaults. For instance, to import the data table of our student example, the user can just write:

```
from modeller import Modeller

grades = Modeller.from_file("CSV", "./path/to/grades.csv")
```

These two lines of code transform Table 1 into Listing 1.2.

To generate our original Listing 1.1, a few customisation options are needed to select $Student \times Course$ as the primary key column range and set the range of the type $Grade$:

```
from modeller import Modeller

path = "./path/to/grades.csv"
```

---
[2] https://gitlab.com/EAVISE/rdv/KeBAP.

```
key = ["Student", "Course"]
config = {Grade: {"values": list(range(0,21))}}

grades = Modeller.from_file("CSV", path,
                            key=key,
                            config_dict= config)
```

The configuration information can also be stored as a JSON file and loaded using the *from_config* method.

As described earlier, we have then used our system to implement a laptop webshop, which is also available online[3]. The data for the webshop comes from two tables, one describing laptops and one describing CPUs. The user interface, shown in Figure 1 is the generic Interactive Consultant [3] interface, which is powered by the IDP-Z3 reasoning engine. It is a flexible interface, which allows the user to enter any information they want (e.g., they can select a laptop feature, or they can select a specific laptop) and then shows all of the consequences of the entered information (e.g., by reducing the list of possible laptops, or by propagating the value of certain features).

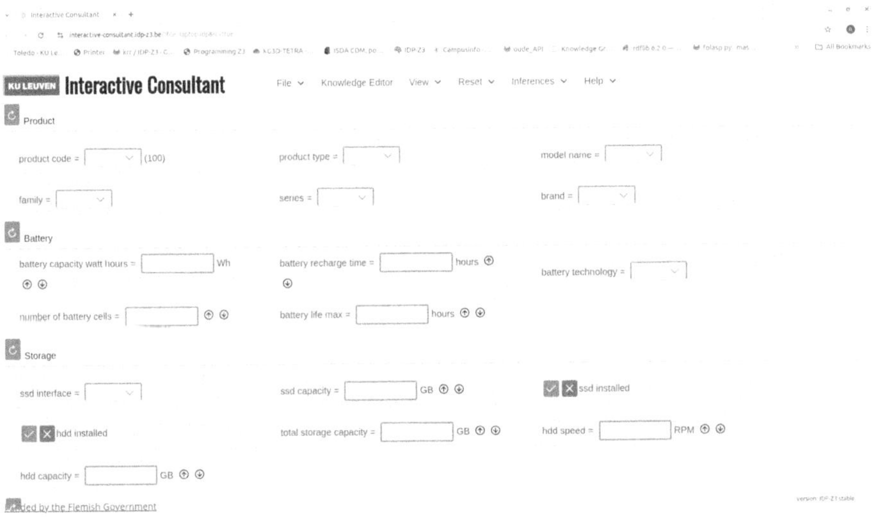

Fig. 1. The online shop for laptops seen in the interactive consultant [3]. Many additional fields can be seen when accessing the online demo. The number between brackets next to the product code indicates how many eligible laptops are left as a consequence of the user's choices.

These powerful components were already available, but using them was not trivial, due to the need for *ad hoc* scripts to link them to the data. Thanks to

---

[3] https://interactive-consultant.idp-z3.be/?file=laptop.idp&ic=true.

our system, this bottleneck has been eliminated and the webshop can now be
implemented with remarkably little effort.

```
from modeller import Modeller
from standard_config_creator import add_default_constants

laptop_file = "./tetra/laptop_split/laptop_100.csv"
processor_file = "./tetra/laptop_split/processor.csv"
save_file = "laptop.idp"

config = {
    "Release_date": {"typing": "Date"},
    "Market_positioning": {"typing": "!Exclude"}
}

laptop_model = Modeller.from_file("CSV",
                                  laptop_file,
                                  key="Product_code",
                                  config_dict=config,
                                  ignore_freevars=True)

processor_model = Modeller.from_file("CSV",
                                     processor_file,
                                     key="Processor_model",
                                     ignore_freevars=True)

laptop_model.merge(processor_model)
laptop_model.model = add_default_constants(laptop_model.model)
laptop_model.translate("IDPZ3", save_file)
```

7 Related Work

In the IDP-Z3 ecosystem, some previous work has focused on making these tools easier to use. For instance, a Python API was developed to allow easy interfacing [14] and several user-friendly input languages were developed to lower the learning curve for FO(.) [11,12]. Our paper is complementary, focusing on easy use of *data* rather than on acquiring *knowledge*.

The IDP-Z3 paradigm and its tools are closely related to the Answer Set Programming (ASP) paradigm, as demonstrated by, e.g., the FOLASP [10] tool that translates FO(.) to ASP. In the ASP world, the ASP Chef framework [2] most closely resembles our work. ASP Chef aims to make it easier to link multiple ASP programs together. Likewise, our application makes it easier to deal with multiple FO(.) specifications. Our projects differ in the sense that, contrary to ASP, IDP adheres to the knowledge base paradigm, which means that our application links data, not programs. This distinction can have important consequences. Both our project and theirs also consider the import of data from CSV files / tables, but where their work simply describes which values can be found in every cell, using a *cell* predicate, our work attempts to find the underlying logic in the data to introduce more meaningful functions and predicates.

Other articles exist that try to facilitate the use of ASP from within procedural code. By way of example we mention [9], which integrates ASP in object-oriented programming languages, such as Python, by introducing a language to formally specify the input and output of the ASP program. Again, this is in contrast to an FO(.) specification that is a bag of knowledge and not a program, and therefore has no input nor output.

Finally, especially in the area of the semantic web, efforts have already been made to extract information from tabular data. These solutions often require custom mappings, for instance in RDF Mapping Language (RML) [8], or rely on existing data to annotate and enhance the tabular data (e.g. [5]). Our work focuses on finding meaningful relations within the data, without consulting any outside sources or predefined categories, and with minimal user intervention. That being said, the annotation and enhancement approaches could be useful as a preprocessing or data augmentation step before using our tool to obtain a logical specification.

8 Conclusions and Future Work

Knowledge-base systems need data to perform inference tasks on. This paper studied the underlying logic of tabular data, one of the most common forms of data, in order to automate the process of deriving a logical vocabulary and structure from it. In each case, we have come up with some practical assumptions to deal with ambiguity. For types, we assume that partially overlapping columns are subtypes of a larger hidden supertype. For functions and predicates, we prefer to explicitly ask a modeller to provide the key columns, but in the absence of this information are able to provide default functions using the index as keys. For missing data, we are unable to determine whether the function is partial or the data is incomplete (or both). We handle this by introducing guard predicates to explicitly inform a modeller of where the function is defined. The modeller has access to both the function's output type, as can be found in its signature, and the domain for which it is implemented, thus making the task of updating the specification a lot easier. In the future, we would like to explore if we can expand this type of analysis to different data formats.

We have further shown the possibilities of combining data sources. Merging the data into a single specification is the most straightforward approach, but requires a human modeller to remove any contradictions between the sources. An interesting area of research is how we can combine information from different sources without merging them into a single specification. We have seen one such example of linking data, but further research is necessary in order to study this option from a logical perspective and deepen our understanding of its possibilities.

We have introduced KeBAP, an API that allows users to easily create FO(.) specifications from different sources and manipulate these specifications (e.g. by merging) after creation. This API is still actively being developed.

Finally, we have shown some additional functionality that is useful to automate knowledge base creation, such as the introduction of standardised constants and associated constraints to deal with user input, and the possibilities to introduce additional custom constraints and categories. In this respect, we have highlighted the option to precalculate the result of applying certain time-consuming constraints, which is made possible because KeBAP provides the necessary flexibility to store and merge these results.

Acknowledgments. This work was funded by Flanders Innovation & Entrepreneurship as part of the Technology Transfer project HBC.2022.0071.

Disclosure of Interests. The authors have no competing interests to declare that are relevant to the content of this article.

References

1. Aerts, B., Deryck, M., Vennekens, J.: Knowledge-based decision support for machine component design: a case study. Expert Syst. Appl. **187**, 115869 (2022). https://doi.org/10.1016/j.eswa.2021.115869, https://www.sciencedirect.com/science/article/pii/S0957417421012288
2. Alviano, M., Cirimele, D., Reiners, L.A.R.: Introducing ASP recipes and ASP chef. In: ICLP Workshops, vol. 3437 (2023)
3. Carbonnelle, P., Aerts, B., Deryck, M., Vennekens, J., Denecker, M.: An interactive consultant. In: Beuls, K., et al. (eds.) Proceedings of the 31st Benelux Conference on Artificial Intelligence (BNAIC 2019) and the 28th Belgian Dutch Conference on Machine Learning (Benelearn 2019), Brussels, Belgium, 6–8 November 2019. CEUR Workshop Proceedings, vol. 2491. CEUR-WS.org (2019). http://ceur-ws.org/Vol-2491/demo45.pdf
4. Carbonnelle, P., Vandevelde, S., Vennekens, J., Denecker, M.: IDP-Z3: a reasoning engine for FO (.). arXiv preprint arXiv:2202.00343 (2022)
5. Dasoulas, I., Yang, D., Duan, X., Dimou, A.: Torchictab: semantic table annotation with Wikidata and language models. In: CEUR Workshop Proceedings, pp. 21–37. CEUR Workshop Proceedings (2023)
6. De Cat, B., Bogaerts, B., Bruynooghe, M., Janssens, G., Denecker, M.: Predicate logic as a modeling language: the IDP system. In: Kifer, M., Liu, Y.A. (eds.) Declarative Logic Programming: Theory, Systems, and Applications, pp. 279–323. ACM, September 2018. https://doi.org/10.1145/3191315.3191321, https://dl.acm.org/citation.cfm?id=3191321
7. Denecker, M., Vennekens, J.: Building a knowledge base system for an integration of logic programming and classical logic. In: Garcia de la Banda, M., Pontelli, E. (eds.) Logic Programming, vol. 5366, pp. 71–76. Springer, Berlin, Heidelberg (2008). https://doi.org/10.1007/978-3-540-89982-2_12
8. Dimou, A., Vander Sande, M., Colpaert, P., Verborgh, R., Mannens, E., Van de Walle, R.: RML: a generic language for integrated RDF mappings of heterogeneous data. LDOW **1184** (2014)
9. Rath, J., Redl, C.: Integrating Answer Set Programming with object-oriented languages. In: Practical Aspects of Declarative Languages: 19th International Symposium, PADL 2017, Paris, France, 16–17 January 2017, Proceedings 19, pp. 50–67. Springer (2017)

10. Van Dessel, K., Devriendt, J., Vennekens, J.: FOLASP: FO (·) as input language for answer set solvers. Theory Pract. Log. Program. **21**(6), 785–801 (2021)
11. Vandevelde, S., Aerts, B., Vennekens, J.: Tackling the DM challenges with cDMN: a tight integration of DMN and constraint reasoning. Theory Pract. Log. Program. 1–24 (2021). https://doi.org/10.1017/S1471068421000491
12. Vandevelde, S., Callewaert, B., Vennekens, J.: Interactive feature modeling with background knowledge for validation and configuration. In: Proceedings of the 26th ACM International Systems and Software Product Line Conference-Volume B, pp. 209–216 (2022)
13. Vandevelde, S., Vennekens, J., Jordens, J., Van Doninck, B., Witters, M.: Knowledge-based support for adhesive selection: will it stick? Theory Pract. Log. Program. 1–21 (2024). https://doi.org/10.1017/S1471068424000024, https://www.cambridge.org/core/product/E58D9C3E3E47548A96D19A7579A8B242
14. Vennekens, J.: Lowering the learning curve for declarative programming: a Python API for the IDP system. In: International Symposium on Practical Aspects of Declarative Languages, pp. 86–102. Springer (2016)

Automated Playing of Survival Video Games with Commonsense Reasoning

Bryant Hargreaves, Dan N. Nguyen[✉], Keegan Krimbell, and Gopal Gupta

Department of Computer Science, The University of Texas at Dallas,
Richardson, TX, USA
{bryant.hargreaves,dan.nguyen,keegan.krimbell,gupta}@utdallas.edu

Abstract. Don't Starve is a non-linear, real-time survival video game where the player's objective is to survive as long as possible. The game is challenging because randomly generated situations and events make it hard to survive this game for a long time. However, the game follows specific rules that can be used to predict future outcomes. We can use these rules to automate its playing. Our preliminary effort reported in this paper uses the answer set programming framework to model the game-playing agent's logic to survive in the game for as long as possible. The agent learns the environment around it and translates the knowledge into facts represented as predicates. A set of commonsense reasoning rules represented in ASP captures the logic that the agent must use to survive. We combined the logic rules with the facts about the environment to compute the best action the agent must take. We use the s(CASP) goal-directed predicate ASP engine and a custom game modification program written in Lua supported by the game environment that can interface with s(CASP). Our results indicate that our preliminary automated game-playing system can outperform novice players. Further refinement should allow our system to survive longer.

Keywords: Video Games · Goal-Directed Answer Set Programming

1 Introduction

Video games are popular with children, teenagers, college students, and adults worldwide; however, playing them can require complex thought and reasoning, especially in randomly generated open-world survival games, where the players face unique situations and can make countless choices. Historically, this complex thinking has been difficult to mimic with software, as too many unique scenarios have to be accounted for [1]. Our motivation for this paper is to develop an autonomous agent that can play the Don't Starve game by just using common sense reasoning and answer set programming. Our goal is to show that automated commonsense reasoning realized through ASP and s(CASP) is an excellent tool for automated survival video game playing.[1][2]

---
[1] https://hargreaves.dev/sCASP-Independent-Study/.
[2] https://youtu.be/asS59Sr3Oww - Unedited Run of the Agent.

2 Background

2.1 Don't Starve

Don't Starve is a real-time survival video game where players must learn to survive in a harsh environment. Don't Starve starts a player out as Wilson, a scientist, who has been mysteriously transported to a strange and deadly world by a demon gentleman. After a quick greeting, the adversaries vanish, and the player has to figure out how to survive [2].

The player's objective is to survive as long as possible. To survive, a player must carry out operations such as scavenging for food, building a campfire to stay warm, etc. If not fed, for example, the player will eventually die. After playing and dying a few times without help from the games, the player will figure out some essential mechanics. The core game mechanics important in the creation of Agent Wilson [3] are discussed next.

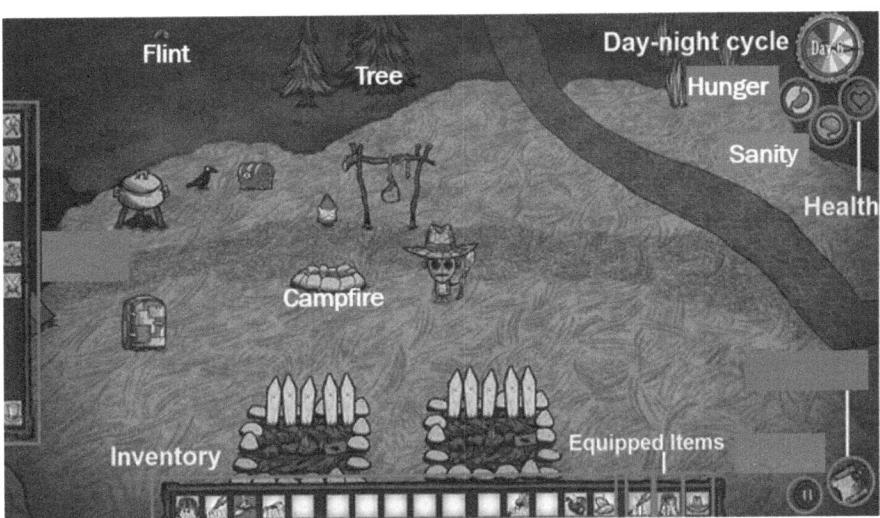

Fig. 1. Player's normal game screen

Hunger: Hunger (or Energy stats) is represented as a yellow icon. When it reaches 0, the player's health will drop drastically until the player dies. Most of the actions that the players perform will deplete their health statistics. Players can always eat food to replenish energy and slow down starvation.

Health: Health is represented as a red icon, and when it reaches 0, the player dies. Health can be drained due to hostile mobs, natural disasters like lightning and fire, or starvation. Eating foods and drinking potions might improve the player's health.

Sanity: Sanity is represented as an orange icon, and when it gets near 0, players will be in a hallucinated state, and hostile mobs will keep spawning to attack the player. The most common cause of decreased sanity is fighting hostile mobs and staying in darkness. Picking flowers usually restore it.

Day/Night Cycle: The Day/Night Cycle of Don't Starve is a constant factor shown in the top right corner of the screen. Each day will have three cycles: Day (yellow section), Dusk (red section), and Night (blue section). It is generally safe during the day but it will get darker when Dusk comes. Finally, when the night arrives, it will become completely dark. The players should have a light source to survive the night.

Inventory: The player's inventory keeps a present record of items gathered, used, and crafted. The inventory also shows if perishable foods (carrots, berries, etc.) will go bad soon in 3 colors (green, yellow, and red, where red usually means the food is spoiled and should not be eaten). The player's inventory is limited to 15 items unless the player is equipped with a backpack.

Equipment: The player has three slots for equipped items: tool, torso, and hat. The player can use equipped tools like an ax to chop trees for wood, a spear to hunt animals, or a torch to light up the pitch-dark night. The player can wear a torso piece and/or hat to reduce the damage from hostile mobs, keep their sanity, or a backpack to expand their inventory slots.

Interaction and Crafting: Interacting with the world is one of the most critical elements of Don't Starve. Interacting can mean various actions, including collecting items, picking berries, gathering flowers, and chopping wood. These actions generally allow the player to obtain items for survival. Furthermore, players can use these items in crafting. Crafting is another core mechanism in Don't Starve that enables players to acquire tools and structures for survival.

2.2 ASP and S(CASP)

Answer Set Programming (ASP) [4,5] is a logic programming paradigm suited for knowledge representation and reasoning that facilitates commonsense reasoning. The s(CASP) system [6] is an answer set programming system that supports predicates, constraints over non-ground variables, uninterpreted functions, and, most importantly, a top-down, query-driven execution strategy. These features make it possible to return answers with non-ground variables (possibly including constraints) and compute partial models by returning only the fragment of a stable model necessary to support the answer.

Complex commonsense knowledge can be represented in ASP and the s(CASP) query-driven predicate ASP system can be used for querying it [7,8]. Commonsense knowledge can be emulated using (i) default rules, (ii) integrity constraints, and (iii) multiple possible worlds, according to [5] and [9]. Default rules are used for jumping to a conclusion in the absence of exceptions, e.g., a bird normally flies, unless it's a penguin.

```
1  flies(X) :- bird(X), not abnormal_bird(X).
2  abnormal_bird(X) :- penguin(X).
```

Integrity constraints allow us to express impossible situations and invariants. For example, a person cannot be dead and alive simultaneously.

```
1  false :- person(X), dead(X), alive(X).
```

Finally, multiple possible worlds allow us to construct alternative universes that may have some parts common but other parts inconsistent. For example, the cartoon world of children's books has a lot in common with the real world (e.g., birds can fly in both worlds), yet in the former, birds can talk like humans, but in the latter, they cannot.

A large number of commonsense reasoning applications have already been developed using ASP and the s(CASP) system: [7,8,10]. Justification for each response can also be given as the s(CASP) system can generate justifications for successful queries as proof trees as shown by [11].

3 Designing Agent Wilson

Our goal in this paper is to automate the playing of the Don't Starve game. For this purpose, we created an autonomous agent that uses goal-directed commonsense reasoning to compute what actions it must take, given the surrounding environment, to survive.

The main parts of creating the autonomous agents are: (i) understanding the current environment and the agents' characteristics; (ii) converting the environment and characteristics into predicates; (iii) combining the predicates, rules, and constraints to compute agent action(s); (iv) executing one of the best actions to continue surviving. The agent also operates in a feedback loop, updating the metrics after each action or change in the state of the game. This dynamic process forms a cycle where the agent gains knowledge about the world and uses it to make decisions and execute the action, repeating until the agent dies.

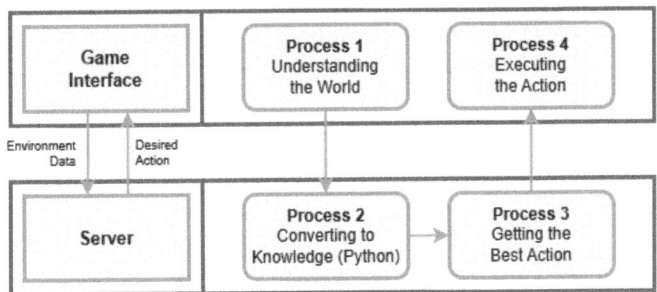

Fig. 2. Diagram of Agent Wilson

The common goal of both the custom game modification interface and the s(CASP) server is to survive the game as long as possible. However, to survive, the agent's game interface's goal is to be the agent's eyes and brawn that can understand the world and execute actions, while the s(CASP) server is the brain that decides what actions it could take. That computed list of actions is the end result (or the goal) of each s(CASP) iteration, so using a top-down execution strategy is advantageous.

3.1 Understanding the World

The base version of Don't Starve relies on a day/night system. During the day, the player can safely explore the world and gather materials [12]. For the agent to explore the world, it needs to understand the world around it. Our custom game modification, supported by the game system, allows us to inject custom Lua code [13] into the game engine that lets the agent know what entities are on the screen and their characteristics and sends that data to the server using TCP networking protocol. In our Lua script, we create a repeating event that reads the environment's data, which includes information about the entities on the screen and their characteristics, cleans it, and sends it as JSON-formatted text to a Python server that invokes the logic coded in s(CASP).

3.2 Converting to Knowledge

For the game engine to communicate the game data to s(CASP), we need to transform the information collected from the game world into a logical form that s(CASP) can understand. s(CASP) is well-suited for reasoning with incomplete information and constraints, making it ideal for complex decision-making scenarios like those in Don't Starve. The decision made by s(CASP) needs to be suitably transformed so that the game engine can update and display its state.

The JSON data from the game world is converted into a set of s(CASP) predicates. These predicates represent the state of the world, the current status of the agent and the entities, and their characteristics. The example below shows facts about an evergreen (a type of tree) with a GUID(Global Unique Identifier) of 108017. It is workable (can be manipulated via a mouse click) and choppable with an axe since it is a tree.

```
1  item_on_screen(evergreen, 108017).
2  guid(108017).
3  workable(108017).
4  choppable(108017).
```

Second, the agent's inventory data will be converted to predicates. For this example, the agents have 2 twigs in one of their inventory slots. Twigs are a fuel source that can keep a campfire burning. If the twigs are on the ground, they can be collected.

```
 6  slot_in_inventory(twigs, 111163).
 7  guid(111163).
 8  fuel(twigs).
 9  collectable(twigs).
10  item_in_inventory(twigs, 2).
```

Third, the agent's equipment data will also be converted to predicate. The data below, for example, tells us that the agent is equipped with an axe.

```
11  equipment(axe, 111191).
12  guid(111191).
13  quantity(111191, 1).
14  equippable(axe).
```

The agent's statistics are also mapped to predicates. The facts below represent that the agent has a high amount of health, sanity, and hunger points (a low hunger bar point means the agent is hungry).

```
17  sanity(high).
18  hunger(high).
19  health(high).
```

Finally, the world characteristics will also be mapped to predicates. These characteristics are the time of day, season, and current biome on which the player stands.

```
20  time(day, early).
21  season(summer).
22  biome(forest).
```

Once the environment has been converted into perdicates, the s(CASP) engine reasons to compute the actions that are possible given the game's current state.

3.3 Computing the Possible Actions

The selection of possible actions for the agent to perform comes after the world state has been transformed into s(CASP) predicates. Using the current environment, player statistics, and resource availability as inputs, the s(CASP) engine is queried to start the decision-making process. In assessing potential courses of action, the engine considers the agent's objectives: survival through self-management of hunger, health, and sanity and ensuring necessary resources to survive through the future (nights, seasons, and hostile monsters). In the s(CASP) program, there is a list of actions that the agent could take, and as of now there are 23 actions that s(CASP) can compute, that are of the form:

`action(short_description_of_action, function_in_lua, function_arguments)`

Finally, we will query the s(CASP) program by using the format below.

`?- action(DESC, FUNC, ARGS).`

After modeling the agent, we run the solver using the command "scasp /path/-to/file.pl -n0" with the "-n0" flag to query all the actions. The "-n0" flag also gives the output ranked by the order in which they appeared in the file. An action that appears first is to be modeled first. For example, if the action that allows the agent to run away from the monster comes first, and the action that allows the agent to chop the tree comes after, and if both actions are possible at the current moment given the state of the game, then the agent will choose the action to run away from the monster as the top choice and the chop-tree action will come later in the priority. But let's say that the current environment is safe for the agent (so there is no need to run away because the model will not output an action to run away). One of the actions that can help it survive the nights is to gather logs to make a campfire. The rule describes the chop-tree action:

```
action(chop_tree, chop_tree, GUID) :-    choppable(GUID), equipment(axe), \\
                         sufficient_amount(log, 10), not time(night)
```

Using the sample data earlier that was converted to s(CASP) knowledge, the chop-tree action can be performed.

```
1   item_on_screen(evergreen, 108017). %An evergreen with GUID of 108017
4   choppable(108017).
11  equipment(axe).
20  time(day).
```

Finally, the predicate "sufficient-amount" uses the powerful negation capabilities of s(CASP) to accurately model whether the agent has enough of a given resource. This predicate holds true if the agent does not have any of that item or has fewer than the maximum desired number of items.

```
1   item_present(X) :- item_in_inventory(X,N), N .>. 0.
2   sufficient_amount(X, MAX) :- not item_present(X).
3   sufficient_amount(X, MAX) :- item_in_inventory(X, N), N .>. 0, N .<. MAX.
```

Without using negation-as-failure, the logic behind entities and items that are not present becomes complicated. Negation-as-failure allows us to search the current world and ensure that there are no cases where "item_present(X)" holds.

With all these rules, finally, the chop-tree action will hold true, with s(CASP) generating the following aciton:

`action(chop_tree,chop_tree,108017)`

Finally, note that chopping trees requires the agent to perform more than one chopping action (or more than one feedback loop). If the agent can see multiple trees, it might attempt a single chop on one tree and another on a different tree, which is not optimal. Therefore, we implement a history system that saves the agent's last action to prevent suboptimal behavior. The action is reselected if it remains feasible given the current state of the world, i.e., the agent will chop the same tree multiple times. The action is ignored if the agent should respond to higher-priority actions, such as running away from hostile mobs.

3.4 Executing the Chosen Action

The final step in creating the agent is executing the s(CASP) server output. Our game agent can perform the following actions received from the s(CASP) module: wandering around the world, walking towards entities, picking up items, foraging entities for items, cooking food, equipping and unequipping items, chopping down trees, running away from hostile entities, eating food, adding fuel to campfires, staying close to entities, and crafting items.

4 Evaluation

Our goal was to have Agent Wilson survive for at least 7 days. This is because we utilized the Don't Starve Wiki guide [3,14]. Table 1 shows Agent Wilson's unassisted attempts at surviving in randomly generated worlds.

In creating the agent, we discovered that while the guide [3] was generally helpful, it did not include some of the small details that a normal player tends to ignore. For example, the guide instructs the reader to avoid spiders and other hostile entities; however, it does not specify the distance a player should keep or how to disengage from them properly. In addition, the guide instructs the player to collect everything in sight. However, it does not suggest what amounts of resources are necessary or if there should be a balance or limit to the items collected. These small details, intuitively understood by human reasoning, must be represented logically and consistently in s(CASP).

Table 1. Summary of Test Results on Causes of Death and Days Lived

Run	Causes of Death	Days Lived
1	Terrorbreak (Out of Sanity)	7
2	Frog (Hostile Mob)	2
3	Starvation	5
4	Hound (Hostile Mob)	5
5	Starvation	6
6	Frog (Hostile Mob)	7
7	Treeguard (Hostile Mob)	6
8	Darkness	4

5 Related Work and Conclusions

There is past work by Almeida in which Behavior Tree Search algorithms are used to play the multiplayer version of Don't Starve called Don't Starve Together. This work aims to make a Non-Playable-Character(NPC) companion for the player [15]. The agent in this work could only survive for an average of 3.9 days, and the bench-marked agent that this work compared to could survive an average of 8.9 days. The bench-marked agent is Artificial Wilson, a work of the anonymous modder KingofTown, which can be found in the public repository https://github.com/KingofTown/DS-AI. One issue of Almeida's work is that for their result, all hostile enemies and any event that could turn a mob into a hostile enemy have been removed from the game, and there are no random external events that could harm the agent. Our system, in contrast, can survive longer, while taking hostile mobs into account.

In this paper, we reported on our experience designing an autonomous agent that can play the survival game "Don't Starve" automatically. The agent stimulates the commonsense reasoning that a human would use to play the game. It uses answer set programming and the s(CASP) goal-directed predicate ASP system to perform commonsense reasoning. Our evaluation shows that our preliminary implementation can play slightly better than the novice level—surviving for 7 days. Future work includes making our agent's reasoning stronger so that it can survive indefinitely.

References

1. Justesen, N., Bontrager, P., Togelius, J., Risi, S.: Deep learning for video game playing. IEEE Trans. Games **12**, 1–20 (2017)
2. Nathan Meunier. Don't starve review. 2014
3. Don't Starve Wiki. Guides/getting started guide. 2024
4. Brewka, G., Eiter, T., Truszczynski, M.: Answer set programming at a glance. Commun. ACM **54**(12), 92–103 (2011)
5. Gelfond, M., Kahl, Y.: Knowledge Representation, Reasoning, and the Design of Intelligent Agents: The Answer-set Programming Approach. Cambridge University Press, Cambridge (2014)
6. Arias, J., Carro, M., Salazar, E., Marple, K., Gupta, G.: Constraint answer set programming without grounding (2018)
7. Chen, Z., Marple, K., Salazar, E., Gupta, G., Tamil, L.: A physician advisory system for chronic heart failure management based on knowledge patterns. Theory Pract. Log. Program. **16**(5–6), 604–618 (2016)
8. Xu, Z., et al.: Jury-trial story construction and analysis using goal-directed answer set programming. In: Proceedings of the PADL, volume 13880 of LNCS, pp. 261–278. Springer, 2023
9. Gupta, G.: Automating common sense reasoning with ASP and s(CASP), 2022. Technical Report. https://utdallas.edu/~gupta/csr-scasp.pdf
10. Sartor, G., Dávila, J.A., Billi, M., Contissa, G., Pisano, G., Kowalski, R.A.: Integration of logical English and s(casp). In: Proceedings of the ICLP Workshops: GDE'22, volume 2970 of CEUR Workshop Proceedings. CEUR-WS.org, 2022
11. Arias, J., Carro, M., Chen, Z., Gupta, G.: Justifications for goal-directed constraint answer set programming. In: Proceedings 36th ICLP (Tech. Comm.), volume 325 of EPTCS, pp. 59–72, 2020
12. Sliva, M.: Don't starve review, 2013
13. Ierusalimschy, R., De Figueiredo, L.H., Filho, W.C.: Lua-an extensible extension language. Softw.: Pract. Exp. **26**(6), 635–652 (1996)
14. Don't Starve Wiki. Food and edible items. 2024
15. Almeida, F., Rui, P.: Creating an Agent-Based Framework for Don't Starve Together. Master's thesis, Instituto Superior Técnico, June 2018

Checking Concurrency Coding Rules

Lars-Åke Fredlund, Ángel Herranz, and Julio Mariño

School of Computer Engineering, Universidad Politécnica de Madrid, Campus de
Montegancedo s/n, Madrid, Spain
{lfredlund,aherranz,jmarino}@fi.upm.es

Abstract. We present an approach for checking that Java programs correctly use libraries such as `java.util.concurrent.locks` for synchronizing concurrent tasks. Concretely, the article develops methods to check that the behaviour of a program is in accordance with a set of coding rules that govern the correct usage of the library. Here such coding rules are formalized as Prolog predicates that judge whether the history of interactions between program and library represents correct usage or not. The history of interactions is obtained by tracing the interactions between the program and the library when executing a representative test suite. The approach is evaluated in a case study in which around 200 independent monitor-based Java implementations of a common specification are analysed to check adherence to the concurrency coding rules.

Keywords: Concurrency Coding Rules · Java · Logic Programming

1 Introduction

Libraries that provide basic mechanisms for multiple tasks to synchronise accesses to shared data structures are often quite hard to use correctly. Elaborate protocols (sequences of calls to library methods) are used to ensure that writes to shared data structures are isolated from other concurrent writes or reads. As an example of such a library, the Java concurrency library `java.util.concurrent.locks` permits arbitrating thread access using locks (similar to monitors) and conditions.

The authors of this article teach an undergraduate course on concurrency at the Universidad Politécnica de Madrid using the Java programming language. Students are required to experiment with different concurrency mechanisms: semaphores, concurrent monitors, message passing, and so on. On a higher abstraction level, students are also taught a particular API design style for ensuring atomic access to shared data: shared resources [9]. A shared resource has a state, and access to that state is through a finite set of actions (or operations). An action is executed atomically. Actions are specified declaratively, using pre and post conditions, and, interestingly using a *concurrency precondition* which permits postponing an action until some logical conditions on the shared state is satisfied (condition synchronization). A great number of control systems can be specified as such shared resources.

Students are expected to, given such a rather abstract shared resource specification, implement the specification as a concrete Java class providing the same behaviour as the shared resource, using concurrency mechanisms such as monitors and message passing libraries. In a typical semester, teachers are faced with the task of aiding students to correctly implementing such shared resources, and grading their efforts.

Implementations are rigorously tested for errors. However, subtle concurrency errors are difficult to detect even using extensive testing. Test cases will typically have to be repeated many times, since only a subset of the executions of a non-deterministic implementation may exhibit the error. In practice, to reduce the number of bugs in the implementation of shared resources using a particular concurrency library, students are taught a number of coding rules, e.g., that a single monitor should be used.

Coding Rules implemented in Prolog. In this work we have formalised, as Prolog predicates, a number of such code rules for the libraries used in the course. These predicates express temporal and data constraints on how programs may use a particular concurrency library to implement a shared resource, and are expressed as predicates over the history of interactions between a shared resource implementation and a particular concurrency programming library. In other words, coding rules are expressed as *behavioural* properties, concerning the observed events of the program under study (how the program behaves), rather than as *static* properties restricting the source or object code of a program (how the program was written).

We have formalised such behavioural coding rules for the task of programming shared resources using the two main concurrency libraries used in the course: a monitor library named CCLIB [8] (similar to java.util.concurrent.locks) and the JCSP message passing library [16]. Due to a lack of space, this article focuses exclusively on the encoding and checking of coding rules for CCLIB. The absence of difficulties in implementing coding rules as Prolog predicates for these two libraries (with quite different APIs) suggest that coding rules for other concurrency libraries may also be developed without major difficulties.

Checking Coding Rules on an Implementation. As a first analysis step a log file resulting from the execution of a test suite on the shared resource implementation is generated, logging events such as calls to shared resource actions, and calls from the implementation to the library. The Byteman tool [4] is used to instrument Java code to log analysis relevant events as Prolog facts. Next, the resulting log file is analysed post-execution to determine whether any of the coding rules expressed as Prolog predicates are violated by the logged execution. In such cases, a detailed feedback is produced, detailing which action implementation(s) failed which coding rule(s).

Article Organisation. The rest of the article is organised as follows. Section 2 introduces the shared resource formalism using a simple Bank API that will be used as the running example throughout the rest of the article. Next, Sect. 3 discusses how to implement a shared resource using the CCLIB monitor library [8]. Section 4 provides details on the collection of event traces from shared resource implementation, and Sect. 5 discusses the formalisation and checking of coding rules in Prolog. In Sect. 6 the resulting approach is evaluated: a large number of independent implementations in Java of the Bank shared resource example are analysed. Finally, Sect. 7 presents an overview of some related works, and Sect. 8 discusses the results, and outlines issues for future work.

Our tool, comprising rules for the derivation of Byteman event logging rules from an implementation to analyse, together with code for encoding and checking concurrency coding rules using SWI-Prolog, is available under a BSD Licence at https://gitlab.com/babel-upm/shared-resources/concurrency-coding-rules.

2 Shared Resources

The *shared resource* notation introduced in [9] expresses process interaction by defining encapsulated state, an interface of *observationally atomic* actions, and a state transition semantics. A shared resource has an encapsulated state and defines a set of actions which provide the only mechanisms to modify the resource internal state. It can be seen as a central controller to serialise conflicting requests. Such methods are guaranteed to be executed atomically from an observational point of view. This means that the concurrent execution of two actions on a resource is either forbidden (mutual exclusion is preserved) or, if allowed, the observed behaviour of executing these actions concurrently is equivalent to some sequential execution [7].

CADT Bank
  ACTION Deposit: **String**[i] × $\mathbb{N}^+$[i]
  ACTION Transfer: **String**[i] × **String**[i] × $\mathbb{N}^+$[i]
  ACTION Balance: **String**[i] × $\mathbb{N}$[o]
  ACTION Alert: **String**[i] × $\mathbb{N}^+$[i]

BEHAVIOUR
  DOMAIN String $\rightarrowtail \mathbb{N}$ **INITIAL self** = {}

  Deposit(c, v) :   **POST**: c $\notin$ **dom self**^{pre} $\Rightarrow$ **self** = **self**^{pre} $\cup$ {c $\mapsto$ v}
                     $\wedge$ c $\in$ **dom self**^{pre} $\Rightarrow$ **self** = **self**^{pre} $\oplus$ {c $\rightarrow$ **self**^{pre}(c) + v}

  Transfer(o, d, v) : **PRE**: o $\neq$ d
                     CPRE: o $\in$ **dom self** $\wedge$ d $\in$ **dom self** $\wedge$ **self**(o) $\geq$ v
                     POST: **self** = **self**^{pre} $\oplus$ {o $\rightarrow$ **self**^{pre}(o) − v, d $\rightarrow$ **self**^{pre}(d) + v}

  Alert(c, m) :   **PRE**: c $\in$ **dom self**
                     CPRE: **self**(c) < m
                     POST: **self** = **self**^{pre}

  Balance(c,r) :   **PRE**: c $\in$ **dom self**
                     POST: **self** = **self**^{pre} $\wedge$ r = **self**(c)

Note: $F \cup \{X \mapsto Y\}$ is a function like F *adding* (X, Y), $F \oplus \{X \mapsto Y\}$ is a function like F *updating* the image of X with Y, $\mathbb{N}^+$ is the set of natural numbers except 0.

Fig. 1. The *Bank* shared resource specification.

Figure 1 depicts the shared resource specification of the running example: a simple API to provide access to bank accounts. There are four actions: Deposit that increases the balance of an account, Transfer for transferring funds between two accounts, Balance which returns the balance of an account, and Alert which is used to alert the caller to a low balance situation in an account. As an example, the Deposit action has two input parameters[1], a String (the account name), and a positive natural number (the amount).

The state of the Bank, specified under **DOMAIN**, is a partial function that relates an account number to its balance. The empty function is the initial state.

Each action is specified using a number of predicates: **PRE** specifies a precondition that must be satisfied for the action to be executed (otherwise its invocation fails, e.g., an exception should be raised by a Java implementation), **POST** expresses how the state is transformed: **self**^{pre} and **self** expresses the state before and after the execution of an action. More novel, the *concurrency precondition* **CPRE** predicate expresses a condition synchronization for *when* the action may be executed; an action invocation that satisfies the **PRE** predicate is suspended until the corresponding **CPRE** predicate holds.

As an example, an invoked Transfer action – for transferring an amount v from an account o to an account d – must specify different origin and destination accounts (precondition), and will be suspended until both accounts exist and the origin account has sufficient funds (the concurrency precondition). If the action is eventually executed, the post condition specifies that the balance of the origin account is reduced by v, and the balance of the destination account increases by v. In contrast, the Deposit(c,v) action has a true precondition and a true concurrency precondition (the defaults), meaning that every invocation succeeds and that the action can be executed at any time (in any state). When executed, it increases the balance of the account c with the amount v; note that the account c may not have existed until the execution of Deposit(c,v). The Balance(c,r) action returns (the output parameter r) the balance of the account parameter c, and the Alert(c,m) action suspends until the balance of the account c is less than m.

In the example below it is assumed that the actions are executed by independent processes a, b, c and d (expressed informally using the "||" operator). Due to the definition of the Bank shared resource, processes a and d suspend initially. However, the processes b and c are executable, creating accounts c1 and c2. Then process d becomes executable, which transfers 10 to account c1. Finally, the process a becomes executable.

a: Transfer(c1,c2,20) || b: Deposit(c1,10) || c: Deposit(c2,10) || d: Transfer(c2,c1,10)

3 Implementing Shared Resources

Shared resources can be implemented in many languages and using many different concurrency libraries. In the following, we focus on implementations in Java that use the CCLIB monitor library. Concretely, a Java class that implements the above resource specification should implement the following action methods:

---

[1] Input parameters are specified using the [i] qualifier; output parameters use the [o] qualifier.

```
void deposit(String c, int v);
void transfer(String o, String d, int v);
void alert(String c, int m);
int balance(String c);
```

The implementation of these methods must provide a behaviour compatible with the resource specification, e.g., a call to `alert(c,m)` should check that the account c exists and if not throw an exception (precondition check), and moreover block until the concurrency precondition holds (the account c has a balance less than m).

The CCLIB monitor library provides a monitor mechanism for Java programs, similar to the functionality provided by the Java `java.util.concurrent.locks` package:

```
m.enter();              // Acquire a monitor m
m.leave();              // Release the monitor m
cnd = m.newCond();      // Create a condition cnd from a monitor m
cnd.await();            // Temporarily suspend a thread
cnd.signal();           // resume a suspended thread
```

Exclusive access between a number of threads is arbitrated by invoking the method `enter()` on a monitor m, which permits access by exactly one thread. The monitor is released by calling the `leave()` method. A thread that has been granted monitor access may relinquish the monitor temporarily by invoking the `cnd.await()` method on a *condition* cnd, created from the monitor m. Another thread that has acquired the monitor may later give permission to a waiting thread to resume its execution by invoking the method `cnd.signal()`; this causes the signalled thread to be resumed (holding the monitor) when the thread that signalled it releases the monitor.

Using the CCLIB monitor library to implement a resource, we should create a number of data structures representing the state of the resource, and create a monitor which ensures that these data structures are accessed by no more than one thread at a time executing a method implementing a resource action. Moreover, we should create a number of conditions on which we should invoke the `await()` method to correctly implement condition synchronisation. The other threads that execute resource actions are then responsible for checking whether such suspended threads can be resumed, and if so, invoking the method `signal()` on the corresponding condition.

In Fig. 2 a typical Java implementation of the Transfer action is shown, together with (a part of) the declaration of the shared resource state. The attribute `accounts` associates account names with balances, and the attribute `monitor` stores a monitor object. Moreover, the attribute `waitingTransfers` associates an account name with a queue of waiting transfer requests (and waiting conditions). The `transfer` method first checks the precondition. Exclusive access is then requested and granted by the monitor (line 8). In lines (9) and (10) the concurrency precondition is checked. If false, a new object corresponding to the call to `transfer` is created (and a new condition), which is stored in a queue of waiting transfer requests[2]. On line (13) the executing thread blocks by calling the `await()` method of the new condition. Next, on line 15, it can be assumed that CPRE holds, either because it was true on line 4, or because the thread

---

[2] Note that the code sketch assumes that every account has a transfer queue.

```
1  // State attributes
2  final Monitor m;
3  final Map< String, FIFO<Transfer> > waitingTransfers;
4  final Map<String,Integer> accounts;
5
6  public void transfer(String o, String d, int v) {
7    if (o.equals(d)) throw new IllegalArgumentException(); // PRE
8    m.enter();  // Enforce single thread execution
9    if (!accounts.containsKey(o) || !accounts.containsKey(d) ||
10       accounts.get(o) < v) { // CPRE does not hold, block
11     Transfer transfer = new Transfer(o,d,v,m);
12     waitingTransfers.get(o).enqueue(transfer);
13     transfer.getCondition().await();
14   }
15   // CPRE holds here; establish POST
16   accounts.put(o,accounts.get(o)-v);
17   accounts.put(d,accounts.get(d)+v);
18
19   // After POST check if other threads can be resumed
20   if (!signalReadyTransfers()) signalAlerts();
21   m.leave();
22 }
```

Fig. 2. An implementation of the transfer action using the CCLIB monitor library.

suspended, and was later resumed by another thread. Lines (16) and (17) implement POST: the modification of the resource state. Next, line (20) attempts to resume a thread that had been previously suspended, either executing a transfer or alert action; resuming is realised by signalReadyTransfers and signalAlerts (not shown). Finally, exclusive access is released on line 21.

Common Implementation Mistakes. As can be seen, the task of implementing the Bank shared resource using the CCLIB monitor library is far from trivial. Students frequently make serious programming errors, which prevent shared resources from functioning correctly and safely. Apart from basic mistakes in implementing pure data calculations (e.g., CPRE checks and POST state modifications), students frequently use the monitor library incorrectly. Below we enumerate a subset of the informal coding rules which express restrictions on the *behaviour* of Java methods implementing shared resource actions. In subsequent sections we shall see how such rules are formalised in Prolog, making their meaning precise, and permitting checking whether resource implementations conform to these rules.

- exactly_one_enter: Action methods should call enter() exactly once.
- exactly_one_leave: Action methods should call leave() exactly once.
- enter_before_leave: Action methods may not release a monitor (leave()) before acquiring it (enter()).
- exactly_one_monitor_in_test: Action methods should use the same monitor.

- `not_access_before_monitor`: The resource state may be accessed only from threads holding the monitor, i.e., preceded by a call to `enter()`.
- `not_access_after_monitor`: The resource state may be accessed only from threads holding the monitor, i.e., accesses must occur before a call to `leave()`.
- `signals_inside_op`: An action method should check whether the CPRE of other actions have become true, and if so, should resume one such action thread.
- `zero_or_one_await`: An action method may call `await()` at most once.
- `no_operation_calls_in_operation`: An action method is not allowed to call a method implementing an action.

4 Trace Collection

Our approach to detect incorrect uses of the CCLIB and JCSP libraries entails as a first step collecting runtime traces from the implementation to verify, as it executes a JUnit test suite. To be able to check the properties in the previous section, a number of significant events must be observable: calls to methods implementing shared resource actions (e.g. calls to a method implementing the `Balance` action), creation of monitors and conditions, calls to (and returns from) monitor and condition methods such as `enter()`, `leave()`, `signal()`, and `await()`. In addition, accesses to the shared resource state, or data structures storing conditions, must also be observed.

The Byteman tool [4] is used to instrument the Java bytecode to emit events, and for logging them. To tailor which events are emitted, it is necessary to specify a set of tracing rules using a simple scripting language. For example, the rule to monitor a call (but not the return) to the `enter` method of a monitor is shown below:

```
RULE Entry to Monitor::enter
CLASS cclib.Monitor
METHOD enter
AT ENTRY
IF true
DO ByteManUtils.makeCall($CLASS,$METHOD,$*)
ENDRULE
```

The rule, named *Entry to Monitor::enter*, specifies that when the method `enter` in the class `cclib.Monitor` is called[3], a call to the `makeCall` method should be invoked, where the $CLASS and $METHOD parameters are Java strings corresponding to the class and method invoked, and $* corresponds to the source object whose `enter` method was invoked followed by all the arguments of the `enter` method. An analogous rule traced the return of a call to the `enter` method.

The `makeCall` helper method logs the corresponding event to a log file in the form of clauses of a Prolog predicate:

`eventAt(29,'Thread-3',call('cclib.Monitor','enter',['•104..'])).`

The `eventAt` predicate has three parameters: an event counter (29), the thread that invoked the call ('Thread-3'), and the event source (a call to `enter`).

---
[3] Byteman permits tracing invocation (entry) and exit (return or throw) of a method call.

The set of rules for monitoring a shared resource implemented using the CCLIB monitor library is comprised of 13 general rules which cater to the observation of e.g. calls to the methods of the CCLIB monitor library, as well as creation of monitors and conditions, and moreover observe the start of a test case being executed. This general set of rules is combined with a rule set specific for the resource being implemented, i.e., tracing the calls to action methods such as e.g. balance. Another set of Byteman rules specific to the implementation being checked observes accesses to shared resource state, and to data structures storing conditions. Using a Java reflection-based byte-code analysis the attributes of the class implementing the shared resource are extracted, and Byteman rules are generated to log reads and writes to these attributes. In Table 1 the rules for tracing an implementation is enumerated. As an example, it is assumed that the main state attribute storing accounts is named "accounts".

Table 1. Byteman rules for tracing an implementation of the Bank resource.

JAVA EVENT TO TRACE	WHAT IS TRACED	EXPLANATION
Generic rules – common for all specifications; written manually		
UnitTest.run	method entry	starting test case
new Monitor()	constructor entry & exit	creating monitor
m.newCond()	method entry & exit	creating condition
m.enter()	method entry & exit	acquire monitor
m.leave()	method entry & exit	release monitor
c.await()	method entry & exit	block thread
c.signal()	method entry & exit	signal thread to continue
Resource specific rules – generated automatically from the specification		
r.deposit(c,v)	method entry & exit & throw	action call
r.transfer(o,d,v)	method entry & exit & throw	action call
r.alert(c,m)	method entry & exit & throw	action call
r.balance(c)	method entry & exit & throw	action call
Implementation specific rules – generated automatically from an implementation		
accounts	attribute read & write	state access
...	attribute read & write	state access

5 Trace Analysis

The principal input to the trace analysis is the log file with trace events represented as Prolog predicates as explained in the previous section. A second input to the analysis is an encoding, as Prolog predicates, of the knowledge of the shared resource that the observed program tries to implement. Concretely, knowledge comprises an enumeration of the shared resource actions with arities, together with manually derived information regarding the behaviour of the shared resource, e.g., which action may, when executed, cause the CPRE of an another action to become true. Figure 3 depicts the information for the Bank example. The `operation_class` describes the name of the Java class that should implement the resource, and the `operation` predicate recognise calls to the shared resource action methods. The `cpreTrue` predicate enumerates the methods that have a trivially true CPRE. Next follows the predicates which express behavioural facts about the shared specification, and which cannot (yet) be derived automatically from the shared resource specification. The `mayThrowEarlyException` predicate enumerates the actions that are permitted to terminate with an exception without first acquiring the monitor. Transfer is such an action, since its precondition (the account parameters differ) does not refer to the shared resource state. Next, the `noCPREchange` predicate enumerates the actions whose execution can never cause the concurrency precondition of other actions to become true. Note that this holds trivially for actions that do not change the shared resource state (e.g., both Balance and Alert).

```
operation_class('BankMonitor').      cpreTrue('deposit').
operation('deposit',2).              cpreTrue('balance').
operation('balance',1).              mayThrowEarlyException('transfer').
operation('alert',2).                noCPREchange('balance').
operation('transfer',3).             noCPREchange('alert').
```

Fig. 3. Prolog facts concerning the Bank shared resource actions.

As a first phase in the analysis of the trace log, the sequence of events `Events` directly caused by the call of a Java method implementing a shared resource action is collected as clauses of the `opCall(Call,Return,Events)` predicate. The `Call` and `Return` parameters are the events corresponding to the call and return of the action method (i.e., as recognised by the `operation` predicate described above), and `Events` is an ordered list of logged events occurring between the call and return events which are *executed by the thread that invoked the action method* (event ordering is determined by the counter parameter of the `eventAt` predicate). Note that a return event can correspond either to a true return from a method, or an abnormal exit due to an uncaught exception, or the symbol `blocking` signifying that the call had not terminated when the corresponding test case terminated (e.g., due to a test case timeout). Note that collecting such event lists entails filtering out events from other threads, as events from all threads are interleaved in the trace log. The set of such predicate clauses (one for each call to an action method during the executed test suite) is tabled [2] to improve analysis speed.

5.1 Formalising Coding Rules

Coding rules are encoded directly in SWI-Prolog, typically as the negation of some desirable property. That is, the Prolog rule tries to find a counterexample to the rule in the event log. Let us examine as an example the rule that checks that a call to a method implementing a shared resource action must acquire a monitor exactly once (`exactly_one_enter`); its negation is shown encoded as a Prolog predicate below.

```
1  not_exactly_one_enter(OpMethod,Enters) :-
2    isOpExec(OpCall),  OpCall = opCall(Call,_,OpInsts),
3    include(isMonitorEnterCall,OpInsts,Enters), length(Enters,Len),
4    callMethod(Call,OpMethod),
5    (Len ≡ 0 → \+ mayThrowEarlyException(OpMethod);   Len \≡ 1).
```

In line 1, the predicate is parametric on the parameters OpMethod (in which method was the rule violated) and Enters (a list of monitors which were acquired). In line 2, the predicate code retrieves a tabled operation call. In line 3, OpCall comprises the call Call, and possibly return events, together with all intermediate logged events OpInts caused by the thread executing the call. Next, in line 4, the predicate include extracts the events corresponding to acquiring monitors Enters during the execution of the call. In line 5, the number of such events is assigned to the Len logical variable. Next, in line 6, callMethod assigns the name of the method call to the OpMethod logical variable. Finally, there is a branch: either (line 7) the number of monitor events was zero, in which case the goal mayThrowEarlyException(OpMethod) *must not* be provable (i.e., the action is *not* allowed to raise an exception without acquiring the monitor), or (line 8) the number of events is different than one (corresponding to multiple monitor enters). The coding of the isMonitorEnterCall predicate which recognises events corresponding to monitor enters is trivial:

```
isMonitorEnterCall(TimedEvent) :-
  event(TimedEvent,Event),
  callClass(Event,'cclib.Monitor'),
  callMethod(Event,'enter').
```

Other concurrency-coding rules are specified in the same manner. As a second example, let us examine the informal coding rule (signals_inside_op) which require that the signal() method be called when appropriate. Deciding when it is appropriate to do so may require a complicated calculation whether the state changes of the resuming thread cause the post condition POST of the resumed thread to become true. The formalisation of the negation of the rule in Prolog instead identifies action methods that *never* (in no execution) call the signal() method on a condition. This is a far weaker condition, but arguably more useful for identifying conceptual misunderstandings in how the library API is to be used: perhaps the student simply has not understood the role of the signal() and await() methods.

Note that an invoked action may, for example, not call signal() simply because there is no suspended thread to resume (or because no thread has a true CPRE). However, if a sufficient number of varied tests are executed, eventually in some execution, the signal() method should have been called. The negation of this rule is expressed as the Prolog predicate below:

```
zero_signals_inside_op(Op) :-
  operation(Op,_),
  findall(NumCalls,
     ( isOpExec(opCall(Call,_,OpInsts)), callMethod(Call,Op),
       include(isSignalCall,OpInsts,AllSignalCalls),
       length(AllSignalCalls,NumCalls) ),
  AllNumCalls),
```

```
list_sum(AllNumCalls,SumCalls), SumCalls is 0,
\+ notInChain(Op).

notInChain(Method) :- cpreTrue(Method), noCPREchange(Method).
```

The Op parameter will be bound to the method that never makes a call to `signal()`. The rule finds all calls to the `signal()` method, inside the execution of the originating method call, counts them, and asserts that it is not the case that the action never needs to call signal (`notInChain(Op)`). The `notInChain(Op)` predicate is true if a method has a true CPRE and cannot modify the CPRE of another call (`noCPREchange(Method)`). Note that it is necessary to include the check that the method CPRE is true, as otherwise the originating method call may form part of a chain of suspended calls being resumed.

Finally, let us examine the encoding in Prolog of the rule which checks that the shared resource state (and condition data structures) is accessed only whilst having acquired the monitor. We express the violation of this property as two predicates, i.e., detecting accesses before holding the monitor and detecting accesses after releasing the monitor. The coding of the second predicate is shown below:

```
access_after_monitor(OpMethod,Accesses) :-
  isOpExec(OpCall), OpCall = opCall(Call,_,OpAccesses),
  callMethod(Call,OpMethod),
  after(isMonitorLeaveReturn,OpAccesses,PreAccesses),
  include(readOrWrite,PreAccesses,Accesses), Accesses \= [],
  callMethod(Call,OpMethod).

readOrWrite(TimedEvent) :- event(TimedEvent,read(_,_,_,_)).
readOrWrite(TimedEvent) :- event(TimedEvent,write(_,_,_,_)).
```

The predicate identifies all reads or writes to class attributes (remember that only accesses to attributes are logged), and asserts that after the moment when the monitor is released, there is a non-empty list of such accesses thus detecting a rule violation. Note that the list of accesses is "returned" as a predicate parameter, to permit debugging.

6 Evaluation

This section provides an evaluation of the behavioural code rule checker by applying it to the task of checking implementations of the Bank example. The Bank example was used as a practical exercise in an undergraduate course on concurrency. The students had to write an implementation of the shared resource using both the CCLIB and the JCSP libraries. To help students submit solutions of a reasonable quality, the submission Web site runs a fixed test suite on each solution, and reports errors to students. Correction of submitted solutions has traditionally been done by running additional tests (derived using property-based testing [3]), and by manual code inspection of the implementations to find violations of coding rules.

6.1 Performance Metrics

In total 209 solutions implemented using CCLIB were handed in, and out of those, 35 solutions had failed the fixed test suite (17%). The average solution had around 240 lines of code. The fixed test suite consisted of 36 tests (with 316 action calls), comprising a number of handwritten test cases together with a number of additional tests automatically derived from the failures observed in implementations submitted during a voluntary pre-submission phase. The resulting test suite was used to drive the event collection process.

The computer used to run the performance benchmarks was a Leno ThinkPad Yoga X1 with a Intel i7-10510U CPU (with 4 cores) and 16GB of memory, running under Ubuntu 20.04. SWI-Prolog version 8.4.2 was used for trace analysis, and Byteman 4.0.18 was used for trace collection.

For every submitted solution, the attributes of the class implementing the resource were computed using Java reflection, and Byteman rules were automatically generated to trace reads and writes to these attributes. This rule set specific to a particular implementation was combined with the general Byteman rule set (e.g., comprising calls to the library API) which are invariant (do not depend on a particular programming exercise). The average number of Byteman rules for these 209 implementations was 70[4].

On average running the fixed test suite on an implementation, and collecting the runtime trace, took 5.5 (real elapsed user) seconds. This figure is dominated by the requirement to frequently wait during the execution of a test case; to judge that an action call is blocking the test harness has to wait a heuristic amount of time. The number of events logged, in the average case, were 39400. However, this is due to a single implementation that was exceptionally buggy and whose execution resulted in around 7.5 million logged events. Excluding that implementation the average number of logged events was 3860.

Eleven (11) coding rules were formulated in Prolog in around 200 lines of code. The average execution time for the analysis of an implementation (excluding the extremely buggy implementation previously mentioned for which the analysis failed) was 5.1 (real elapsed user) seconds.

6.2 Examples of Analysis Output

To exemplify the analysis, many students had problem coping with the checking of the precondition of Alert(c), i.e.: **PRE**: c ∈ **dom self**. A good implementation of the precondition check would (i) first acquire the monitor (since the precondition concerns the shared resource state), (ii) then check the condition, and (iii) if it failed raise an exception *but first* releasing the monitor. A common erroneous implementation was to check the precondition without acquiring the monitor (and removing the need to release the monitor), which permitted the test suite to pass:

```
public void alert(String c) {
  if (!accounts.containsKey(c)) throw new IllegalArgumentException();
```

---

[4] The number of rules vary as the implementations are free to organise the shared state in different ways, and Byteman rules must trace all such accesses.

```
...
}
```
giving rise to an error signalled by the rule checker:

```
*** ERROR: solution xxxx satisfies access_before_monitor but should not:
    operation alert has reads/writes [read(alert,accounts)]
```

Another common error was to acquire the monitor correctly, and check the precondition, and if it failed, the exception was raised but forgetting to release the monitor first. This caused a test suite failure. However, unfortunately the testing error was reported in the next action call, since it was unable to acquire the monitor (which was never released by the previous call), thus greatly confusing the students. Example code:

```
public void alert(String c) {
  mutex.enter();
  ... // complex code checking the state if c exists
  if (!found) throw new IllegalArgumentException();
  ...
}
```

Such bugs were detected by rule checker since the implementation failed the property `return_implies_not_exactly_one_leave` that checks that upon action return (or throw) `leave()` has been called exactly once.

6.3 Quality of Analysis

Table 2 summarizes the program errors detected by the automatic analysis. In total 77 implementations failed at least one property; note that it is common for implementations to fail multiple properties.

Table 2. Errors detected by the analysis.

any_property_failed	77 (35%)
return_implies_not_exactly_one_leave	62 (30%)
not_exactly_one_enter	54 (26%)
access_before_monitor	42 (20%)
access_after_monitor	36 (17%)
more_than_one_leave	26 (12%)
number_of_enters_and_leaves_differs	22 (11%)
zero_signals_inside_op	21 (10%)
nonzero_operation_calls_in_operation	15 (7%)
multiple_awaits	4 (2%)
not_exactly_one_monitor_in_test	1 (1%)

A strict comparison with manual correction turned out to be impossible. Early trials showed that errors were detected much more reliably using the automatic behavioural analysis than by manual code inspection, and therefore inevitably automatic analysis was adopted as an integral part of the correction process. In essence, manual correction became largely an exercise in confirming the presence of an error detected by the automatic analysis and checking more stylistic coding criteria, e.g., a lack of comments.

Even though manual correction had access to the result of the automatic analysis, we can still evaluate the efficacy of the automatic analysis by focusing on the cases where the manual correction corrected analysis errors, or identified additional errors.

First, no false positives were detected; all buggy implementations detected by automated analysis were confirmed by manual correction to be buggy. However, in one case, the error indicated was misleading. The property prop_zero_signals_inside_op tries to detect the absence of calls to the signal() method even though needed. The property simply counts the number of such calls, and if the underlying implementation was very buggy, in some cases the method was never called during the test run although the call was present in the source code. The tool reported that the implementation was buggy (correctly), and that signals property failed (correctly, no signals were issued), but raised doubts about the implementation of signalling (possibly incorrectly).

Second, the tool diagnostics can be improved. There were several cases where manual correction just reported one of several bugs detected by the automatic analysis, although it had access to the generated analysis report. This is understandable, as a single program bug can give rise to multiple coding rules failing.

Thirdly, there were a small number of implementations (around 5%) where automatic analysis failed to detect a real problem (a false negative), which was detected during manual correction. There were two causes for such problems:

- The test suite run did not check all the functionality of the shared resource. Concretely, it failed to execute any call to the balance(c) method when the account c had not been created. As a result, no bugs were detected in the implementation of the precondition check for balance(c). Clearly, any verification method which relies on behavioural data for its analysis should carefully consider the scenarios in which the program-under-verification is executed.
- Naturally, manual correction pointed out "style errors which are not behavioural errors". As an example, in instructions to students, it is frowned upon to check a concurrency precondition within a loop, and manual correction regularly finds and penalises such code. Whether our behavioural analysis points out such errors depends on whether a call to await() – corresponding to a failed CPRE check – is ever executed twice. As an example, the following code fragment was not signalled to be faulty by the automatic analysis but was penalised during manual correction:

```
while (!found && i<accounts.length) {
  account = accounts[i++];
  if (account.name().equals(c)) {
    found = true;
    if (account.amount() < transferSum) cond.await();
  }
}
```

7 Related Work

The work presented here is part of a broader effort to improve the quality of concurrent Java applications through the use of formal models. For example, code synthesis is explored in [12] and testing in [6].

Runtime analysis and verification has already been applied to concurrent systems [5]. In [1] potential deadlocks are detected for programs using semaphores and monitors as synchronization mechanisms. In [11] trace analysis is used to discover locking rules used by the Linux kernel and automatically generate documentation for them.

A key feature of our proposal is the use of APIs to reduce the "granularity" of the traces. In [15] legal sequences of calls to an API are specified in temporal logic and then verified using model checking. In [13] coding rules were also encoded as Prolog predicates, as in this work. However, the rules only consider structural properties of C++ programs, using the AST and static analyses to extract information regarding the program-under-study instead of using behavioural tracing as in this work.

The SimRacer [17] tool analyzes traces using happens-before analysis to identify potential order violations according to test oracles provided by the developers. The analysis is done by using a problem specific algorithm that cannot be easily generalized. Cafa [10] detects a specific form of order violation in event-driven programs resulting in a use-after-free violation. Finally [14] monitors execution traces in JavaScript client code that executes multiple callbacks asynchronously and detected events, such as cookies updates, that cannot be reordered. In this case, authors describe the analysis with a set of formal rules specifically designed for the problem.

8 Discussion and Future Work

This article has described our approach to checking code guidelines for concurrent code, which entails logging significant program events during runtime, and analysing such logs post-execution to find situations where the code guidelines, expressed as restrictions on program *behaviour*, are violated by the program-under-study.

The resulting coding rule checking approach is "cheap" in terms of development effort. General purpose tools such as Byteman and SWI-Prolog are reused for event logging and trace analysis. A mature logic programming language implementation like SWI-Prolog is helpful in expressing coding rules cleanly and succinctly, and in implementing reasonable efficient code search procedures for detecting violations of the coding rules. Although coding such rules in Prolog is a learned skill, in our experience it is a quickly learned skill. Moreover, the manner in which Prolog facilitates expressive queries about the program state (the event logs) made debugging faulty coding rules a quick and painless task.

The resulting coding rule checker was evaluated in a study in which a large number of shared resource implementations written by undergraduate students (as part of a course on concurrent programming in Java) were checked for violations of concurrency coding rules. The results were very positive: real bugs were frequently found which had not been detected by traditional manual code inspection, with little effort. Since that initial evaluation the coding rule checker has been adopted as a standard correction tool in the undergraduate course.

The study also revealed issues for future work. We need to more carefully consider how the program-under-study is executed during the logging phase. Obviously if a test suite does not stimulate a piece of buggy code, then the bug will stay hidden from a behavioural analysis. Secondly, a number of code guidelines are more natural to express as restrictions on code, rather than code behaviour. For this reason we would like to experiment with static analysis-based code checking too, and evaluate whether the costs (in terms of development effort as well as in terms of false positives or negatives) merit either replacing the behavioural analysis, or complementing it.

Acknowledgements. This work has been partly funded by the Ministerio de Ciencia e Innovación of Spain (SAFER project, ref. PID2019-104735RB-C44).

References

1. Agarwal, R., Stoller, S.D.: Run-time detection of potential deadlocks for programs with locks, semaphores, and condition variables. In: Proceedings of the 2006 Workshop on Parallel and Distributed Systems: Testing and Debugging, PADTAD 2006, pp. 51–60. ACM, New York (2006)
2. Chen, W., Warren, D.S.: Tabled evaluation with delaying for general logic programs. J. ACM **43**(1), 20–74 (1996)
3. Claessen, K., Hughes, J.: Quickcheck: a lightweight tool for random testing of haskell programs. In: Proceedings of the Fifth ACM SIGPLAN International Conference on Functional Programming, ICFP 2000, pp. 268–279. ACM, New York (2000)
4. Dinn, A.E.: Flexible, dynamic injection of structured advice using byteman. In: Borba, P., Chiba, S. (eds.) Companion Volume of the 10th International Conference on Aspect-Oriented Software Development, AOSD 2011, pp. 41–50. ACM (2011)
5. Falcone, Y., Krstic, S., Reger, G., Traytel, D.: A taxonomy for classifying runtime verification tools. Int. J. Softw. Tools Technol. Transf. **23**(2), 255–284 (2021). https://doi.org/10.1007/S10009-021-00609-Z
6. Fredlund, L., Mariño, J., Alborodo, R.N.N., Herranz, A.: A testing-based approach to ensure the safety of shared resource concurrent systems. Proc. Inst. Mech. Eng. Part O: J. Risk Reliab. (2015)
7. Herlihy, M.P., Wing, J.M.: Linearizability: a correctness condition for concurrent objects. ACM Trans. Program. Lang. Syst. **12**(3), 463–492 (1990)
8. Herranz, A., Mariño, J.: A verified implementation of priority monitors in Java. In: Proceedings of the 2011 International Conference on Formal Verification of Object-Oriented Software, FoVeOOS 2011, pp. 160–177. Springer, Heidelberg (2012)
9. Herranz, A., Mariño, J., Carro, M., Moreno Navarro, J.J.: Modeling concurrent systems with shared resources. In: Alpuente, M., Cook, B., Joubert, C. (eds.) Formal Methods for Industrial Critical Systems. LNCS, vol. 5825, pp. 102–116. Springer, Cham (2009)
10. Hsiao, C.H., et al.: Race detection for event-driven mobile applications. SIGPLAN Not. **49**(6), 326–336 (2014). https://doi.org/10.1145/2666356.2594330
11. Lochmann, A., Schirmeier, H., Borghorst, H., Spinczyk, O.: Lockdoc: trace-based analysis of locking in the linux kernel. In: Candea, G., van Renesse, R., Fetzer, C. (eds.) Proceedings of the 14th EuroSys Conference 2019, Dresden, Germany, pp. 11:1–11:15. ACM (2019)
12. Mariño, J., Alborodo, R.N.N., Fredlund, L., Herranz, Á.: Synthesis of verified concurrent Java components from formal models. Softw. Syst. Model. (2016)

13. Marpons-Ucero, G., Mariño-Carballo, J., Carro, M., Herranz-Nieva, Á., Moreno-Navarro, J.J., Fredlund, L.: Automatic coding rule conformance checking using logic programming. In: PADL 2008. LNCS, vol. 4902, pp. 18–34. Springer, Cham (2008)
14. Mutlu, E., Tasiran, S., Livshits, B.: Detecting Javascript races that matter. In: Proceedings of the 2015 10th Joint Meeting on Foundations of Software Engineering, ESEC/FSE 2015, pp. 381–392. Association for Computing Machinery, New York (2015). https://doi.org/10.1145/2786805.2786820
15. Song, F., Touili, T.: Model-checking software library API usage rules. In: Johnsen, E.B., Petre, L. (eds.) Integrated Formal Methods, 10th International Conference, IFM 2013, Turku, Finland, 10–14 June 2013. LNCS, vol. 7940, pp. 192–207. Springer, Cham (2013)
16. Welch, P.H., Brown, N., Moores, J., Chalmers, K., Sputh, B.H.C.: Integrating and extending JCSP. In: McEwan, A.A., Schneider, S.A., Ifill, W., Welch, P.H. (eds.) The 30th Communicating Process Architectures Conference, CPA 2007. Concurrent Systems Engineering Series, vol. 65, pp. 349–370. IOS Press (2007)
17. Yu, T., Srisa-an, W., Rothermel, G.: Simracer: an automated framework to support testing for process-level races. In: Proceedings of the 2013 International Symposium on Software Testing and Analysis, ISSTA 2013, p. 167–177. Association for Computing Machinery, New York (2013). https://doi.org/10.1145/2483760.2483771

A Weighted Bipolar Argumentation Framework and Its ASP-Based Implementation

Yan Yan[1], Junru Li[2], Fangzhou Liu[2], Zerong Wang[2], and Zhizheng Zhang[2,3](✉)

[1] School of Cyber Science and Engineering, Southeast University, Nanjing 211189, China
[2] School of Computer Science and Engineering, Southeast University, Nanjing 211189, China
seu_zzz@seu.edu.cn
[3] Key Laboratory of New Generation Artificial Intelligence Technology and Its Interdisciplinary Applications (Southeast University), Ministry of Education, Nanjing, China

Abstract. A novel Weighted Bipolar Argumentation Framework (WBAF) is proposed in this paper, which deals with attack and support relations equally and takes into account the weight of arguments and relations, and is a more general extension of the classical AF. The semantics of WBAF - minimum-penalty preferred extensions is introduced, which refers to the maximal acceptable argument set inclusions. Furthermore, this paper designs and realizes an ASP-based WBAF reasoning tool - ASPWBART (Answer Set Programming Based Weighted Bipolar Argumentation Reasoning Tool). This tool supports the incorporation of weighted arguments and weighted relations, and culminates in the generation of minimum-penalty preferred extensions.

Keywords: Argumentation framework · Answer set programming · Weighted argumentation · Bipolar argumentation

1 Introduction

The Abstract Argumentation Framework (AF) [10] proposed by Dung is the core form for many applications in the field of abstract argumentation, which considers the arguments and the attacks between them. Each internally consistent subset output by AF is called an extension [19], and each type of extensions corresponds to one semantics. Various studies have extended AF from different perspectives [28], including semantics [1], expressivity [18,20] and algorithms [9]. Moreover, Answer set Programming (ASP), a declarative programming paradigm, is recognized as a powerful tool for knowledge representation and reasoning in AF.

Cayrol C and Lagasquie-Schiex M C proposed Bipolar Argumentation Framework (BAF) [4] to handle both the attack and support relations. However, their method of transforming support relations into additional attack relations cannot deal with the relations equally [5]. Potyka proposed a new deductive semantics that symmetrically defines attack and support relations to address this issue [25]. On the other hand, Bench-Capon proposed Value-based Argumentation Framework (VAF) [2], arguing that the strength of each argument is different; while Dunne et al. proposed Weighted Argumentation Framework (WAF) [11], focusing on the weight of attack relations. On the basis of BAF and WAF, the concept of Weighted Bipolar Argumentation Framework (WBAF) is proposed. Most of the WBAFs only consider one of the weights of arguments or relations [7,21,22,24,26]. However, Trust-affected BWAF (T-BWAF) proposed in [23] takes the both weights into account, which focuses on the acceptability of a single argument. [14] proposed General Argumentation Framework (GAF), encompassing AF, BAF, WAF and WBAF, but did not put forward the corresponding semantics.

In summary, the various WBAF models and their variants currently proposed are not without flaws. These deficiencies manifest in several ways: some fail to comprehensively address additional information (two relations and two weights); others neglect to consider the acceptability of the argument sets; and still others lack a dedicated semantic structure. However, in the practical context of case-based reasoning, it is customary to encounter a variety of elements including deterministic evidence, uncertain testimonies, relations between them, as well as the associated credibility levels. The objective is to identify the complete and acceptable evidence chains through argumentation. Extension semantics, as another commonly used semantics, is mainly used to evaluate the acceptability of argument sets. Therefore, we propose a new WBAF and its preferred semantics based on the principles of extension semantics, which enable the comprehensive processing of additional information and the assessment of the argument sets' acceptability. Moreover, a reasoning tool based on ASP (ASPWBART - Answer Set Programming Based Weighted Bipolar Argumentation Reasoning Tool) is designed, enabling users to input weighted arguments and weighted relations, upon which it autonomously performs reasoning in WBAF.

This paper is organized as follows: the basics of two classical argumentation frameworks are recalled in Sect. 2. The definitions of WBAF and its semantics are introduced and compared with other frameworks in Sect. 3. Section 4 introduces the implementation of ASPWBART and evaluates its efficiency. Section 5 summarizes conclusions and gives future prospects.

2 Background Knowledge

Dung's Abstract Argumentation Framework (AF) has been instrumental in the study of argumentation, providing a structured approach to identifying consistent sets of arguments. This section revisits the essential concepts of AF and its extensions, which serve as the theoretical basis for our proposed Weighted Bipolar Argumentation Framework (WBAF).

2.1 Argumentation Framework

We begin with a concise review of Dung's AF [13], which elegantly captures the fundamental aspects of argument interactions through a model of attacks between arguments.

Definition 1. *A Dung Abstract Argumentation Framework is a pair $F = (A, R)$, where A is a finite set of arguments and $R \subseteq A \times A$ represents the attack relations between* arguments. a attacks b if the pair $(a,b) \in R$. A set $S \subseteq A$ attacks b if $(a,b) \in R$ for some $a \in S$. A set $S \subseteq A$ defends a if S attacks each b with $(b,a) \in R$.

The semantics of the argumentation framework is defined as function σ. For an argumentation framework F, the set $S \in \sigma(F)$ is called a σ-extension of F. Some acceptance criteria have been proposed, including grounded, complete, preferred, stable, semi-stable and ideal semantics. Preferred semantics can be regarded as the maximal set inclusions among the acceptable argument sets, which align more closely with the objective in the context of case reasoning scenarios. Therefore, we focus on the preferred extensions ($\sigma = prf$). In order to illustrate the definition of preferred extension, it is necessary to clarify the definitions of conflict-free extension ($\sigma = cf$) and admissible extension ($\sigma = adm$).

Definition 2. *Let $F = (A, R)$ be an AF. A set $S \subseteq A$ is conflict-free, if there are no $a, b \in S$ with $(a, b) \in R$. A set $S \subseteq A$ is admissible, if $S \in cf(F)$ and S defends each $a \in S$. A set $S \subseteq A$ is preferred, if $S \in adm(F)$ and there is no $T \supset S$ such that $T \in adm(F)$.*

From the above definition, we can see that preferred extensions can be regarded as the maximum set inclusions among the admissible extensions.

2.2 Bipolar Argumentation Framework

Building upon the established foundation of AF, the BAF extends the model to include support relations, offering a more nuanced representation of argumentation. This advancement acknowledges the supportive as well as confrontational dimensions of arguments.

Definition 3. *A Bipolar Argumentation Framework is a tuple $F = (A, Att, Sup)$, where A is a finite set of arguments, $Att \subseteq A \times A$ represents the attack relations and $Sup \subseteq A \times A$ represents the support relations. $Att(A) \subseteq \{B|(B, A) \in Att\}$ denotes the set of attackers of A, and $Sup(A) \subseteq \{B|(B, A) \in Sup\}$ denotes the set of supporters of A.*

In order to achieve equal treatment of attack and support relations, we refer to the method proposed by Potyka [25]. For convenience, Potyka employs labellings to clarify the definition, a method that has been demonstrated to be equivalent to the extension approach [3]. A labelling is a function $L : A \rightarrow \{in, out, und\}$ which assigns a label to each argument, indicating accepted, rejected and undecided respectively. On this basis, we can provide the definition of deductive extension ($\sigma = ded$).

Definition 4. *Let $F = (A, Att, Sup)$ be a BAF. We call a labelling L deductive, if it satisfies that for all $a \in A$,*

- *if $L(a) = in$, then $L(b) = out$ for all $b \in Att(a)$;*
- *if $L(a) = out$, then $L(b) = out$ for all $b \in Sup(a)$;*
- *if $L(b) = in$ for some $b \in Att(a)$, then $L(a) = out$;*
- *if $L(b) = in$ for some $b \in Sup(a)$, then $L(a) = in$.*

A set $S = \{a|a \in A, L(a) = in\}$ where L is a deductive labelling is deductive.

As can be seen from the above definition, a labelling can correspond to an extension. Similar to the definition of preferred semantics in AF, the preferred semantics in BAF on the basis of deductive semantics are defined as follows ($\sigma = prf_{ded}$).

Definition 5. *Let $F = (A, Att, Sup)$ be a BAF. For a deductive set $S \in ded(F)$, $S \in prf_{ded}(F)$ if there is no $T \supset S$ such that $T \in ded(F)$.*

In BAF, preferred extensions can be regarded as the maximum set inclusions among all deductive extensions.

3 Weighted Bipolar Argumentation Framework

Different from the above argumentation frameworks, on one hand, this paper attempts to consider attack and support relations equally; on the other hand, this paper tries to consider both the weight of arguments and the weight of relations. Therefore, we propose a new Weighted Bipolar Argumentation Framework, which will be introduced and evaluated in detail in this chapter.

3.1 Relevant Definitions

Definition 6. *A Weighted Bipolar Argumentation Framework is a tuple $F = (A, Att, Sup, w_A, w_{Att}, w_{Sup})$ where (A, Att, Sup) is a BAF, $w_A : A \to \mathbb{R}_{\geq 0}$ is a function that assigns a non-negative real number to each argument, and $w_{Att} : Att \to \mathbb{R}_{\geq 0}$ ($w_{Sup} : Sup \to \mathbb{R}_{\geq 0}$) is a function that assigns a non-negative real number to each attack (support).*

In line with the aforementioned definitions, the WBAF introduced in this study takes into account the weight of arguments and relations, which can be interpreted as their acceptability. [12] presented a traditional methodology for weights within the context of WAF, where the central notion is the inconsistency budget, signifying the degree of inconsistency that is deemed tolerable. Building upon this approach, this paper proposes the concept of minimum-penalty deductive semantics in WBAF ($\sigma = mpded$). To illustrate this semantics, we first introduce the concepts of violate and penalty.

Definition 7. *Given a weighted bipolar argumentation framework $F = (A, Att, Sup, w_A, w_{Att}, w_{Sup})$ and an argument set $S \subseteq A$, the corresponding bipolar argumentation framework is $F^{(BAF)} = (A, Att, Sup)$. For an argument $a \in A$, if $a \notin S$, we say a is violated in S. For a relation $(a, b) \in Att \cup Aup$, if (a, b) results in S failing to satisfy the deductive semantics in $F^{(BAF)}$, we say (a, b) is violated corresponding to S. In other words, an attack $(a, b) \in Att$ is violated corresponding to S, if $a \in S$ and $b \in S$; a support $(a, b) \in Sup$ is violated corresponding to S, if $a \in S$ and $b \notin S$. Then the penalty of S in F is defined as:*

$$penalty_F(S) = \sum_{a \in \bar{S}} w_A(a) + \sum_{att \in \overline{Att_S}} w_{Att}(att) + \sum_{sup \in \overline{Sup_S}} w_{Sup}(sup), \tag{1}$$

where $\bar{S}$ represents the set of arguments which are violated in S, and $\overline{Att_S}$ and $\overline{Sup_S}$ represent the set of attacks and set of supports which are violated corresponding to S respectively.

From an intuitive perspective, when arguments or relations contravene the constraints established within the argumentation framework, their corresponding weights are factored into the computation of penalty values. We aim to minimize the overall value of these penalties. Next, the definition of minimum-penalty deductive extension in WBAF is given.

Definition 8. *Given a weighted bipolar argumentation framework $F = (A, Att, Sup, w_A, w_{Att}, w_{Sup})$, a set $S \subseteq A$ is minimum-penalty deductive if there is no $T \subseteq A$ such that $penalty_F(T) < penalty_F(S)$.*

In line with the preceding definition, it is feasible to establish the preferred semantics in WBAF, grounded on the principles of minimum-penalty deductive semantics ($\sigma = prf_{mpded}$).

Definition 9. *Let $F = (A, Att, Sup, w_A, w_{Att}, w_{Sup})$ be a weighted bipolar argumentation framework, for a minimum-penalty deductive set $S \in mpded(F)$, $S \in prf_{mpded}(F)$ if there is no $T \supset S$ such that $T \in mpded(F)$.*

An AF can be described as a directed graph where arguments are represented as nodes and relations are represented as arrows. In a similar vein, the WBAF can be conceptualized as a directed graph through the incorporation of numerical values to nodes and arrows to denote the associated weights. Elements that are not marked with numbers are considered to have a weight of 0. For ease of representation, we use α to represent the case where the weight is positive infinite. Under ideal conditions, when the weight value is α, the corresponding relation or argument must be accepted. However, if such argument or relation is violated in reality, its penalty value will still be taken into account.

Example 1. As shown in Fig. 1, each node a_i represents an argument, the solid arrow represents attack relation, and the dashed arrow represents support relation. Furthermore, the number on each arrow represents the weight of the relation, and the number next to each node represents the weight of the argument. In the succeeding sections of this paper, F_{eg1} consistently denotes the WBAF pertaining to Example 1. According to the definition, $prf_{mpded}(F_{eg1}) = \{\{a_1, a_3, a_4, a_5\}\}$ contains one argument set whose penalty is 0.

3.2 Semantic Comparison

We will contrast the prf_{mpded} semantics in WBAF with prf semantics in AF and prf_{ded} semantics in BAF from two distinct perspectives, to realize the evaluation of prf_{mpded} semantics. To facilitate comprehension, we employ Example 1 for illustrative purposes.

On one hand, we weaken WBAF to AF and BAF, and compare their semantics to evaluate the expressivity of the preferred semantics in WBAF.

$F_{eg1} = (A, Att, Sup, w_A, w_{Att}, w_{Sup})$ can be projected to the corresponding AF $F_{eg1}^{(AF)} = (A, Att)$ (Fig. 2) and BAF $F_{eg1}^{(BAF)} = (A, Att, Sup)$ (Fig. 3) as follows.

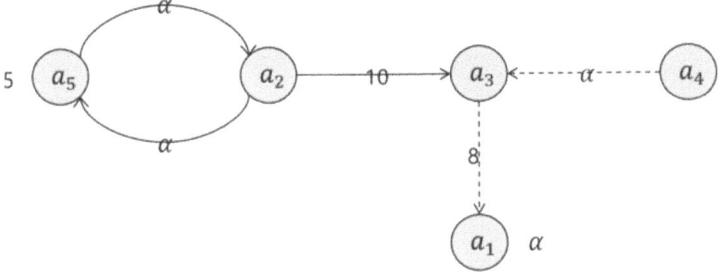

Fig. 1. An example of WBAF (Example 1)

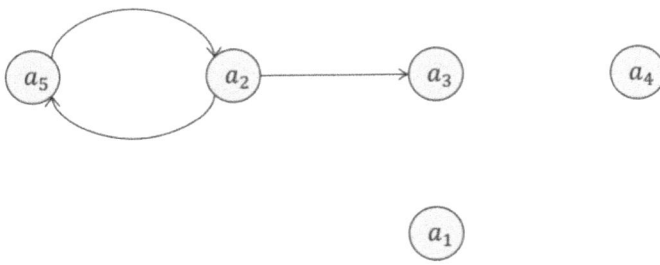

Fig. 2. WBAF mapped to AF (Example 1)

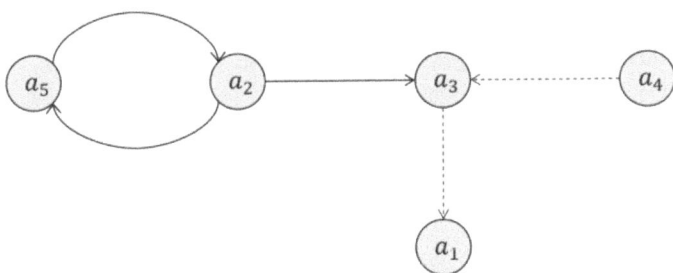

Fig. 3. WBAF mapped to BAF (Example 1)

The corresponding extensions are calculated in these frameworks[1] as shown in Table 1. "-" indicates that the semantics is not defined in the current argumentation framework.

As can be seen from Table 1, the preferred extension set in WBAF is a subset of the preferred extension set in AF or in BAF. Intuitively, the preferred semantics in WBAF considers more constraints than those in other frameworks, resulting in a more limited extension set. Despite the numerous inclusive relationships depicted in Table 1, it is essential to recognize that these are not absolute. Considering the essential difference

---
[1] Please find the calculation program from https://github.com/11neflibata/ASPWBART/tree/main/experiment.

Table 1. Preferred extensions in different frameworks

	prf	prf_{ded}	prf_{mpded}
$F_{eg1}^{(AF)}$	$\{\{a_1,a_2,a_4\}, \{a_1,a_3,a_4,a_5\}\}$	-	-
$F_{eg1}^{(BAF)}$	-	$\{\{a_1,a_2\}, \{a_1,a_3,a_4,a_5\}\}$	-
F_{eg1}	-	-	$\{\{a_1,a_3,a_4,a_5\}\}$

that AF only deals with attacks and BAF/WBAF deals with both attacks and supports, it becomes straightforward to present counter-examples.

Theorem 1. *For a WBAF $F = (A, Att, Sup, w_A, w_{Att}, w_{Sup})$, the corresponding BAF $F^{(BAF)} = (A, Att, Sup)$, when the minimum penalty in F is 0, there exists $prf_{mpded}(F) \subseteq prf_{ded}(F^{(BAF)})$.*

Proof. When the minimum penalty in F is 0, for each $S \in mpded(F)$, there exists $penalty_F(S) = 0$. According to the definition of penalty, $penalty_F(S) = 0$ indicates that no attack or support relation corresponding to S is violated; in other words, S satisfies the deductive semantics in $F^{(BAF)}$ ($S \in ded(F^{(BAF)})$). So when the minimum penalty in F is 0, there exists $mpded(F) \subseteq ded(F^{(BAF)})$, which naturally leads to $prf_{mpded}(F) \subseteq prf_{ded}(F^{(BAF)})$.

To summarize, the prf_{mpded} semantics in WBAF are capable of accommodating more constraints (additional information) compared to the other two semantics, thereby demonstrating enhanced expressiveness.

On the other hand, we strengthen AF and BAF into equivalent WBAF, and evaluate the universality of the preferred semantics in WBAF.

We proceed with Example 1. The AF $F_{eg1}^{(AF)} = (A, Att)$ and the BAF $F_{eg1}^{(BAF)} = (A, Att, Sup)$ can be mapped to the equivalent WBAFs $F_{eg1(AF)} = (A, Att, Sup = \emptyset, w_A : A \to \{0\}, w_{Att} : Att \to \{\alpha\}, w_{Sup} : \emptyset)$ (Fig. 4) and $F_{eg1(BAF)} = (A, Att, Sup, w_A : A \to \{0\}, w_{Att} : Att \to \{\alpha\}, w_{Sup} : Sup \to \{\alpha\})$ (Fig. 5) respectively.

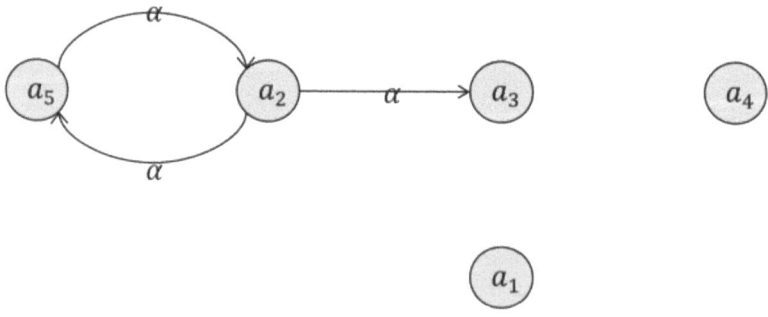

Fig. 4. AF (Fig. 2) mapped to WBAF

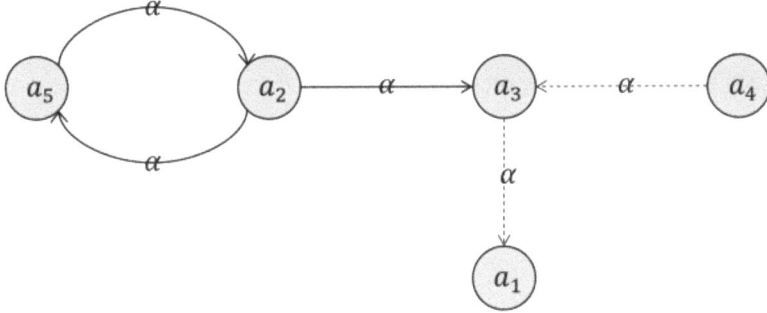

Fig. 5. BAF (Fig. 3) mapped to WBAF

The preferred extensions of $F_{eg1(AF)}$ and $F_{eg1(BAF)}$ are calculated respectively, as shown in Table 2.

Table 2. Preferred extensions in different frameworks

	prf_{mpded}
$F_{eg1(AF)}$	$\{\{a_1, a_2, a_4\}, \{a_1, a_3, a_4, a_5\}\}$
$F_{eg1(BAF)}$	$\{\{a_1, a_2\}, \{a_1, a_3, a_4, a_5\}\}$

By comparison with Table 1 and Table 2, there are $prf_{mpded}(F_{eg1(AF)}) = prf(F_{eg1}^{(AF)})$ and $prf_{mpded}(F_{eg1(BAF)}) = prf_{ded}(F_{eg1}^{(BAF)})$. Certainly, considering the essential difference between AF and BAF/WBAF, it becomes evident that this equation is not invariably valid. For example, for AF $F^{(AF)} = (\{a, b, c\}, \{(a, b), (b, c)\})$, its preferred extension set is $\{\{a, c\}\}$, and the preferred extension set of its equivalent WBAF is $\{\{a, c\}, \{b\}\}$. The fundamental reason is that deductive semantics has adjusted the semantics in classical AF to ensure that attack and support relations are treated equally. Even if the framework consists solely of attack relations, the impact of support relations will also be taken into account.

Theorem 2. *Given a BAF $F^{(BAF)} = (A, Att, Sup)$, the corresponding equivalent WBAF is $F = (A, Att, Sup, w_A : A \to \{0\}, w_{Att} : Att \to \{\alpha\}, w_{Sup} : Sup \to \{\alpha\})$. If the deductive preferred extensions of $F^{(BAF)}$ exist, there exists $prf_{mpded}(F) = prf_{ded}(F^{(BAF)})$.*

Proof. If the deductive preferred extensions of $F^{(BAF)}$ exist ($prf_{ded}(F^{(BAF)}) \neq \emptyset$), it is inferred that there exists $ded(F^{(BAF)}) \neq \emptyset$. For each $S \in ded(F^{(BAF)})$, S satisfies the deductive semantics in $F^{(BAF)}$; in other words, there is no attack or support relation corresponding to S is violated in F. Furthermore, when $F^{(BAF)}$ is mapped to F, the weights on all arguments are set to 0. Consequently, this configuration ensures that no argument is violated in S. By integrating the aforementioned two aspects, we derive $penalty_F(S) = 0$; consequently, it follows that $S \in mpded(F)$ exists. Then for each $S \in ded(F^{(BAF)})$, there exists $S \in mpded(F)$, which naturally leads to $prf_{ded}(F^{(BAF)}) \subseteq prf_{mpded}(F)$. According to Theorem 2, $prf_{mpded}(F) \subseteq prf_{ded}(F^{(BAF)})$ is deduced. Therefore, it can be proved that $prf_{mpded}(F) = prf_{ded}(F^{(BAF)})$.

In summary, the prf_{mpded} semantics in WBAF encompasses the prf_{ded} semantics in BAF under specific conditions. Its enhancement of prf_{ded} semantics in BAF is smooth, while its improvement of prf semantics in AF is alternative.

3.3 A Case Study

[15] applied classical AF, WAF and VAF to analyze the Avetrana Murder Case, revealing the pivotal role of abstract argumentation in the reasoning processes inherent to case analysis and judicial trials. Analogously, we apply the WBAF to analyze one panel categorized in reference [15], thereby demonstrating the practical applicability of the framework. Table 3 summarizes the arguments that the panel extracts from the case, their source and the arguments they attack or support.

Table 3. Arguments and relations in the formalization of Avetrana Murder Case

	argument	source	attacks	supports
a_1	The evening of August 25th Sabrina didn't fight with Sarah.	Sabrina	-	-
a_2	The evening of August 25th Sabrina had a fight with Sarah.	Sabrina's friends	a_1	-
a_3	Sabrina was angry with Sarah due to Ivano's attentions for Sarah.	Sarah's diary	a_1	a_2
a_4	The relationship between Sabrina and Sarah was not relaxed.	Sabrina	a_1	a_2

A brief explanation of Table 3 is as follows: Sabrina initially denied arguing with Sarah the night before her disappearance (a_1), but her friend said otherwise (a_2). Furthermore, Sarah wrote in her own diary that Sabrina was angry with her on that particular evening because of Ivano's excessive attention towards her (a_3). Sabrina later admitted that she and Sarah did not get along (a_4). Thus, arguments a_2, a_3 and a_4 attack argument a_1, while arguments a_3 and a_4 support argument a_2.

It should be noted here that the definition of relations between arguments is rather ambiguous and lacks objective criteria. For instance, in this context, we could consider both a_2 attacking a_1 and a_1 attacking a_2; however, we only take into account a_2's attack on a_1. Given that our search pertains to the acceptable argument sets, a simplified set of relations typically does not affect the primary outcome. Therefore, we have adopted only the attack relations mentioned in [15] without delving deeper into it.

Subsequently, we allocate appropriate weights to the arguments and relations. The weight of an argument is mainly affected by its source. As the prime suspect in the case, the credibility of Sabrina and her friend's testimony remains to be scrutinized; hence, it is justifiable not to assign weights to the corresponding arguments at this stage. The diary written by Sarah, the victim of the case, is considered to be more credible ($w_A(a_3) = 7$). The weight of the relation depends mainly on the strength of the attack or support. a_1 and a_2 are completely opposite claims ($w_{Att}(a_2, a_1) = \alpha$). Neither

Sabrina being angry with Sarah (a_3) nor Sabrina and Sarah not getting along (a_4) necessarily means that they had a quarrel (a_2). And a_3 is more likely to cause a_2 than a_4 ($w_{Sup}(a_3, a_2) = 9 > w_{Sup}(a_4, a_2) = 7$). Finally, we model the case as the corresponding WBAF, as shown in Fig. 6.

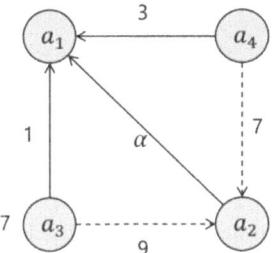

Fig. 6. WBAF graph representation of Avetrana Murder Case

The single preferred extension of this WBAF is calculated to be $\{a_2, a_3, a_4\}$, whose penalty is 0, consistent with the conclusion in the original case: Sabrina and Sarah had an argument (a_2). We are able to swiftly ascertain the testimony or argument that aligns with a_2 through this extension. Given the assumption that Sabrina and Sarah did not quarrel ($w_A(a_1) = \alpha$), the only preferred extension will be a_1 and its penalty is 7. It is evident that the incorporation of supplementary information (weight) can exert a pivotal impact on the outcome of argumentation. The WBAF introduced in this study possesses the capability to accommodate this necessity adeptly and adjust the result accordingly.

4 Implementation

To facilitate the implementation of automated reasoning within WBAF, we transform the issue of argumentation into a format that is compatible with an existing ASP solver. This paper implements ASPWBART[2] a reasoning tool of WBAF based on ASP, which can generate corresponding preferred extensions according to the arguments and relations provided by users. The process includes two parts: representing the arguments and their relations, and solving the extensions under target semantics.

4.1 Representation of Arguments and Relations

ASPWBART needs to represent weighted arguments, weighted attacks and weighted supports, as shown in Table 4, where represents the number of the weighted rule. The number between arguments cannot be repeated, nor can the number between relations.

---

[2] Please find the implementation program of ASPWBART from https://github.com/11neflibata/ASPWBART/tree/main/aspwbart.

Table 4. Representation of arguments and relations supported by ASPWBART

representation	meaning
$in(a, w, i)$	Argument a is accepted with weight w.
$attack(a, b, w, i)$	Argument a attacks argument b with weight w.
$support(a, b, w, i)$	Argument a supports argument b with weight w.

4.2 Solution of Preferred Extensions

ASPWBART aims at solving the preferred extensions in WBAF, whose underlying semantics lies in deductive semantics. Therefore, in order to solve the target extensions, we aim to employ ASP as a means to achieve this function: if the semantic rule is violated, then calculate the corresponding penalty. Based on this foundation, we are able to calculate the minimum penalty and the associated extensions.

The corresponding decomposition rules are given according to the definition of deductive semantics, as shown in Table 5. For example, $w : out(b) \leftarrow in(a)$ represents the weight of the rule "if argument a holds, argument b does not hold" is w. The rest of the rules can be interpreted similarly. The decomposition rules serve merely as an intermediary form that facilitates understanding; they are not directly expressible in ASP.

Table 5. Deductive semantic decomposition in ASPWBART

representation	decomposition rules
$attack(a, b, w, i)$	$w : out(b) \leftarrow in(a)$
	$w : out(a) \leftarrow in(b)$
$support(a, b, w, i)$	$w : in(b) \leftarrow in(a)$
	$w : out(a) \leftarrow out(b)$

In order to calculate the penalty, the definition of weak constraint in ASP is given here. Weak constraint is a special constraint rule in ASP, different from ordinary constraints in that the answer sets can not satisfy the weak constraints in the program. The basic syntax form of weak constraints is shown as follows [16]:

$$\leftsquigarrow b_1, \cdots, b_m, not\ c_1, \cdots, not\ c_n.[weight : level, i], \qquad (2)$$

where *weight* represents the weight of the weak constraint, *level* represents the level of the weight, and i is used to distinguish between the different weak constraints. For an answer set X, the ASP solver will calculate the penalty of X at different levels according to the weak constraints violated by, with the higher level penalty as small as possible, to find the optimal answer sets. Therefore, the minimum-penalty deductive extensions can be solved by using the mechanism of weak constraints.

It should be noted that the above decomposition rules do not conform to the syntax in ASP. [17] provides a method to convert a rule $w_i : r_i$ into an ASP program.

Theorem 3. *For each rule $w_i : r_i$, the corresponding ASP program contains the following rules:*

$$unsat(i) \leftarrow b(r_i), not\ h(r_i). \qquad (3)$$

$$h(r_i) \leftarrow b(r_i), not\ unsat(i). \qquad (4)$$

$$\leftsquigarrow unsat(i).[weight : level, i], \qquad (5)$$

where $b(r_i)$ represents the body of r_i, $h(r_i)$ represents the head of r_i, and $unsat(i)$ is a newly introduced atom representing r_i is not satisfied. Moreover, if $w_i = \alpha$, then weight = 1 and level = 1, otherwise weight = w_i and level = 0.

It is evident that if the rule with a weight of α is violated, the corresponding penalty value will be taken into account, which cannot be achieved through hard constraints.

The decomposition rules in Table 5 can be transformed into corresponding ASP programs through the above transformation method[3], and the results will be minimum-penalty deductive extensions. Based on this, we search for the maximum set inclusions as the final results of ASPWBART. Following the aforementioned rationale, it is feasible to implement ASPWBART with the help of clingo API in Python (clingo is an ASP solver).

4.3 Evaluation of Efficiency

Initially, we conduct a comprehensive analytical examination on a typical case (see Sect. 3.3). In the given case, both the weighted arguments and weighted relations are encoded in a manner compliant with the format prescribed by ASPWBART (see Table 4). ASPWBART is employed for the purposes of reasoning and validating the outcome, with its execution duration being tested. The experimental environment is shown in Table 6.

Table 6. Experimental environment configuration

	configuration information
operating system	Windows 11 Pro(64 bit)
development language	Python 3.11.5
dependency package	clingo 5.7.1
CPU	13th Gen Intel(R) Core(TM) i5-13400F
GPU	NVIDIA GeForce RTX 4060
memory	16G

---

[3] A representation supported by ASPWBART necessitates decomposition into two rules of the form $w_i : r_i$, and each such rule requires transformation through the introduction of a unary atom *unsat(i)*. To facilitate the conversion process, we extend the atom to be binary in the actual implementation, thereby enabling each representation to transition simultaneously into two rules.

The results demonstrate that ASPWBART is capable of accurately calculating the sole preferred extension $\{a_2, a_3, a_4\}$ for this case, and it computes the corresponding penalty to be 0. The procedure executes within a duration of approximately 2 ms. Subsequently, we employ a dataset to assess the efficiency of ASPWBART. Owing to the absence of a standardized dataset, we generate a set of arguments and relations along with their respective weights as test datasets at random[4]. Specifically, in each experiment, we designate a set number of arguments and then randomly generate twice the number of relations associated with these arguments. The distribution between attacks and supports is determined at random. These are then input into ASPWBART for analysis. Maintaining a consistent running environment and testing methodology, the outcomes are illustrated in Fig. 7.

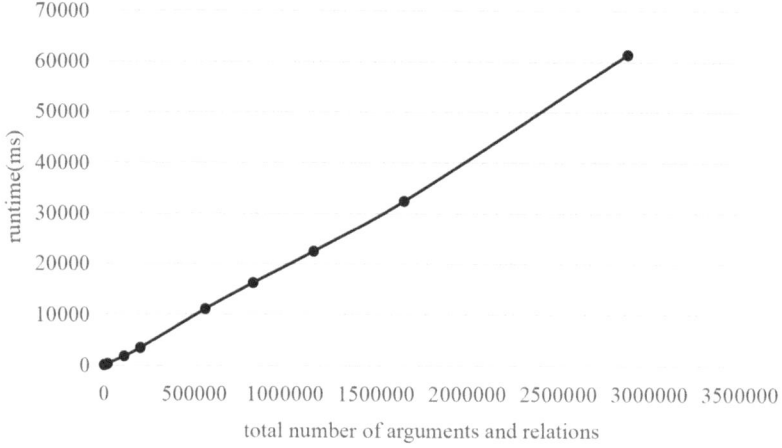

Fig. 7. Tests on the efficiency of ASPWBART

The results show that the runtime is almost proportional to the total number of arguments and relations. ASPWBART can find the results in seconds when the total number is on the scale of 100,000; ASPWBART can find the results in one minute when the scale is in the millions. When the scale reaches ten million or higher, ASPWBART takes a long time to solve the problem. It can be seen that ASPWBART can achieve high solving efficiency under a certain problem scale, but its efficiency needs to be improved in the face of large-scale problems.

5 Conclusion and Future Work

This paper proposes a new Weighted Bipolar Argument Framework (WBAF), which aims to consider the attack and support relations between arguments equally, and to

---

[4] Please find the evaluation program of ASPWBART from https://github.com/11neflibata/ASPWBART/blob/main/aspwbart/evaluate.py.

handle the weights of arguments or their relations by calculating the penalty. Furthermore, we propose the minimum-penalty deductive preferred semantics in WBAF and design the corresponding reasoning tool - ASPWBART.

Compared with other frameworks, the WBAF and its preferred semantics proposed in this paper incorporate an expanded set of constraints, enabling a more diverse range of representations. This development holds significant implications for practical research endeavors. Nevertheless, there remain numerous aspects that necessitate further refinement. Firstly, the way of dealing with weights in this paper still has room for improvement. There is no comprehensive study on the reasonable range and treatment of the weights between arguments and relations. And there is no strict distinction when we handle the weights of arguments and the weights of relations. In subsequent work, we will explore more appropriate ways of dealing with argument weights and relation weights [27], and even consider higher-order attack and support relations [6,8]. Secondly, by comparing the minimum-penalty preferred semantics in WBAF with the semantics in other argumentation frameworks, it can be seen that the semantics proposed in this paper only makes smooth improvements on the deductive preferred semantics in BAF. In subsequent work, we will explore ways to apply refined adjustments in other semantic context. Thirdly, the WBAF proposed in this paper represents a novel model, for which there currently exists no standardized dataset. In contrast, several mature datasets are available for traditional AFs, such as those utilized in the International Competition on Computational Models of Argumentation (ICCMA). Therefore, we intend to refine these existing datasets by implementing strategies such as the stochastic generation of weights, with the aim of conducting a comprehensive test analysis for ASPWBART in the future.

Acknowledgments. This work is supported by (1)State Grid Corporation of China Science and Technology Project Funding (Task Book Number: 5108-202340062A-1-1-ZN) and (2)the Fundamental Research Funds for the Central Universities (2242024k30035).

Disclosure of Interests. The authors have no competing interests to declare that are relevant to the content of this article.

References

1. Baroni, P., Giacomin, M., Guida, G.: SCC-recursiveness: a general schema for argumentation semantics. Artif. Intell. **168**(1), 162–210 (2005). https://doi.org/10.1016/j.artint.2005.05.006. https://www.sciencedirect.com/science/article/pii/S0004370205000962
2. Bench-Capon, T.J.M.: Persuasion in practical argument using value-based argumentation frameworks. J. Log. Comput. **13**(3), 429–448 (2003)
3. Caminada, M.W.A., Gabbay, D.M.: A logical account of formal argumentation. Studia Logica **93**, 109–145 (2009). https://api.semanticscholar.org/CorpusID:7749403
4. Cayrol, C., Lagasquie-Schiex, M.C.: On the acceptability of arguments in bipolar argumentation frameworks. In: Godo, L. (ed.) Symbolic and Quantitative Approaches to Reasoning with Uncertainty, pp. 378–389. Springer, Heidelberg (2005)
5. Cayrol, C., Lagasquie-Schiex, M.C.: Bipolarity in argumentation graphs: towards a better understanding. Int. J. Approximate Reasoning **54**(7), 876–899 (2013). https://doi.org/10.1016/j.ijar.2013.03.001. https://www.sciencedirect.com/science/article/pii/S0888613X13000509, special issue: Uncertainty in Artificial Intelligence and Databases

6. Cohen, A., Gottifredi, S., García, A.J., Simari, G.R.: An approach to abstract argumentation with recursive attack and support. J. Appl. Log. **13**(4), 509–533 (2015)
7. Cordeiro, R., Alcântara, J.: Generalising semantics to weighted bipolar argumentation frameworks. In: Xavier-Junior, J.C., Rios, R.A. (eds.) Intelligent Systems, pp. 520–534. Springer, Cham (2022)
8. Doutre, S., Lafages, M., Lagasquie-Schiex, M.C.: Argumentation frameworks with higher-order attacks: labellings and complexity. In: 2020 IEEE 32nd International Conference on Tools with Artificial Intelligence (ICTAI), pp. 1210–1217 (2020). https://doi.org/10.1109/ICTAI50040.2020.00183
9. Dung, P., Kowalski, R., Toni, F.: Dialectic proof procedures for assumption-based, admissible argumentation. Artif. Intell. **170**, 114–159 (2006). https://doi.org/10.1016/j.artint.2005.07.002
10. Dung, P.M.: On the acceptability of arguments and its fundamental role in nonmonotonic reasoning, logic programming and n-person games. Artif. Intell. **77**(2), 321–357 (1995)
11. Dunne, P.E., Hunter, A., McBurney, P., Parsons, S., Wooldridge, M.: Inconsistency tolerance in weighted argument systems. In: Proceedings of The 8th International Conference on Autonomous Agents and Multiagent Systems, AAMAS 2009, vol. 2, pp. 851–858. International Foundation for Autonomous Agents and Multiagent Systems, Richland, SC (2009)
12. Dunne, P.E., Hunter, A., Mcburney, P., Parsons, S., Wooldridge, M.: Weighted argument systems: basic definitions, algorithms, and complexity results. Artif. Intell. **175**(2), 457–486 (2011)
13. Dvořák, W., Rapberger, A., Wallner, J.P., Woltran, S.: Aspartix-v19 - an answer-set programming based system for abstract argumentation. In: Herzig, A., Kontinen, J. (eds.) Foundations of Information and Knowledge Systems, pp. 79–89. Springer, Cham (2020)
14. Ferilli, S.: Introducing general argumentation frameworks and their use. In: Baldoni, M., Bandini, S. (eds.) AIxIA 2020 - Advances in Artificial Intelligence, pp. 136–153. Springer, Cham (2021)
15. Ferilli, S., Leuzzi, F.: An analysis of the avetrana murder case through abstract argumentation. In: AI^3@AI*IA (2019). https://api.semanticscholar.org/CorpusID:210472385
16. Gelfond, M., Kahl, Y.: Knowledge Representation, Reasoning, and the Design of Intelligent Agents: The Answer-Set Programming Approach. Cambridge University Press (2014)
17. Lee, J., Talsania, S., Wang, Y.: Computing LPMLN using ASP and MLN solvers. Theory Pract. Logic Program. **17**(5–6), 942–960 (2017). https://doi.org/10.1017/S1471068417000400
18. Li, H., Oren, N., Norman, T.J.: Probabilistic argumentation frameworks. In: Modgil, S., Oren, N., Toni, F. (eds.) Theory and Applications of Formal Argumentation, pp. 1–16. Springer, Heidelberg (2012)
19. Morveli Espinoza, M., Possebom, A.T., Tacla, C.A.: Argumentation-based agents that explain their decisions. In: 2019 8th Brazilian Conference on Intelligent Systems (BRACIS), pp. 467–472 (2019). https://doi.org/10.1109/BRACIS.2019.00088
20. Nielsen, S.H., Parsons, S.: A generalization of dung's abstract framework for argumentation: Arguing with sets of attacking arguments. In: Maudet, N., Parsons, S., Rahwan, I. (eds.) Argumentation in Multi-Agent Systems, pp. 54–73. Springer, Heidelberg (2007)
21. Nishihana, K., Nomura, S., Takahashi, K.: Hybrid reasoning using weighted bipolar argumentation framework for legal simulation. In: Proceedings of JURISIN, pp. 68–81 (2021)
22. Pazienza, A., Ferilli, S., Esposito, F.: Constructing and evaluating bipolar weighted argumentation frameworks for online debating systems. In: Bistarelli, S., Giacomin, M., Pazienza, A. (eds.) Proceedings of the 1st the Italian Association for Artificial Intelligence (AI*IA 2017), Bari, Italy, 16–17 November 2017. CEUR Workshop Proceedings, vol. 2012, pp. 111–125. CEUR-WS.org (2017). http://ceur-ws.org/Vol-2012/AI3-2017_paper_12.pdf

23. Pazienza, A., Ferilli, S., Esposito, F.: On the gradual acceptability of arguments in bipolar weighted argumentation frameworks with degrees of trust. In: Kryszkiewicz, M., Appice, A., Ślęzak, D., Rybinski, H., Skowron, A., Raś, Z.W. (eds.) Foundations of Intelligent Systems, pp. 195–204. Springer, Cham (2017)
24. Potyka, N.: Continuous dynamical systems for weighted bipolar argumentation. In: The 16th International Conference on Principles of Knowledge Representation and Reasoning (2018)
25. Potyka, N.: Abstract argumentation with Markov networks. In: European Conference on Artificial Intelligence (2020). https://api.semanticscholar.org/CorpusID:221714427
26. de Tarlé, L.D.: A gradual semantic to model opinion using bipolar argumentation graphs. JIAF-JFPDA, p. 20 (2023). https://api.semanticscholar.org/CorpusID:261700472
27. Yamaguchi, K., Matsuda, Y.: Cost-based framework for natural language argumentation analysis. In: 2021 19th International Conference on Information Technology Based Higher Education and Training (ITHET), pp. 1–10 (2021). https://doi.org/10.1109/ITHET50392.2021.9759813
28. Zhang, H., Zhang, S.: A divide-and-conquer method for computing preferred extensions of argumentation frameworks. In: 2021 IEEE International Conference on Big Knowledge (ICBK), pp. 1–7 (2021). https://doi.org/10.1109/ICKG52313.2021.00039

Haskell Based Spreadsheets

Ignacio Ballesteros[1,2](✉), Luis Eduardo Bueso de Barrio[1], and Julio Mariño[1]

[1] Universidad Politécnica de Madrid, Madrid, Spain
{luiseduardo.bueso.debarrio,julio.marino}@upm.es
[2] IMDEA Software Institute, Madrid, Spain
ignacio.ballesteros@upm.es

Abstract. Spreadsheet programs are one of the most widespread information processing tools used by end-users. Their importance lies not only in their extensive use by people with little or no knowledge of programming but because of their relevance as a decision-making tool by executives in many companies. In spite of this long-term success, many studies have found plenty of pitfalls that make spreadsheets widely faulty, hence potentially leading to risky decisions. Because of these problems several analysis tools have been proposed to help find errors easily. In this project we present a different approach, more oriented to prevent the appearance of errors through a change in the way users interact with them. We focus on the *declarative* essence of spreadsheets and propose to refound them on the grounds of modern functional programming languages. Our tool uses a subset of *Haskell* as the expression language for its cells and takes advantage of its rich type system to support a safer way of spreadsheet programming that prevents the appearance of certain errors and helps to understand the meaning of programs, as new data types can be introduced from cell aggregates. Haskell is also used for defining reusable, user-defined functions and external modules. We show a working prototype incorporating the ideas above and point towards new features based on advanced functional programming technologies.

Keywords: Spreadsheets · Haskell · End-user Programming · Functional Programming

1 Introduction

If you are reading this, you are very likely to have plenty of experience using spreadsheets. You have probably enjoyed their ease of use, the visual appeal of the grid arrangement, the immediate feedback provided by automatic recalculation, the possibility of cutting and pasting rectangular regions and, more recently, the feature of sharing content hosted on the cloud. You have probably also experienced the frustration of writing overly complicated formulas in a single line, as soon as you go beyond the basic "adding and multiplication" usage, the unexpected results from operating with empty cells, unnoticed errors, etc.

Despite all these well-known nuisances, spreadsheet applications remain one of the most successful end-user computation models. Since the introduction of *VisiCalc* in 1979, the basic idea has remained relatively stable, with new actors appearing – *Lotus 1-2-3* (1983), *Excel* (1985) or *Google SpreadSheets* (2006) [1]. Radical changes have been avoided due to the huge user base, with the requirement of *backwards compatibility* being a big deterrent to finding a solution to their problems. Indeed, it was estimated that MS Excel alone had 750 million users in 2010 [2]. Although there is not a full disclosure of exact number of users, comments by Microsoft's CEO Satya Nadella in 2016 stated that around 1200 million people used Office Suite [3]. Moreover, spreadsheets are one of the most used tools by managers and executives for budget preparation, financial reports or scenario-based decision-making [4].

Due to the relevance of spreadsheets use, a number of studies have tried to quantify the risks caused by the errors in them [4–6]. It has been estimated that 94% of spreadsheets used in companies contain some kind of error and that an average of 5,2% of the cells in these spreadsheets contain errors [4]. A European interest group on spreadsheet risks was created recently, and a comprehensive set of *horror stories* can be found in their web page [7]. Such stories do not cease to appear, with the recent loss of COVID-19 related data in the UK receiving extensive coverage in general and specialized media [8].

Several proposals have been made to avoid and detect errors in spreadsheets. In [9] a development methodology is proposed in order to improve reliability through data consistency and error traceability. Other approaches advocate the use of *static analysis* techniques to improve error detection in spreadsheets [10].

In a sense, these works try to bring techniques and features used to ensure quality in standard software development to the end-user setting. Then, why not turn to functional programming? This seems a natural choice. On one hand, spreadsheets are basically a declarative, side-effect-free computation model – where even *maps* and *folds* occur naturally – and that makes functional programming a close relative. On the other hand, functional programming is in itself one of the safest ways of developing software, with recent studies showing how statically-typed functional languages influence software quality [11].

In fact, some typical spreadsheet errors, such as confusion between alphanumeric and non-alphanumeric values, absence of static checks prior to function application or inconsistent coercions – both from actual data and also empty cells – can be connected to the nonexistence of an acceptable type system. Additionally, modern functional programming languages support further means to increase safety, such as *declarative debugging*, *property-based testing*, etc.

Our approach, then, is to improve on existing spreadsheet systems by incorporating features from modern functional programming languages, especially static type checks. Our proposal, *Haskcell* [12,13], consists of a spreadsheet system where the cell language is Haskell mildly sugared to ease working with cell rectangles. Haskell is also used for user-defined functionality and the whole sheet (grid plus extra definitions) is saved as a standalone Haskell program. Of course, users interact with the sheet in the usual WYSIWYG way, thanks to a client-server architecture that performs the usual update/refresh cycle.[1]

1.1 Related Work

Various works have explored the relation of functional programming with spreadsheets and have tried to provide better semantic foundations for them. In [14] an extension to Excel is proposed that facilitates adding user-defined functions. This paper is the base for subsequent work done at Microsoft Research by Gordon and Peyton-Jones in the *Calc Intelligence* group. Another proposal related to MS Excel is Funcalc [15] by Sestoft et al. This, like those mentioned before assume backwards compatibility with an existing system.

Haxcel [16] proposes a new interface for spreadsheet environments backed by a Haskell interpreter. This approach is centered on a new interface on top of a Haskell code module using an array library. Operations between ranges are made using this library and the interface provides a visualization window for each value declaration.

In the work of David Wakeling [17], the proposal is an integration between Haskell and Microsoft Excel using custom function definitions through comments in the cells.

There have also been some proposals to provide a *relational* rather than functional foundation for spreadsheets, so that deductive capabilities can be added [18,19] While this is a quite interesting direction, which can address issues such as incomplete information and circular references, the goals pursued in this work are, say, more mundane in the sense that we are now focusing in how to better do what users are already doing with spreadsheets rather than extending their functionality.

1.2 Paper Organization

Next section provides details about the choices made in the design of Haskcell and its main features. Section 3 discusses one key aspect of spreadsheets: the treatment of blank cells. A high-level presentation of the language used for cells and the transformation rules that guide the *desugaring* process into Haskell code is given in Sect. 4. An actual experiment where an existing Excel spreadsheet is recreated by Haskcell is presented in Sect. 5. Finally, Sect. 6 concludes and briefly comments on work in progress and future improvements. For those readers interested in further technical details, these are provided in the appendices.

2 Design

It is tempting to connect a spreadsheet interface with all the power of a functional programming language, but that could probably result in a tool far too

---
[1] HaskCell is available at https://gitlab.com/babel-upm/haskcell.

	A	B	C	D	E	F	G	H
0	YEAR	SUBJECT	ECTS	GRADE	QUAL	VAL	TOTAL	60
1	1	Algebra	6	5	A	ok	creds 1	30
2	1	Calculus	6	7.1	N	ok	creds 2	6
3	1	Logic	6	7	N	ok	creds 3	9
4	1	Programming I	6	9	S	ok	creds 4	15
5	1	Programming II	6	8.8	N	ok		
6	2	Concurrency	3	7.8	N	ok	AVG	7.95
7	2	Data Bases	3	5.4	A	ok	avg 1	7.38
8	3	Middleware	3	8	N	ok	avg 2	6.60
9	3	Operating Systems	6	8.1	N	ok	avg 3	8.05
10	4	Practicum	12	9.6	S	ok	avg 4	9.56
11	4	Computability	3	9.4	S	ok		

Fig. 1. A sample spreadsheet with courses and grades.

complicated for the typical user of this kind of systems. The next subsection explains some of the design compromises we had to consider when starting the project. The main functionality of Haskcell will be explained later. The example sheet in Fig. 1 will be used. Finally, some implementation details are given.

2.1 Design Principles

No Backwards Compatibility. Haskcell will show no compliance with existing operator languages or type systems. Natural, since we are targetting a different kind of user – unhappy spreadsheet users with some knowledge of FP.

WYSIWYG. The user should interact with Haskcell mostly through the grid interface, although a separate editor will be available for external functions – the so-called *external module*.

Simple Cells vs. Aggregates. In accordance with the previous requirement, single cells will contain *simple* data, not collections, as common spreadsheet usage dictates. This means that the information shown in each cell will typically be numeric; boolean, strings, atoms, etc. In order to process structured data, it is advised to aggregate data, e.g. from adjacent columns, as is also common practice when using standard spreadsheets. These new data types will be managed using the external function facility. Similar principles apply to higher-order values. While it does not seem practical to have cells of higher-order types, higher-order functions are routinely used inside cells formulae and external functions.

Separation Between Appearance and Internal Representation. In order to prevent errors and enforce data consistency, the internal representation of the contents of the cells may correspond to different datatypes even when the appearance is indistinguishable. This will be supported by Haskell's constructors and constructor classes – i.e. the Show class. The restrictions stated in the previous paragraph are actually helpful to achieve this. For example, the data stored in columns labelled A and C of the example in Fig. 1 may be of different types although their appearance is the same.

Haskell Compatibility. In order to take advantage of all the advanced features of Haskell, the whole spreadsheet can be stored faithfully as a (standalone) Haskell program. In fact, this approach is a transformational one. This will bring various benefits. On one hand, unlimited possibilities of extending spreadsheets with Haskell libraries that are expected to be far more reliable than similar extensions written in proprietary languages for existing systems. Also, the standard semantics for Haskell will be the Haskell semantics for the generated program, which will be useful for users already familiar with Haskell.

2.2 Main Features

Cell Language. Haskcell compiles the text introduced by the user in a cell and, if syntactically correct, recompiles the Haskell code and refreshes the view offered to the user. Basically, the cell language is a subset of Haskell enhanced with operators for range and rectangle support. Whole rows (1:1), columns (A:A), rectangles (A1:C5) and intersections of the former are supported. Haskcell provides two operators to manipulate ranges:

$$(1) \quad range \;\rightarrow\; [\; cell\!:\!cell\;]$$
$$(2) \quad\qquad\quad |\;\; (\; cell\!:\!cell\;)$$

(1) corresponds to the traditional semantics of spreadsheet ranges, and treats the cells as a data collection. (2) is a new operator to interact with ranges. It takes the indices in the range given and passes them as arguments to some function. For instance, sum [C1:C3] is rewritten as sum [C1, C2, C3], but date (C1:C3) is rewritten as date C1 C2 C3. This new syntax has been devised to ease working with cell aggregates and data constructors.

Cell translation is done in several steps: range reduction, dependency and empty cell checking, and dereferencing. For example, the formula used for the overall sum of credits in cell H1 is just

sum [C1:C11]

The formula that computes the overall average grade of all the courses is basically a "scalar product" combining grades and credits and the resulting sum is divided by the overall count of credits, previously stored in cell H0:

H6 = (sum $ zipWith (*) [C1:C11] [D1:D11]) / H0

External Functions. Several helper types and functions have been defined in the external module for the grades example. For instance, symbolic grades can be represented with the sum type

```
data SymbGrade = A | B | C | D | F
```

The actual appearance of cells containing `SymbGrade` data will be governed by providing an implementation of the `Show` function. Translation between numeric and symbolic grades is implemented by an external function:

```
num2symb :: Grade -> Either Error SymbGrade
num2symb (Grade n)
  | n >= 0 && n < 5 = Right F
  | n >= 5 && n < 7 = Right C
  | n >= 7 && n < 9 = Right B
  | n >= 9 && n <= 10 = Right A
  | otherwise = Left "wrong grade"
```

Again, the actual appearance of *right* and *wrong* cells is governed by some show-like function.

The formula that adds the credits filtering them by year tuples corresponding cells in the CREDIT and YEAR columns, and builds a list that is filtered out later:

```
H2 = sum $ map snd $ filterYear 1 $ zip [A1:A11] [C1:C11]
```

where `filterYear` is defined as:

```
filterYear :: Integer -> [(Integer,a)] -> [(Integer,a)]
filterYear n = filter (\x -> n == (fst x))
```

Tagged Types. The introduction of constructors allows Haskcell to distinguish between data that would be treated uniformly in a conventional spreadsheet system. For instance, in our example we have different kinds of numeric values:

```
newtype Year = Year Integer
newtype ECTS = ECTS Integer
newtype Grade = Grade Float
```

By using different types we can avoid errors resulting from inadvertently combining different sources. Also, it makes sense to add credits and to add grades but perhaps years should also be used as ordinals. The typeclass mechanism is really handy here, using `GeneralizedNewtypeDeriving` users can automatically generate typeclass instances to deal with the arithmetic operations they need for their types.

Aggregates. In our example it would be reasonable to treat data in columns A to C as a single entity – in the database sense. Haskcell provides mechanisms to group sets of cells and generates the corresponding type definitions:

```
data Subject = Subject
  { year :: Year, name :: String, ects :: ECTS, grade :: Grade }
  deriving Eq
```

To use the `Subject` constructor in a cell we can write the expression:
```
F1 = Subject (A1:D1)
```

Data Validators. Another useful feature, often used along with data aggregators, is the possibility of defining data validators. The main purpose of validators is to check the correctness of the data introduced in the spreadsheet.

Haskcell provides a default implementation of a `Validation` data type defined on top of `Either` with its correspondent applicative instance:

```
newtype Validation e r = Validation (Either e r) deriving (Eq, Functor)

instance Monoid m => Applicative (Validation m) where
  pure = Validation . pure
  Validation (Left x) <*> Validation (Left y) = Validation . Left $ x <> y
  Validation f <*> Validation r = Validation $ f <*> r
```

Using Validation a user can write new validators for its own types. For example if the user wants to check that the name of a subject is never empty:

```
validateName :: String -> Validation [Error] String
validateName n
  | n /= "" = Validation $ Right n
  | otherwise = Validation $ Left ["incorrect name"]
```

After defining validation for each field of an aggregate type, these can be easily combined using applicatives, which is a common technique in the functional-programming community:

```
validateSubject :: Year -> String -> ECTS -> Grade
               -> Validation [Error] Subject
validateSubject year name ects grade = pure Subject
  <*> validateName name
  <*> grade'
  <*> validateGrade grade
  <*> validateECTS ects
  <*> validateYear year
  where grade' = Validation $ Right grade
```

This validator can be used with the expression `validateSubject(A1:D1)`. After cell evaluation this cell will show `ok` if validation succeeded or a list of errors with the reasons why it failed otherwise.

Data Generators for Property-Based Testing. Haskcell provides an interface with Haskell QuickCheck that provides data generators for the basic and user-defined types, hence allowing for the generation of randomly populated spreadsheets for testing.

Referencing Blank Cells. We will devote next section to discuss this issue.

3 Treatment of Blank Cells

Blank cells are an essential feature of spreadsheets, and also a cause behind some of their more error-prone constructs. When a user starts interacting with a spreadsheet most of their cells are empty and the possibility of performing calculations in the presence of incomplete data is, at first, perceived as something positive. In the most basic "additive" usage of spreadsheets, blank cells are routinely treated as zeroes and there is usually no problem with that. However, as soon as the usage goes beyond basic addition, problems do arise. In nonarithmetic contexts blank cells may be confused with empty strings and the user is forced to write complex formulas dealing with special cases. The following is a real example taken from an apparently unsophisticated spreadsheet to compute grades from the students' various assessment activities:

```
=IF(AND(ISBLANK(M2);AA2="absent");"absent";IF(AND(ISNUMBER(AA2);
ISNUMBER(M2);AA2>4,9;M2>4,9);(M2+AA2)/2;"FAIL"))
```

In this particular example blank cells correspond to students not delivering some assignment or examination paper, which requires a logical, rather than arithmetic treatment. Using the built-in function ISBLANK the case of blanks is recognized and then blanks must be converted into some symbolic representation, which must be encoded using strings. This, in turn, brings another complication: now cells can contain numbers *or* strings and this requires some sort of *runtime type checking* via the ISNUMBER built-in function. Of course, this is the kind of situations where we expect a Haskell-based spreadsheet system to be superior: algebraic datatypes will allow us to consider different subcases inside a type via pattern matching, as we will see in the full example.

Automatic conversion of blank cells into zeroes can also be problematic in arithmetic contexts. Consider, for example, division by zero, which often leads to overly complex formulae where cases now depend on some "exception handling" via the ISERROR function:

```
=IF(ISERROR(SUM(K24:K33)+SUM(M24:M33)*SUM(W24:W33)/G17+SUM(N24:N33)*
SUM(Y24:Y33)/G17);0;SUM(K24:K33)+SUM(M24:M33)*SUM(W24:W33)/G17+
SUM(N24:N33)*SUM(Y24:Y33)/G17)
```

Again, this is an example brought from a quite dull spreadsheet to compute teaching credits.

We considered different approaches for dealing with blank cells in a strongly typed functional spreadsheet and, to be honest, we do not consider the matter fully settled. One possibility was to have a *blank* value present in every type, but that had problems of diverse nature. It was problematic from the point of view of Haskell's type system, was not consistent with the intuition that blanks are *not* values that can be returned by expressions, but the absence of definition for a given cell and, more importantly, was impractical, as it led to the same kind of lengthy formulae as those shown above.

Finally, we have adopted a solution that generalizes the standard solution in classical spreadsheet systems without breaking strong typing – *default values*. A default value is a value that acts as a replacement for the missing content of a cell. Of course, our defaults must be consistent with the type expected by the expression referring to that cell.

There are several ways of specifying default values. The simplest is to declare the replacement value directly, e.g.:

```
(A4 ? 1) * B4
```

If $A4$ is not empty, the product $A4 \cdot B4$ is computed. If $A4$ is an empty cell, the expression is evaluated as if it were a 1, which is what appears to be useful in this multiplicative context. It is relevant to note that Haskcell performs this substitution *at compile time*, i.e. an actual Haskell rule

```
a4 = 1
```

is generated if cell $A4$ happens to be empty. A consequence of this transformational approach is that cell $A4$ must have a *unique default value*. That is, it is not allowed to refer to $A4$ from another expression that would assume it to behave as a 0 instead. We do not consider this a limitation but, instead, a virtue since we find the possibility of multiple replacement values for a cell a potential source for errors.

We have devised ways of saving time for users when specifying default values. One piece of syntactic sugar that has proven useful in practice is *default lists*:

```
mult ([A4:F4] ? 1)
```

multiplies the values in the cells after replacing empty cells with 1's. Default values can also be associated with specific parameters of functions. A function declared as

```
f :: (Int ? 0) -> (String ? "") -> Bool
```

will replace its first parameter with 0 when applied to a blank reference and, analogously, the second one will be replaced by the empty string. A similar scheme can be applied for dealing with product types:

```
g :: ((Int ? 0) , (String ? "")) -> Bool
```

For the moment we only allow this kind of type transformation for monomorphic types although under some conditions polymorphic default values can be safely generated:

```
h :: ([a] ? []) -> [a] -> [a]
```

Finally, default values can be declared for a whole datatype, e.g. by considering a type class `Default` providing a `default` function. As this lacks the flexibility of the previous idioms, we consider this option a *fallback* or last resort when no other replacement instructions are found for a cell.

4 A Static Semantics

The semantics of a spreadsheet is given by the Haskell semantics of the generated code. This is considerably simpler than having to specify a full operational semantics for cell evaluation as done in [15], as only the source to source transformation must be specified, leaving the main part of the behaviour to the standard semantics for the generated code. In the following paragraphs we just formalise the main properties and operations required in the translation process.

As we mentioned before, a spreadsheet is just a (partial) mapping from addresses to Haskell terms with ranges and defaults:

$$address = \mathbb{N} \times \mathbb{N} \quad (1)$$
$$spreadsheet = address \nrightarrow haskell^+ \quad (2)$$

A *workspace* is composed of a spreadsheet and an external module:

$$workspace = spreadsheet \times extmod \quad (3)$$

By $haskell^+$ we mean the subset of Haskell terms extended with specific constructs that we allow as cell definitions. Nonempty cells are those in the domain of the spreadsheet, $\text{dom}(s)$.

Cell definitions may refer to other cells. The set of addresses referenced from a given one is given by function $\text{deps} : spreadsheet \to address \to Set(address)$:

$$\text{deps } s\ a = \text{refs } s\ (s\ a) \quad (4)$$
$$\text{refs } s\ x = \{x\} \cup (\text{deps } s\ x), x \in address \quad (5)$$
$$\text{refs } s\ (f\ t) = (\text{refs } s\ f) \cup (\text{refs } s\ t) \quad (6)$$

etc., where $\text{refs} : spreadsheet \to haskell^+ \to Set(address)$ returns the set of addresses referenced by some expression in the spreadsheet. For the time being we do not allow circularity in references, that is:

$$\forall x \in address. x \notin \text{deps } s\ x \quad (7)$$

Dependencies are used to trigger reevaluation of cells once one of them has been modified by the user. The property in formula 7 ensures termination of the reevaluation procedure.

The *sugared* syntax for cells allows for references inside cell *ranges*. As we will see, range evaluation – *removal* – is necessary for the spreadsheet evaluation process to take place using plain Haskell. Range removal is achieved by iteratively applying the function $\text{range} : haskell^+ \to haskell^+$ that satisfies

$$\text{range}([x_1y : x_2y\ ]) = [x_1y, \ldots, x_ny] \quad (8)$$
$$\text{range}(f\ (x_1y : x_2y\ )) = f\ x_1y\ \ldots\ x_ny \quad (9)$$

Range removal terminates because addresses – thus neither ranges – cannot appear in external modules, so they cannot be reintroduced during cell (re)evaluation. In other words, addresses and ranges are not first class citizens and may not be manipulated in an external module like any other Haskell datatype.

Default values, needed to deal with blank cells, are a different issue. They may appear in cells, but also in type and function definitions of the external module. As removal of default expressions will, in general, have side effects on the spreadsheet under consideration, we will make use of a function $\texttt{default} : haskell^+ \times spreadsheet \rightarrow haskell^+ \times spreadsheet$.

The simplest case is when a default term of the form $(x?v)$ is found inside a cell:[2]

$$\texttt{default}(x?v, s) = (x, s) \qquad \text{if } x \in \texttt{dom}(s) \tag{10}$$

$$\texttt{default}(x?v, s) = (x, s \oplus \{x \mapsto v\}) \qquad \text{if } x \notin \texttt{dom}(s) \tag{11}$$

Note that this treatment of default values ensures that blank cells are given a single default value. It does not ensure, however, that the value assigned to a blank cell is independent of the order of application of the $\texttt{default}$ rules when inconsistent default rules coexist. It is up to the user to guarantee the consistency of default rules. Of course, typing errors introduced by a misuse of default rules will be detected when compiling the desugared Haskell code.

As mentioned before, a useful piece of syntactic sugar allows to declare a single replacement value for a range expression. An expression of the form $[x_1y : x_2y]\,?v$ is firstly rewritten into $[x_1y, \ldots, x_ny]\,?v$ via the $\texttt{range}$ function, and then, using the $\texttt{defrange} : haskell^+ \rightarrow haskell^+$ function in the following way:

$$\texttt{defrange}([x_1y, \ldots, x_ny]\,?v) = [(x_1y?v), \ldots, (x_ny?v)] \tag{12}$$

Finally, default values for blank cells can be specified in the external module, using *default type* declarations. At the moment, the syntax supported by Haskcell is the following, although it can be easily extended to cope with equivalent curried definitions.

$$DefaultType ::= (OptType_1 \times \cdots \times OptType_k) \rightarrow \tau \tag{13}$$

$$OptType ::= \mu?v \mid \tau \tag{14}$$

where τ is some Haskell type or type scheme, μ is a *monomorphic* Haskell type and $v \in \mu$. Given a function declaration in the external module with default type $f :: (ot_1, \ldots, ot_k) \rightarrow \tau$ a new constant definition $f_i = v_i$ is added for each $ot_i \equiv \mu_i?v_i$, and ot_i is replaced by just μ_i. Resolution of blank cell references is then performed when invoking f from a cell definition using the $\texttt{default}$ function:

$$\texttt{default}(f(t_1, \ldots, x, \ldots, t_k), s) = (f(t_1, \ldots, x, \ldots, t_k), s)$$
$$\text{if } x \in \texttt{dom}(s) \tag{15}$$

$$\texttt{default}(f(t_1, \ldots, x, \ldots, t_k), s) = (f(t_1, \ldots, f_i, \ldots, t_k), s \oplus \{x \mapsto f_i\})$$
$$\text{if } x \notin \texttt{dom}(s) \tag{16}$$

---

[2] Here $\oplus$ denotes a *function update*, as in the Z mathematical toolkit [20].

where x is an address, i.e. a cell reference.

The main idea of the source transformation procedure is that the two desugaring functions defined above, `range` and `default`, should provide a terminating and somewhat confluent rewriting mechanism that ensures *sugar-freeness* of the generated code. The following lemmas formalise these notions:

Lemma 1. *Repeated application of the* `range` *function will eventually lead to a spreadsheet where no cell contains appearances of range terms.*

Lemma 2. *Repeated application of* `default` *and* `defrange` *on a spreadsheet with no appearances of range terms will eventually lead to a spreadsheet with no appearances of neither default terms nor range terms.*

At this point, the spreadsheet and its associated external module are considered sugar-free and ready for execution in Haskell, according to the execution scheme detailed in the following section.

5 A Realistic Example

In this section we will adapt an existing Excel spreadsheet to Haskcell to illustrate its unique features. This spreadsheet must compute the grades of a course. For conciseness, we only show the formulas for a single student. During a course, a student must address different assignments divided into theory and practice. In order to pass the course, she must succeed in both parts, but not all the assignments in each one are mandatory. Furthermore, some assignments have a minimum required grade to be taken into account.

We can summarize the existing core formulas with the following expressions:

1. Calculate the mean if both grades are above the threshold.

    ```
    =IF(AND(B8>=3.75,B11>=3.75),(B8+L2)/2,"FAIL")
    ```

2. Check mandatory assignments, minimum grade and apply weights for each assignment.

    ```
    =IF(AND(Y2="p",Z2="p"),"p",IF(OR(X2<3,Y2<3,Z2<3,Y2="p",Z2="Absent"),
        "FAIL",X2*0.2+Y2*0.4+Z2*0.4))
    ```

3. Blank cell and type checks for grades, like the ones shown in Sect. 3.

    ```
    =IF(AND(ISBLANK(M2);AA2="absent");"absent";IF(AND(ISNUMBER(AA2);
        ISNUMBER(M2);AA2>4,9;M2>4,9);(M2+AA2)/2;"FAIL"))
    ```

Figure 2 shows the spreadsheet, now written with our tool, so cells contain Haskell expressions, possibly making use of auxiliary types and function definitions contained in a separate Haskell file. Cells containing grade values use the following type definitions:

```
newtype NumericGrade = NG { getNumericGrade :: Double }
  deriving (Show, Eq, Ord, Num)

data Grade = Fail | Absent | Grade NumericGrade deriving (Show, Eq, Ord)

data Projects = Projects
  { p1 :: Grade ? Absent, p2 :: Grade ? Absent, p3 :: Grade ? Absent }
  deriving (Show, Eq)
```

The `NumericGrade` type wraps a number (`Double`) to differentiate it from other kinds of numbers used, such as the weights for the assignments. The data type `Grade` defines the three possible values for a grade. Finally, a `Project` collects the grades for each assignment, `p1` – `p3`, with a default grade of `Absent`.

	A	B	C	D
0		THEORY		
1		EXERCISES		FINAL
2	EXAM 1	NG 2.92	NG 1.20	B2 + C2
3	EXAM 1 (R)	NG 5.67	NG 0.75	B3 + C3
4	EXAM 1 (BEST)			max D2 D3
5	EXAM 2	NG 3	NG 1.5	B5 + C5
6	FINAL	meanWithThreshold (NG 3.75) ([D4, D5]?NG 0)		
7		PRACTICE		
8	PROJECT 1	Grade (NG 6.7)		
9	PROJECT 2	Grade (NG 4.5)		
10	PROJECT 3			
11	FINAL	projectGrade (Projects (B8:B10))		
12		FINAL GRADE		
13		finalGrade B6 B11		

Fig. 2. A spreadsheet to compute student grades.

The spreadsheet in Fig. 2 is divided in three parts: THEORY (rows 0 to 6), PRACTICE (rows 7 to 11), and FINAL GRADE (rows 12 and 13). The THEORY part of the spreadsheet contains: two exams (EXAM 1 and EXAM 2); the retake of the first exam EXAM 1 (R), and EXAM 1 (BEST) which computes the best grade for the first exam. Each exam contains two exercises, for instance, EXAM 1 (row 2) has the scores of each exercise (cells B2 and C2), and the final exam score is calculated in cell D2.

The function (+) overrides the `Prelude` definition of addition, including the default value 0:

```
(+) :: Double ? 0 -> Double ? 0 -> Double
(+) = Prelude.(+)
```

The final THEORY grade (cell B6) is calculated using the auxiliary function `meanWithThreshold`, defined as follows:

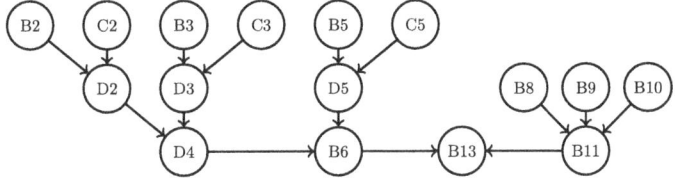

Fig. 3. Dependency graph.

```
meanWithThreshold :: NumericGrade -> [NumericGrade] -> Grade
```

The function `meanWithThreshold` receives two arguments, a minimum threshold score and a list of grades to compute the mean. For example, cell B6 in Fig. 2 uses a threshold of 3.75 and replaces any blank cell of the list [D4, D5] with NG 0.

The PRACTICE section of the spreadsheet, in rows 7 to 11, contains the grades for each project. In cell B11, a `Project` value is built from cells B8 to B10. Notice that cell B10 is empty, which is replaced by `Absent` according to the default value definition of the `Projects` data type. The final PRACTICE grade uses the `Projects` value and the auxiliary function `projectGrade`:

```
projectGrade :: Projects -> Grade
```

The `projectGrade` function calculates the final grade considering three cases. First, if a mandatory project is `Absent`, the final grade is `Absent`. Second, if any submitted project is below the threshold of 3, the final project grade is `Fail`. Otherwise, it computes the grades according to some weights for each project using an auxiliary function, named `gradeWithWeights`, with the following signature:

```
gradeWithWeights :: [Weight] -> [Grade] -> Grade
newtype Weight = Weight { getWeight :: Double } deriving (Show, Eq, Num)
```

The weights used to compute the final grade are numeric values (`Double`) encapsulated in a `newtype` definition. This tagged types are useful to differentiate between the numeric lists arguments `weights` and `grades`. A function definition using the `Double` values without tagged types could lead to an error when arguments are switched. Tagged types help to prevent this error at the type level and provides clear error messages if confused.

Finally, cell B13 calculates the final grade of a student using the auxiliary function `finalGrade`:

```
finalGrade :: [Grade] -> Grade
```

Cell Content Evaluation. The evaluation of cell expressions involves two files: one derived from the module containing auxiliary definitions and another containing cell expressions. Before generating these files, Haskcell performs a dependency analysis on the expressions in the cells. Figure 3 shows the resulting dependency graph after analyzing the running example. If the graph contains a circularity, an error is reported to the user. At this point, a file containing the cell expressions is produced. Each line of this file contains a function, with the name of the referenced cell; for instance, the function that corresponds to D2 is d2 = b2 + c2.

Desugaring Cell Contents. In Haskcell, cell expressions may contain default expressions, so they must be rewritten into standard Haskell code before evaluation. This program transformation is performed using Template Haskell (TH) [21]. First, let us recall the definition of (+) used in the running example. After applying the transformation, the resulting function is:

```
(+) :: Double -> Double -> Double
(+) = Prelude.(+)
arg1 = 0
arg2 = 0
```

where the default values in the type signature have been moved to new argument constants. Assuming that cell C2 is empty, let us illustrate the desugaring of the expression in cell D2 as a sequence of rewrites:

$$d2 = b2 + c2 \;\rightarrow\; d2 = (b2\ ?\ arg1) + (c2\ ?\ arg2) \;\rightarrow\; d2 = b2 + arg2$$

First, the (+) operator is rewritten to introduce the default arguments. After that, the default resolution over expressions leaves b2 untouched and introduces arg2 in place of c2.

6 Conclusion

Our initial goal when we started this project was to find out, *from an empirical standpoint*, whether it was possible to alleviate some problems of existing spreadsheet systems by incorporating features and ideas from functional programming. In order to run these experiments we needed a tool and now, we have an open source system that can be used by anyone interested in end-user programming and extended in several ways.

The running prototype is functional enough to test the concepts advocated in our project. We can affirm that a spreadsheet system based on Haskell is, not only possible, but not way harder to use than a traditional one – provided that the user has some knowledge of FP.

From the point of view of efficiency, user interaction is a bit slower than that of a professional spreadsheet system which is, of course, to be expected given the implementation techniques used, but the prototype is still usable. Also, our prototype does not take advantage of incremental compilation after edits.

Our experiments show that the functional syntax of Haskell and its type system can be leveraged to improve on existing spreadsheets in several aspects. Our formulas are more concise – thus readable, less prone to errors and favor reuse of code. We can conceive that, for a certain kind of user, functional spreadsheets could eventually be a natural replacement for the ones currently in use.

There is a lot of room for improvement regarding user interaction. For instance, on how to connect *user gestures* with actual definitions, e.g. range selection for data aggregator definition. Also, it would be nice to have the possibility of "tagging" areas of the spreadsheet with implicit type constructors so that users do not have to actually provide the data constructors when editing the cells. The connection of the property-based features of Haskcell with the user interface is still missing. Being a system based on program transformation it is tricky to connect the outcome of the errors detected in the generated code to its source.

Many errors in actual spreadsheets are related to *dimensions* and *units* issues, and we are already studying the possibility of incorporating dimension types into a future version of Haskcell.

Acknowledgments. The authors are partly funded by the Spanish Government through the SAFER project from the MCI-AEI (PID2019-104735RB-C44), the PROCODE project (PID2019-108528RB-C21/MCIN/AEI/10.13039/501100011033) and the PRODIGY project (TED2021-132464B-I00/MCIN/AEI/10.13039/501100011 033).

This work has also been funded by the European Union via the NextGenerationEU/PRTR (GA No. 101061343). Views and opinions expressed are however those of the author(s) only and do not necessarily reflect those of the EU, which can not be held responsible for them.

References

1. Zynda, M.R.: The first killer app: a history of spreadsheets. Interactions **20**(5), 68–72 (2013). https://doi.org/10.1145/2509224
2. Foley, M.J.: About that 1 billion Microsoft Office figure... (2010). https://www.zdnet.com/article/about-that-1-billion-microsoft-office-figure/
3. Nadella, S., Nadella, S., Myerson, T.: Build 2016 (2016). https://news.microsoft.com/speeches/satya-nadella-and-terry-myerson-build-2016/
4. Panko, R.R.: What we know about spreadsheet errors. J. End User Comput. **10**(2), 15–21 (1998). http://dl.acm.org/citation.cfm?id=287893.287899
5. Panko, R.: What we don't know about spreadsheet errors today: the facts, why we don't believe them, and what we need to do, CoRR abs/1602.02601 (2016). arXiv:1602.02601
6. Powell, S.G., Baker, K.R., Lawson, B.: A critical review of the literature on spreadsheet errors. Decis. Support Syst. **46**(1), 128–138 (2008). https://doi.org/10.1016/j.dss.2008.06.001. http://www.sciencedirect.com/science/article/pii/S0167923608001127
7. EuSpRIG, Original horror stories (2019). http://www.eusprig.org/stories.htm
8. Parker, M.: UK Government loses COVID data because of Excel mistake (2020). https://youtu.be/zUp8pkoeMss. Accessed 06 May 2021
9. Ronen, B., Palley, M.A., Lucas, H.C., Jr.: Spreadsheet analysis and design. Commun. ACM **32**(1), 84–93 (1989). https://doi.org/10.1145/63238.63244
10. Barowy, D.W., Berger, E.D., Zorn, B.: Excelint: automatically finding spreadsheet formula errors. Proc. ACM Program. Lang. **2**(OOPSLA), 148:1–148:26 (2018). https://doi.org/10.1145/3276518

11. Ray, B., Posnett, D., Devanbu, P., Filkov, V.: A large-scale study of programming languages and code quality in github. Commun. ACM **60**(10), 91–100 (2017). https://doi.org/10.1145/3126905
12. Ballesteros, I.: Diseño de una librería para el apoyo a hojas de cálculo funcionales, Escuela Técnica Superior de Ingenieros Informáticos (2019)
13. Bueso de Barrio, L.E.: Entorno de ejecución para un sistema de hojas de cálculo basado en programación funcional, Escuela Técnica Superior de Ingenieros Informáticos (2019)
14. Jones, S.P., Blackwell, A., Burnett, M.: A user-centred approach to functions in Excel. SIGPLAN Not. **38**(9), 165–176 (2003). https://doi.org/10.1145/944746.944721
15. Bock, A.A., Bøgholm, T., Sestoft, P., Thomsen, B., Thomsen, L.L.: On the semantics for spreadsheets with sheet-defined functions. J. Comput. Lang. **57**, 100960 (2020). https://doi.org/10.1016/j.cola.2020.100960. https://www.sciencedirect.com/science/article/pii/S2590118420300204
16. Lisper, B., Malmström, J.: Haxcel: a spreadsheet interface to Haskell. In: 14th International Workshop on the Implementation of Functional Languages, Forthcoming, pp. 206–222 (2002)
17. Wakeling, D.: Spreadsheet functional programming. J. Funct. Program. **17**(1), 131–143 (2007). https://doi.org/10.1017/S0956796806006186
18. Fernández-Soriano, A.M., Mariño, J., Herranz, Á.: A tool for the integration of constraint solving in spreadsheets. Electron. Notes Theor. Comput. Sci. **282**, 35–45 (2012). Proceedings of the XI Spanish Conference on Programming and Languages, PROLE 2011. https://doi.org/10.1016/j.entcs.2011.12.004. https://www.sciencedirect.com/science/article/pii/S1571066111001939
19. Cervesato, I.: The Deductive Spreadsheet, Springer, Cham (2013)
20. Spivey, J.: The Z Notation. Prentice-Hall (1987)
21. Sheard, T., Jones, S.P.: Template meta-programming for Haskell. In: Proceedings of the 2002 ACM SIGPLAN Workshop on Haskell, Haskell 2002, pp. 1–16. Association for Computing Machinery, New York (2002). https://doi.org/10.1145/581690.581691

Leveraging LLM Reasoning with Dual Horn Programs

Paul Tarau

Department of Computer Science and Engineering, University of North Texas, Denton, USA
`paul.tarau@unt.edu`

Abstract. Dual Horn clauses mirror key properties of Horn clauses. We revisit Dual Horn clauses as enablers of a form of constructive negation that supports goal-driven forward reasoning and is valid both intuitionistically and classically. In particular, we explore the ability to falsify hypotheses in the context of a background theory expressed as a Dual Horn clause program. With Dual Horn clause programs, by contrast to negation as failure, the variable bindings in their computed answers provide explanations for the reasons why a statement is successfully falsified. We devise a compilation scheme from Dual Horn clause programs to Horn clause programs, ensuring their execution with no performance penalty and we design the embedded SymLP language to support combined Horn clause and Dual Horn clause programs. As a (motivating) application, we cast LLM reasoning chains into propositional Horn and Dual Horn clauses that work together to constructively prove and disprove goals and enhance Generative AI with explainability of reasoning chains.

Keywords: Dual Horn clauses · constructive negation · theory falsification · LLM generated logic programs · compilation to Prolog

1 Introduction

The concept of negation in logic programming traditionally relies on "negation as failure", which infers the negation of a proposition if the proposition itself cannot be proven. This approach, while useful, often lacks the ability to provide clear explanations for why a proposition is considered false (given the absence of variable bindings). This is a problem, especially in complex scenarios where understanding the reasoning process is crucial.

In fact, negation as failure tacitly reflects a meta-level property about the proof procedure into the object-language, and as this can be iterated on, the resulting semantics is unavoidably subtle requiring carefully designed guardrails for both practical programming uses and theoretical foundations. In practical terms, it conflates interpretations of failure to prove as meaning "unknown" or "false" depending on the open or closed world semantics of the logic program.

Curiosity about the possibility of a simpler and more informative negation mechanism in Logic Programming brings us to our "back to the future" revisiting of Dual Horn clauses.

Dual Horn clauses have emerged as an interesting set of propositional formulas in Schaefer's *"dichotomy theorem"*, that classifies propositional formulas in P-complete vs. NP-complete classes [14], by falling in the P-complete class together with their Horn clause cousins.

Surprisingly, while their theoretical properties have been well known for very long time, we have found no evidence of their uses in programming or knowledge representation tasks and no mentions of uses in more expressive logic languages beyond the propositional case.

In part, this motivates revisiting them simply as logic programming expressiveness enhancers. Another motivation comes from the ability to generate interesting propositional Dual Horn clause programs with LLMs, when the problem we focus on involves forward reasoning from a fact to its consequences. This contrasts to Prolog's usual backward reasoning elaboration of a goal into progressively more solvable alternatives and subgoals.

As we will show next, it turns out that the significance of Dual Horn clauses centers around their ability to constructively handle negation, moving beyond the limitations of negation as failure. By enabling *goal-driven forward reasoning*, Dual Horn clauses support the exploration and falsification of hypotheses in the presence of negative factual information. This capability is particularly valuable in fields where reasoning that supports decisions processes is important. With constructive logic in mind, we will also point out the properties shared between Horn clause and Dual Horn clause programs that also hold in Intuitionistic Logic when represented in implicational form (Sect. 2).

The formal structure of Dual Horn clauses enables a compilation scheme that transforms Dual Horn clause programs into conventional Horn clause programs allowing their execution with no performance penalty. This development ensures that the enhanced capabilities of Dual Horn clauses can be seamlessly integrated into existing logic programming systems, leading to a sketch of an embedded language accommodating Horn clauses and Dual Horn clause working together, SymLP (Sect. 3). We will describe, using the notations of SymLP several examples of reasoning patterns including default reasoning, theory falsification, decision on conflicting information and interactions with negation as failure (Sect. 4).

We will also expand the utility of Dual Horn clauses by exploring their application in the context of Generative AI and Large Language Models (LLMs). By casting the reasoning steps of LLMs into propositional Horn and Dual Horn clauses, we provide a framework that not only supports the proving or disproving of goals but also enhances the explainability of the LLMs' decision-making processes. The ability to explain AI decisions transparently is crucial for building trust and for the practical deployment of AI systems in sensitive or impactful domains (Sect. 5).

After discussing related work (Sect. 6) we conclude the paper and discuss future work (Sect. 7).

The SWI-Prolog code described in the paper is available online[1].

---

[1] https://github.com/ptarau/TypesAndProofs/tree/master/symlp.

2 Background on Dual Horn Clauses

A *Horn clause* is a disjunction of literals with at most one positive literal. A *Definite Horn clause* is a disjunction of literals with exactly one positive literal. A *Dual Horn clause* is a disjunction of literals with at most one negative literal. A *Definite Dual Horn clause* is a disjunction of literals with exactly one negative literal. *A Horn clause Program* is a conjunction of Horn clauses. A *Dual Horn clause program* is a conjunction of Dual Horn clauses.

The following formulas describe Horn clauses (1) and (2), vs. Dual Horn clauses (3) and (4). Note the disjunctive forms as expressed, for instance, in resolution theory and the implicational forms as expressed in Prolog or Answer Set Programming (ASP) programs.

Horn

$$p_0 \vee \neg p_1 \vee \ldots \vee \neg p_n. \tag{1}$$

$$p_0 \leftarrow p_1 \wedge \ldots \wedge p_n. \tag{2}$$

Dual Horn

$$\neg p_0 \vee p_1 \vee \ldots \vee p_n. \tag{3}$$

$$p_0 \rightarrow p_1 \vee \ldots \vee p_n. \tag{4}$$

Similarly, the two forms make sense when extending Definite Horn clauses with integrity constraints called *denials* [8] (see (5) and (6)), asserting that at least one p_i must be false and their duals (see (7) and (8)), asserting that at least one p_i must be true.

Horn

$$\neg p_1 \vee \ldots \vee \neg p_n. \tag{5}$$

$$false \leftarrow p_1 \wedge \ldots \wedge p_n. \tag{6}$$

Dual Horn

$$p_1 \vee \ldots \vee p_n. \tag{7}$$

$$true \rightarrow p_1 \vee \ldots \vee p_n. \tag{8}$$

While the usual assumption about the underlying logic in Prolog and SAT solvers is classical logic (CL) or the underlying logic of the ASP systems, the proof-theoretical semantics [12] of Horn clause Logic in implicational form has been known to be compatible also with its reading in Intuitionistic Logic (IL). We will keep this in mind when covering some key properties of both Horn clause and Dual Horn clause programs.

Proposition 1. – *(1) implies (2) in IL and (1) is equivalent to (2) in CL.*
- *(3) implies (4) in IL and (3) is equivalent to (4) in CL.*
- *(5) implies (6) in IL and (5) is equivalent to (6) in CL.*
- *(7) and (8) are equivalent both in IL and CL.*

Proofs of the CL statements are trivial using De Morgan and definition of material implication. The implicational forms in IL are weaker given that De Morgan holds only one way. Proofs in IL are otherwise easy using a sequent calculus system like [6] or its corresponding sound and complete theorem prover [16].

Proposition 2. *Satisfiability of Horn clause and Dual Horn clause formulas with or without integrity constraints is P-complete.*

This follows from Schaefer's dichotomy theorem classifying propositional formulas [14] in P-complete vs. NP-complete types. Note that finding a renaming that might turn a set of clauses into a set of Horn or Dual Horn clauses is also polynomial [3].

Example 1. *We start with a small Dual Definite program, adopting Prolog-like syntax, with $\rightarrow$ represented as "=>" and $\vee$ represented as ";".*

```
p => q ; r.
q => r ; s.
r => false.
s => false.
```

Note also that "s => false" represents a negated fact (in either CL or IL), the same way as "s :- true" would represent a positive fact. Let's proceed with p as our goal, similarly as if we would evaluate a Horn clause program. Assuming that p were true, we would infer that at least one of q, r and s should be true. Thus at least one of r and s should be true, but both r and s implies false. The falsity of s and r and then backpropagates and falsifies the initial goal p. Note that this reasoning is also intuitionistically valid, similarly to its Horn clause counterpart.

We conclude from this example that we have a goal oriented *falsification* process for Dual Horn programs that mimics *verification* in Horn programs via SLD-resolution. It is easy to see that programs with variable bindings generated via unification will work also in a similar way.

More generally, the falsification process relies on the following fact:

Proposition 3. *The relations (9) and (10) hold both in IL and CL.*

$$(p_0 \leftarrow p_1 \wedge \ldots \wedge p_n) \wedge p_1 \wedge \ldots \wedge p_n \rightarrow p_0 \tag{9}$$

$$(p_0 \rightarrow p_1 \vee \ldots \vee p_n) \wedge \neg p_1 \wedge \ldots \neg p_n \rightarrow \neg p_0 \tag{10}$$

Thus, based on (10), to falsify p_0 we need to falsify all the disjuncts p_i that are consequences of p_0, the essence of a goal-driven falsification process, operationally similar to SLD-resolution proof procedure on Horn clause programs as illustrated by (9). Note that inference using (9) reduces to applying *modus ponens* and inference using (10) reduces to applying *modus tollens*.

3 Symmetric Logic Programming (SymLP): The Two Sides of the Mirror, Together

The next step is to design a mechanism for the "safe cohabitation" of Horn clauses and Dual Horn clauses in the same program. To ensure that their predicates defining rules and facts are disjoint (for instance, to avoid contradictions) we will place the Horn clause component in module `true` and the Dual Horn clause component in module `false`. Note that using modules, is mostly a syntactic simplification for implementing them in Prolog, as any mechanism ensuring that the predicate symbols are distinct would do (e.g., by prefixing predicate names with symbols `true` and `false`).

3.1 Syntax

To embed the SymLP language that combines Horn clauses and Dual Horn clauses into Prolog, we will use a few operators. We use "+" to mark facts that are true and "-" to mark facts that are false. We will use "=>" to represent implication and "<=" to represent reverse implication. Note also that -p can be seen as a shortcut for p=>false and that similarly, +p can be seen as a shortcut for p<=true. We will borrow from Prolog the usual notation for conjunction ",'' and disjunction ";".

Next, we will describe a surprisingly simple mechanism to implement a goal-oriented execution mechanism for Dual Horn programs, inspired by the SLD-resolution mechanism of Prolog. In the case of Dual Horn clauses it will map the falsification process of forward reasoning rules to the goal-driven elaboration process that Prolog's SLD-resolution uses. To this end, we will devise a compilation mechanism directly derived from the duality between successful proofs of Horn clause programs a and successful falsification of Dual Horn clause programs.

3.2 The Compilation of Symmetric Logic Programs to Prolog Clauses

The similarity between proving a goal by backward reasoning in Horn Clause programs and falsifying a claim via forward reasoning about its consequences in Dual Horn programs suggests that a simple compilation scheme from Dual Horn clauses to Horn clauses must exist, noting that when extended to the case of SymLP programs, it will just keep Horn clauses invariant.

Let us note the following classically and intuitionistically valid transformation applied to Dual Horn clause

$$p_0 \to p_1 \vee \ldots \vee p_n.$$

into a Horn Clause

$$p_0 \leftarrow p_1 \wedge \ldots \wedge p_n.$$

Clearly, successful proof of the resulting Horn clause program maps step-by-step into successful falsification of the transformed Dual Horn clause program. Thus we will convert Dual Horn clauses occurring in a Prolog program to corresponding Horn clauses that, when executed, follow the semantics of the Dual Horn clause program. We will implement this using Prolog's term_expansion[2] that overloads the Prolog reader with a call to

```
compile_clauses(SymLPclause, EquivalentPrologclause)
```

We will distinguish successful falsification from successful proof of the "compiled" Horn program simply by placing the result of the term_expansion/2 of Horn clauses into the module true and the result for Dual Horn clauses into the module false.

After defining "<=" (reverse implication) and "=>" (implication) as operators, the predicate compile_clauses will be called at term expansion time to convert the Dual Horn clauses to Horn clauses to be placed in module "false". Note also that in the bodies of Dual Horn clauses disjunctions will be converted to conjunctions. Facts marked with "-" will be placed in module false. The action on Horn clauses introduced by "<=" is just replacing "<=" with ":-" to be then added together with facts marked with "+" to the module "true".

```
:- multifile(term_expansion/2).

:-op(1199,xfx,(=>)).
:-op(1199,xfx,(<=)).
```

```
compile_clauses(C,_):-var(C),!,fail.

compile_clauses((H<=B),true:(H:-B)):-!,nonvar(H),nonvar(B).
compile_clauses((+H),true:H):-!,nonvar(H).

compile_clauses((H=>B),R):-nonvar(H),nonvar(B),!,dual2clause((H=>B),R).
compile_clauses((-H),false:H):-nonvar(H).
```

```
dual2clause((H=>false),false:(H)):-!.
dual2clause((H=>B),false:(H:-CB)):-disj2conj(B,CB).
dual2clause((-H),false:H).

disj2conj((A;B),(CA,CB)):-nonvar(A),nonvar(B),!,
    disj2conj(A,CA),
    disj2conj(B,CB).
disj2conj(A,A).
```

Example 2. *As the Horn clauses get compiled simply by replacing* <= *with* :-, *we will illustrate next what happens to a Dual Horn clause program:*

```
:-include('compile_clauses.pro').

p => q ; r.
q => r ; s.
r => false.
s => false.
```

---
[2] https://www.swi-prolog.org/pldoc/man?predicate=term_expansion/2

becomes:

```
p :- q , r.
q :- r , s.
r :- true.
s :- true.
```

Then, querying it with:

```
?- false:p.
true
```

the success confirms that p *is indeed falsifiable.*

4 Reasoning Patterns Expressed in SymLP

We will next overview a few reasoning patterns expressed as SymLP programs.

4.1 Default Reasoning, a Dual View

Example 3. *Dually to the usual way to express defaults and exceptions, we just declare which birds are not challenged when defining which of them can fly.*

```
:-include('compile_clauses.pro').

fly(X) <= bird(X),false:challanged_bird(X).
```

```
+bird(tweety).
+bird(chicken_little).
+bird(eagle_joe).
+bird(humming_jenny).

-challanged_bird(eagle_joe).
-challanged_bird(humming_jenny).
```

```
?- true:fly(X).
X = eagle_joe ; X = humming_jenny.
```

4.2 Dual Horn Programs and the Logic of Theory Falsification

Falsifiability of a theory has been known for a long time [13] as instrumental to make the theory predictive and testable, and thus useful in practice. In terms of Dual Horn programs, this is expressed by saying that something should fail if its consequences fail and by observing that falsity propagates back from false facts to rules that rely to them. This suggests a proof procedure to be applied to Dual Horn clauses described in formula (4).

Example 4. *We will clarify this by working out an example of "theory falsification"*[3].

```
:-include('compile_clauses.pro').

'Negative gravity fields are possible' =>
    'Planets and stars would disperse' ;
    'Atmospheres of planets would be pushed away from their surfaces' ;
    'Unresolvable paradoxes in physics'.

'Planets and stars would disperse' => false.
```

```
'Unresolvable paradoxes in physics' =>
    'Relativity theory is incorrect' ;
    'Quantum field theory is incorrect'.

'Relativity theory is incorrect' => false.
'Quantum field theory is incorrect' => false.

'Atmospheres of planets would be pushed away from their surfaces' => false.
```

The result of the "execution" of this Dual Horn clause program could be expressed by a query goal of the form:

```
?- false:'Negative gravity fields are possible'.
true
```

confirming that "Negative gravity fields are possible" has been successfully falsified in the context of our accepted background knowledge about physics.

4.3 Combining Positive and Negative Advice in a SymLP Program

The next example of SymLP program will have calls across the true and false modules. Note that the include statement will trigger the compilation process, as explained in Subsect. 3.2.

Example 5. *Combining nuances of (a fictional example) of advice on stocks.*

```
:-include('compile_clauses.pro').

cautious_buy(X)<=recommended(X),safe(X).

safe(X) <= false:volatile(X).
safe(X) <= false:overvalued(X).
safe(X) <= true:stable(X).
```

---

[3] Obtained by edits of an LLM request to explain problems with assuming the existence of negative gravity fields.

```
+recommended(qqq).
+recommended(bitcoin).
+recommended(apple).
+recommended(meta).
+recommended(berkshire).

+stable(att).
+stable(berkshire).
```

```
volatile(X) => big_price_changes_last_month(X).
```

```
-big_price_changes_last_month(apple).
-big_price_changes_last_month(meta).
-big_price_changes_last_month(comcast).

-overvalued(qqq).
```

After combining positive and negative facts and inferences drawn from them in Horn module true *and Dual Horn module* false *the call to* cautious_buy(X) *in module* true *will generate the following answers:*

```
?- true:cautious_buy(X).
X = qqq ;
X = apple ;
X = meta ;
X = berkshire.
```

At this point, one might want to ask the legitimate question:

> Why would we represent negation by explicitly listing negative facts, knowing that something like not(white(swan,X)) will include not just "black swans" but also an infinite set of unrelated entities (e.g., "globular galaxies") ?

First, like in the stock market advising in Example 5, decisions are justified by a small set of positive or negative facts from where a decision process initiates. Next, reasoning with Machine Learning datasets (including those used in Inductive Logic Programming) relies on finite sets of positive and negative facts. In particular, in Generative AI, a way to control hallucinations is by implementing, as part of a multi-agent framework, generation of positive and negative facts and rules relying on them.

4.4 Negation as Failure to Prove and Affirmation as Failure to Disprove

Assuming that we have compiled our SymLP e program into the modules true and false, negation as failure (unverifiable/1) and its dual (unfalsifiable) are implemented as follows:

```
unverifiable(X):-not(true:X).
unfalsifiable(X):-not(false:X).
```

Note that combining modules true and false into one program has the same complexity as Horn clause programs. Thus it has a single minimal model that can be computed in polynomial time in the propositional case. This holds true also if not/1 calls between modules true and false result in a stratified compiled program [7]. Otherwise, we are back to the usual pitfalls of Prolog's negation as failure. Therefore, a semantically safe and simple use of Prolog's not/1 would be to only apply it to predicates in modules true and false from *outside* (e.g., from Prolog's module "user").

Example 6. *Using Prolog's* not/1 *in a SymLP program.*

```
:-include('compile_clauses.pro').

exonerated(X) <= suspect(X),false:proven_guilty(X).

investigated(X) <= suspect(X),not(false:proven_guilty(X)).

+suspect(alice).
+suspect(bob).

proven_guilty(X) => found_of(X,dna) ; found_of(X,fingerprints).

-found_of(alice,_anything).
```

Not falsifiable *that Bob is* proven_guilty *only entails that he is still investigated (vs. exonerated if not proven guilty in the case of Alice).*

```
?- exonerated(X).
X = alice.

?- investigated(X).
X = bob.
```

Let us just mention that, similarly to ASP and s(CASP) [1], concepts related to epistemic modalities emerge, when combining the independent opinions originating on the two sides:

- things that are clearly unknown: failure to prove and failure to disprove
- things that are strongly accepted as known: successfully proven and failing to disprove
- things that are very likely to be impossible: successfully falsified and failing to prove.

Let us also note here an important distinction between the disjunction added in Classical Logic to implement negation

```
:- p,q.
p v q.
```

and omitting the disjunction in the case of its Intuitionistic Logic interpretation of the integrity constraints.

Instead of explicitly using negation, integrity constraints of the form (6) for Horn Clause programs and (8) for Dual Horn Clause programs can be used with similar expressive power while staying with the Intuitionistic semantics of Horn Clause and Dual Horn Clause programs. As an added benefit, the absence of the disjunctive clause, in the propositional case keeps complexity polynomial.

5 LLM Generated Dual Horn Programs

Generative AI, with often human-like language skills is shifting focus from typical search engines to more conversational interactions. Yet, the challenge remains that humans must still process and verify this information, an often tedious task.

An answer to this, as implemented in the DeepLLM system [18] is to automate the entire process. We start with a simple "initiator goal" and let the LLM dive recursively in its parametric memory and deliver a detailed answer focused on the initiator and the trace of the LLM's chain of steps. These are summarized as the short term-memory maintained via the DeepLLM API. DeepLLM also helps to minimize common issues like inaccuracies, made-up information, and biases that are often associated with LLMs by using ground truth and oracle agents that constrain its generative steps.

We refer to [17, 18] for details of implementation of the DeepLLM system, as well as to its open-source code[4] and its online demo[5].

The DeepLLM system's active components (subclasses of the Agent class) are Interactors, Recursors, and Refiners:

- Interactors manage input prompts and task breakdown
- Recursors handle iterative exploration of subtasks
- Refiners enhance clarity and relevance of LLM responses

  To validate its reasoning steps, the system also relies on stored knowledge resources:

  Ground truth facts: sentences collected from online sources or local documents
- Vector store: enabler of "semantic search" via embeddings of sentences

Starting from a succinct prompt (typically a nominal phrase or a short sentence describing the task) an Interactor will call the LLM via its API, driven by a Recursor that analyzes the LLM's responses and activates new LLM queries as it proceeds to refine the information received up to a given depth.

Refiners are Recursor subclasses that rely on semantic search in an embeddings store containing ground-truth facts as well as on oracles implemented as specialized Interactors that ask the LLM for advice on deciding the truth of, or the rating of hypotheses. Besides returning a stream of answers, Recursors and Refiners compile their reasoning steps to a propositional Horn clause program available for inspection by the user or subject for execution and analysis with logic programming tools (in particular, with its model builder – a fast propositional Horn clause theorem prover).

---

[4] https://github.com/ptarau/recursors/.
[5] https://deepllm.streamlit.app.

5.1 Generating Propositional Horn Clause Programs with the DeepLLM App

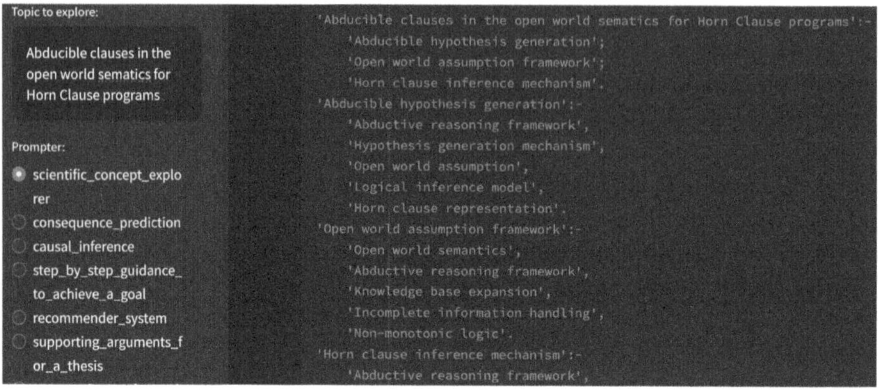

Fig. 1. DeepLLM app

In the case of the interaction shown in Fig. 1, the initiator goal "Abducible clauses in the open world semantics for Horn Clause programs" starts the "scientific concept explorer" option and generates in the right side window a Horn clause program describing successive refinements of the initiator goal.

The DeepLLM app, written with the `Streamlit`[6] webapp generator lets the user choose between the Recursor, Advisor and Rater agents, providing for the latter a threshold level slider. The threshold informs the Rater oracle to accept or reject a generated rule head or fact (the higher the threshold the stricter the accept decision). Options to set the maximum recursion depth and activate relation extraction and visualization are also available.

The application starts once the user enters the topic to explore, chooses the prompter template and activates the LLM. Besides the output produced in the right window, when run locally, it saves the generated logic program and its computed minimal model as Prolog code files.

Given the ability to steer an LLM to explore recursively a given topic while staying focussed on the objective specified by an initiator goal the LLM can be used to generate large sets of high quality positive or negative facts as well as rules describing their inference steps, to be all exported as a Prolog program.

5.2 The LLM-Generated Dual Horn Clause Programs

When targeting Dual Horn clause programs, the generation mechanism is dual to asking LLMs to solve a problem by decomposing it into simpler steps (a form of backward reasoning). When asking an LLM to explore the consequences (a form of forward reasoning) enables a decision maker to understand via the Dual Horn Clause falsification mechanism their far reaching impacts.

---
[6] https://streamlit.io/.

Example 7. *The following is a complete example of a propositional Dual Horn clause program[7] generated from a recursively explored (up to depth = 2) initiator goal asking to falsify the misguided belief about:* "escalation risks after use of tactical nuclear weapons":

The initiator goal expands into a disjunction of implications that would all need to be falsified.

```
'escalation risks after use of tactical nuclear weapons'=>
    'Global nuclear war';
    'Uncontrollable retaliation cycles'.
```

The same applies to each of the disjuncts, which, if successfully falsified, with back-propagate failure to the initiator goal.

```
'Global nuclear war'=>
    'Widespread radioactive fallout',
    'Massive civilian casualties',
    'Long-term environmental damage',
    'Global economic collapse',
    'Irreversible climate change',
    'Extensive agricultural failure'.
'Widespread radioactive fallout'=>
    'Long-term environmental damage';
    'Massive civilian casualties'.
```

We will skip the details of the generated Dual Horn Clause program and just illustrate a set of unwanted consequences (implemented as negative facts), that have been reached by DeepLLM at recursion level 2.

```
-'Sudden geopolitical shifts'.
-'Massive displacement waves'.
-'Severe resource shortages'.
-'Intensified disease outbreaks'.
-'Heightened conflict incidents'.
-'Severe job losses'.
-'Market instability'.
-'Investment crashes'.
-'Supply chain disruptions'.
-'Increased poverty rates'.
-'Currency devaluation'.
-'Overburdened local resources'.
-'Increased social tensions'.
-'Strained healthcare systems'.
-'Environmental degradation'.
-'Widespread famine outbreaks'.
-'Mass displacement waves'.
-'Severe medical shortages'.
-'Intensified poverty levels'.
```

---

[7] Ready to be tried out online with the DeepLLM system at https://deepllm.streamlit.app/.

```
-'International trade paralysis'.
-'Financial sector instability'.
-'Intensified food shortages'.
-'Increased child mortality'.
```

Note that the "-" operator marking negation is interpreted here as an unwanted outcome, from which, a rational agent would propagate back the denial of the initiator goal, implying that *"escalation risks after use of tactical nuclear weapons"* is something to avoid, given its consequences.

Similar initiator queries can cover recursive descent in consequences of things like unobservable/unmeasurable claims, undesirable outcomes of planned actions, implications of hidden legalese in contracts as well as untruthful advertisements or political persuasion hyperbolae.

By default, the DeepLLM system [18] generates propositional programs together with their unique minimal model[8] and its low complexity polynomial solver can support scaling to very large programs aggregating positive and negative knowledge snippets consisting of facts and rules of Horn and Dual Horn programs. By asking an LLM to decompose recursively a task into subtasks organized as an AND-OR tree, the generated Prolog file will be a Horn clause program. Dually, by asking an LLM to explore consequences of an undesirable state of the world or of a hypothesis that one would want to reject, the results will take the shape of a Dual Horn clause program.

This abundance of positive and negative information offers a fully explainable and semantically straightforward alternative to default reasoning and alleviates the contrast between the underlying open vs. closed world assumptions, given that arbitrary positive or negative information and constructive inference based on it is available on demand.

6 Related Work

Horn clause formulas and Dual Horn clause formulas (called weakly negative and, respectively, weakly positive in [14]) are proven in his "dichotomy theorem" (under the assumption $P \neq NP$) to be among the classes of propositional formulas that are in P. A graph-based linear algorithm exists for Horn clause formulas, described in [5] and given the linear renaming algorithm of propositional variables in [3], the same applies to Dual Horn formulas. Along these lines, as a follow-up of [5], the Hornlog system, a logic programming alternative to Prolog covering (besides definite programs) the handling of denial integrity constraints has been implemented [9].

A salient question one might ask is *"If Dual Horn clauses have been known for a long time, why they haven't been widely used until now?"*.

A possible explanation is that the practical usefulness of negation as failure in Prolog and the related theoretical ramifications, culminating with the stable model semantics [10] and the emergence of Answer Set Programming as an alternative logic programming execution model have provided enough expressive power to deal with more subtle nuances of negative information.

---

[8] https://github.com/ptarau/recursors.

Another is that constructive negation algorithms, going back to [2, 15] and present in goal-directed ASP systems like s(CASP) [1], have provided, in the form of constraints on variable bindings, similar explanations covering the reasons of negative outcomes. Also, a compilation scheme from normal logic programs to definite programs under given stratification constraints has been devised in [11]. Note however that constructive negation expressed as a set of "is different from" constraints on a set of variables is fundamentally weaker than inferring in Dual Horn clause logic where the actual values should be based on known negative facts. More precisely, in the case of classical constructive negation, these results were expressed as disjunction of conjunctions of the form X\=T where T is a (usually ground) term, thus describing what X cannot be, while in the case of Dual Horn programs the result is a positive binding of the form X=T saying what X actually is. Thus, while the classical "constructive" negation in combination with constraint solvers provides an efficient filtering mechanism over a potentially infinite set of terms, it shares with negation as failure the fact that it can only reject bindings constructed elsewhere in the program but it cannot actually *construct* variable bindings as its name would (somewhat inadvertently) suggest.

7 Conclusion and Future Work

We have revisited Dual Horn clauses as a "back to the future" endeavor, motivated by their syntactic simplicity and straightforward semantics. As a result, we have devised a compilation scheme that integrates them into Prolog programs. This enables our SymLP embedded language as a practical programming tool that reasons with explicitly specified positive and negative facts and rules. In case of the possibly very large propositional programs generated by LLMs, the low polynomial complexity[9] ensures tractability – a key requirement for practical applications.

To some extent, the utility of Dual Horn program relies on the assumption that full knowledge of positive and negative facts can be acquired given their encapsulation in LLMs or traditional knowledge bases. This leaves open the possibility of unknown facts (e.g., those reached at the DeepLLM recursion depth limit) that can be seen as *abducibles*, i.e., verifiable if passing integrity constraints on the Horn clause side (formula (6)) or falsifiable if passing the corresponding constraints on the Dual Horn side (formula (8)). Future work will be needed to study these in full detail, while aware that their presence, in the propositional case will keep complexity polynomial.

This also opens the possibility to rely on soft-unification [4], relevant especially in the presence of LLM-generated facts stored as embeddings into a vector database. For instance, closeness via cosine-similarity to positive or negative facts could decide rules on which side would adopt these facts as abducibles, another future work direction worth to be explored.

Acknowledgements. We thank the PADL'2025 reviewers fort heir careful reading of the paper, their insightful comments and their constructive suggestions on improving its presentation.

---

[9] Actually linear if using the graph-based algorithm of [5]).

References

1. Arias, J., Carro, M., Salazar, E., Marple, K., Gupta, G.: Constraint answer set programming without grounding. Theory Pract. Logic Program. **18**(3–4), 337–354 (2018). https://doi.org/10.1017/S1471068418000285
2. Chan, D.: Constructive negation based on the completed database. In: Kowalski, R.A., Bowen, K.A. (eds.) Logic Programming, Proceedings of the Fifth International Conference and Symposium, Seattle, Washington, USA, 15–19 August 1988 (2 Volumes), pp. 111–125. MIT Press (1988)
3. Chandru, V., Coullard, C.R., Hammer, P.L., Montañez, M., Sun, X.: On renamable Horn and generalized Horn functions. Ann. Math. Artif. Intell. **1**(1-4), 33–47 (1990). https://doi.org/10.1007/BF01531069
4. Cingillioglu, N., Russo, A.: Learning invariants through soft unification (2020). https://doi.org/10.48550/arXiv.1909.07328
5. Dowling, W.F., Gallier, J.H.: Linear-time algorithms for testing the satisfiability of propositional horn formulae. J. Log. Program. **1**(3), 267–284 (1984). https://doi.org/10.1016/0743-1066(84)90014-1
6. Dyckhoff, R.: Contraction-free sequent calculi for intuitionistic logic. J. Symb. Log. **57**(3), 795–807 (1992). https://doi.org/10.2307/2275431
7. Eiter, T., Fink, M., Tompits, H., Woltran, S.: Complexity results for checking equivalence of stratified logic programs. In: IJCAI, pp. 330–335 (2007)
8. Eshghi, K., Kowalski, R.A.: Abduction compared with negation by failure. In: Levi, G., Martelli, M. (eds.) Logic Programming, Proceedings of the Sixth International Conference, Lisbon, Portugal, 19–23 June 1989, pp. 234–254. MIT Press (1989)
9. Gallier, J.H., Raatz, S.: HORNLOG: a graph-based interpreter for general Horn clauses. J. Logic Program. **4**(2), 119–155 (1987). https://doi.org/10.1016/0743-1066(87)90015-X. https://www.sciencedirect.com/science/article/pii/074310668790015X
10. Gelfond, M., Lifschitz, V.: The stable model semantics for logic programming. In: Kowalski, R.A., Bowen, K.A. (eds.) Logic Programming, Proceedings of the Fifth International Conference and Symposium, Seattle, Washington, USA, 15–19 August 1988 (2 Volumes), pp. 1070–1080. MIT Press (1988)
11. Kanchanasut, K., Stuckey, P.: Eliminating negation from normal logic programs. In: Kirchner, H., Wechler, W. (eds.) Algebraic and Logic Programming, pp. 217–231. Springer, Heidelberg (1990)
12. Miller, D.: A survey of the proof-theoretic foundations of logic programming. CoRR abs/2109.01483 (2021). https://arxiv.org/abs/2109.01483
13. Popper, K.R.: The Logic of Scientific Discovery. Hutchinson, London (1934)
14. Schaefer, T.J.: The complexity of satisfiability problems. In: Proceedings of the Tenth Annual ACM Symposium on Theory of Computing, STOC 1978, pp. 216–226. Association for Computing Machinery, New York (1978). https://doi.org/10.1145/800133.804350
15. Stuckey, P.: Negation and constraint logic programming. Inf. Comput. **118**(1), 12–33 (1995). https://doi.org/10.1006/inco.1995.1048. https://www.sciencedirect.com/science/article/pii/S0890540185710486
16. Tarau, P.: Abductive reasoning in intuitionistic propositional logic via theorem synthesis. Theory Pract. Logic Program. **22**(5), 693–707 (2022). https://doi.org/10.1017/S1471068422000254
17. Tarau, P.: Full automation of goal-driven LLM dialog threads with and-or recursors and refiner oracles arXiv:2306.14077 (2023)
18. Tarau, P.: System description: deepllm, casting dialog threads into logic programs. In: Gibbons, J., Miller, D. (eds.) Functional and Logic Programming, pp. 117–134. Springer, Singapore (2024). https://doi.org/10.1007/978-981-97-2300-3_7

ASP for Language Documentation and Reclamation: A Derivational Stemming Tool for Myaamia

Daniela Inclezan[1(✉)], Hunter Lockwood[1,2], Anita Baral[1], Jitendra Sharma[1], and Pratiksha Shrestha[1]

[1] Miami University, Oxford, OH 45056, USA
inclezd@miamioh.edu
[2] Myaamia Center, Oxford, OH 45056, USA

Abstract. This paper presents a practical application of Answer Set Programming (ASP) in the field of Language Documentation and Reclamation (LDR). LDR involves the systematic recording, preservation, analysis, and revitalization of endangered or dormant languages to protect linguistic diversity and cultural heritage. In collaboration with linguists working on the Myaamia language, we developed a derivational stemming tool that decomposes stems into their smallest meaningful units called morphemes. We explored different solvers and representations of stems and morphemes to identify the most efficient approach for several language documentation and research tasks. The tool's accuracy was assessed by comparing its output with the stem decompositions documented in the ILDA database for Myaamia. The stemming tool for Myaamia–a reawakening Algonquian language with a growing number of second-language speakers–can serve as a model for stemming tools that can be adapted for other Algonquian languages based on the methods detailed in this paper.

Keywords: ASP · linguistics · Language Documentation and Reclamation

1 Introduction

This paper presents a practical application of Answer Set Programming (ASP) [14,15] in the field of Language Documentation and Reclamation (LDR). LDR is a field concerned with the systematic recording, preservation, analysis, and revitalization of endangered or dormant languages, necessary to protect cultural heritage and linguistic diversity. Our work focuses on the Myaamia language, a reawakening language in the Algonquian family which today is used by a growing number of second language speakers, including members of the Miami Tribe of Oklahoma. In collaboration with linguists working at The Myaamia Center, a Miami Tribe of Oklahoma initiative, we developed a tool for derivational stem decomposition, which refers to the identification of the smallest constituents carrying lexical meaning that combine to form a word. While a preliminary version of this tool was briefly introduced elsewhere [4], we focus here on performance results and quality improvements based on the analysis of the preliminary tool.

The Myaamia Center has been developing the Indigenous Languages Digital Archive (ILDA), an online platform where communities are in control of the analysis and display of materials at every step of the process. In our work, we will reference the ILDA dictionary for Myaamia language and the database that supports it. ILDA however provides support to several other indigenous languages and tribal communities who participate in the National Breath of Life Archival Institute for Indigenous Languages.

Using declarative logic programming languages like ASP for Language Documentation and Reclamation offers significant benefits to both linguists and tribal communities. For linguists, the notation used in logic programming closely aligns with the formal structures they are familiar with, making it more intuitive for expressing linguistic rules. Additionally, the accessibility of ASP tools-such as the DLV solver, which requires only a simple text editor and an executable file-lowers the barrier to entry for both researchers and community members. For communities leading LDR efforts, the transparency of logic programs is a key advantage over black-box machine learning (ML) systems. Data sovereignty, which encompasses control over language data, access rights, and storage locations, is a priority for these communities. Unlike many ML systems that often necessitate sharing data with external parties, logic programming ensures that the data remains local, safeguarding the community's autonomy over their cultural and linguistic resources.

Logic programming, including ASP, has a long history of being used in linguistics and NLP research (e.g., [3,9–11,17,18,20,26–28]), complementing other rule-based approaches reducible to finite-state transducers (FSTs) [6,19]. A work similar to ours explores the use of Prolog for Uzbek morphological parsing [23], while other researchers have applied Inductive Logic Programming to the linguistic task of recognizing monosyllables in a language [24]. Our preliminary stem decomposition tool (or *stemmer*) [4] demonstrated the following contributions to Myaamia language documentation: proposing new stem derivation possibilities; enabling testing of linguistic theories; and facilitating the identification of errors and inconsistencies in the database for improved documentation. While currently focusing on Myaamia, the tool can be adapted for other Algonquian languages within the ILDA database in the future.

From a technical perspective, this project involved working with and manipulating a large volume of strings. We chose ASP for its advantages in representing linguistic defaults and exceptions, as well as its ability to generate multiple interpretations. Although the current project does not fully utilize ASP's capabilities, they are instrumental in building an additional phonological component. The DLV[1] [1] and DLV2[2] [2] solvers were selected for their built-in capabilities

---

[1] https://www.dlvsystem.it/dlvsite/.
[2] https://dlv.demacs.unical.it/home.

to handle text/words, with DLV and DLV2 representing strings as lists, while DLV2 also supports direct string manipulation. For the logic programming community, particularly those working with ASP, this paper offers a comparative analysis of solvers (DLV vs. DLV2) and string representations (lists vs. strings) when managing large volumes of input data.

In particular, this paper addresses the following research questions:

RQ1 Which representation of stems and morphemes-as lists or strings-and which ASP solver-DLV or DLV2-is more efficient when the derivational stemming tool is applied to (a) the entire collection of stems and morphemes vs. (b) decomposing a single stem (using the full set of morphemes) vs. (c) the testing of linguistic theories?

RQ2 What specific improvements can be made to the derivational stemmer to enhance its accuracy and performance?

RQ3 What are the current limitations of the derivational stemmer, and what future developments could be explored to further improve its quality and capabilities?

In Sect. 2 we provide background information on Myaamia derivational stem decomposition and ASP. In Sect. 3, we present the derivational stem decomposition tool and outline the experimental setup. Sections 4 through 6 detail the experiments conducted to address research questions *RQ1* through *RQ3*, respectively. The paper ends with conclusions in Sect. 7.

2 Background

2.1 The Indigenous Languages Digital Archive (ILDA)

For the Myaamia language, the ILDA platform [25] stores archival documents, such as Jesuit manuscripts, that contain Myaamia data or translations between Myaamia and French or English. It also includes a database [29] developed by Myaamia linguists, which records the known stems and morphemes identified to date from these documents. ILDA database entries for both stems and morphemes consist of a unique ID, the stem/morpheme itself in Myaamia language, its English translation, an identifier denoting its part-of-speech classification, and other fields not relevant to our task. Some examples of stems are *nawi-* meaning *"go get (?)"* [sic][3] and *apikaateesi-* meaning *"warm one's feet."* Figure 1 displays the ILDA entry for the stem *apikaateesi-* as seen through the ILDA interface. Some stems have already been fully or partially decomposed by linguists, and these decompositions are documented in the "Associated Morphemes" section of the dictionary entry.

---

[3] The question mark in parentheses appears in the actual ILDA database entry for *nawi-*. Given the incomplete language knowledge often available, it reflects the ongoing process of editing, updating, and revision that is inherent in LDR work.

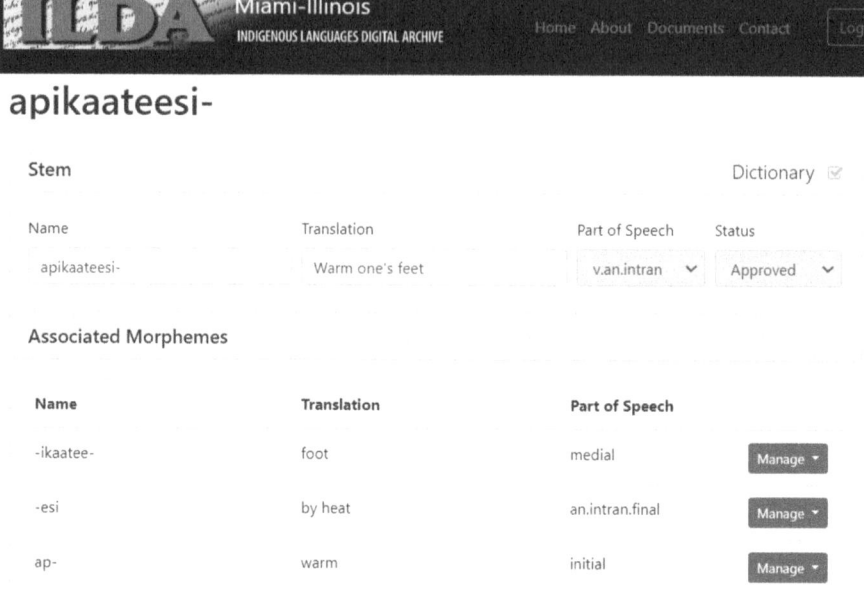

Fig. 1. ILDA Entry for the Stem *apikaateesi-*.

In Algonquian languages like Myaamia, morphemes can be initial, medial, or final, which is noted in the ILDA Database by a dash symbol at the position where the morpheme may be attached to other morphemes/stems. Some examples of morphemes as specified in the ILDA Database are:

- **initial**: *naw-* meaning *"go and, andative"*; *ap-* meaning *"warm"*
- **medial**: *-ikaatee-* meaning *"foot"*
- **final**: *-i* indicating an *"abstract final"*; *-esi* meaning *"by heat"*

2.2 Myaamia Derivational Stem Decomposition

Before discussing the linguistic task addressed in this paper, we will first introduce some key linguistic terms. See Macaulay and Salmons [21] for a thorough discussion of the particulars of Algonquian morphological analysis. A stem is the base of a word, associated with its core lexical meaning (or propositional content) and syntactic category (or part of speech). A morpheme is the smallest meaningful or functional unit of language. Broadly speaking, there are two types of morphemes: inflectional and derivational. Inflectional morphemes attach to the stem and are often called affixes (e.g. prefixes, suffixes, infixes). Derivational morphemes combine into stems, and in Algonquian linguistics are often called components [16,21]. Stem decomposition is the process of breaking stems down into derivational morphemes. Although we have begun work on inflection, this paper focuses exclusively on derivation, with inflectional decomposition left for future research.

Primary Derivation. In Myaamia, a stem can be derivationally decomposed according to the following three cases outlined by Goddard [16] cf. Macaulay and Salmons [21]:

1. The stem itself is an initial morpheme.
2. The stem is an initial morpheme followed by a final morpheme.
3. The stem is an initial morpheme, followed by a medial morpheme, followed by a final morpheme.

An example of primary derivation, as described in case 2 above, is provided below for the stem *nawi-*, presented in a format adapted from linguistics scholars, a so-called *interlinear gloss* [8]:

```
nawi = naw               + i
       go and, andative  + abstract final
       initial           + an.intran.final
       'go get (?)'
```

The first line of the interlinear gloss specifies the decomposition of a stem into morphemes; the second line captures the English translation of the morphemes; the third line represents the part-of-speech classification of the morphemes; the last line is the English translation of the stem to be decomposed.

Secondary Derivation. In Myaamia and other Algonquian languages, secondary stem decomposition occurs when a stem created through primary derivation (as described so far) is further extended with another final to form a new stem. There is a limited number of finals used for secondary derivation. One such final is *-aakan*, which indicates an instrument.

An example of a secondary derivation is *maawihšinaakan-* meaning *"band, hunting party,"* obtained from the stem *maawihšin-* and the suffix *-aakan*:

```
maawihšinaakan = maawihšin                       + aakan
                 head of a band or hunting party + instrument
                 v.an.intran                     + n.final
                 'band, hunting party'
```

where *maawihšin-* is obtained through primary derivation as follows:

```
maawihšin = maaw              + ihšin
            together, collect + be in position, lie
            initial           + an.intran.final
            'head of a band or hunting party'
```

2.3 Answer Set Programming

Answer Set Programming (ASP) [13–15,22] is a logic-based knowledge representation language [5]. A logic program of ASP is a specification for the set of beliefs held by a rational agent. It consists of a set of rules over a signature Σ. Each rule is a statement of the form:

$$l_1 \text{ or } \ldots \text{ or } l_i \leftarrow l_{i+1}, \ldots, l_m, \text{not } l_{m+1}, \ldots, \text{not } l_n$$

where $l_1, \ldots, l_n$ are literals of Σ (i.e., atoms or their negation), the symbol "*or*" denotes epistemic disjunction, and the symbol "not" denotes default negation, read as "there is no reason to believe." The following shorthands are normally used to refer to the components of a rule: $head(r) =_{def} \{l_1, \ldots, l_i\}$; $pos(r) =_{def} \{l_{i+1}, \ldots, l_m\}$; and $neg(r) =_{def} \{l_{m+1}, \ldots, l_n\}$.

The semantics of ASP are given in terms of *answer sets* of a program. Informally, an *answer set* A of a logic program Π over Σ is a consistent set of literals of Σ that corresponds to a set of beliefs held by the rational agent, such that A satisfies the rules of Π and the rationality principle: *Believe nothing you are not forced to believe*. A rule r with variables is viewed as the set of its possible ground instantiations. A ground set S of literals *satisfies* a rule r if any of the following conditions holds: $pos(r) \not\subseteq S$; $neg(r) \cap S \neq \emptyset$; or $head(r) \cap S \neq \emptyset$.

An *answer set* of Π is a set S of ground literals such that

1. If Π does not contain default negation, then S is a consistent and minimal set that satisfies all the rules in Π.
2. If Π contains default negation, then S is an answer set of the *reduct* of Π wrt S, Π^S, obtained by removing all rules containing "not" such that $l \in S$, and then removing all other premises containing "not."

While the LDR project described in this paper does not employ classical negation or epistemic disjunction, these features are necessary for the phonological component, which is crucial for developing a high-quality stem decomposition tool and will be addressed in future work.

2.4 ASP Solvers: DLV and DLV2

Answer sets of ASP programs are computed by answer set solvers (e.g., DLV, DLV2, Clingo), which support additional ASP constructs including *choice rules*

Table 1. List Manipulation Facilities in DLV and DLV2

DLV	DLV2	Description
$\#append(X,Y,Z)$	$\&append(X,Y;Z)$	Z is a list obtained by appending the elements of Y to X
$\#length(X,Y)$	$\&length(X;Y)$	Y is the size of list X
$\#getnth(X,Y,Z)$	$\&member(X,Y;Z)$	Z is the element at position Y in list X
$\#delnth(X,Y,Z)$	$\&delNth(X,Y;Z)$	Z is a list obtained by deleting the element of list X at position Y

and *aggregates* [7,12]. We selected DLV and DLV2 for this work due to their list and string manipulation capabilities. We represent Myaamia stems and morphemes as lists, utilizing the built-in facilities of DLV and DLV2 shown in Table 1.

Similar facilities are available in DLV2 for string manipulation, including: $\&append\_str(X,Y;Z)$ – Z is a string obtained by concatenating string Y to string X; $\&length\_str(X;Z)$ – Z is the length of string X; $\&sub\_str(X,Y,W;Z)$ – Z is the substring of W starting from index X to Y.

3 Derivational Stem Decomposition Tool and Experimental Setup

Let us now introduce the initial Myaamia derivational stem decomposition tool, which was developed using the DLV system and Python. The tool's underlying process is described in Fig. 2. Initially, information about stems and morphemes was downloaded from the ILDA Database in the form of csv files (*stems.csv* and *morphemes.csv* respectively) that were pre-processed by a Python script to produce a DLV program consisting of facts, *facts.lp*. This file together with an additional DLV program in which we encoded the stem decomposition rules of Myaamia language, *stemmer.lp*, were fed together into the DLV system. The resulting answer sets were post-processed by a second Python script that produced a more readable output in the *interlinear gloss* format [8].

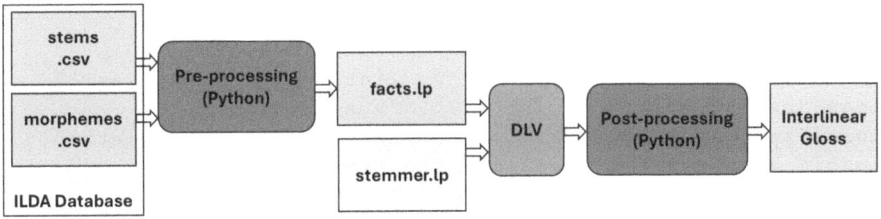

Fig. 2. Stem Decomposition Tool for Myaamia Language.

In the *facts.lp* file, predicate *stem* denoted Myaamia stems coming from the *stems.csv* file, and the predicates *initial*, *medial*, and *final* represented the three different types of Myaamia morphemes in the *morphemes.csv* file. Each stem or morpheme was represented as a list of characters and the initial and/or final dash symbol was omitted, as shown in the facts below:

```
stem(["n","a","w","i"]).
stem(["a","p","i","k","a","a","t","e","e","s","i"]).
initial(["n","a","w"]).
initial(["a","p"]).
medial(["i","k","a","a","t","e","e"]).
final(["i"]).
final(["e","s","i"]).
```

Additionally, we captured the other pieces of information for stems and morphemes using a predicate *gloss* with four parameters: the Myaamia stem/morpheme, its type (which could be stem, initial, medial, or final), its English translation, and its part-of-speech classification. Here are the glosses for the stem and morphemes introduced in Sect. 2.1:

```
gloss(["n","a","w","i"], stem, "go get (?)", "v.an.intran").
gloss(["a","p","i","k","a","a","t","e","e","s","i"], stem,
    "warm one's feet", "v.an.intran").
gloss(["n","a","w"], initial, "go and, andative", "initial").
gloss(["a","p"], initial, "warm", "initial").
gloss(["i","k","a","a","t","e","e"], medial, "foot",
    "medial").
gloss(["i"], final, "abstract final", "an.intran.final").
gloss(["e","s","i"], final, "by heat", "an.intran.final").
```

We marked stems used for secondary derivation using the predicate *secondary_ derivation_final*, as in:

```
secondary_derivation_final(["a","a","k","a","n"].
```

In our experimental setup to address research questions *RQ1-RQ3*, we introduced two additional tools where the DLV solver was replaced by the DLV2 solver: one where stems and morphemes were still represented as lists, and another where they were represented as strings. In both cases, the *stemmer.lp* file was adapted to match the syntactic format of the built-in list and string functions in DLV2. The representation of stems and morphemes as strings (for DLV2) in the *facts.lp* looks as follows:

```
stem("nawii"). stem("apikaateesi"). initial("naw").
initial("ap"). medial("ikaatee"). final("i"). final("esi").
gloss("nawi", stem, "go get (?)", "v.an.intran").
gloss("apikaateesi", stem, "warm one's feet", "v.an.intran").
gloss("naw", initial, "go and, andative", "initial").
gloss("ap", initial, "warm", "initial").
gloss("ikaatee", medial, "foot", "medial").
gloss("i", final, "abstract final", "an.intran.final").
gloss("esi", final, "by heat", "an.intran.final").
secondary_derivation_final("aakan").
```

In our experiments, we focused on three key derivational stem decomposition tasks that Myaamia linguists might perform: (a) analyzing the decomposition results for the entire collection of stems, (b) decomposing a single stem, and (c) testing different linguistic theories related to stem decomposition. In all cases, the complete set of morphemes in the database needed to be considered.

The first task involves a maintenance process to be executed after each substantial update of the database (i.e., following multiple additions, updates, or corrections of stem/morpheme entries). This task helps identify potential inconsistencies in the database, such as a final morpheme incorrectly entered as a medial morpheme, which could result in erroneous decompositions, as demonstrated in our preliminary work. Additionally, it can reveal decomposition patterns that may require further attention from linguists. The second task would be valuable when a linguist identifies a stem in the ILDA database that lacks associated morphemes (i.e., its decomposition into morphemes has not yet been analyzed or recorded). In the future, the goal is to enable the derivational stemmer tool to be accessed directly from the ILDA interface, providing decomposition suggestions. Once reviewed and approved by the linguist, these suggestions could then be added to the database. The third task is more theoretical in nature, aimed at exploring potential research questions in Myaamia linguistics.

The ILDA database for Myaamia currently contains 3,387 stems and 564 morphemes. All experiments described in the following three sections were conducted on a computer with the following processor specification: 13th Gen Intel(R) Core(TM) i5-1335U, 1300 Mhz, 10 Cores, 12 Logical Processors. Each experiment was run 10 times, and the average time and standard deviation were calculated in seconds. A timeout of 30 min was applied for each run.

4 Experiment 1: Stemmer Efficiency

In this experiment, we compared the relative performance of two representations of stems and morphemes-lists and strings-and two solvers, DLV and DLV2. Specifically, we evaluated three tools: the original Myaamia derivational stem decomposition tool using lists in DLV, as well as two additional tools, one using lists in DLV2 and the other using strings in DLV2. Recall that DLV does not offer built-in functions for string manipulation. We were particularly interested in evaluating the performance of the tool using strings in DLV2. Working with list representations proved to be challenging, especially when it came to reading and interpreting the stem information in the DLV output. In contrast, representing Myaamia stems and morphemes as strings was more intuitive and easier to manage.

The encoding for primary and secondary derivation in the file *stemmer.lp*, compatible with DLV and the list representation of stems and morphemes, looks as follows:

```
% Primary Decomposition - Case 1: S = I
decompose_1(S, S) :- stem(S), initial(S).
% Primary Decomposition - Case 2: S = I + F
decompose_2(S, I, F) :- stem(S), initial(I), final(F),
                        #append(I, F, S).
% Primary Decomposition - Case 3: S = I + M + F
decompose_3(S, I, M, F) :- stem(S), initial(I), medial(M),
                           final(F), #append(I, M, T),
                           #append(T, F, S).
% Secondary Decomposition: S = S1 + F
sec_decompose(S, S1, F) :- stem(S), stem(S1), S1 != S,
                           secondary_derivation_final(F),
                           #append(S1, F, S).
```

Since the built-in list functions in DLV2 use a slightly different syntax, the rules were adjusted accordingly, as shown in the example for the third case of primary decomposition:

```
% Primary Decomposition - Case 2: S = I + F
decompose_2(S, I, F) :- stem(S), initial(I), final(F),
                        &append(I, F; S).
```

Using the string representation of stems and morphemes for the same example resulted in the following form of rules in DLV2. This example corresponds to the second case of primary decomposition:

```
% Primary Decomposition - Case 2: S = I + F
decompose_2(S, I, F) :- stem(S), initial(I), final(F),
                        &append_str(I, F; S).
```

A new *stemmer.lp* file was created to evaluate the performance of the solvers and different representations while testing linguistic theories. Specifically, we tested the "dropped w" hypothesis from our preliminary work. This hypothesis, a basic version of morphophonological rules, suggests that the 'w' at the end of a morpheme can be dropped when additional morphemes are appended during the stem derivation process in Myaamia. We introduced new predicates, *decompose_2_w*, *decompose_3_w*, and *sec_decompose_w* to encode this hypothesis, allowing us to distinguish potential new decompositions from those generated by the standard rules for primary and secondary derivation. There are three distinct rules for *decompose_3_w*, corresponding to cases where (1) the initial, (2) the medial, or (3) both the initial and medial morphemes end in 'w'.

```
% "Dropped w" Hypothesis
% Primary Decomposition - Case 2: S = I + F
decompose_2_w(S, I, F) :-
    stem(S), initial(I), final(F), #length(I, N),
    #getnth(I, N, "w"), #delnth(I, N, New_I),
    #append(New_I, F, S).
% Primary Decomposition - Case 3: S = I + M + F
decompose_3_w(S, I, M, F) :-
    stem(S), initial(I), medial(M), final(F), #length(I, N),
    #getnth(I, N, "w"), #delnth(I, N, New_I),
    #append(New_I, M, T), #append(T, F, S).
decompose_3_w(S, I, M, F) :-
    stem(S), initial(I), medial(M), final(F),
    #append(I, M, T), #length(T, N1),
    #getnth(T, N1, "w"), #delnth(T, N1, New_T),
    #append(New_T, F, S).
decompose_3_w(S, I, M, F) :-
    stem(S), initial(I), medial(M), final(F), #length(I, N),
    #getnth(I, N, "w"), #delnth(I, N, New_I),
    #append(New_I, M, T), #length(T, N1),
    #getnth(T, N1, "w"), #delnth(T, N1, New_T),
    #append(New_T, F, S).
% Secondary Decomposition : S = S1 + F
sec_decompose_w(S, S1, F) :-
    stem(S), stem(S1), S1 != S,
```

```
secondary_derivation_final(F),
#length(S1, N), #getnth(S1, N, "w"),
#delnth(S1, N, New_S1), #append(New_S1, F, S).
```

Table 2 presents the running time for the three tasks outlined in Sect. 3: (a) decomposing all stems, (b) decomposing a single stem, and (c) decomposing all stems while applying additional derivation rules to test linguistic theories. For the single stem decomposition, we analyzed two scenarios: one where the stem is expected to be successfully decomposed by our stemmer, and another where it is not, due to phonological transformations that prevent the stem from being a straightforward concatenation of its morphemes. For the former case, we used the stem *aalimat-* composed of morphemes *aalim-* and *-at*. In the latter case, we used the stem *aahsantee-*, which is derived from morphemes *aahsam-* and *-etee* through a phonological transformation not addressed by our tool.

Table 2. Relative Performance for DLV vs DLV2 and list vs string representation (T (s) - average runtime over 10 runs in seconds; SD - standard deviation; (y) - stem expected to be decomposed by our stemmer; (n) - stem not expected to be decomposed by our stemmer; '-' means the test did not complete within the 30-minute timeout)

Solver	DLV		DLV2			
Representation	lists		lists		strings	
	T (s)	SD	T (s)	SD	T (s)	SD
All stems	**49.393**	2.235	-	-	-	-
1 stem (y)	14.193	0.400	10.313	1.061	**3.998**	0.005
1 stem (n)	14.204	0.411	9.803	0.387	**4.304**	0.444
Dropped "w" hypothesis	**63.810**	0.999	-	-	-	-

The results indicate that the answer to research question *RQ1* depends on the specific task being considered. DLV with the list representation of stems and morphemes is more efficient for analyzing all stems, including when testing new linguistic theories. In contrast, the string representation in DLV2 performs better for analyzing a single stem. Notably, the list representation in DLV2 was less efficient than in DLV, as the test did not complete within the 30-minute timeout. Similarly, the string representation in DLV2 also failed to finish before the timeout. To investigate further, we tested the decomposition of 25 stems using both the list and string representations in DLV2, and in both cases, the computation successfully completed and produced the expected results.

Additional efficiency improvements were explored, such as matching the first letter of the stem with the first letter of the initial morpheme:

```
% Primary Decomposition - Case 2: S = I + F
decompose_2(S, I, F) :- stem(S), initial(I), final(F),
                       #getnth(S, 1, C), #getnth(I, 1, C),
                       #append(I, F, S).
```

Although this approach yielded some performance improvements, it is linguistically inaccurate. Phonological transformations that occur when an initial morpheme combines with another can result in a stem with a different initial letter. For instance, *ahkipak-* combined with *-eekin* results in the stem *ihkipakiikin*, not *ahkipakeekin*.

5 Experiment 2: Improving Stemmer Quality

Based on the analysis of the output from the preliminary derivational stem decomposition tool [4], we identified several necessary improvements. First, stems extended with final morphemes for secondary derivation are currently categorized as initials in the morpheme table. However, they are not true initials, as indicated by their part-of-speech information, which differs from the "initial" designation used for other initial morphemes (e.g., "n.inan" for inanimate nouns, "v.tran.an" for transitive animate verbs). Second, final morphemes used for secondary derivation should not be applied in primary decomposition. These two issues led to incorrect decompositions.

We attempted two different approaches to address these issues. The first was to refine the ASP rules for primary decomposition, as shown below for the DLV representation using lists:

```
pos_not_for_initial_primary("n.inan").
pos_not_for_initial_primary("v.tran.an").
% Other such facts omitted here

% Primary Derivation - Case 1: S = I
decompose_1(S, S) :-
   stem(S), initial(S), gloss(S, initial, _, PI),
   not pos_not_for_initial_primary(PI).
% Primary Derivation - Case 2: S = I + F
decompose_2(S, I, F) :-
   stem(S), initial(I), final(F),
   not secondary_derivation_final(F), #append(I, F, S).
% Primary Derivation - Case 3: S = I + M + F
decompose_3(S, I, M, F) :-
   stem(S), initial(I), medial(M), final(F),
   not secondary_derivation_final(F),
   #append(I, M, T), #append(T, F, S).
```

The second approach involved improving the Python pre-processing code that generates facts for the predicates *stem, initial, medial, final,* and *gloss*. This was done to ensure that (1) stems would no longer be incorrectly categorized as *initial*s, and (2) final morphemes used exclusively in secondary derivation would be categorized only as *secondary_derivation_final*, and not also as *final*.

In Table 3, we compare the two improvement approaches with the original representation that resulted in erroneous decompositions due to these issues. The results show that the improved Python pre-processing strategy yields better efficiency. Additionally, it keeps the ASP encodings for primary derivation clearer and more straightforward, while remaining independent of database implementation details. These findings address research question *RQ2*, demonstrating the effectiveness of enhancing the pre-processing step to improve the accuracy of stem decomposition in an efficient way.

Table 3. Relative Performance for Two Quality Improvement Strategies (T (s) - average runtime over 10 runs in seconds; SD - standard deviation; (y) - stem expected to be decomposed by stemmer; (n) - stem not expected to be decomposed by stemmer)

	Solver & Represent.	Basic ASP Encoding		Improved Encoding		Improved Pre-processing	
		T (s)	SD	T (s)	SD	T (s)	SD
All stems	DLV - lists	49.393	2.235	142.399	0.445	**41.304**	2.830
1 stem (y)	DLV - lists	14.193	0.400	13.992	0.030	**8.797**	0.583
1 stem (n)	DLV - lists	14.204	0.411	14.197	0.780	**8.604**	0.469
1 stem (y)	DLV2 - strings	3.998	0.005	5.394	0.472	**3.609**	0.465
1 stem (n)	DLV2 - strings	4.304	0.444	4.698	0.447	**3.699**	0.621

6 Experiment 3: Preliminary Quality Analysis Through Comparison with ILDA-Decomposed Stems

The ILDA database documents known decompositions of stems into morphemes, including partial decompositions. As an example see the "Associated Morphemes" section in Fig. 1 for stem *apikaateesi-*. Partial decompositions occur when a morpheme of a Myaamia stem has been identified, but the meanings of the remaining parts of the stem are either not yet identified or not yet recorded in the database. We extended our ASP code to track the number of stems decomposed by ILDA but not by the stemmer, and vice versa, along with the total number of stems decomposed by both ILDA and the stemmer (see results in Fig. 3).

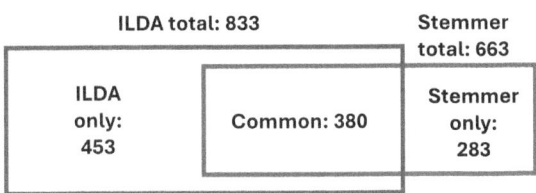

Fig. 3. Stem Decomposition: ILDA vs Stemmer.

Next, we examined the 453 stems that were decomposed in ILDA but could not be decomposed by our stemmer. The reasons for this fell into three categories:

- Morphophonological transformations occur as morphemes combine, which our tool does not currently account for. For instance, *apikaateesi-* is derived from *apikaatee-* and *-esi*, but the three *e*'s are contracted into a long-*e* (i.e., two *e*'s).
- ILDA documents partial decompositions, whereas our tool currently processes only complete decompositions. For example, a partial decomposition in ILDA might identify that the stem *ciilitee-* contains the morpheme *ciil-*, but the remaining portion of the word has not yet been identified.
- Inconsistencies in the morpheme table. For example, *-enam* is a final morpheme but is incorrectly listed in the database as a medial, as in *-enam-*. This causes our tool to miss certain decompositions.

Examining the decompositions generated by the stemmer that were not recorded in ILDA, we identified the following issues:

- Morphemes that are homophones (i.e., share the same form but have different meanings) can result in incorrect decompositions. The stemmer currently does not account for meaning, such as the English translation of stems and morphemes. In the future, we may be able to leverage existing linguistic resources such as WordNet to identify the most appropriate homophone for a given context.
- Stem class mismatch occurs when the part of speech of the stem does not align with that of the final morpheme. These cases can be addressed by identifying all incompatible classes and adjusting the rules accordingly. For example, the decomposition of stem *nawi-* is incorrect because an 'adverb formative' cannot be appended to a verb; it can only be added to an adverb.

```
nawi = naw                + i
       go and, andative   + adverb formative
       initial            + final
       'go get (?)'
```

- Inflectional compositions are incorrectly classified as derivational by the stemmer due to homophonic final morphemes. For example, the tool incorrectly decomposed *alamoni-* ("*red ocher, paint, vermillion*"), as shown below:

```
alamoni = alamon             + i
          ochre, vermillion   + abstract final
          n.inan              + an.intran.final
          'red ocher, paint, vermillion'
```

when, in this case, the final *-i* is an inflection for nouns that marks gender.

Finally, we sought to evaluate the correctness of the decompositions in the group common to both ILDA and the stemmer. We began by identifying how many stems in the stemmer's output had multiple decompositions. There were 24 such cases, with all but 4 also decomposed in ILDA. When comparing the stemmer's decompositions with those recorded in ILDA, we found that the majority were decomposed based on Cases 2 and 3 of primary decomposition. Linguists and ILDA confirm that Case 2, which decomposes a stem into two morphemes rather than three, is preferred. In the future, we can implement a preference for decomposing into fewer morphemes.

As an example, our tool produced two different decompositions for the stem *ciileelim-* meaning *"like him, think well of him, think highly of him:"*

```
ciileelim = ciil      + eelim
            intense + by thought
            initial + tran.an.final
            'Like him, think well of him, think highly of him'
ciileelim = ciil         + eeli         + m
            intense    + by boat     + (abstract final)
            initial    + tran.an.final + tran.an.final
            'Like him, think well of him, think highly of him'
```

While the first decomposition is correct and documented in ILDA, the second one is not. Examining the interlinear gloss for the decomposition into three morphemes reveals an incompatibility between the meanings of the morphemes (second line of the interlinear gloss) and the meaning of the decomposed stem (last line of the interlinear gloss). This incorrect decomposition occurred because the morpheme *eeli* with the meaning *"by boat"* was marked incorrectly as a medial morpheme in the database via the use of dashes, as in *-eeli-*. Instead, this should have been marked as a final morpheme, stated as *-eeli*.

To answer research question $RQ3$, we see two main avenues for improving the stemmer. The first is to integrate a phonological component that addresses the phonological transformations that occur when morphemes combine to form stems. The second is to incorporate the meanings (translations) of stems and morphemes into the stemmer. This would enable the selection of the most plausible decomposition in cases of homophones and help eliminate decompositions that are semantically incorrect due to meaning mismatches.

7 Conclusions

In this paper, we presented a practical application of logic programming to Language Documentation and Reclamation by introducing a tool for Myaamia derivational stem decomposition. We explored different solvers and representations of stems and morphemes to determine which would be most efficient for various maintenance, documentation, and research tasks. Our findings showed that the list representation in DLV is most efficient for decomposing all stems in the database, while the string representation in DLV2 is faster for decomposing individual stems. We also concluded that the quality of the stemmer can be improved-without compromising the clarity of linguistic rule representation-by enhancing the pre-processing phase, which converts database entries into logic programming facts. Finally, we identified future research directions, including the integration of morpheme meanings to refine stem decomposition.

Since our work focused on handling large volumes of strings, the efficiency analysis and results may be of interest to other researchers in the field and could contribute to the development of more efficient solvers.

References

1. Adrain, W.T., et al.: The ASP system DLV: advancements and applications. Künstliche Intell. **32**(2–3), 177–179 (2018). https://doi.org/10.1007/S13218-018-0533-0
2. Alviano, M., et al.: The asp system dlv2. In: Balduccini, M., Janhunen, T. (eds.) Logic Programming and Nonmonotonic Reasoning, pp. 215–221. Springer International Publishing (2017)
3. Balduccini, M., Baral, C., Lierler, Y.: Knowledge representation and question answering. In: van Harmelen, F., Lifschitz, V., Porter, B.W. (eds.) Handbook of Knowledge Representation, Foundations of Artificial Intelligence, vol. 3, pp. 779–819. Elsevier (2008). https://doi.org/10.1016/S1574-6526(07)03020-9
4. Baral, A., Shrestha, P., Sharma, J., Lockwood, H., Inclezan, D.: An exploration of datalog applications to language documentation and reclamation. In: Alviano, M., Lanzinger, M. (eds.) Proceedings 5th International Workshop on the Resurgence of Datalog in Academia and Industry (Datalog-2.0 2024) co-located with the 17th International Conference on Logic Programming and Nonmonotonic Reasoning (LPNMR 2024), Dallas, Texas, USA, October 11, 2024. CEUR Workshop Proceedings, vol. 3801, pp. 23–29. CEUR-WS.org (2024). https://ceur-ws.org/Vol-3801/short2.pdf
5. Baral, C., Gelfond, M.: Logic programming and knowledge representation. J. Log. Program. **19**(20), 73–148 (1994)
6. Beesley, K.R., Karttunen, L.: Finite State Morphology, CSLI Studies in Computational Linguistics, vol. 3. CSLI Publications (2003). http://www.stanford.edu/group/cslipublications/cslipublications/site/1575864347.shtml
7. Calimeri, F., et al.: ASP-core-2 input language format. Theory Pract. Log. Program. **20**(2), 294–309 (2020). https://doi.org/10.1017/S1471068419000450
8. Chelliah, S.L., Burke, M., Heaton, M.: Using interlinear gloss texts to improve language description. Indian Linguist. **82**(1-2) (2021). https://par.nsf.gov/biblio/10383818
9. Drescher, C., Walsh, T.: Modelling grammar constraints with answer set programming. In: Gallagher, J.P., Gelfond, M. (eds.) Technical Communications of the 27th International Conference on Logic Programming, ICLP 2011, July 6–10, 2011, Lexington, Kentucky, USA. LIPIcs, vol. 11, pp. 28–39. Schloss Dagstuhl - Leibniz-Zentrum für Informatik (2011). https://doi.org/10.4230/LIPICS.ICLP.2011.28
10. Erdem, E.: Applications of answer set programming in phylogenetic systematics. In: Balduccini, M., Son, T.C. (eds.) Logic Programming, Knowledge Representation, and Nonmonotonic Reasoning. LNCS (LNAI), vol. 6565, pp. 415–431. Springer, Heidelberg (2011). https://doi.org/10.1007/978-3-642-20832-4_26
11. Erdem, E., Lifschitz, V., Ringe, D.: Temporal phylogenetic networks and logic programming. Theory Pract. Log. Program. **6**(5), 539–558 (2006). https://doi.org/10.1017/S1471068406002729
12. Gebser, M., et al.: Potassco User Guide, 2 ed. University of Potsdam (2015)
13. Gelfond, M., Kahl, Y.: Knowledge Representation, Reasoning, and the Design of Intelligent Agents. Cambridge University Press, Cambridge (2014). https://doi.org/10.1017/CBO9781139342124
14. Gelfond, M., Lifschitz, V.: The stable model semantics for logic programming. In: Proceedings of the International Conference on Logic Programming (ICLP88), pp. 1070–1080 (1988)

15. Gelfond, M., Lifschitz, V.: Classical negation in logic programs and disjunctive databases. New Gener. Comput. **9**(3/4), 365–386 (1991). https://doi.org/10.1007/BF03037169
16. Goddard, I.: Primary and secondary stem derivation in algonquian. Int. J. Am. Linguist. **56**(4), 449–483 (1990)
17. Inclezan, D.: An application of answer set programming to the field of second language acquisition. Theory Pract. Log. Program. **15**(1), 1–17 (2015). https://doi.org/10.1017/S1471068413000653
18. Kanazawa, M.: Parsing and generation as datalog queries. In: Proceedings of the 45th Annual Meeting of the Association of Computational Linguistics, pp. 176–183. ACL (2007)
19. Koskenniemi, K.: Two-level morphology: a general computational model for word-form recognition and production. University of Helsinki (1983). publication 11
20. Lierler, Y., Schüller, P.: Parsing combinatory categorial grammar via planning in answer set programming. In: Erdem, E., Lee, J., Lierler, Y., Pearce, D. (eds.) Correct Reasoning. LNCS, vol. 7265, pp. 436–453. Springer, Heidelberg (2012). https://doi.org/10.1007/978-3-642-30743-0_30
21. Macaulay, M., Salmons, J.: Synchrony and diachrony in Menominee derivational morphology. Morphology **27**, 179–215 (2017)
22. Marek, V.W., Truszczynski, M.: Stable models and an alternative logic programming paradigm. In: Apt, K.R., Marek, V.W., Truszczynski, M., Warren, D.S. (eds.) The Logic Programming Paradigm - A 25-Year Perspective, pp. 375–398. Artificial Intelligence, Springer, Cham (1999). https://doi.org/10.1007/978-3-642-60085-2_17
23. Matlatipov, G., Vetulani, Z.: Representation of Uzbek morphology in prolog. In: Marciniak, M., Mykowiecka, A. (eds.) Aspects of Natural Language Processing. LNCS, vol. 5070, pp. 83–110. Springer, Heidelberg (2009). https://doi.org/10.1007/978-3-642-04735-0_4
24. Nerbonne, J., Konstantopoulos, S.: Phonotactics in inductive logic programming. In: Kłopotek, M.A., Wierzchoń, S.T., Trojanowski, K. (eds.) Intelligent Information Processing and Web Mining, pp. 493–502. Springer, Heidelberg (2004).https://doi.org/10.1007/978-3-540-39985-8_58
25. Pérez Báez, G., Morio, K.L., Lapointe, A.L., Baldwin, D.: On the impact of the national breath of life archival institute for indigenous languages: developing an assessment model for archive-based revitalization. Lang. Documentation Conserv. **16**, 130–184 (2023)
26. Scherl, R., Inclezan, D., Gelfond, M.: Automated inference of socio-cultural information from natural language conversations. In: 2010 IEEE Second International Conference on Social Computing, pp. 480–487 (2010). https://doi.org/10.1109/SocialCom.2010.76
27. Schüller, P.: Flexible combinatory categorial grammar parsing using the CYK algorithm and answer set programming. In: Cabalar, P., Son, T.C. (eds.) Logic Programming and Nonmonotonic Reasoning, pp. 499–511. Springer, Heidelberg (2013)
28. Schüller, P.: Answer set programming in linguistics. Künstliche Intell. **32**(2–3), 151–155 (2018). https://doi.org/10.1007/S13218-018-0542-Z
29. Thapa, S.: Use Case Driven Evaluation of Database Systems for ILDA. Master's thesis, Miami University (2022)

Enhancing a Hierarchical Graph Rewriting Language Based on MELL Cut Elimination

Kento Takyu[✉] and Kazunori Ueda[iD]

Waseda University, Tokyo 169-8555, Japan
{takyu,ueda}@ueda.info.waseda.ac.jp

Abstract. Hierarchical graph rewriting is a highly expressive computational formalism that manipulates graphs enhanced with box structures for representing hierarchies. It has provided the foundations of various graph-based modeling tools, but the design of high-level declarative languages based on hierarchical graph rewriting is still a challenge. For a solid design choice, well-established formalisms with backgrounds other than graph rewriting would provide useful guidelines. Proof nets of Multiplicative Exponential Linear Logic (MELL) is such a framework because its original formulation of cut elimination is essentially graph rewriting involving box structures, where so-called promotion boxes with an indefinite number of non-local edges may be cloned, migrated and deleted. This work builds on LMNtal as a declarative language based on hierarchical (port) graph rewriting, and discusses how it can be extended to support the above operations on promotion boxes of MELL proof nets. LMNtal thus extended turns out to be a practical graph rewriting language that has strong affinity with MELL proof nets. The language features provided are general enough to encode other well-established models of concurrency. Using the toolchain of LMNtal that provides state-space search and model checking, we implemented cut elimination rules of MELL proof nets in extended LMNtal and demonstrated that the platform could serve as a useful workbench for proof nets.

Keywords: Graph Rewriting Language · Linear Logic · Proof Nets

1 Introduction

Connectivity and hierarchy are the two major structuring mechanisms that often occur simultaneously in modeling various phenomena ranging from computing to human societies. In organizational charts and system configuration diagrams, connectivity is represented by lines, whereas the hierarchy of groups is represented by box-like structures. Because of their universality, it is desirable to have a computational model and a programming language that formally handles this structure which we call *hierarchical graphs*.

There exist diverse *formalisms* for hierarchical graph rewriting [2,4,12,13,25,27,37]. However, designing a practical high-level declarative *language* based on hierarchical graph rewriting is still a challenge. Well-established formal systems potentially related to graph rewriting could provide guidelines of a solid design. Multiplicative Exponential Linear Logic (MELL) [16] is such a formalism related to hierarchical graph rewriting, in which *proof nets* were formulated for representing proofs graphically, abstracting some of the symmetries in sequent-based proofs. In particular, cut elimination rules for exponentials are represented as the migration, cloning, and deletion of box structures called *promotion boxes*.

In this study, we start with the hierarchical (port) graph rewriting language LMNtal [37] and refine its language constructs to establish strong affinity with the operations on proof nets. We build on LMNtal because it is formalized in the standard style of programming languages with abstract syntax and structural operational semantics. It also allows interpretation as a logic programming language based on intuitionistic linear logic [37].

An encoding of MELL proof nets using the original constructs of LMNtal was outlined in a poster [32], showing a promising direction, but we show that the operations on proof nets can be fully supported only with newly designed and implemented constructs. Formalization of graph cloning and deletion has been a challenge also in the (mainstream) algebraic approach of graph rewriting [5,8,29], but the main theme of the present work is to introduce the constructs for graph cloning and deletion through boxes into a practical declarative language.

The main contributions of this paper are threefold. Firstly, we extend the hierarchical graph rewriting language LMNtal to make it possible to describe the operations of promotion boxes in MELL proof nets, define operations corresponding to the duplication and deletion of promotion boxes, and implement them (Sect. 4). Secondly, we demonstrate that the extended LMNtal serves as a workbench for proof nets (Sect. 5.1). Thirdly, we demonstrate that the proposed constructs are sufficiently general by showing an encoding of the Ambient Calculus, a model of concurrency with box-like structures (Sect. 5.2).

2 LMNtal: A Hierarchical Graph Rewriting Language

We briefly explain the hierarchical graph rewriting language LMNtal [37]. LMNtal consists of (i) term-based syntax, (ii) structural congruence on terms that provides interpretation of terms as graphs, and (iii) small-step reduction relation. For lack of space, we skip detailed syntactic conditions of (i) and introduce (ii) and (iii) informally, and give further details in Appendix of [33], an extended version of this paper. A tutorial introduction to LMNtal can be found in [38] and the full formal definition in [37].

2.1 Overview of LMNtal

The syntax of LMNtal is given in Fig. 1, where three syntactic categories, link names (denoted by X), atom names (denoted by p), and possibly empty membrane names (denoted by m), are presupposed.

$$
\begin{aligned}
(process)\ P &::= \mathbf{0} \mid p(X_1,\ldots,X_n) \mid P,P \mid m\{P\} \mid T \mathbin{:\!\text{-}} T \\
(process\ template)\ T &::= \mathbf{0} \mid p(X_1,\ldots,X_n) \mid T,T \mid m\{T\} \mid T \mathbin{:\!\text{-}} T \\
&\mid @p \mid \$p[X_1,\ldots,X_n|A] \mid p(*X_1,\ldots,*X_n) \\
(residual)\ A &::= [\,] \mid *X
\end{aligned}
$$

Fig. 1. Syntax of LMNtal.

Since LMNtal was originally developed as a model of concurrency, the hierarchical graphs of LMNtal are also called *processes*. **0** is an inert process, $p(X_1,\ldots,X_n)\,(n \geq 0)$ is an *n-ary atom* (a.k.a. node) with *ordered links* (a.k.a. edges) $X_1,\ldots,X_n$, P,P is parallel composition, $m\{P\}$ is a *cell* formed by wrapping P with an optionally named *membrane* { }, and $T \mathbin{:\!\text{-}} T$ is a *rewrite rule*.

Occurrences of a link name represent endpoints of a one-to-one link between atoms (or more precisely, atom arguments). For this purpose, each link name in a process P is allowed to occur at most twice (Link Condition). A link whose name occurs only once in P is called a *free link* of P. Links may cross membranes and connect atoms located at different "places" of the membrane hierarchy. A graph in which each node has its own arity and totally ordered links, like an LMNtal graph, is often called a *port graph*.

Process templates on both sides of a rewrite rule allow *process contexts*, *rule contexts*, and *aggregates* [37,39]. A process context, denoted $\$p[X_1,\ldots,X_n|A]$ $(n \geq 0)$, works as a *wildcard* that matches "the rest of the processes" (except rewrite rules that are matched by a rule context @p) within the membrane in which it appears. The arguments specify what free link names may or must occur. $X_1,\ldots,X_n$ are the link names that must occur free in $\$p$. When the residual A is of the form $*X$ (*bundle*), links other than $X_1,\ldots,X_n$ may occur free, and $*X$ stands for the sequence of those optional free links. When A is of the form $[\,]$ (in which case the "$|\,[\,]$" may be omitted), no other free links may occur. An aggregate, denoted $p(*X_1,\ldots,*X_n)$ $(n > 0)$, represents a multiset of atoms with the name p, whose multiplicity coincides with the number of links represented by the argument bundles, denoted $|*X_i|$. The detailed syntactic conditions on aggregates are given in [37].

Rewrite rules must observe several syntactic conditions [37] so that the Link Condition is preserved in the course of program execution. Most importantly, link names in a rewrite rule must occur exactly twice, and each process context must occur exactly once at the top level of distinct cells in the LHS of a rule.

A rewrite rule repeatedly acts on an LMNtal graph located in the same "place" of the membrane hierarchy. As an example of rewriting using process contexts and bundles, consider the following program:

```
o(B), {i(A,B), a(A,G1), b(G2)}, g(G1), g(G2).   // initial graph
o(B), {i(A,B), $p[A|*X]} :- n(A), $p[A|*X].      // rewrite rule
```

The first line is a text representation of the graph of Fig. 2(a) (left). The rule in the second line (Fig. 2(b)) rewrites this to the graph of Fig. 2(a) (right), where

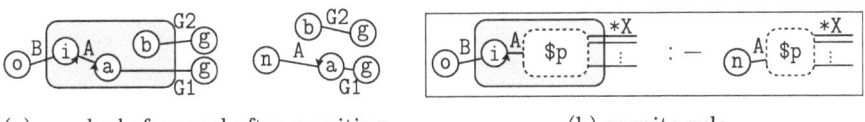

(a) graphs before and after rewriting   (b) rewrite rule

Fig. 2. Rewriting an LMNtal graph using process contexts and bundles. An arrowhead of each non-unary atom indicates the first argument and the ordering of atoms.

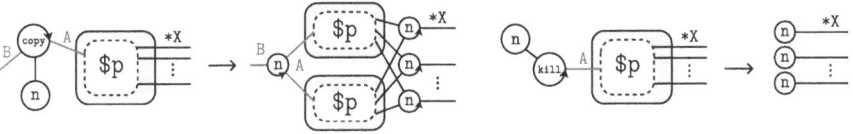

(a) `nlmem.copy(A,B,C),n(B),{$p[A|*X]}`   (b) `nlmem.kill(A,B),n(B),{$p[A|*X]}`

Fig. 3. Operations of the `nlmem` library.

the process context `$p` matches atoms `a` and `b`, and the bundle `*X` matches the free links `G1`, `G2` of `$p`.

The application of rules in LMNtal is nondeterministic because (i) a rule may be able to rewrite different subgraphs of a given graph, and (ii) different rules may be able to rewrite the same graph. The LMNtal runtime SLIM [18] provides a nondeterministic execution mode that constructs the whole state space of rewriting, which can also be visualized using the visualization tool StateViewer [3]. Furthermore, SLIM provides an LTL model checker of the state space [18].

2.2 Nonlinear Membranes

When process contexts with a bundle in the LHS of a rule are cloned or deleted in the RHS, the endpoints of the links matched by the bundle must be connected to some atom to avoid dangling links. Aggregates are a construct provided for this purpose, but instead of providing them in full generality, the LMNtal implementation has provided its functionalities as a wrapper library called `nlmem` (nonlinear membrane) [21]. The library implements `nlmem.copy` (Fig. 3(a)), which copies the membrane with an unspecified number of free links, and `nlmem.kill` (Fig. 3(b)), which removes a membrane with an unspecified number of free links. Note that the semantics of these operations can be defined using aggregates [23].

3 MELL Proof Nets

This study focuses on Multiplicative Exponential Linear Logic (MELL) [16], a fragment of linear logic which extends Multiplicative Linear Logic (MLL) with two exponential operators '!' and '?' to allow non-linear, "classical" handling of resources. The (standard) definition of MELL is given in Appendix of [33].

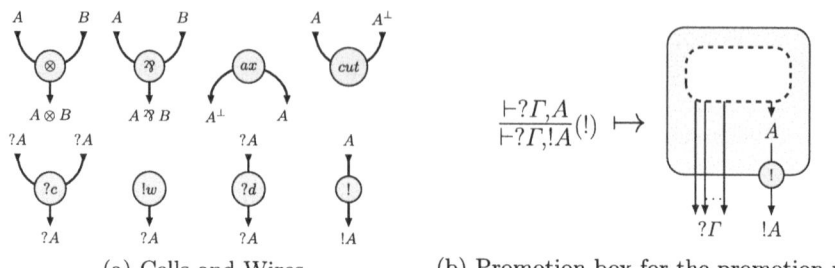

Fig. 4. The components of MELL proof structure.

Proof Structure and Proof Nets. We define *proof nets* [16] corresponding to the sequent proofs of MELL (with mix rules [14]), following the style of [41]. First, we define *proof structures*.

Definition 1. *An MELL proof structure is a directed acyclic multigraph that combines the cells (not to be confused with cells m{P} of LMNtal) and wires shown in Fig. 4(a) and the promotion box shown in Fig. 4(b).*

Each component of Fig. 4(a) consists of (i) cells (nodes) labeled with MELL inference rules and (ii) wires (edges) labeled with MELL formulas. The cells ⊗ and ⅋ have two *ordered* inputs, while the inputs of other cells are *unordered*.

The inference rule for the bottom-right component of Fig. 4(a), called *promotion*, is a *contextual rule*; that is, the rest of the formulas of the sequent containing the !A must come with '?'s. To handle this constraint, a structure called a *promotion box* (Fig. 4(b), also simply called a box) is used as a standard mechanism to protect its contents from rewriting and control the order of proof reductions [16]. Here, the conclusion with '!' is called the *principal door* of the box, while the (bundle of) conclusions with '?' are called the *auxiliary doors*.

A proof structure does not necessarily correspond to a proof tree, but proof structures satisfying a "correctness criterion" have corresponding proofs of sequent calculus and are called *proof nets*. There are several known correctness criteria that are equivalent, but we adopt the popular Danos-Regnier correctness [9] based on *switching graphs* [28] formed by non-deterministically selecting and cutting either the left or right input of the ⅋ and ?c cells.

Definition 2. *A proof net is a proof structure whose switching graphs have no undirected cycles and such that the content of each box is a proof net, inductively.*

Figure 5 shows examples of MELL proof nets. Since every undirected cycle contains a ⅋, and all the switching graphs have no undirected cycles, the Danos-Regnier correctness is satisfied. The proof tree corresponding to Fig. 5(a) is attached in Appendix of [33].

Cut Elimination. Cut elimination of MELL proof nets is expressed as graph rewriting rules. Figures 6(a)–6(c) show examples of cut elimination rules involving (a) migration, (b) deletion, and (c) cloning of boxes, whose concise representation in a graph rewriting language is the topic of the next sections. (A full list of cut elimination rules is attached in Appendix of [33].)

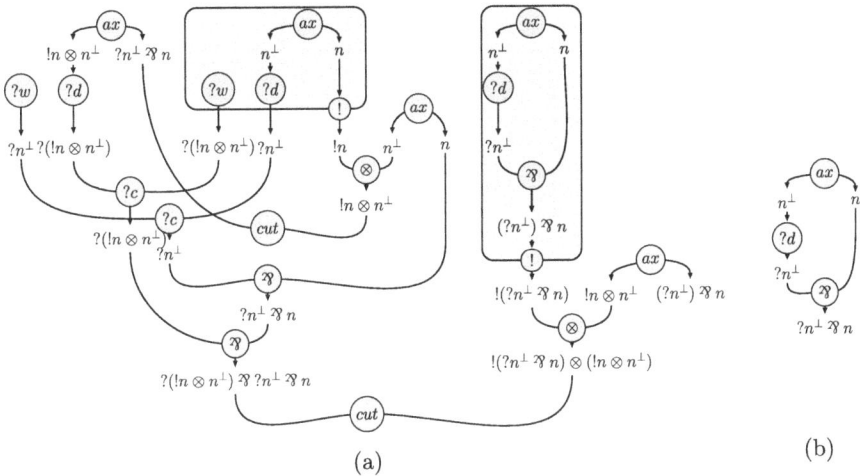

Fig. 5. Examples of MELL proof nets, where applying cut elimination to (a) results in (b) (See Sect. 5.1 also).

The following hold for cut elimination of MELL proof nets [16,17,30]:

1. **(Cut Elimination)** All cuts of an MELL proof net can be eliminated.
2. **(Stability)** An MELL proof net is still a proof net after cut elimination.
3. **(Confluence)** Cut elimination is confluent on MELL proof nets.
4. **(Strong Normalization)** Cut elimination is strongly normalizing.

4 Refining LMNtal's Box Constructs

A design challenge of a practical declarative language for graph rewriting is the design of high-level constructs for the manipulation of subgraphs of non-fixed shape and size (as opposed to individual elements). This can be divided into

1. how to specify subgraphs for rewriting, and
2. how to rewrite (esp. copy/delete/migrate) them.

One direction was studied in [42] to find the right notion of *ground graphs* (a graph counterpart of *ground terms*) for HyperLMNtal, a hypergraph extension of LMNtal, with applications to the encoding of formal systems with name binding, but it focused on *operations based on connectivity*. We focus on the manipulation of subgraphs delimited by membranes, that is, *operations based on hierarchy*.

An approximate solution with bundles and aggregates was proposed (Sect. 2), and the nlmem API (Sect. 2.2) has already been put in practice. This included the attempt of encoding MELL proof nets (Sect. 1) using nlmem designed totally independently of proof nets. However, we found that the solution was only approximate. Whereas the functionality of nlmem (Fig. 3(a)(b)) looks similar to that of promotion box operations (Fig. 6(c)(b), respectively), a refinement is necessary to allow straightforward encoding because:

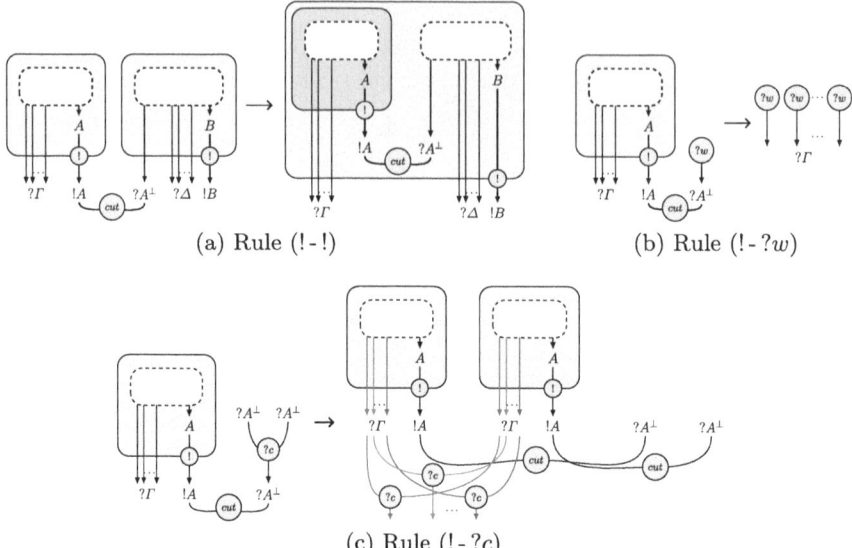

Fig. 6. Some of cut elimination rules of MELL proof nets involving box operations.

1. the functionality did not distinguish between principal and auxiliary doors of boxes, requiring post-processing to obtain the desired result, and
2. while the processing of (the free links of) bundles was the key design issue, the only functionality provided was to reconfigure them with the collection of atoms, which was found to be restrictive.

4.1 Extension of LMNtal Syntax: Aggregates of Process Contexts

We propose an extension of LMNtal that solves the above issues and provides constructs for cloning and deleting membranes with indefinitely many free links.

First, we extend the syntax of process templates to allow *aggregates of process contexts* (in addition to atom aggregates):

$$T ::= \ldots \quad | \quad \$p\texttt{[}*X_1,*X_2,\ldots,*X_n\texttt{]} \quad (n > 0)$$

where each $*X_i$ is a bundle that appears in the process context with the same name, which implies that $|*X_1| = |*X_2| = \ldots = |*X_n|$, where $|*X_i|$ stands for the number of links represented by $*X_i$ upon the present rewriting. This extends the notion of aggregates to a process context, representing $|*X_i|$ process contexts each with n free links. As a practical decision, this functionality is provided as an API as was the case of nlmem.

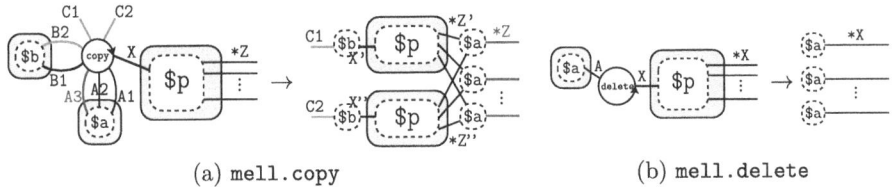

(a) mell.copy (b) mell.delete

Fig. 7. Schematic illustrations of the mell library.

4.2 API Rules Supporting Typical Use Cases

Copying a Membrane with a Bundle of Free Links. We first give a construct for copying a membrane with an indefinite number of free links, which can be specified as follows and illustrated in Fig. 7(a):

```
mell.copy(X, A1,A2,A3, B1,B2, C1,C2),
{$p[X|*Z]}, {$a[A1,A2,A3]}, {$b[B1,B2]}
                :- {$p[X'|*Z']}, {$p[X''|*Z'']},
                   $a[*Z',*Z'',*Z], $b[X',C1], $b[X'',C2].
```

The first argument of mell.copy (where mell is the prefixed module name) is linked to the membrane to be copied. We call the occurrence of X in $p[X|*X] the *principal port* of $p. The next five arguments (A1, A2, A3, B1, B2) are linked to structures ($a, $b) to be connected to the free links of the copies of $p. All these process contexts are enclosed by membranes because the subgraphs matched by the process contexts are determined by delimiting membranes.

The arguments A1, A2, A3 are linked to $a for handling copies of the links *X connected to $p's non-principal ports. The arguments B1 and B2 are linked to $b for handling copies of X connected to $p's principal port. The arguments C1 and C2 will be linked to the principal ports of the two copies of $p *via copies of* $b. After the reduction, the structure {$p[X|*Z]} is cloned, generating {$p[X'|*Z']} and {$p[X''|*Z'']}. Each of the process contexts obtained by cloning $a connects a member of *Z' and a member of *Z'' to a member of the original bundle *Z. The two copies of $b connect X' and X'' of the principal ports of $p to C1 and C2, respectively. Thus, mell.copy separates the treatment of the principal port from that of non-principal ports.

Deleting a Membrane with a Bundle of Free Links. Next, we define a construct for deleting a membrane with an unspecified number of free links defined as follows and illustrated in Fig. 7(b):

```
mell.delete(X,A), {$p[X|*X]}, {$a[A]} :- $a[*X].
```

This is a generalization of nlmem.kill to allow non-atomic structures to terminate the members of *X (which would otherwise become dangling links).

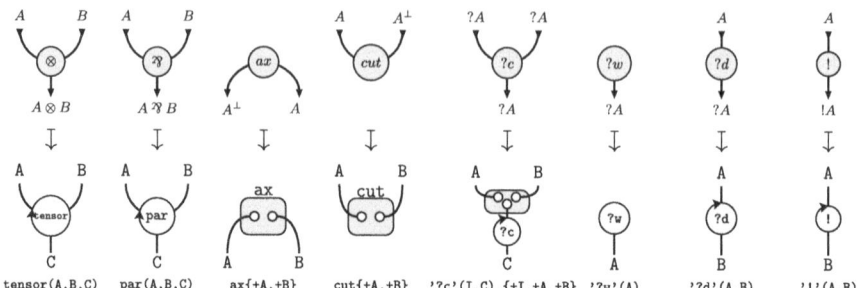

Fig. 8. Encoding of cells and wires (MELL in red, LMNtal in blue henceforth); where a small circle in a membrane stands for a unary atom named '+' and may be written as a prefix operator in textual representation. (Color figure online)

Implementation. The mell library was implemented in the LMNtal runtime SLIM[1]. We have confirmed that all the examples[2] in the following sections work.

5 Examples of Encoding

5.1 Encoding of MELL Proof Nets and Cut Elimination Rules

This section shows how we can (i) encode the cut elimination rules of MELL proof nets using the constructs introduced in Sect. 4 and (ii) use the model checker of LMNtal to verify the properties of proof nets, meaning that LMNtal serves as a useful workbench for proof nets.

MELL Proof Nets. First, we encode the components of the proof structure (Fig. 4). Figure 8 shows the encoding of cells and wires. The non-commutativity of inputs to ⊗ and ⅋ cells is represented by atoms, while the commutativity of the arguments of ax and cut is represented using membranes. A ?c cell with commutative inputs and a single output is represented by using both an atom and a membrane.

Figure 9 shows the encoding of a promotion box (Fig. 4(b)). The outer frame of the promotion box is represented by a membrane. The context ?Γ is represented by a bundle *X, and the blank part is represented by a process context $p[X1|*X].

As described above, all the components of a proof structure can be encoded directly, and the entire proof structure can be encoded by combining these encodings. An example encoding of a proof structure is given in Appendix of [33].

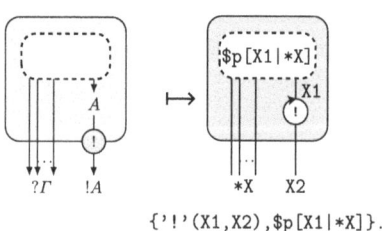

Fig. 9. Encoding of a promotionbox.

---

[1] https://github.com/lmntal/slim/tree/develop.
[2] The complete source code used in the examples in Sect. 5 can be found in https://lmntal.github.io/mell-library-examples.

Cut Elimination Rules. We encode the cut elimination rules (Fig. 6) into the rewrite rules of LMNtal.

Rule (!-!) is encoded as follows (although not shown in Fig. 1, each LMNtal rule may be given an optional rule name followed by @@).

```
promotion_promotion@@
{'!'(X1,X2), $p[X1|*X]}, {$q[X3|*Y]}, cut{+X2,+X3}
  :- {{'!'(X1,X2), $p[X1|*X]}, $q[X3|*Y], cut{+X2,+X3}}.
```

Figure 10 shows the corresponding illustration. We can see that the encoding using LMNtal's bundles and membranes is quite straightforward. Furthermore, under the Occurrence Conditions of bundles [37], the rewrite rule is guaranteed not to generate dangling links.

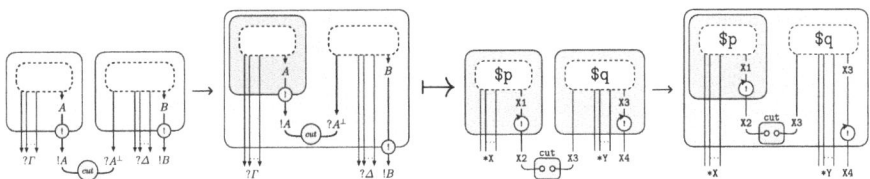

Fig. 10. Encoding of Rule (!-!).

Other cut elimination rules can be encoded in a similarly concise manner (the full encoding is given in Appendix of [33]), of which the weakening and contraction rules involve non-trivial operations and need to be encoded using the constructs introduced in Sect. 4, as described below.

Rule (!-?w) is encoded as follows.

```
promotion_weakening@@
{'!'(X1,X2), $p[X1|*X]}, cut{+X2,+X3}, '?w'(X3)
  :- mell.delete(X,A), {$p[X|*X]]}, {'?w'(A)}.
```

Figure 11 (upper) shows the corresponding illustration. By using `mell.delete`, the ?w atoms are connected to the links previously connected to the non-principal ports of the promotion box. Note that the encoded rewriting is done in two steps due to the API call.

Rule (!-?c) is encoded as follows.

```
promotion_contraction@@
{'!'(X1,X2), $p[X1|*X]}, '?c'(I,X3), {+I,+C1,+C2}, cut{+X2,+X3},
  :- mell.copy(X2, A1,A2,A3, B1,B2, C1,C2),
     {'!'(X1,X2), $p[X1|*X]},
     {'?c'(I, A3), {+I,+A1,+A2}}, {cut{+B1,+B2}}.
```

Figure 11 (lower) shows the corresponding illustration. The second to fourth arguments of `mell.copy` are linked to the structure corresponding to the ?c cell.

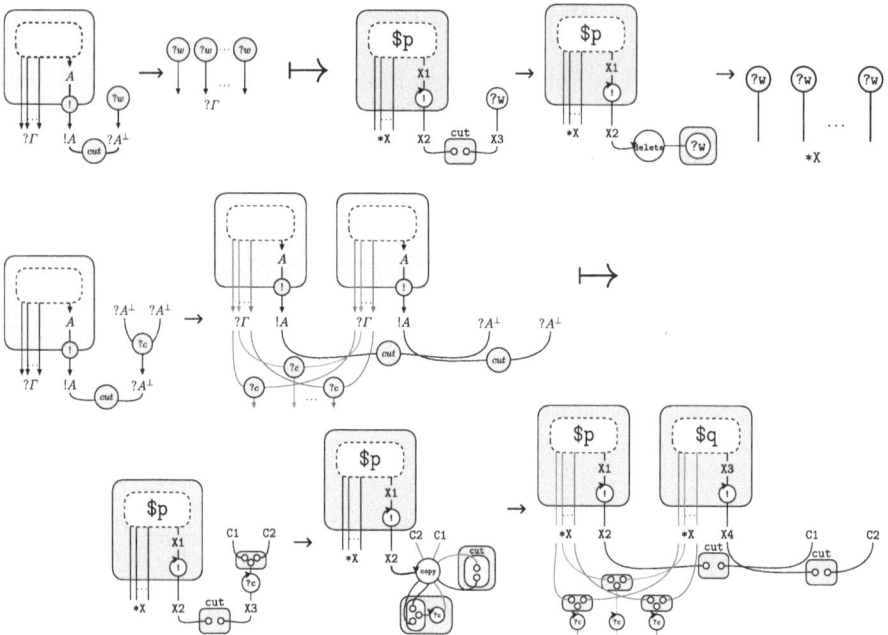

Fig. 11. Encoding of Rule (!-?w) and Rule (!-?c) with the `mell` library.

The main reason for allowing non-atomic structures in `mell.copy` lies in this encoding. The fifth and sixth arguments correspond to the *cut* cell. The seventh and eighth arguments are linked to the input side of the contraction before cut elimination to build the structure around the principal port after cut elimination. With `nlmem.copy`, it was necessary to use multiple rules and unbounded reduction steps to reconfigure free links using non-atomic structures and to handle the principal port, but with the introduction of `mell.copy`, it is now possible to encode it with a single rule.

Correctness of the Encoding. Regarding the correctness of the encoding, we note that Figs. 8, 9, 10 and 11 show clear correspondence between proof nets with cut elimination rules and their LMNtal encodings. When a formal proof is required, it is necessary to establish a correspondence between the mathematical representation of each side, but we omit the details in this paper.

Example: State space of β-Reduction by Cut Elimination We represent simply typed λ-calculus in proof nets. By $(A \to B) \mapsto (?A^\perp \mathbin{\bindnasrepma} B)$, the typing of functions can be embedded into MELL proof nets [16, 20]. As is well-known, cut elimination corresponds to β-reduction, and the proof net after eliminating all cuts corresponds to the normal form of the λ-term. Figure 5(a) shows the representation of the typed λ-term $(\lambda f : n \to n.\lambda x : n.fx)(\lambda x : n.x) \to (\lambda x : n.x)$ as a proof net. The initial net is the same as the one in Fig. 5(a), which corresponds

$$\dfrac{\overline{f:n\to n, x:n \vdash f:n\to n}\ \text{T-Var} \quad \overline{f:n\to n, x:n \vdash x:n}\ \text{T-Var}}{\dfrac{f:n\to n, x:n \vdash fx:n}{\dfrac{f:n\to n \vdash \lambda x:n.fx:n\to n}{\vdash \lambda f:n\to n.\lambda x:n.fx:n\to n\to n}\ \text{T-Abs}}\ \text{T-Abs}}\ \text{T-App} \qquad \dfrac{\overline{x:n \vdash x:n}\ \text{T-Var}}{\vdash \lambda x:n.x:n\to n}\ \text{T-Abs}$$

$$\vdash (\lambda f:n\to n.\lambda x:n.fx)(\lambda x:n.x):n\to n$$

$$\leadsto^{*} \quad \dfrac{\overline{x:n \vdash x:n}\ \text{T-Var}}{\vdash \lambda x:n.x:n\to n}\ \text{T-Abs}$$

Fig. 12. $(\lambda f:n\to n\,.\,\lambda x:n\,.\,f\,x)\,(\lambda x:n\,.\,x) \to_\beta (\lambda x:n\,.\,x)$

to the proof tree of Fig. 12 (upper). $(\lambda f:n\to n\,.\,\lambda x:n\,.\,f\,x)(\lambda x:n\,.\,x)$ is reduced by β-reduction to the normal form $\lambda x:n\,.\,x$, whose corresponding proof tree is in Fig. 12 (lower), and the corresponding net is the proof net of Fig. 5(b).

Figure 13 shows the state space of the cut elimination of this example visualized by LaViT (the LMNtal Visual Tool) [3]. Note that the rules using the mell library involve extra reduction steps (Fig. 11), but LaViT allows one to visualize the states before and after their application as a single abstract state (shown as squares rather than circles in Fig. 13). The initial net is reduced to the net corresponding to the normal form $\lambda x:n\,.\,x$ in 10 or more steps. Furthermore, since all reduction paths eventually stop at

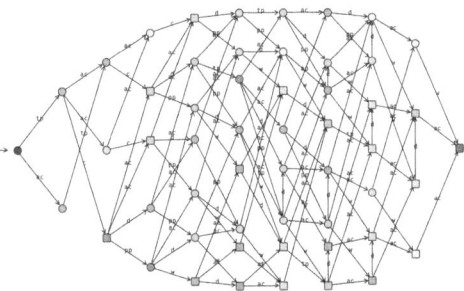

Fig. 13. State space of cut elimination applied to the proof net of Fig. 5.

a single final state (the red node in the figure), we can easily observe that the confluence and strong normalization are satisfied for this example.

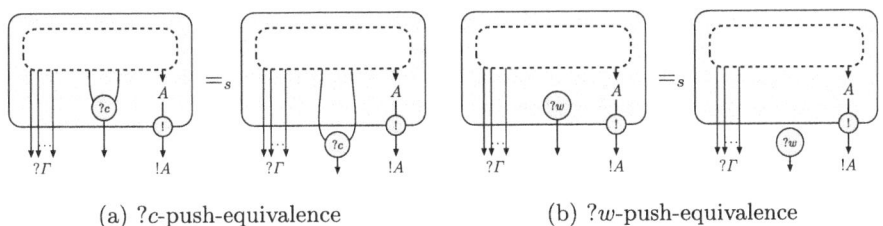

(a) ?c-push-equivalence

(b) ?w-push-equivalence

Fig. 14. Push-equivalence.

```
contraction_pull@@    // ?c_{pull}
  {'!'(X1,X2), '?c'(I,X5), {+I,+X3,+X4}, $p[X1,X3,X4|*X]}
    :- {'!'(X1,X2), $p[X1,X3,X4|*X]}, '?c'(I,X5), {+I,+X3,+X4}.
contraction_push@@    // ?c_{push}
  {'!'(X1,X2), $p[X1,X3,X4|*X]}, '?c'(I,X5), {+I,+X3,+X4},
    :- {'!'(X1,X2), $p[X1,X3,X4|*X], '?c'(I,X5), {+I,+X3,+X4}}.
weakening_pull@@      // ?w_{pull}
  {'!'(X1,X2), '?w'(X3), $p[X1|*X]}
    :- {'!'(X1,X2), $p[X1|*X]}, '?w'(X3).
weakening_push@@      // ?w_{push}
  {'!'(X1,X2), $p[X1|*X]}, '?w'(X3)
    :- {'!'(X1,X2), '?w'(X3), $p[X1|*X]}.
```

Fig. 15. LMNtal encoding of each rule in Fig. 14.

Example: Adding Push-Equivalence Rules. One advantage of the direct encoding of rewrite rules for proof nets into LMNtal is that one can easily modify and/or add rewrite rules and observe their consequences.

For example, an equivalence relation $=_s$, called *push-equivalence*[3] (Fig. 14), has been proposed [35,40]. Rules like this were devised in the context of explicit substitution calculus [10,11] and were also used in the proofs of strong normalization that do not depend on confluence [1]. However, they come with some subtleties, and the precise definition (e.g., whether it is an equivalence relation or should be applied only in one way) varies in the literature. In this section, we introduce these rules into our encoding and verify how they affect confluence and normalization when applied in parallel with cut elimination.

Figure 15 shows the LMNtal encoding of Fig. 14. We represented the equivalence relation as a pair of symmetric rewrite rules. The left-to-right direction (taking elements out of the promotion box) is often called *pull*, and the right-to-left direction (putting elements into the promotion box) is often called *push*. We represent them as a pair of one-step rewrite rules rather than as structural congruence because we want to analyze each direction of rewriting separately.

Using the proof net of Fig. 16 corresponding to $(\lambda f : n \to n \,.\, \lambda x : n \,.\, f\,(f\,x))$ $(\lambda\,x : n\,.\,x)$, we investigated the changes in the state space (number of states, transitions, and end states) caused by the addition of each of these rules to the cut elimination rules. Table 1 shows the results.

---

[3] This name comes from [35].

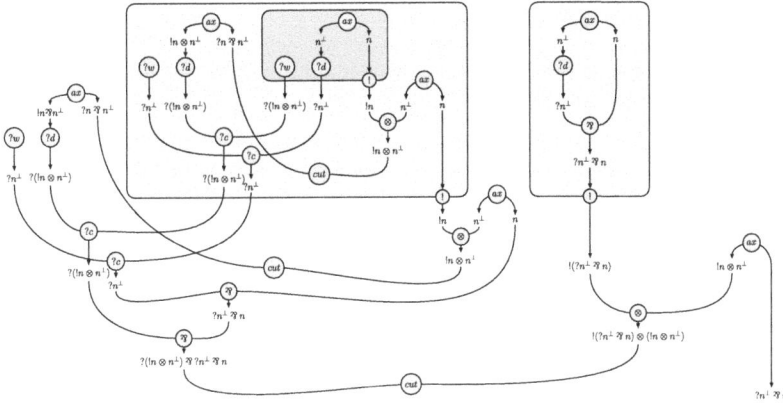

Fig. 16. Proof net corresponding to $(\lambda f : n \to n \, . \, \lambda x : n \, . \, f \, (f \, x)) \, (\lambda x : n \, . \, x)$.

Firstly, we added the ?c-push-equivalence rules (Rows 2–4). For ?c, confluence and strong normalization are proved in [1,11]. Using LaViT, it is easy to see that these properties are preserved. When each rule was added one by one (Rows 2 and 3), they all reached a single end state in a finite number of steps. When both pull and push rules were added (Row 4), strong normalization was lost because of the additional symmetric transitions due to the push rule, but the number of states was preserved from Row 2.

Table 1. Number of states when each rule of Fig. 15 is included/excluded.

$?c_{pull}$	$?c_{push}$	$?w_{pull}$	$?w_{push}$	# of states	# of transitions	# of end states
				476	1592	1
✓				1808	7204	1
	✓			476	1592	1
✓	✓			1808	7832	1
		✓		756	2700	1
			✓	41216	204680	16
		✓	✓	∞	—	—

For ?w, things are more complicated. Indeed, some previous work did not consider the moving of ?w [11], and some allowed pulling only [1]. For pull, it was confirmed that both confluence and strong normalization were maintained, meaning that it is a rule that can be safely handled (Row 5). This result is consistent with the results in [1]. However, when push was added, the number of states increased, and confluence was lost (Row 6). When both pull and push were added, the state space exploded (Row 7). Note that $?w_{push}$ is an interaction between disconnected graph elements (a ?w-cell and a box), which may have properties different from the rewriting of connected components. Whereas discussing the conditions under which Fig. 14(b) hold is out of the scope of the present paper, we can say that the design of correct rewrite/equivalence rules can greatly benefit from a language like LMNtal and a tool like LaViT that allow us to encode the rules straightforwardly and explore the resulting state space.

5.2 Encoding of Process Calculi

The proposed language construct for hierarchical graph rewriting, defined based on the cut elimination of MELL proof nets, is expected to be general enough to describe systems with box structures that involve their cloning, migration and deletion. A typical motivating example is the encoding of the Ambient Calculus [6] that features replication (!), `in`, `out` and `open` operations on box structures called ambients. Due to space limitations, we give some concrete encoding results in Appendix of [33] based on the idea described in [36].

We note that box structures such as promotion boxes of proof nets are sometimes a subject of research towards doing things *without* boxes [19], especially when rewriting of bounded-size redexes is pursued. However, being able to encode and test box operations would still be important because (i) many existing computational formalisms come with primitive operations of unbounded size (e.g., substitution in the λ-calculus) and (ii) hierarchical structures themselves play important roles in modeling (e.g., the Ambient Calculus).

6 Related Work

Graph rewriting systems enhanced with the notion of hierarchies have been proposed in various forms, from mathematical foundations to programming languages [2,4,12,13,25,27,37]. The Chemical Abstract Machine (CHAM) [4] and Bigraphical Reactive Systems (BRS) [25] are graph rewriting formalisms proposed in the context of concurrency theory. Hierarchical Graph Transformation [12] introduces hierarchy into the algebraic graph transformation formalism. Attributed Hierarchical Port Graphs (AHP) [13] adds hierarchical representation to the graphical port graph rewriting tool PORGY [31].

Hierarchical graph rewriting systems based on proof nets include Interaction Nets [24] with boxes [2] and Hypernet with tokens [27]. These proved to be useful as models of functional languages, but they are not designed as general-purpose modeling languages.

The correspondence between graph transformation and logical systems is studied in [34] (graph transformation by double pushout vs. linear logic formulas) and [37] (conversion of LMNtal expressions into linear logic formulas). However, the logical interpretation of the box operations is not yet obvious.

The cloning of boxes in this study atomically clones all graph elements inside the box. In the categorical approach to graph transformation, Sesqui-Pushout (SePO) [8] and PBPO+ [29] have been proposed towards graph cloning. DLGRS [5] and BRS [25] also provide cloning constructs for graph elements. Other graph rewriting systems that provide copying include Pattern Graph Rewrite Systems [22] derived from the ZX-calculus [7].

In this study, we proposed the use of aggregates of process contexts to generate an indefinite number of graph structures for the proper handling of (otherwise dangling) graph edges. As a method of handling an indefinite number of graph elements, GROOVE [15] and QLMNtal [26] propose representations using quantifiers. However, the quantifiers in these formalisms are for the expressive power of an unspecified number of atoms, whereas the present paper is concerned also with handling an unspecified number of free links in port graph rewriting.

7 Conclusion and Future Work

In this work, we extended the syntax of the declarative language LMNtal based on hierarchical graph rewriting with aggregates of process contexts, enabled straightforward description of the operations of promotion boxes of MELL proof nets, defined operations corresponding to the cloning and deletion of promotion boxes, and implemented them via the `mell` API in the full-fledged implementation. LMNtal, extended in this way, has become a practical hierarchical graph rewriting language with strong affinity with MELL proof nets. Furthermore, by describing several examples, we have demonstrated that LMNtal serves as a workbench for proof nets (with many different formulations) and that it is possible to encode concurrency models involving the reconfiguration of hierarchical structures. Thus, the bidirectional consideration from proof nets and from hierarchical graph rewriting languages proved to be beneficial for both sides.

We address future work not mentioned so far. Firstly, the cloning of boxes in this study is limited to generating a single clone, but it might make sense to be able to generate multiple clones at once. This could be realized by extending the `mell` library, but the extension needs non-obvious re-design to allow $a of Fig. 7 to have an unbounded number of free links. Secondly, we plan to accommodate hyperlinks with multiple endpoints [42] in our extension. Since the structure formed by a tree of ?c cells is essentially a hyperlink, it makes sense to allow hyperlinks into our extension, both theoretically and in practice. Finally, LMNtal currently does not allow the rewriting of two atoms connected by a link crossing an indefinite number of membranes ("remote reaction"). Remote reaction across multiple boxes has been proposed in some formulation of proof nets [1]. Allowing this requires major language extension and is a challenging research topic.

Acknowledgments. The authors are indebted to anonymous reviewers for their valuable comments. This work is partially supported by Grant-In-Aid for Scientific Research (23K11057), JSPS, Japan, and Waseda University Grant for Special Research Projects (2024C-432).

References

1. Accattoli, B.: Linear logic and strong normalization. In: van Raamsdonk, F. (ed.) 24th International Conference on Rewriting Techniques and Applications (RTA 2013). Leibniz International Proceedings in Informatics (LIPIcs), vol. 21, pp. 39–54. Dagstuhl, Germany (2013). https://doi.org/10.4230/LIPIcs.RTA.2013.39
2. Alves, S., Fernández, M., Mackie, I.: A new graphical calculus of proofs. In: Electronic Proceedings in Theoretical Computer Science, vol. 48 (2011). https://doi.org/10.4204/EPTCS.48.8

3. Ayano, T., Hori, T., Iwasawa, H., Ogawa, S., Ueda, K.: LMNtal model checking using an integrated development environment. Comput. Softw. **27**(4), 4197–4214 (2010). https://doi.org/10.11309/jssst.27.4_197
4. Berry, G., Boudol, G.: The chemical abstract machine. Theor. Comput. Sci. **96**(1), 217–248 (1992). https://doi.org/10.1016/0304-3975(92)90185-I
5. Brenas, J.H., Echahed, R., Strecker, M.: Verifying graph transformation systems with description logics. In: Lambers, L., Weber, J. (eds.) ICGT 2018. LNCS, vol. 10887, pp. 155–170. Springer, Cham (2018). https://doi.org/10.1007/978-3-319-92991-0_10
6. Cardelli, L., Gordon, A.D.: Mobile ambients. Theor. Comput. Sci. **240**(1), 177–213 (2000). https://doi.org/10.1016/S0304-3975(99)00231-5
7. Coecke, B., Kissinger, A.: Picturing Quantum Processes: A First Course in Quantum Theory and Diagrammatic Reasoning. Cambridge University Press, Cambridge (2017)
8. Corradini, A., Heindel, T., Hermann, F., König, B.: Sesqui-pushout rewriting. In: Corradini, A., Ehrig, H., Montanari, U., Ribeiro, L., Rozenberg, G. (eds.) ICGT 2006. LNCS, vol. 4178, pp. 30–45. Springer, Heidelberg (2006). https://doi.org/10.1007/11841883_4
9. Danos, V., Regnier, L.: The structure of multiplicatives. Arch. Math. Logic **28**(3), 181–203 (1989). https://doi.org/10.1007/bf01622878
10. Di Cosmo, R., Kesner, D.: Strong normalization of explicit substitutions via cut elimination in proof nets. In: Proceedings of Twelfth Annual IEEE Symposium on Logic in Computer Science, pp. 35–46 (1997). https://doi.org/10.1109/LICS.1997.614927
11. Di Cosmo, R., Guerrini, S.: Strong normalization of proof nets modulo structural congruences. In: Narendran, P., Rusinowitch, M. (eds.) RTA 1999. LNCS, vol. 1631, pp. 75–89. Springer, Heidelberg (1999). https://doi.org/10.1007/3-540-48685-2_6
12. Drewes, F., Hoffmann, B., Plump, D.: Hierarchical graph transformation. J. Comput. Syst. Sci. **64**(2), 249–283 (2002). https://doi.org/10.1006/jcss.2001.1790
13. Ene, N.C., Fernández, M., Pinaud, B.: Attributed hierarchical port graphs and applications. Electron. Proc. Theor. Comput. Sci. EPTCS **265**, 2–19 (2018). https://doi.org/10.4204/eptcs.265.2
14. Fleury, A., Retoré, C.: The mix rule. Math. Struct. Comput. Sci. **4**(2), 273–285 (1994). https://doi.org/10.1017/S0960129500000451
15. Ghamarian, A., de Mol, M., Rensink, A., Zambon, E., Zimakova, M.: Modelling and analysis using GROOVE. Int. J. Softw. Tools Technol. Transfer **14**(1), 15–40 (2012). https://doi.org/10.1007/s10009-011-0186-x
16. Girard, J.Y.: Linear logic. Theoret. Comput. Sci. **50**(1), 1–101 (1987). https://doi.org/10.1016/0304-3975(87)90045-4
17. Girard, J.Y.: Linear logic: a survey. In: Bauer, F., Brauer, W., Schwichtenberg, H. (eds.) Logic and Algebra of Specification. NATO ASI Series, vol. 94, pp. 63–112. Springer, Heidelberg (1993). https://doi.org/10.1007/978-3-642-58041-3_3
18. Gocho, M., Hori, T., Ueda, K.: Evolution of the LMNtal runtime to a parallel model checker. Comput. Softw. **28**(4), 137–157 (2011). https://doi.org/10.11309/jssst.28.4_137
19. Gonthier, G., Abadi, M., Lévy, J.J.: Linear logic without boxes. In: [1992] Proceedings of the Seventh Annual IEEE Symposium on Logic in Computer Science, pp. 223–234 (1992). https://doi.org/10.1109/LICS.1992.185535
20. Guerrini, S.: Proof nets and the λ-Calculus. In: Ehrhard, T., Girard, J.Y., Ruet, P., Scott, P. (eds.) Linear Logic in Computer Science, pp. 65–118. London Mathe-

matical Society Lecture Note Series, Cambridge University Press (2004). https://doi.org/10.1017/CBO9780511550850.003
21. Inui, A., Kudo, S., Hara, K., Mizuno, K., Kato, N., Ueda, K.: LMNtal: the unifying programming language based on hierarchical graph rewriting. Comput. Softw. **25**(1), 1124–1150 (2008). https://doi.org/10.11309/jssst.25.1_124
22. Kissinger, A., Merry, A., Soloviev, M.: Pattern graph rewrite systems. Electron. Proc. Theor. Comput. Sci. **143**, 54–66 (2012). https://doi.org/10.4204/EPTCS.143.5
23. Kudo, S., Kato, N., Ueda, K.: Design and implementation of operation constructs of graph structures in the LMNtal system. Inf. Technol. Lett. **4**, 9–12 (2005). http://id.nii.ac.jp/1001/00147815/
24. Lafont, Y.: Interaction nets. In: Proceedings of the 17th ACM SIGPLAN-SIGACT Symposium on Principles of Programming Languages, pp. 95–108. POPL 1990, Association for Computing Machinery, New York, NY, USA (1989). https://doi.org/10.1145/96709.96718
25. Milner, R.: Bigraphical reactive systems. In: Larsen, K.G., Nielsen, M. (eds.) CONCUR 2001. LNCS, vol. 2154, pp. 16–35. Springer, Heidelberg (2001). https://doi.org/10.1007/3-540-44685-0_2
26. Mishina, H., Ueda, K.: Introducing quantification into a hierarchical graph rewriting language. In: 34th International Symposium on Logic-Based Program Synthesis and Transformation (LOPSTR 2024). LNCS, vol. 14919, pp. 220–239. Springer, Cham (2024). https://doi.org/10.1007/978-3-031-71294-4_13
27. Muroya, K.: Hypernet semantics of programming languages. Ph.D. thesis, University of Birmingham (2020)
28. Nguyên, L.T.D.: Unique perfect matchings, forbidden transitions and proof nets for linear logic with mix. Log. Methods Comput. Sci. **16** (2019). https://doi.org/10.23638/LMCS-16(1:27)2020
29. Overbeek, R., Endrullis, J., Rosset, A.: Graph rewriting and relabeling with PBPO$^+$. In: Gadducci, F., Kehrer, T. (eds.) ICGT 2021. LNCS, vol. 12741, pp. 60–80. Springer, Cham (2021). https://doi.org/10.1007/978-3-030-78946-6_4
30. Pagani, M., Falco, L.T.D.: Strong normalization property for second order linear logic. Theor. Comput. Sci. **411**(2), 410–444 (2010). https://doi.org/10.1016/j.tcs.2009.07.053
31. Pinaud, B., Melançon, G., Dubois, J.: PORGY: a visual graph rewriting environment for complex systems. Comput. Graph. Forum **31**(3), 1265–1274 (2012). https://doi.org/10.1111/j.1467-8659.2012.03119.x
32. Takyu, K., Ueda, K.: Encoding MELL cut elimination into a hierarchical graph rewriting language. In: The 21st Asian Symposium on Programming Languages and Systems SRC & Posters (2023)
33. Takyu, K., Ueda, K.: Enhancing a hierarchical graph rewriting language based on MELL cut elimination (2024). https://doi.org/10.48550/arXiv.2411.14802
34. Torrini, P., Heckel, R.: Towards an embedding of graph transformation in intuitionistic linear logic. In: Electronic Proceedings in Theoretical Computer Science, vol. 12, pp. 99–115 (2009). https://doi.org/10.4204/EPTCS.12.7
35. Tranquilli, P.: Confluence of pure differential nets with promotion. In: Grädel, E., Kahle, R. (eds.) CSL 2009. LNCS, vol. 5771, pp. 500–514. Springer, Heidelberg (2009). https://doi.org/10.1007/978-3-642-04027-6_36
36. Ueda, K.: Encoding distributed process calculi into LMNtal. Electron. Notes Theor. Comput. Sci. **209**, 187–200 (2008). https://doi.org/10.1016/j.entcs.2008.04.012
37. Ueda, K.: LMNtal as a hierarchical logic programming language. Theoret. Comput. Sci. **410**(46), 4784–4800 (2009). https://doi.org/10.1016/j.tcs.2009.07.043

38. Ueda, K.: Gentle introduction to LMNtal: language design and implementation. In: Tutorial given at the 17th International Conference on Graph Transformation (ICGT 2024) (2024). https://conf.researchr.org/details/icgt-2024/icgt-2024-research-papers/17/Gentle-Introduction-to-LMNtal-Language-Design-and-Implementation
39. Ueda, K., Kato, N.: LMNtal: a language model with links and membranes. In: Proceedings Fifth International Workshop on Membrane Computing (WMC 2004). LNCS, vol. 3365, pp. 110–125 (2005). https://doi.org/10.1007/978-3-540-31837-8_6
40. Vaux, L.: λ-calcul différentiel et logique classique : interactions calculatoires. Theses, Université de la Méditerranée - Aix-Marseille II (2007). https://theses.hal.science/tel-00194149
41. Vaux, L.: Proof nets. In: Tutorial given at the 5th International Workshop on Trends in Linear Logic and Applications (TLLA 2021) (2021). https://lipn.univ-paris13.fr/TLLA/2021/
42. Yasen, A., Ueda, K.: Revisiting graph types in HyperLMNtal: a modeling language for hypergraph rewriting. IEEE Access **9**, 133449–133460 (2021). https://doi.org/10.1109/ACCESS.2021.3112903

C3G: Causally Constrained Counterfactual Generation

Sopam Dasgupta[1]( ), Farhad Shakerin[2], Joaquín Arias[3],
Elmer Salazar[1], and Gopal Gupta[1]

[1] University of Texas at Dallas, Richardson, TX 75080, USA
{sopam.dasgupta,elmer.salazar,gupta}@utdallas.edu
[2] Microsoft, Redmond, USA
fshakerin@microsoft.com
[3] CETINIA, Universidad Rey Juan Carlos, Madrid, Spain
joaquin.arias@urjc.es

Abstract. Machine learning models that automate decision-making are increasingly being used in consequential areas such as loan approvals, pretrial bail approval, hiring, and many more. Unfortunately, most of these models are black-boxes, i.e., they are unable to reveal how they reach these prediction decisions. A need for transparency demands justification for such predictions. An affected individual might also desire explanations to understand why a decision was made. Ethical and legal considerations may require informing individuals of changes needed to produce a desirable outcome. This paper focuses on this problem through the automatic generation of *counterfactual explanations*. We propose a framework *Causally Constrained Counterfactual Generation (C3G)* that utilizes Answer Set Programming (ASP) and the s(CASP) goal-directed ASP system to automatically generate counterfactual explanations from rules generated by *rule-based machine learning (RBML)* algorithms. Unlike traditional causal based approaches such as MINT, which relies on Structural Causal Models (SCMs) with predefined structural equations, C3G leverages the flexibility of Answer Set Programming (ASP) to model causal dependencies through logical rules, allowing for broader applicability across various domains. In our framework, we show how counterfactual explanations are computed and justified by imagining worlds where some or all factual assumptions are altered/changed. More importantly, we show how we can navigate between these worlds, namely, go from our original world/scenario where we obtain an undesired/negative outcome to the imagined world where we obtain a desired/positive outcome.

Keywords: Causal reasoning · Counterfactual reasoning · Explainable Artificial Intelligence (XAI)

1 Introduction

Predictive models in automated decision-making, like job filtering or loan approval, often function as black boxes, making decision reasoning difficult to understand. Many decisions made by these models have significant consequences for the affected individuals, who desire satisfactory explanations for undesired/negative outcomes. This need for transparency is essential whether decisions are made by automated systems or humans. Certain approaches [28] proposed generating counterfactuals to explain decisions and inform users on how to achieve desired/positive outcomes. Our contribution is a framework called *Causally Constrained Counterfactual Generation (C3G)* that generates counterfactual explanations from *rule-based machine learning (RBML)* algorithms. We answer the question, "What can be done to achieve the desired outcome given an undesired one?" Our framework models various scenarios: the current scenario/world with a negative outcome and an imagined scenario/world with a positive outcome. The goal is to move from a negative scenario to a positive one, assuming the decision-making process remains static. This is achieved through *interventions*, by changing input *feature values* while considering *causal dependencies*. Our framework uses commonsense reasoning through Answer Set Programming (ASP) [18], specifically the goal-directed s(CASP) ASP system [5].

2 Background

Counterfactual Reasoning. Humans use explanations to understand decisions. Counterfactual explanations offer meaningful insights to understand a decision and guide actions to change the outcome to a desired one. For example, in the case of being denied a loan, a counterfactual explanation might state: "If John were married, his loan application would have been approved." The key idea behind counterfactual explanations is to imagine a different world where the desired outcome holds. This alternate world should be reachable from the current one. Therefore, the concept of "closest" or "close possible worlds" envisions alternative, reasonably plausible scenarios/worlds where such a desired outcome is achievable.

For a binary classifier used for prediction, given by $f : X \rightarrow \{0,1\}$, we define a set of counterfactual explanations $\hat{x}$ for a factual input $x \in X$ as $CF_f(\hat{x}) = \{\hat{x} \in X | f(x) \neq f(\hat{x})\}$. This set of counterfactual explanations contains all the inputs ($\hat{x}$) that lead to a different prediction under f compared to the original input x.

We demonstrate how counterfactual reasoning can be performed using the s(CASP) query-driven predicate ASP system [5] while accounting for *causal dependencies* between features. By leveraging s(CASP)'s ability to compute *dual rules* (as described in Sect. 2), which enable the execution of negated queries, counterfactual explanations are naturally obtained. Given a predicate p defined as a rule in ASP, its corresponding dual rule allows us to prove ¬ p, where ¬/not represents *negation as failure* [22]. We use these dual rules to construct alternate worlds that lead to counterfactual explanations, considering causal dependencies between features.

Causality. Traditional approaches to explainability often rely of correlations rather than causal reasoning, limiting their ability to generate realistic explanations [11]. Some approaches [31] highlight the necessity of structural causal assumptions for performing valid causal inference from observational data. Inspired by the *Structural Causal Model (SCM)* approach [23], *MINT* [21] showed that ignoring causal relations in counterfactual explanations produces unrealistic results. *MINT* focused on generating counterfactual explanations through interventions to change the predicted label. In earlier approaches [20,27], assumptions were made that changes from interventions were independent across features, which may not hold in reality. As shown in Fig. 1, the counterfactuals while at a minimum distance from the original instance were unrealistic as they did not model the causal dependencies that exist amongst features. Hence, causal relationships should be considered to generate realistic counterfactual explanations. For instance, changing one's marital status without considering related features like relationship status and gender might not yield realistic results. Modeling these causal relationships ensures that downstream changes are realistically represented.

ASP, S(CASP) and Common Sense Reasoning. Answer Set Programming (ASP) is a well-established paradigm for knowledge representation and reasoning, with applications in automating commonsense reasoning [6,10,18]. We use ASP to encode knowledge about features, their domains, properties, decision-making rules, and causal rules, which facilitates automatic generation of counterfactual explanations. s(CASP) is a goal-directed ASP system that executes programs in a top-down manner without grounding [5,19]. Its query-driven nature supports commonsense and counterfactual reasoning by utilizing proof trees. To ensure facts are $TRUE$ only by specified rules, s(CASP) adopts *program completion*, which replaces a set of *"if"* rules with *"if and only if"* rules. In s(CASP) this is done by introducing **dual rules**- for every rule that says $p \Rightarrow q$, add a complementary rule saying $\neg p \Rightarrow \neg q$. The effect ensures that q is $TRUE$ *"if and only if"* p is $TRUE$.

Unlike *MINT* [21], which relies on *Structural Causal Model (SCM)* to capture and reason about causal dependencies, *C3G* leverages Answer Set Programming (ASP) for this task. *SCMs* require predefined structural equations, which may not always generalize across applications. ASP, on the other hand, allows for a more flexible and declarative way to represent and reason about causality. This makes *C3G* more adaptable to diverse domains where causal dependencies can be encoded through logical rules rather than equations. This eliminates the need for manually defining *SCMs* and expands the range of applications where *C3G* can generate actionable counterfactuals.

Commonsense knowledge in ASP is emulated using default rules, integrity constraints, and multiple possible worlds [18,19]. We assume the reader is familiar with ASP and s(CASP). An introduction to ASP can be found in Gelfond and Kahl's book [18], while a fairly detailed overview of the s(CASP) system can be found elsewhere [4,5].

FOLD-SE. FOLD-SE [29] is an efficient and explainable *rule-based machine learning (RBML)* algorithm for classification tasks. For given input data (numerical and categorical), FOLD-SE generates a set of default rules (a stratified normal logic program) from input data. The explainability obtained through FOLD-SE is scalable. It maintains a small number of learned rules and literals regardless of dataset size, while achieving good accuracy compared to other *RBML* approaches like RIPPER [13]. FOLD-SE's accuracy is comparable to traditional tools like XGBoost [12] and Multi-Layer Perceptrons (MLP), with the added benefit of explainability.

3 Overview

The Problem. When an individual (represented as a set of features) receives an undesired negative decision (loan denial), they can seek necessary changes to flip it to a positive one. *C3G* automatically identifies these changes. In *C3G*, we refer to the state/world/scenario corresponding to the negative decision as a *pre-intervention state i* while the positive one is referred to as a *post-intervention state g*. For example, if John is denied a loan (*pre-intervention state i*), *C3G* models the various (positive) scenarios (*post-intervention states $g \in G$*) where he obtains the loan. Obviously, the (negative) decision in the *pre-intervention state i* should not apply to any scenario in the *set of post-intervention states G*. The query goal '?- reject_loan(john)' should be True in the state i and False for all states in G. The objective is to find the interventions, namely, changes to feature values, that will take us from i to $g \in G$.

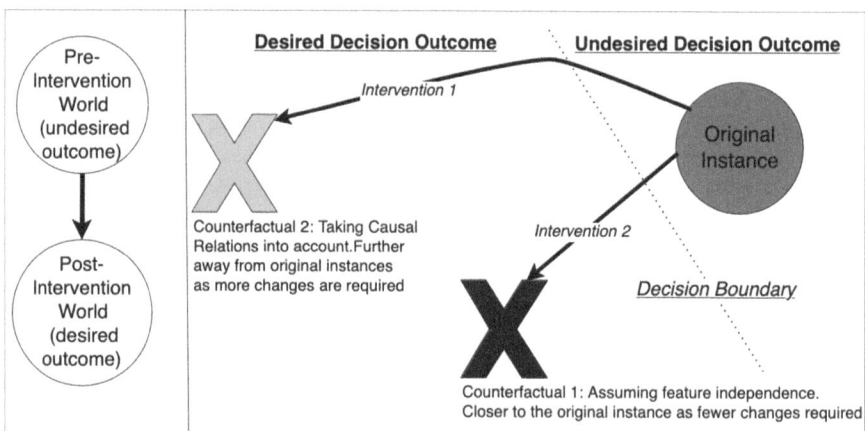

Fig. 1. Left: Transition from *Pre-Intervention World* to the *Post-Intervention World*. **Right:** *Intervention takes the original instance to the other side of the decision boundary. With feature independence, the new counterfactual is closer to the original instance. With causal dependencies, the new counterfactual is further away as more changes are made to the original instance.*

Solution- *C3G* Approach. The *C3G* approach involves transitioning from a *pre-intervention* state i to a *post-intervention* state g (as shown in Fig. 1), with each state represented as feature-value pairs (e.g., credit score: 600; age: 24). There can be multiple post-intervention states representing the positive outcome (set of states G where $g \in G$). The goal is to convert a negative decision (*pre-intervention* state i) into a positive one (*post-intervention* state g) by changing feature values, so that the query goal '?- not reject_loan(john)' will succeed for $g \in G$. Given an instance where the decision query (e.g., '?- reject_loan/1') succeeds (negative outcome), *C3G* finds the state where this query fails (i.e., the query '?- not reject_loan/1' succeeds), constituting the *post-intervention* state g.

In ASP terms, the problem can be described as follows: given a *pre-intervention* state/world where a query succeeds, compute the necessary feature changes (considering causal dependencies) to reach a *post-intervention* state/world where the negation of the query succeeds. The transition from *pre-intervention* to *post-intervention* states/worlds must be viable with respect to the rules.

We use the s(CASP) query-driven predicate ASP system [5] for this purpose. s(CASP) automatically generates dual rules, allowing us to execute negated queries (such as '?- not reject_loan/1') constructively.

Example: Consider a loan application scenario. There are 3 feature-domain pairs: 1) Debt: {*no_debt*, $\leq$ 10000,$>$ 10000}, 2) Bank Balance: {$0, ..., $1 *million*} and 3) Credit Score: {300 *points*, ..., 850 *points*}.

John ($>$ $10000, $40000, 599 *points*) applies for a loan. The bank has a rejection rule: Deny loans to individuals with a *bank balance* of **less than** $60000, and with a *credit score* below 600. John ($>$ $10000, $40000, 599 *points*) is denied a loan (negative outcome) but wishes to get it approved (positive outcome).

Without the knowledge of causal dependencies, a solution might be the following: **Pre-Intervention state**: John ($>$ $10000, $40000, 599 *points*) is denied a loan. **Post-Intervention state**: John ($>$ $10000, $60000, 620 *points*) is approved for a loan. **Interventions**: 1) Change the *bank balance* to $60000, and 2) the *credit score* to 620 *points*. However, *credit score* cannot be changed directly. Hence this solution is unrealizable.

To realistically increase the credit score, the bank's guidelines suggest **1) having no debt**. This leads to a causal dependency between *debt* and *credit score*. Incorporating this, *C3G* provides: **Pre-Intervention state**: John ($>$ $10000, $40000, 599 *points*) is denied a loan. **Post-Intervention state**: John (*no_debt*, $60000, 620 *points*) is approved for a loan. **Interventions**: 1) John changes his *bank balance* to $60000, and 2) *clears his debt* to increase his *credit score*. As shown in Fig. 1, this intervention takes the original instance to the other side of the decision boundary. The unrealistic counterfactual where the *credit_score* is directly altered while having *debt* of $>$ $10000 is closer to the original instance in terms of distance/cost. However it is unrealistic as it incorrectly assumes feature independence. The realistic counterfactual is further away as it requires more changes but is realizable. This is showcased in Fig. 1.

220   S. Dasgupta et al.

4 Methodology

In this section we define the methodology employed by our proposed framework *C3G* for generating counterfactual instances (that produce a *desired/positive outcome*) from an original instance (that produces an *undesired/negative outcome*). While we shall use a simple example to denote our process, we have run experiments (as show in Sect. 5) on the following datasets: adult [7], car [9], titanic [14], dropout [24], mushroom [3] and voting [2].

Example. Consider the loan application scenario from Sect. 3. We represent the loan rejection rules as follows:
`reject_loan(john(X,Y,Z)):- bank_balance(Y),`
  `Y#=<60000, credit_score(Z), Z<600.`

The above rule classifies individuals with their *loans rejected* through their value of the '*bank_balance*' and '*credit_score*' feature, i.e. *bank_balance* less than $60000; and *credit_score* less than 600. For an individual with their loan rejected (negative outcome), assuming that they wish to have their loan approved (positive outcome), what would they have to do to not be rejected i.e. be approved for the loan? We provide a step-by-step flowchart showing how to navigate from an undesired negative outcome to a desired positive outcome in Fig. 2. We elaborate on our methodology as follows:

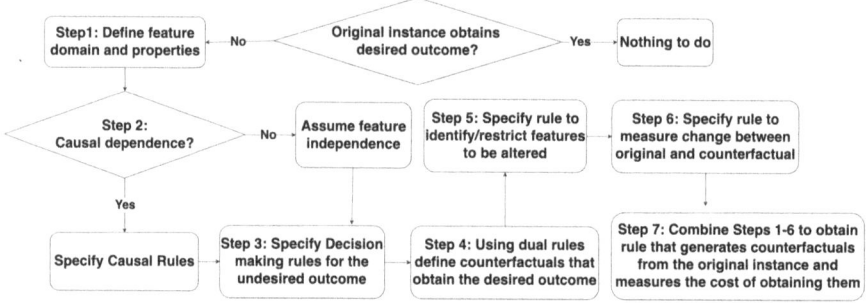

Fig. 2. Methodology of the *Causally Constrained Counterfactual Generation (C3G)*

4.1 Step 1: Defining Domain and Properties of Features

Defining Domains. To determine the necessary changes for obtaining the desired outcome, we must understand the features' properties and their possible values. Continuing with our running example from Sect. 3, for categorical features, we declare domain values as facts, e.g.,:
1. `f_domain(debt,`no_debt`).`
2. `f_domain(debt,`$\leq \$10000$`).`
3. `f_domain(debt, `$> \$10000$`).`

The above facts represent the various values that the categorical feature '*debt*' can take: *no_debt*, ≤ $10000 and > $10000.

For numerical features, we define ranges, e.g.,:
4. `f_domain(bank_balance,X):-X#>=0,X#=<1000000.`
5. `f_domain(credit_score,X):-X#>=300,X#=<850.`

The rule for *bank_balance* (line 4) defines $0 – $1 million as the range of values for the numeric feature *bank_balance*. The feature *credit_score* is defined having the range 300 – 850 (line 5).

These rules specify the possible values that features like '*debt*,' '*bank_balance*,' and '*credit_score*' can take. This understanding is crucial for identifying viable changes to achieve the desired outcome. After defining the domain of the features, the next step involves specifying their properties.

Specifying Feature Properties. We define two worlds: **pre-intervention** (negative outcome) and **post-intervention** (positive outcome).

Pre-intervention: The original world where the negative outcome occurs (e.g., loan rejection). **Post-intervention:** The imagined world where the positive outcome is achieved (e.g., loan approval).

We need to specify the properties corresponding to each world to generate pre and post-intervention worlds (what properties are $TRUE$ **pre-intervention** may not be $TRUE$ **post-intervention**).

Numerical Features: Properties are defined with rules specifying pre- and post-intervention worlds. For example, properties for the feature '*credit_score*' is as follows:
6. `pre_credit_score(X):- f_domain(credit_score,X).`
7. `post_credit_score(X):- f_domain(credit_score,X).`

Categorical Features: Properties are explicitly defined to ensure mutual exclusivity. This is done to prevent unrealistic scenarios such as one where a person has both '*no debt*' as well as '> $10000 in debt' simultaneously:
8. `not_pre_debt(X):- f_domain(debt,Y), pre_debt(Y), Y \= X.`
9. `pre_debt(X) :- not not_pre_debt(X).`

The above rules specify the **pre-intervention** properties for the feature '*debt*.'
10. `not_post_debt(X):- f_domain(debt,Y), post_debt(Y), Y \= X.`
11. `post_debt(X) :- not not_post_debt(X).`
The above rules specify the **post-intervention** properties for the feature '*debt*.'

4.2 Step 2: Incorporating Causal Rules for Modeling Realistic Solutions

In the real world, it is seldom true that the features used are independent. More often than not, a causal dependency exists among features. To ensure realistic counterfactuals, we model causal dependencies between features.

Identifying and Defining Causal Rules. Using knowledge from domain experts or common sense knowledge, we identify features with cause-effect relations. We then run *RBML* algorithms to obtain rules defining the causal relations we can incorporate into our algorithm. For our running example, we obtain rules corresponding to the cause-effect relations between the features '*debt*' and '*credit_score*'- *no_ debt* implies *credit_score* greater ≥ 620.

12. `causal_credit_score_debt(X,Y):- X #>=620, Y` = no_debt.

Using External Knowledge in the Absence of Rules. The rule in line 12 defines the causal dependency of a '*credit_score*' between $620 - 850$ *points* points on '*debt*.' Without a rule for '*credit_score*' in the $300 - 619$ range, we can't generate counterfactuals for those scores. For example, generating John($>$ \$10000, \$60000, 599 *points*) would be impossible without a rule for a $599 - point$ *credit_score*. Thus, we use common-sense or expert knowledge to specify these rules. *C3G* allows incorporating user-defined rules due to its use of explainable *RBML* algorithms.

13. `causal_credit_score_debt(X,Y):- X #>=300, X #=<619, Y` = '$> \$10000$'.

14. `causal_credit_score_debt(X,Y):- X #>=300, X #=<619, Y` = '$\leq \$10000$'.

The user generated rules (line 14,15) imply that if a person is in *debt*, their *credit_score* will be in the $300 - 619$ range.

Incorporating Causality for a Realistic Solution. Since we wish to model realistic solutions, we must take into account the causal rules defined in lines 12, 13 and 14. By combining these rules with the feature domains and feature properties defined in Sect. 4.1, we define rules that generate realistic instances that follow the causal rules that govern the world. Hence, we define the following rules:

15. `pre_realistic(X,Y,Z):- f_domain(debt,X),f_domain(bank_balance,Y),`
    `f_domain(credit_score,Z), pre_debt(X), pre_bank_balance(Y),`
    `pre_credit_score(Z), causal_credit_score_debt(Y,Z).`

The above rule generates realistic instances for the pre-intervention scenario. Similarly, after making changes to obtain a counterfactual instance, we wish for such instances to be realistic, so we define a rule to generate realistic instances post-intervention. This is expressed as follows:

16. `post_realistic(X,Y,Z):- f_domain(debt,X),f_domain(bank_balance,Y),`
    `f_domain(credit_score,Z), post_debt(X), post_bank_balance(Y),`
    `post_credit_score(Z), causal_credit_score_debt(Y,Z).`

By incorporating the rules in lines 15 and 16 into our overall function as we shall do later, we constrain our solutions to be realistic in nature and model the reality of the world.

Causally Independent Features. Assuming that no causal dependency exists amongst the features, then we slightly modify the rules from lines $15 - 16$.

15. `pre_realistic(X,Y,Z):-`

```
    f_domain(debt,X),f_domain(bank_balance,Y),
    f_domain(credit_score,Z), pre_debt(X),
    pre_bank_balance(Y),pre_credit_score(Z).
```

The above rule generates the instances for the pre-intervention scenario where the features are independent and are not constrained by causal dependencies.

```
16. post_realistic(X,Y,Z):-
    f_domain(debt,X),f_domain(bank_balance,Y),
    f_domain(credit_score,Z),post_debt(X),
    post_bank_balance(Y),post_credit_score(Z).
```

The above rule generates the instances for the post-intervention scenario where the features are independent and none of the features are constrained by causal dependencies.

4.3 Step 3: Decision-Making Rules for Undesired Outcomes

In our running example, we have the decision rules provided to us. Alternatively, we can also run an *RBML* algorithm (FOLD-SE) to obtain the decision-making rules that produce the negative outcome and express it in the ASP/s(CASP) syntax as follows:
`reject_loan(john(X,Y,Z)):-bank_balance(Y),Y#=<60000,credit_score(Z),Z<600.`

The above rules states that an individual having both 1) a *bank_balance* less then $60000, and 2) a *credit_score* less than 600 *points* shall have their loan rejected. However in order to work in our *C3G* framework, we need to rewrite these rules as follows:
`17. lite_reject_loan(X,Y,Z):-Y#=<60000,Z#<600.`

The rule in line 17 specifies the decision-making component of our overall rule (as defined later in line 18) that determines if an individual has their loan *rejected* as per our original decision-making rule. The rule in line 17 will be $TRUE$ if the variable Y has a value *less than 60000* and if the variable Z has a value *less than 600*.

Now we need to incorporate the domain and properties of the features as mentioned in Step 1 (Sect. 4.1) and Step 2 (Sect. 4.2). Our overall rule with the domain and feature properties defined for the pre-intervention scenario is defined as follows:
```
18. reject_loan(X,Y,Z) :-f_domain(debt,X), f_domain(bank_balance,Y),
    f_domain(credit_score,Z), pre_debt(X), pre_bank_balance(Y),
    pre_credit_score(Z), lite_reject_loan(X,Y,Z).
```

By querying the rules described in line 15 and 18 and leaving the variables unassigned, we can obtain the feature values for all the possible realistic individuals that are classified to have their loans rejected.
`?- reject_loan(X,Y,Z),pre_realistic(X,Y,Z).`

In the query shown above, X is the variable that represents the feature '*debt*,' and Y is the variable that represents the feature '*bank_balance*.' Z is the variable that represents the feature '*credit_score*.' By leaving the variables X, Y, and Z unassigned, the executed query above gives a symbolic representation of the solution space for all individuals classified to have their loan *rejected* (negative outcome). The second component `pre_realistic(X,Y,Z)` generates realistic instances while the first component `reject_loan(X,Y,Z)` constrains these realistic instances to achieve the original *negative* decision outcome.

4.4 Step 4: Counterfactuals in s(CASP)

In the running example, to obtain counterfactuals for individuals whose loans are *rejected*, we need rules that classify individuals whose loans are *approved*.

Procedure to Obtain Counterfactual Rules. Our procedure for defining the counterfactual rules is as follows:

- Define the domain of the features as per the original decision making rules.
- Define the features' properties per the original decision-making rules but only change pre-intervention property to post-intervention property (By definition, counterfactual instances are ones that we obtain **post/after** making an intervention). For example, if the property of the feature '*debt*' in the original decision-making rules is given by `pre_debt(X)`, we define the properties of the counterfactual instance as `post_debt(X)` in the counterfactual formula.
- Negate the decision-making component of the original decision-making rules. For example, in the original decision-making rule (line 18), the predicate `lite_reject_loan(X,Y,Z)` defines the decision-making component. We replace '`lite_reject_loan(X,Y,Z)`' with '`not lite_reject_loan(X,Y,Z)`' for the counterfactual rule.

Overall Counterfactual Rule: For our running example, by following the procedure in Sect. 4.4, we express the counterfactual rule that identifies counterfactual instances that disagree with the original decision making rule:
19. `cf_accept(X1,Y1,Z1):-f_domain(debt,X1),f_domain(bank_balance,Y1),`
    `f_domain(credit_score,Z1),post_debt(X1),post_bank_balance(Y1),`
    `post_credit_score(Z1), not lite_reject_loan(X1,Y1,Z1).`

By querying the rules described in line 16 and 19 and leaving the variables unassigned, we can obtain the feature values for all the possible individuals do **not** have their loan *rejected*, i.e., have their loan *approved*.
`?-cf_accept(X1,Y1,Z1), post_realistic(X1,Y1,Z1).`

In the query shown above, $X1$ is the variable that represents the feature '*debt*,' and $Y1$ is the variable that represents the feature '*bank balance*.' $Z1$ is the variable that represents the feature '*credit score*.' By leaving the variables $X1$, $Y1$, and $Z1$ unassigned, the executed query above gives a symbolic representation of the solution space for all individuals classified to **not** have their loan *rejected*, i.e., have their loans *approved* (positive outcome). The second component `post_realistic(X1,Y1,Z1)` generates realistic instances while the first component `cf_accept(X1,Y1,Z1)` constrains these realistic instances to achieve the counterfactual *positive* decision outcome.

4.5 Step 5: Restricting Features Taking Mutability and Immutability of Features into Account

Our goal is to suggest interventions on the original instance (that produces a negative outcome) that will lead to a counterfactual instance (that produces the positive outcome). In many cases, we wish to restrict the kinds of changes that are done to reach the counterfactual. For our running example, take the case of the feature '*credit_score*'. Suppose we wish to be approved for the loan without changing '*credit_score*'. Then a counterfactual that recommends changing the value of the '*credit_score*' will be has no utility to the user.

Hence to tackle this problem, we introduce rules that **constrain/restrict** the kind of changes (interventions) that can be made to the features in the process of generating counterfactuals.

If a certain feature is declared as immutable, its value cannot be changed. On the other hand, if a feature is mutable, it is allowed to change its value. If no such declaration is made for a feature, it can be treated as a mutable feature, if the need arises.

Constraining/Restricting Categorical Features. We aim to define the rules that constrain/restrict the kind of interventions/changes that can be made to categorical features.
20. f_domain(restrict_C,0).
21. f_domain(restrict_C,1).

The facts (line 20, 21) define the kind of interventions that restrict categorical features. If the second argument is 0, the feature is immutable and if it is 1 then the feature's value has to be changed.
22. compare_C(Pre_X,Post_X,Z):- f_domain(restrict_C,Z), Z=0,Pre_X=Post_X.
23. compare_C(Pre_X,Post_X,Z):- f_domain(restrict_C,Z),Z=1,Pre_X\=Post_X.

The above rules (lines 22-23) restrict the kind of pre- and post-intervention on categorical features. If $Z = 0$ the feature remains unchanged or is immutable before and after intervention. If $Z = 1$ the pre-intervention value of the feature changes post-intervention, i.e., the feature values changes after intervention.

Constraining/Restricting Numeric Features. We aim to define the rules that constrain/restrict the kind of interventions/changes that can be made to numeric features.
24. f_domain(restrict_N,0).
    f_domain(restrict_N,1).
    f_domain(restrict_N,-1).

The facts above define kind of interventions that restrict numeric features. 0 indicates a feature is immutable.1 indicates that the value of the numeric feature will increase and -1 indicates that the value will decrease after intervention.
25. compare_N(Pre_X,Post_X,Z):-f_domain(restrict_N,Z), Z=0, Pre_X=Post_X.
26. compare_N(Pre_X,Post_X,Z):-f_domain(restrict_N,Z),Z=1,Pre_X#<Post_X.
27. compare_N(Pre_X,Post_X,Z):-f_domain(restrict_N,Z),Z=-1,Pre_X#>Post_X.

The above rules in lines 25–27 restrict the kind of intervention on numeric features, pre and post intervention (before and after making an intervention). If $Z = 0$ the feature is immutable or does not change pre and post intervention. If $Z = 1$ the post intervention value of the feature is higher than the pre-intervention value, i.e., the feature value increases after intervention. If $Z = -1$ the post intervention value of the feature is lower than the pre-intervention value, i.e., the feature value decreases after intervention.

Overall Rule Restricting Interventions Between the Original and Counterfactual Instances. Taking our running example, we define an overall rule for restricting the interventions between an original instance and counterfactual instances by using the rules defined in Sects. 4.5 and 4.5.

28. `id_restrict(original(X1,X2,X3),id(Z1,Z2,Z3), counterfactual(Y1,Y2,Y3))`
    `:- compare_C(X1,Y1,Z1),compare_N(X2,Y2,Z2),compare_N(X3,Y3,Z3).`

The predicate defined in the rule in line 28 takes 3 arguments; $original(X1, X2, X3)$ representing the instance with three features $X1$, $X2$ and $X3$ before any intervention, $counterfactual(Y1, Y2, Y3)$ representing the counterfactual instance with three features $Y1$, $Y2$ and $Y3$ generated after intervention, and $id(Z1, Z2, Z3)$ representing the kind of restriction allowed on the features. $Z1$ indicates the restriction on the feature $X1$ as its value changes to $Y1$, $Z2$ indicates the restriction on the feature $X2$ as its value changes to $Y2$ and $Z3$ indicates the restriction on the feature $X3$ as its value changes to $Y3$. Additionally, by leaving any of the variables $Z1, Z2$ and $Z3$ unassigned, we put **no restriction** on the corresponding features, i.e., their values can change if needed.

4.6 Measuring the Cost of Interventions

To ensure that we do not make unnecessary interventions that require an investment of time and effort, we measure the cost of making interventions on the original instance in the process of generating counterfactuals. Our definition of the cost involves the sum total of all features that have been intervened on in the process of generating the counterfactual. Our approach to this is simple, we identify intervened categorical features (features that have been changed) by the value $\{1\}$ and immutable categorical features by the value $\{0\}$ as shown in Sect. 4.5. Similarly we identify intervened numeric features by the values $\{1, -1\}$ and immutable numeric features by the value $\{0\}$ as shown in Sect. 4.5. We simply sum up the categorical values and sum of the squares of the numerical values and add both the sums to obtain the total cost. Hence the maximum value for the cost of intervention is equal to the total number of features.

Step 6: Measuring the Cost of Changed Features. As per our running example 4, we define a rule for computing the total number of features that have been intervened which we measure as the cost of making interventions.

29. `measure(Z1,Z2,Z3,W1,W2,W3,X):- f_domain(restrict_C,Z1),`

```
f_domain(restrict_N,Z2), f_domain(restrict_N,Z3),
Q2 #= Z2*Z2, Q3 #= Z3*Z3, X #= (W1*Z1)+(W2*Q2)+(W3*Q3).
```
The above rule in line 29 calculates the total cost of making changes to the original instance. Here Z1, Z2 and Z3 are the **restriction** variables that can also indicate whether a feature has changed after intervention. They have the domain $\{0,1,\}$ for categorical features and $\{0,1,-1\}$ for numerical features. For the above rule in line 29, Z1 indicates the restriction on the categorical features whereas Z2, Z3 indicates the restriction on the numeric feature. For categorical features, as mentioned earlier, simply summing up the values will give the total number of features that have been intervened on/changed. For numerical features the value $\{-1\}$ indicates that the counterfactual feature value was decreased after intervention. So in order to measure the cost, we square the restriction variables for the numerical features. Hence 0 will remain 0, 1 will remain 1 and -1 will become 1. By summing them up, we can compute the total number of numeric features that have been intervened on. Adding the overall sums/cost for the numerical and categorical features provides the overall cost of making interventions (total number of features that have been intervened on). Additionally, W1, W2, W3 are the weights assigned to measure the cost of making changes to the corresponding features. If changing certain features is more difficult than others, this is reflected in the weight. For example, changing *credit score* is more difficult than changing *bank balance*, i.e., $W3 > W2$. A counterfactual involving only altering the *credit score* will have a lower cost compared to one involving altering the *bank balance*.

4.7 Step 7: Obtaining Counterfactual from the Original Instance

As per our running example, we incorporate all the rules from Steps 1 through 6 into one final rule to obtain:
```
30. refined(original(A,B,C),id(Z1,Z2,Z3),counterfactual(A1,B1,C1),
    weights(W1,W2,W3),X):- reject_loan(A,B,C), pre_realistic(A,B,C),
    cf_accept(A1,B1,C1), post_realistic(A1,B1,C1),
    id_restrict(original(A,B,C), id(Z1,Z2,Z3),
    counterfactual(A1,B1,C1)), measure(Z1,Z2,Z3,W1,W2,W3,X).
```
The **first** argument $original(A, B, C)$ represents the original feature values that led to the undesired decision. **Second** argument $id(Z1, Z2, Z3)$ represents the constraints on each of the features. **Third** argument $counterfactual(A1, B1, C1)$ represents the counterfactual values. **Fourth** argument $weights(W1, W2, W3)$ represents the *weights* indicating the difficulty of intervening/ altering certain features. **Fifth** argument X represents the cost of making the interventions.
```
?- refined(original(A,B,C),id(Z1,Z2,Z3),
   counterfactual(A1,B1,C1), weights(W1,W2,W3),X).
```
By leaving the variables A, B, C, $Z1$, $Z2$, $Z3$, $A1$, $B1$, $C1$, $W1$, $W2$, $W3$, X unassigned, the executed query above gives a symbolic representation of the solution space for possible paths that can be taken by original instances (that were subject to an undesired outcome) in the process of generating counterfactual

instances. It also specifies the cost that will be incurred by the original instance in taking a path to achieving a particular counterfactual. Additionally, by specifying the respective feature values for the original instances, we can obtain a possible counterfactual solution $(A1, B1, C1)$ with the cost incurred (X).

```
?- refined(original(>$10000,$40000,599), id(Z1,Z2,Z3),
   counterfactual(A1,B1,C1), weights(W1,W2,W3),X).
```

Consider the query for our running example:

```
?- refined(original(>$10000,$40000,599), id(Z1,Z2,Z3),
   counterfactual(A1,B1,C1), weights(W1,W2,W3),1).
```

By specifying the value of the fifth argument (X), as shown in the query above, we can restrict the solution space for all paths to have a specific cost $(X=1)$.

Table 1. Time for Computing the Counterfactual for Various Datasets

Dataset	Training Size	FOLD-SE		RIPPER	
		Features Used	Avg. Time Taken (ms)	Features Used	Avg. Time Taken (ms)
Adult	26048	6	291	12	2869
Titanic	891	3	84	1	14
Dropout	3539	4	67	16	807
Voting	348	5	779	2	75
Cars	1382	4	807	6	75
Mushroom	6499	5	600	9	3911

5 Experiments

For our running example, we defined a rule in Sect. 4.7 that provides *original instance-counterfactual* pairs, indicating possible paths from a negative outcome to a counterfactual. It calculates the cost of reaching the counterfactual while allowing flexibility in the types of interventions permitted in the process of generating such counterfactuals. We applied our *C3G* framework to rules generated by *RBML* algorithms, specifically FOLD-SE [29] and RIPPER [13], using datasets such as adult [7], car [9], titanic [14], dropout [24], mushroom [3] and voting [2]. In the adult dataset, which includes demographic information with labels indicating income ('=<$50k/year' or '> $50k/year'), our *RBML* algorithms generate rules to predict income. Given decision-making rules specifying an undesired outcome ('=<$50k/year'), the goal is to find a path to a counterfactual instance where the income is '>$50k/year'. We have shown our results in Table 1. Further details on the code and the experiments are available in the supplement [1].

For each dataset in Table 1, there are 3 columns denoting the following: 1) **Training Size:** Size of the training data used to generate the decision making and causal rules; 2) **FOLD-SE**: Shows the metrics of the FOLD-SE algorithm; 3) **RIPPER**: Similar to FOLD-SE, it shows the metrics of the RIPPER algorithm. Additionally, for each of the **FOLD-SE** and **RIPPER** algorithms, there exists 2 columns denoting the following: 4) **Number of Features:** Count of the features that were used in generating *original instance-counterfactual* pairs. This depends on the features defined in the decision making rules (Step 4.3) and causal rules (Step 4.2); and 5) **Average Time Taken:** Average Time taken to produce a *(original instance, counterfactual)* pair.

As shown in Table 1, our *C3G* framework generates counterfactuals regardless of the *RBML* algorithm that specifies the decision making rules. We see that the time taken does not depend on the size of the training data (*C3G* takes longer for the voting dataset than the adult dataset) but more on the **Number of Features** (FOLD-SE has fewer features used versus RIPPER).

6 Discussion and Related Work

Existing approaches address transparency by providing explanations for undesired outcomes [28]. These methods generate counterfactual explanations to guide actions for changing outcomes, using both model-specific and optimization-based approaches [25,26]. *Actionable Recourse* [27] emphasizes algorithmic recourse through actionable changes. *MACE* [20], a model agnostic approach improves on this by generating counterfactuals that consider feature immutability, avoiding impractical suggestions like changing 'gender' or 'age'. *CLEAR* [30] uses counterfactual explanations to enhance model performance and accuracy.

Both *Actionable Recourse* and *MACE* assume feature independence, whereas real-world scenarios often involve causal dependencies. *MINT* [21] improves on these by modeling causal dependencies for realistic counterfactuals but lacks the '*if and only*' property, crucial for incorporating causal effects. Other methods [8] rectified this by utilizing Answer Set Programming (ASP) but rely on grounding, which can disconnect variables from their associations. In contrast, *C3G* uses the goal-directed s(CASP) system, supporting complex logic without grounding.

Certain frameworks [17] generate contrastive explanations in ASP, focusing on why one outcome occurred instead of another. While contrastive explanations identify and compare the assumptions leading to different outcomes, *C3G* goes further by incorporating causal dependencies, ensuring that the generated counterfactuals are realistic and achievable. An extension of C3G lies in adding a step-by-step path of actions from the undesired to the desired outcome [15].

Our framework, *Causally Constrained Counterfactual Generation (C3G)*, uses the answer set programming (ASP) paradigm to generate counterfactual explanations [16], accommodating any *RBML* algorithm and allowing user-defined rules. *C3G* ensures realistic counterfactuals by considering causal dependencies. This paper demonstrates that complex tasks like imagining possible scenarios can be modeled with s(CASP) while considering causal dependencies.

The s(CASP) system enables imagining and reasoning about counterfactual situations, providing detailed explanations for decisions.

7 Conclusion

This paper addresses the challenge of generating counterfactual explanations for undesired outcomes predicted by machine learning models. Our framework, *Causally Constrained Counterfactual Generation (C3G)*, utilizes ASP and the goal-directed s(CASP) system to generate counterfactual explanations, regardless of the *RBML* algorithm used. By supporting negation as failure and dual rules, s(CASP) generates alternative worlds to find reachable counterfactuals. We methodically demonstrate how to reach counterfactuals, identify and constrain features to be altered, and measure the cost of interventions. This approach allows specifying intervention costs and integrating user-defined rules, enhancing the transparency and explainability of machine learning models. The implementation of *C3G* has been made available at [1].

References

1. Supplement: C3G: Causality Constrained Counterfactual Generation. https://github.com/sopam/PADL-2025/tree/main
2. Congressional Voting Records: UCI Machine Learning Repository (1987). https://doi.org/10.24432/C5C01P
3. Mushroom. UCI Machine Learning Repository (1987). https://doi.org/10.24432/C5959T
4. Arias, J., Carro, M., Chen, Z., Gupta, G.: Modeling and reasoning in event calculus using goal-directed constraint answer set programming. Theory Pract. Log. Program. **22**(1), 51–80 (2022). https://doi.org/10.1017/S1471068421000156
5. Arias, J., Carro, M., Salazar, E., Marple, K., Gupta, G.: Constraint answer set programming without grounding. Theory Pract. Logic Program. **18**(3–4), 337–354 (2018). https://doi.org/10.1017/S1471068418000285
6. Baral, C.: Knowledge Representation, 1st edn. Reasoning and Declarative Problem Solving. Cambridge University Press, USA (2010)
7. Becker, B., Kohavi, R.: Adult. UCI Machine Learning Repository (1996). https://doi.org/10.24432/C5XW20
8. Bertossi, L.E., Reyes, G.: Answer-set programs for reasoning about counterfactual interventions and responsibility scores for classification. In: Katzouris, N., Artikis, A. (eds.) ILP 2021. LNCS, vol. 13191, pp. 41–56. Springer, Cham (2021). https://doi.org/10.1007/978-3-030-97454-1_4
9. Bohanec, M.: Car Evaluation. UCI Machine Learning Repository (1997). https://doi.org/10.24432/C5JP48
10. Brewka, G., Eiter, T., Truszczyński, M.: Answer set programming at a glance. Commun. ACM **54**(12), 92–103 (2011). https://doi.org/10.1145/2043174.2043195
11. Carloni, G., Berti, A., Colantonio, S.: The role of causality in explainable artificial intelligence. CoRR **abs/2309.09901** (2023). https://doi.org/10.48550/ARXIV.2309.09901

12. Chen, T., Guestrin, C.: Xgboost: a scalable tree boosting system. In: Proceedings of the 22nd ACM SIGKDD International Conference on Knowledge Discovery and Data Mining, pp. 785–794. KDD 2016, Association for Computing Machinery, New York, NY, USA (2016). https://doi.org/10.1145/2939672.2939785
13. Cohen, W.W.: Fast effective rule induction. In: Prieditis, A., Russell, S. (eds.) Machine Learning Proceedings 1995, pp. 115–123. Morgan Kaufmann, San Francisco (CA) (1995). https://doi.org/10.1016/B978-1-55860-377-6.50023-2, https://www.sciencedirect.com/science/article/pii/B9781558603776500232
14. Cukierski, W.: Titanic - machine learning from disaster (2012). https://kaggle.com/competitions/titanic
15. Dasgupta, S., Arias, J., Salazar, E., Gupta, G.: Cogs: causality constrained counterfactual explanations using goal-directed ASP. CoRR **abs/2407.08179** (2024). https://doi.org/10.48550/ARXIV.2407.08179
16. Dasgupta, S., Shakerin, F., Salazar, E., Arias, J., Gupta, G.: Causally constrained counterfactual generation using ASP. In: Arias, J., Azzolini, D., Basu, K., Dahl, V., Hecher, M., Pacenza, F., Saribatur, Z.G., Varanasi, S.C. (eds.) Workshop Proceedings of the 40th International Conference on Logic Programming (ICLP-WS 2024) co-located with the 40th International Conference on Logic Programming (ICLP 2024), Dallas, TX, USA, October 12th and 13th, 2024. CEUR Workshop Proceedings, vol. 3799. CEUR-WS.org (2024). https://ceur-ws.org/Vol-3799/paper5GDE24.pdf
17. Eiter, T., Geibinger, T., Oetsch, J.: Contrastive explanations for answer-set programs. In: Gaggl, S.A., Martinez, M.V., Ortiz, M. (eds.) JELIA 2023. LNCS, vol. 14281, pp. 73–89. Springer, Cham (2023). https://doi.org/10.1007/978-3-031-43619-2_6
18. Gelfond, M., Kahl, Y.: Knowledge Representation, Reasoning, and the Design of Intelligent Agents: The Answer-Set Programming Approach. Cambridge University Press, Cambridge (2014)
19. Gupta, G., et al.: Automating commonsense reasoning with asp and s(casp) * (2022). https://api.semanticscholar.org/CorpusID:251793743
20. Karimi, A., Barthe, G., Balle, B., Valera, I.: Model-agnostic counterfactual explanations for consequential decisions. In: Chiappa, S., Calandra, R. (eds.) The 23rd International Conference on Artificial Intelligence and Statistics, AISTATS 2020, 26-28 August 2020, Online [Palermo, Sicily, Italy]. Proceedings of Machine Learning Research, vol. 108, pp. 895–905. PMLR (2020). http://proceedings.mlr.press/v108/karimi20a.html
21. Karimi, A., Schölkopf, B., Valera, I.: Algorithmic recourse: from counterfactual explanations to interventions. In: Elish, M.C., Isaac, W., Zemel, R.S. (eds.) FAccT 2021: 2021 ACM Conference on Fairness, Accountability, and Transparency, Virtual Event / Toronto, Canada, March 3-10, 2021, pp. 353–362. ACM (2021). https://doi.org/10.1145/3442188.3445899
22. Lloyd, J.W.: Foundations of logic programming. In: Symbolic Computation (1987). https://api.semanticscholar.org/CorpusID:46408498
23. Pearl, J.: Causal inference in statistics: an overview. Stat. Surv. **3**, 96–146 (2009). https://doi.org/10.1214/09-SS057
24. Realinho, V., Vieira Martins, M., Machado, J., Baptista, L.: Predict students' dropout and academic success. UCI Mach. Learn. Repository (2021). https://doi.org/10.24432/C5MC89
25. Russell, C.: Efficient search for diverse coherent explanations. In: Proceedings of the Conference on Fairness, Accountability, and Transparency, pp. 20–28. FAT*

2019, Association for Computing Machinery, New York, NY, USA (2019). https://doi.org/10.1145/3287560.3287569
26. Tolomei, G., Silvestri, F., Haines, A., Lalmas, M.: Interpretable predictions of tree-based ensembles via actionable feature tweaking. In: Proceedings of the 23rd ACM SIGKDD International Conference on Knowledge Discovery and Data Mining, pp. 465–474. KDD 2017, Association for Computing Machinery, New York, NY, USA (2017). https://doi.org/10.1145/3097983.3098039
27. Ustun, B., Spangher, A., Liu, Y.: Actionable recourse in linear classification. In: danah boyd, Morgenstern, J.H. (eds.) Proceedings of the Conference on Fairness, Accountability, and Transparency, FAT* 2019, Atlanta, GA, USA, January 29-31, 2019, pp. 10–19. ACM (2019). https://doi.org/10.1145/3287560.3287566
28. Wachter, S., Mittelstadt, B., Russell, C.: Counterfactual explanations without opening the black box: automated decisions and the GDPR. Harvard J. Law Technol. **31**(2), 841–887 (2018)
29. Wang, H., Gupta, G.: FOLD-SE: an efficient rule-based machine learning algorithm with scalable explainability. In: Gebser, M., Sergey, I. (eds.) PADL 2024. LNCS, vol. 14512, pp. 37–53. Springer, Cham (2024). https://doi.org/10.1007/978-3-031-52038-9_3
30. White, A., d'Avila Garcez, A.S.: Measurable counterfactual local explanations for any classifier. In: Giacomo, G.D., Catalá, A., Dilkina, B., Milano, M., Barro, S., Bugarín, A., Lang, J. (eds.) ECAI 2020 - 24th European Conference on Artificial Intelligence, 29 August-8 September 2020, Santiago de Compostela, Spain, August 29 - September 8, 2020 - Including 10th Conference on Prestigious Applications of Artificial Intelligence (PAIS 2020). Frontiers in Artificial Intelligence and Applications, vol. 325, pp. 2529–2535. IOS Press (2020). https://doi.org/10.3233/FAIA200387
31. Xia, K., Lee, K., Bengio, Y., Bareinboim, E.: The causal-neural connection: expressiveness, learnability, and inference. In: Ranzato, M., Beygelzimer, A., Dauphin, Y.N., Liang, P., Vaughan, J.W. (eds.) Advances in Neural Information Processing Systems 34: Annual Conference on Neural Information Processing Systems 2021, NeurIPS 2021, December 6-14, 2021, virtual, pp. 10823–10836 (2021). https://proceedings.neurips.cc/paper/2021/hash/5989add1703e4b0480f75e2390739f34-Abstract.html

Exploring Answer Set Programming for Provenance Graph-Based Cyber Threat Detection: A Novel Approach

Fang Li[1]( ) , Fei Zuo[2] , and Gopal Gupta[3]

[1] Oklahoma Christian University, Edmond, OK 73013, USA
fang.li@oc.edu
[2] University of Central Oklahoma, Edmond, OK 73034, USA
fzuo@uco.edu
[3] University of Texas at Dallas, Richardson, TX 75080, USA
gupta@utdallas.edu

Abstract. Provenance graphs are useful and powerful tools for representing system-level activities in cybersecurity; however, existing approaches often struggle with complex queries and flexible reasoning. This paper presents a novel approach using Answer Set Programming (ASP) to model and analyze provenance graphs. We introduce an ASP-based representation that captures intricate relationships between system entities, including temporal and causal dependencies. Our model enables sophisticated analysis capabilities such as attack path tracing, data exfiltration detection, and anomaly identification. The declarative nature of ASP allows for concise expression of complex security patterns and policies, facilitating both real-time threat detection and forensic analysis. We demonstrate our approach's effectiveness through case studies showcasing its threat detection capabilities. Experimental results illustrate the model's ability to handle large-scale provenance graphs while providing expressive querying. The model's extensibility allows for incorporation of new system behaviors and security rules, adapting to evolving cyber threats. This work contributes a powerful, flexible, and explainable framework for reasoning about system behaviors and security incidents, advancing the development of effective threat detection and forensic investigation tools.

Keywords: Provenance Graphs · Answer Set Programming · Cyber Threat Detection

1 Introduction

In an era of increasingly sophisticated cyber threats, the ability to effectively detect, analyze, and respond to security incidents has become paramount. Provenance graphs, which capture the relationships and interactions between system entities such as processes, files, and network connections, have emerged as a powerful tool for representing and reasoning about system-level activities in cybersecurity contexts. These graphs provide a comprehensive view of information flow and causal relationships within a system, making them invaluable for both real-time threat detection and post-incident forensic analysis.

However, as cyberattacks become more complex and multi-staged, traditional approaches to analyzing provenance graphs often fall short. Many existing methods struggle with expressing complex queries, performing flexible reasoning about system behaviors, and adapting quickly to new threat patterns. There is a pressing need for more expressive, adaptable, and powerful techniques for modeling and analyzing provenance graphs in cybersecurity applications.

This paper introduces a novel approach to addressing these challenges by leveraging Answer Set Programming (ASP) to model and analyze provenance graphs. ASP, a declarative logic programming paradigm, offers several key advantages in this context:

1. **Expressiveness:** ASP allows for the concise and intuitive expression of complex relationships and queries.
2. **Flexibility:** The declarative nature of ASP facilitates easy modification and extension of analysis rules.
3. **Reasoning capabilities:** ASP supports various forms of reasoning, including deductive, abductive, and counterfactual reasoning.
4. **Efficiency:** Modern ASP solvers can handle large-scale problems efficiently.

Our ASP-based approach enables a wide range of sophisticated analysis tasks, including:

- Tracing attack paths through complex system interactions
- Identifying data exfiltration attempts
- Detecting privilege escalation
- Matching complex patterns of suspicious behavior
- Performing temporal and causal reasoning about system events

By representing provenance graphs in ASP, we create a powerful and flexible framework for cybersecurity analysis that can adapt to the ever-evolving landscape of cyber threats. This approach not only enhances the capabilities of security analysts but also paves the way for more advanced, automated threat detection and response systems.

In this paper, we present the theoretical foundations of our ASP-based provenance graph model, demonstrate its practical applications through a series of case studies, and evaluate its performance and expressiveness compared to traditional approaches. We also discuss the implications of this work for the future of cybersecurity analysis and outline potential directions for further research.

Our contributions include:

1. A novel ASP-based representation of provenance graphs tailored for cybersecurity applications

2. A set of ASP rules for performing various types of security analyses on provenance graphs
3. Case studies demonstrating the effectiveness of our approach in real-world scenarios
4. A discussion of the broader implications and future directions for ASP-based security analysis

The rest of this paper is organized as follows: Sect. 2 provides background on provenance graphs and Answer Set Programming. Section 3 details our ASP-based provenance graph model. Section 4 presents case studies and experimental results. Section 5 discusses the implications and limitations of our approach. Finally, Sect. 6 concludes the paper and outlines future work.

2 Background

2.1 Provenance Graphs

Provenance graphs are a powerful and versatile tool for representing and analyzing the lineage, history, and relationships of entities within a system [13]. In the context of cybersecurity, these graphs provide a detailed record of system activities, data flows, and causal relationships, making them invaluable for threat detection, forensic analysis, and system understanding.

Definition and Structure. A provenance graph $G = (V, E)$ is a directed graph where:

- V is a set of vertices representing system entities
- E is a set of edges representing interactions or relationships between these entities

   More formally:

- $V = \{v \mid v \text{ is a process, file, network connection, or other system entity}\}$
- $E = \{(v1, v2, l, t) \mid v1, v2 \in V, l \text{ is an interaction type}, t \text{ is a timestamp}\}$

Vertices: A vertex in a provenance graph typically represents a system entity. For different operating systems, the types of entities could be different. Some common examples of system entities include:

1. Process: Running programs or tasks within the system
2. File: Data objects stored in the file system
3. Network Socket: Endpoints for sending and receiving data across a network

Edges: Edges in a provenance graph represent interactions or relationships between entities. Common types of edges include:

1. Process-to-File: `read`, `write`, `open`, `close`
2. Process-to-Process: `fork`, `exec`, `clone`

3. Process-to-Network: `connect, bind, listen, accept`

In reality, depending on the system monitoring application used, edges are often labeled with different information [17]. The following are some common attributes:

- The type of interaction that is usually described using syscalls (e.g., `read, write, fork`)
- A timestamp indicating when the interaction occurred
- Additional metadata such as amount of data transferred, access permissions, etc.

Properties and Characteristics. Provenance graphs have several important properties:

1. Directed: Edges have a direction, indicating the flow of information or control.
2. Acyclic: In most cases, provenance graphs are acyclic, as events in the past cannot be influenced by future events.
3. Time-ordered: Edges are typically ordered by their timestamps, allowing for temporal analysis.
4. Multi-relational: Multiple types of relationships can exist between the same pair of entities.

Applications in Cybersecurity. Provenance analysis has several key applications in cybersecurity. First, provenance-based intrusion detection techniques have been developed to identify suspicious patterns of system behavior and detect known attack signatures in system activities [9,22]. Secondly, in forensic analysis, provenance data has been widely used to reconstruct the sequence of events leading to a security incident, trace the origin and impact of a malicious file or process, and eventually uncover the initial point of compromise in an attack [19,21]. Thirdly, some systems based on provenance data were designed to monitor system activities in real time, track access to sensitive data and resources, and verify that they comply with security policies and regulations [11,12]. Lastly, provenance analysis helps to link attack patterns to known threat actors or groups, and identify commonalities across multiple security incidents, therefore playing a significant role in attack attribution [10,20].

Challenges in Provenance Analysis. Despite their utility, analyzing provenance data presents several challenges in practice. First, nowadays, an organization may have hundreds or thousands of endpoints. Consequently, systems generate vast amounts of provenance data every day, resulting in extremely large and complex graphs that can be challenging to store and analyze efficiently. Second, not all captured provenance data is relevant to security analysis, necessitating techniques for pruning and focusing on important subgraphs. Furthermore, the collection of system-level provenance data is limited by various factors, such as the accuracy and granularity of the specific tools used. Therefore, the data may be incomplete or tampered with, which negatively impacts the reliability of subsequent analysis. Lastly, many important security queries require complex graph traversals and pattern matching, which can be challenging to express in traditional query languages. These challenges highlight the need for more advanced, flexible, and efficient approaches to provenance graph analysis in cybersecurity, motivating our exploration of Answer Set Programming as a powerful framework for addressing these issues.

2.2 Answer Set Programming

Logic programming [1] has been applied to many areas such as fault diagnosis, databases, planning, natural language processing, knowledge representation and reasoning. During decades of exploration, researchers have developed various semantics for solving different reasoning tasks. Among those semantics, the stable model semantics based answer set programming (ASP) [14] paradigm is popular for knowledge representation and reasoning as well as for solving combinatorial problems. Though computing ASP programs is considered to be NP-hard, there are a lot of ASP solvers (e.g., CLINGO [7], DLV [2], s(CASP) [3]) that can compute stable models of an ASP program efficiently.

Answer Set Programming (ASP) is a declarative paradigm that extends logic programming with negation-as-failure. ASP is a highly expressive paradigm that can elegantly express complex reasoning methods, including those used by humans, such as default reasoning, deductive and abductive reasoning, counterfactual reasoning, constraint satisfaction [4,8]. ASP supports better semantics for negation (*negation as failure*) than does standard logic programming and Prolog. An ASP program consists of rules that look like Prolog rules. The semantics of an ASP program Π is given in terms of the answer sets of the program ground(Π), where ground(Π) is the program obtained from the substitution of elements of the *Herbrand universe* for variables in Π [4]. Rules in an ASP program are of the form shown as below (Rule 1):

$$p \;:\!\!-\; q_1, \;...,\; q_m, \textbf{ not } r_1, \;...,\; \textbf{not } r_n. \tag{1}$$

where $m \geq 0$ and $n \geq 0$. Each of p and q_i ($\forall i \leq m$) is a literal, and each **not** r_j ($\forall j \leq n$) is a *naf-literal* (**not** is a logical connective called *negation-as-failure* or *default negation*). The literal **not** r_j is true if proof of r_j *fails*. Negation as failure allows us to take actions that are predicated on failure of a proof. Thus, the rule r :- not s. states that r can be inferred if we fail to prove s. Note that in Rule 1, p is optional. Such a headless rule is called a constraint, which states that conjunction of q_i's and **not** r_j's should yield *false*. Thus, the constraint :- u, v. states that u and v cannot be both true simultaneously in any model of the program (called an answer set).

The declarative semantics of an Answer Set Program P is given via the Gelfond-Lifschitz transform [4,8] in terms of the answer sets of the program ground(Π). More details on ASP can be found elsewhere [4,8].

Key Features of ASP. Key features of ASP include:

1. Declarative Semantics: Programs describe the problem rather than the solution algorithm.
2. Non-monotonic Reasoning: ASP supports default reasoning and the ability to draw conclusions based on the absence of information.
3. Efficient Solvers: Modern ASP solvers can handle large-scale problems efficiently.

ASP in Related Domains. ASP is a powerful tool for solving optimization and reasoning-related problems, especially in areas where traditional methods struggle. In the past few years, we have witnessed their intriguing applications of ASP in diverse fields, such as bioinformatics [6,16], planning and scheduling [5]. While applying ASP to provenance graph analysis is novel, it has already made significant progress in other security domains. For example, Sterlicchio et al. leveraged ASP to detect patterns of attacks to network security [18]. Rezvani et al. explored the capability of ASP in specifying and verifying web access control policies [15]. These successful applications in related fields suggest the potential of ASP for enhancing provenance graph analysis in cybersecurity.

In the following section, we will detail our novel approach to representing and analyzing provenance graphs using ASP, leveraging the strengths of both provenance graphs and ASP to create a powerful framework for cybersecurity analysis.

3 ASP-Based Provenance Graph Model

This section introduces our innovative approach to modeling and analyzing provenance graphs using ASP. Our model harnesses ASP's expressive power and advanced reasoning capabilities to facilitate sophisticated analysis of system behaviors and security incidents. For this research, we employ the s(CASP) ASP solver, chosen for its top-down execution strategy. This characteristic makes s(CASP) particularly efficient for threat detection tasks, which typically involve query-style operations. The s(CASP) solver's approach aligns well with the nature of cybersecurity analyses, where specific patterns or behaviors are often queried against a large set of system events.

3.1 Graph Representation in ASP

We represent the provenance graph using a set of ASP facts and rules. The basic structure of our model is as follows:

Node Representation. Nodes in the provenance graph are represented using the following predicates:

```
process(ID).
file(ID).
network_connection(ID).
user(ID).
memory_object(ID).
```

Where ID is a unique identifier for each entity.

Edge Representation. Edges are represented using the predicate:

    edge(From, To, Type, Timestamp).

Where:

- From and To are node IDs
- Type is the interaction type (e.g., read, write, fork)
- Timestamp is the time of the interaction

Additional Metadata. We also include predicates for additional metadata, such as:

    process_name(ProcessID, Name).
    file_path(FileID, Path).
    network_address(ConnectionID, Address).
    user_name(UserID, Name).
    memory_address(MemoryID, Address).
    sensitive_file(FileID).
    authorized_process(ProcessID).
    compromised_node(ID).

3.2 Core ASP Rules

We define a set of core ASP rules to enable basic reasoning about the provenance graph:

Reachability:

    reachable(X, Y) :- edge(X, Y, _, _).
    reachable(X, Z) :- reachable(X, Y), edge(Y, Z, _, _).

Temporal Ordering:

    before(X, Y) :- edge(X, _, _, T1),
                    edge(Y, _, _, T2), T1 < T2.

Causal Dependency:

    causal_dependency(X, Y) :- edge(X, Y, _, _).
    causal_dependency(X, Z) :- causal_dependency(X, Y),
                               causal_dependency(Y, Z).

3.3 Advanced Analysis Rules

Building upon the core representation, we can define rules for more sophisticated analysis. The flexibility and expressiveness of ASP allow us to formulate a wide range of advanced analysis rules tailored to specific security concerns. The following examples demonstrate the power and versatility of our approach, showcasing just a few of the many possible advanced analyses that can be performed:

Attack Path Tracing:
```
attack_path(X, Y, D) :-
                process(X),
                process(Y),
                reachable(X, Y, D),
                D <= 10.
```

Data Exfiltration Detection:
```
data_exfiltration(Process, File, Connection) :-
                sensitive_file(File),
                edge(Process, File, read, T1),
                edge(Process, Connection, send_data, T2),
                network_connection(Connection),
                T2 > T1.
```

Privilege Escalation Detection:
```
privilege_escalation(P1, P2) :-
                edge(P1, P2, create_process, _),
                process_privilege(P1, LowPriv),
                process_privilege(P2, HighPriv),
                HighPriv > LowPriv.
```

Root Cause Analysis:
```
root_cause(Event) :- compromised_node(Node),
                causal_dependency(Event, Node),
                not causal_dependency(_, Event).
```

Alert Generation:
```
generate_alert(Process,
    "Unauthorized access to sensitive file") :-
                sensitive_file(File),
                accessed_file(Process, File),
                not authorized_process(Process).
```

3.4 Customization and Extension

One of the key advantages of our ASP-based model is its flexibility and extensibility. New types of analysis can be easily added by defining additional rules. For example:

Policy Enforcement:

```
policy_violation(Process) :- send_data(Process, _, _),
                             not whitelisted_process(Process).
```

Anomaly Detection:

```
anomalous_process(Process) :-
        count_distinct_files_accessed(Process, Count),
        threshold(Threshold),
        Count > Threshold.

count_distinct_files_accessed(Process, FileCount) :-
    findall(File, edge(Process, File, read, _), List),
    length(List, FileCount).
```

What-if Analysis:

```
potential_compromise(Node) :-
                    compromised_node(Initial),
                    reachable(Initial, Node).
```

In conclusion, our ASP-based provenance graph model provides a powerful, flexible, and extensible framework for cybersecurity analysis. By leveraging the declarative nature and reasoning capabilities of ASP, we enable sophisticated querying and analysis of system behaviors, facilitating more effective threat detection and forensic investigation.

4 Case Studies and Experimental Results

In this section, we present a series of case studies to demonstrate the effectiveness of our ASP-based provenance graph analysis approach. We used synthetic data generated by a custom Python script to simulate various cybersecurity scenarios. This approach allows us to test our model against a wide range of attack patterns and system behaviors while maintaining control over the complexity and scale of the data.

4.1 Data Generation

We developed a Python script to generate synthetic provenance graph data. This script creates a diverse set of system entities (processes, files, network connections) and their interactions, simulating both normal system activities and various attack scenarios. The key features of our data generation process include:

- Customizable graph size and complexity
- Simulation of multi-stage attacks
- Incorporation of temporal aspects in entity interactions
- Generation of both benign and malicious activity patterns
- Ability to inject specific attack scenarios (e.g., data exfiltration, privilege escalation)

4.2 Experimental Setup

We tested our ASP-based model using the following setup:

- ASP Solver: s(CASP)
- Hardware: Apple Macbook Pro (m1 processor)
- Dataset Sizes: We generated and tested datasets ranging from 1,000 to 10,000 nodes
- Attack Scenarios: We simulated 5 different attack patterns, including data exfiltration, privilege escalation

Note that given the complex nature of ASP reasoning, we may adopt different ASP solvers according to specific tasks.

4.3 Case Study 1: Multi-Stage Attack Detection

Scenario: We simulated a multi-stage attack involving initial compromise, privilege escalation, and data exfiltration.

ASP Rules:

```
multi_stage_attack(InitialProcess, EscalatedProcess,
   ExfiltratedFile, ExitPoint) :-
            initial_compromise(InitialProcess),
            privilege_escalation(InitialProcess,
               EscalatedProcess),
            data_exfiltration(EscalatedProcess,
               ExfiltratedFile, ExitPoint).
```

Query:

```
?- multi_stage_attack(Ip, Ep, Ef, Ep).
```

Results: Our model successfully identified the complete attack path, linking the initial compromise to the final data exfiltration. The ASP query efficiently traced the causal relationships between different stages of the attack. For a dataset of 100,000 nodes, the query execution time averaged 0.259 milliseconds.

4.4 Case Study 2: Anomaly Detection in Process Behavior

Scenario: We injected anomalous process behaviors, such as accessing an unusually high number of sensitive files or establishing multiple unauthorized network connections. This case study illustrates the extensibility of our ASP-based model, by definition of customization rules.

ASP Rules:

```
anomalous_process(Process) :- process(Process),
    count_distinct_files_accessed(Process, FileCount),
    count_network_connections(Process, NetCount),
    threshold(FileThreshold, NetThreshold),
    FileCount > FileThreshold.

anomalous_process(Process) :- process(Process),
    count_distinct_files_accessed(Process, FileCount),
    count_network_connections(Process, NetCount),
    threshold(FileThreshold, NetThreshold),
    NetCount > NetThreshold.

% Helper predicates
count_distinct_files_accessed(Process, FileCount) :-
    findall(File, edge(Process, File, read, _), List),
    length(List, FileCount).

count_network_connections(Process, NetCount) :-
    findall(Conn, edge(Process, Conn, connect, _), List),
    length(List, NetCount).

length([],0).
length([_|Xs],C) :- length(Xs,Cs), C is Cs + 1.
```

Query:

```
?- anomalous_process(P).
```

Results: Our model demonstrated high accuracy in identifying all anomalous processes. For a dataset of 100,000 nodes, the average query execution time was 1302 milliseconds. The declarative nature of ASP allowed us to easily adjust and fine-tune the anomaly detection criteria.

4.5 Performance Evaluation

We evaluate the performance of our ASP-based approach across datasets of different sizes. The results are summarized in Table 1:

Our ASP-based approach showed good scalability, with query execution times increasing sub-linearly with dataset size. The declarative nature of ASP allowed for intuitive expression of complex security patterns, resulting in shorter development time for new types of analyses.

Table 1. Evaluation Results

Dataset Size	Query Type	Average Execution Time (ms)
1,000	multi-stage	0.22
1,000	anomaly	21
10,000	multi-stage	0.26
10,000	anomaly	1302

5 Discussion

The application of Answer Set Programming (ASP) to provenance graph analysis for cyber threat detection represents a significant advancement in the field of cybersecurity. Our research demonstrates that this novel approach offers several key advantages over traditional methods, while also presenting some challenges and opportunities for future work.

5.1 Advantages of the ASP-Based Approach

Expressiveness and Flexibility. One of the most notable strengths of our ASP-based approach is its exceptional expressiveness and flexibility. Traditional query languages and graph databases often struggle to capture the complex, multi-faceted nature of cyber attacks. In contrast, ASP's declarative paradigm allows security analysts to express sophisticated attack patterns and system behaviors in a more natural and intuitive manner. This expressiveness is particularly evident in our ability to easily define rules for complex scenarios such as multi-stage attacks, data exfiltration, and privilege escalation.

The flexibility of our model is further demonstrated by its extensibility. As new types of threats emerge or as organizations need to incorporate domain-specific knowledge, our ASP-based approach allows for seamless integration of new rules and patterns. This adaptability is crucial in the ever-evolving landscape of cybersecurity, where the ability to quickly respond to new threats can make the difference between a successful defense and a costly breach.

Reasoning Capabilities. Another significant advantage of our approach is the advanced reasoning capabilities inherent in ASP. Unlike traditional graph traversal algorithms, ASP allows for sophisticated logical inference, including default reasoning, abductive reasoning, and counterfactual analysis. This enables our model to not only detect known attack patterns but also to reason about potential vulnerabilities and attack vectors that may not have been explicitly programmed.

For instance, our model's ability to perform temporal and causal reasoning allows it to uncover subtle connections between seemingly unrelated events, potentially revealing hidden attack paths or identifying the root cause of a security incident. This level of analysis is particularly valuable in the context of advanced persistent threats (APTs) and other sophisticated attack scenarios that may unfold over extended periods.

Performance Considerations. While our experimental results demonstrate the feasibility of using ASP for provenance graph analysis, it's important to address the performance implications of this approach. ASP solvers have made significant advancements in recent years, but the NP-hard nature of ASP computation can still pose challenges for very large-scale graphs.

Explainability and Transparency. A significant advantage of our ASP-based approach is its inherent explainability. Unlike black-box machine learning models, the logical rules in our ASP programs provide clear, human-readable explanations for why a particular conclusion was reached. This transparency is crucial in cybersecurity contexts, where analysts need to understand and trust the reasoning behind automated threat detection systems.

The explainable nature of our model also facilitates easier auditing and validation of security policies. Organizations can review and verify the logical rules governing their threat detection system, ensuring alignment with their security policies and regulatory requirements.

5.2 Limitations and Challenges

Despite its many advantages, our ASP-based approach does face some challenges. One primary concern is the potential for state space explosion when dealing with extremely large or complex provenance graphs. While our model handles typical scenarios well, edge cases involving highly interconnected graphs or very long causal chains may require additional optimization techniques.

Another challenge lies in the knowledge engineering aspect of our approach. Effectively capturing the nuances of complex system behaviors and attack patterns in ASP rules requires both domain expertise in cybersecurity and proficiency in logic programming. This may present a learning curve for some security analysts and necessitates close collaboration between ASP experts and cybersecurity professionals.

5.3 Future Directions

Looking ahead, there are several exciting avenues for further research and development of our ASP-based provenance graph analysis approach:

1. Developing domain-specific libraries of ASP rules for common attack patterns and security policies to facilitate easier adoption by security professionals.
2. Real-time Analysis: Developing incremental ASP solving methods for real-time provenance graph analysis.
3. Incorporating probabilistic reasoning to better handle uncertainty and incomplete information in provenance data.
4. Integration with Machine Learning: Combining ASP with machine learning techniques to enhance anomaly detection and automate rule generation.

6 Conclusion

This paper presented a novel approach to modeling and analyzing provenance graphs using Answer Set Programming for enhanced cybersecurity threat detection and forensic analysis. Our ASP-based model offers a powerful, flexible, and explainable framework for reasoning about complex system behaviors and security incidents. Through case studies and experimental results, we demonstrated the effectiveness of our approach in uncovering multi-stage attacks and detecting anomalous behaviors.

As cyber threats continue to evolve in complexity, approaches like ours that offer both power and adaptability will be crucial in staying ahead of attackers. Future work will focus on addressing scalability challenges, incorporating machine learning techniques, and extending the model for real-time analysis.

By bridging the gap between provenance graphs and the expressive power of ASP, this work opens new avenues for advanced cybersecurity analysis and paves the way for more intelligent, adaptive threat detection and response systems.

References

1. Abiteboul, S., Hull, R., Vianu, V.: Foundations of databases, vol. 8. Addison-Wesley Reading, San Francisco (1995)
2. Adrian, W., Alviano, M., Calimeri, F.: Others: the ASP system DLV: advancements and applications. Künstl. Intell. **32**, 177–179 (2018)
3. Arias, J., Carro, M., Salazar, E., Marple, K., Gupta, G.: Constraint answer set programming without grounding. Theory Pract. Logic Program. **18**(3–4), 337–354 (2018)
4. Baral, C.: Knowledge Representation, Reasoning and Declarative Problem Solving. Cambridge University Press, Cambridge (2003)
5. Cao Tran, S., Pontelli, E., Balduccini, M., Schaub, T.: Answer set planning: a survey. Theory Pract. Logic Program. **23**(1), 226–298 (2023)
6. Dal Palù, A., Dovier, A., Formisano, A., Pontelli, E.: Exploring life: answer set programming in bioinformatics, pp. 359–412. Association for Computing Machinery and Morgan & Claypool (2018)
7. Gebser, M., Kaminski, R., Kaufmann, B., Schaub, T.: Clingo= asp+ control. arXiv preprint arXiv:1405.3694 (2014)
8. Gelfond, M., Kahl, Y.: Knowledge Representation, Reasoning, and The Design of Intelligent Agents: The Answer-Set Programming Approach. Cambridge University Press, Cambridge (2014)
9. Han, X., Pasquier, T., Seltzer, M.: Provenance-based intrusion detection: opportunities and challenges. In: 10th USENIX Workshop on the Theory and Practice of Provenance (2018)
10. Hassan, W.U., Bates, A., Marino, D.: Tactical provenance analysis for endpoint detection and response systems. In: IEEE Symposium on Security and Privacy, pp. 1172–1189. IEEE (2020)
11. Irshad, H., et al.: Trace: enterprise-wide provenance tracking for real-time APT detection. IEEE Trans. Inf. Forensics Secur. **16**, 4363–4376 (2021)
12. Jenkinson, G., et al.: Applying provenance in APT monitoring and analysis: practical challenges for scalable, efficient and trustworthy distributed provenance. In: 9th USENIX Workshop on the Theory and Practice of Provenance (2017)

13. Li, Z., Chen, Q.A., Yang, R., Chen, Y., Ruan, W.: Threat detection and investigation with system-level provenance graphs: a survey. Comput. Secur. **106** (2021)
14. Marek, V.W., Truszczyński, M.: Stable models and an alternative logic programming paradigm. In: The Logic Programming Paradigm, pp. 375–398. Springer (1999)
15. Rezvani, M., Rajaratnam, D., Ignjatovic, A., Pagnucco, M., Jha, S.: Analyzing XACML policies using answer set programming. Int. J. Inf. Secur. **18**, 465–479 (2019)
16. Schaub, T., Thiele, S.: Metabolic network expansion with answer set programming. In: International Conference on Logic Programming, pp. 312–326. Springer (2009)
17. Shrestha, M., et al.: ProvSec: open cybersecurity system provenance analysis benchmark dataset with labels. Int. J. Netw. Distrib. Comput. **11**(2), 112–123 (2023)
18. Sterlicchio, G., Lisi, F.A.: Detecting patterns of attacks to network security in urban air mobility with answer set programming. In: European Conference on Artificial Intelligence, pp. 1285–1292. IOS Press (2024)
19. Tabiban, A., Zhao, H., Jarraya, Y., Pourzandi, M., Wang, L.: Vincidecoder: automatically interpreting provenance graphs into textual forensic reports with application to openstack. In: Nordic Conference on Secure IT Systems, pp. 346–367. Springer International Publishing (2022)
20. Wang, Z., Zhou, Y., Liu, H., Qiu, J., Fang, B., Tian, Z.: Threatinsight: innovating early threat detection through threat-intelligence-driven analysis and attribution. IEEE Trans. Knowl. Data Eng. (2024)
21. Xie, Y., Feng, D., Liao, X., Qin, L.: Efficient monitoring and forensic analysis via accurate network-attached provenance collection with minimal storage overhead. Digit. Investig. **26**, 19–28 (2018)
22. Zipperle, M., Gottwalt, F., Chang, E., Dillon, T.: Provenance-based intrusion detection systems: a survey. ACM Comput. Surv. **55**(7), 1–36 (2022)

Author Index

A
Areias, Miguel 1
Arias, Joaquín 215

B
Ballesteros, Ignacio 146
Baral, Anita 179
Bueso de Barrio, Luis Eduardo 146

C
Ceresa, Martin 53
Costa, Vítor Santos 1

D
Dasgupta, Sopam 215
De Vogelaere, Robin 88

F
Fredlund, Lars-Åke 113

G
Gorostiaga, Felipe 53
Gupta, Gopal 104, 215, 233

H
Hansen, Zachary 71
Hargreaves, Bryant 104
Herranz, Ángel 113

I
Inclezan, Daniela 179

K
Krimbell, Keegan 104

L
Li, Fang 233
Li, Junru 130
Libby, Steven 35
Lierler, Yuliya 71

Liu, Fangzhou 130
Lockwood, Hunter 179

M
Mariño, Julio 113, 146

N
Newton, Jim 18
Nguyen, Dan N. 104

R
Robinson, Vincent 35

S
Salazar, Elmer 215
Sánchez, César 53
Shakerin, Farhad 215
Sharma, Jitendra 179
Shrestha, Pratiksha 179

T
Takyu, Kento 196
Tarau, Paul 163

U
Ueda, Kazunori 196

V
Van Dessel, Kylian 88
Vennekens, Joost 88

W
Wang, Zerong 130

Y
Yan, Yan 130

Z
Zhang, Zhizheng 130
Zuo, Fei 233

The manufacturer's authorised representative in the EU is Springer Nature Customer Service Centre GmbH, Europaplatz 3, 69115 Heidelberg, Germany. If you have any concerns regarding our products, please contact ProductSafety@springernature.com

Printed and bound by CPI Group (UK) Ltd, Croydon, CR0 4YY

26/03/2026

02078935-0009